AF278347

Volume 17

DIRECTORY OF
WORLD CINEMA
LATIN AMERICA

Edited by Isabel Maurer Queipo

intellect Bristol, UK / Chicago, USA

First published in the UK in 2013 by
Intellect Books, The Mill, Parnall Road, Fishponds, Bristol, BS16 3JG, UK

First published in the USA in 2013 by Intellect Books, The University of Chicago Press,
1427 E. 60th Street, Chicago, IL 60637, USA

A catalogue record for this book is available from the British Library.

Publisher: May Yao
Publishing Manager: Melanie Marshall

Cover photograph: Laberinto del fauno, El / Pan's Labyrinth, 2006, Baquero, Ivana,
   del Toro, Guillermo, Tequila Gang / WB / The Kobal Collection.
Cover designer: Holly Rose
Copy-edited by Emma Rhys
Typesetting: John Teehan

Directory of World Cinema ISSN 2040-7971
Directory of World Cinema eISSN 2040-798X

Directory of World Cinema: Latin America ISBN 978-1-84150-618-0
Directory of World Cinema: Latin America eISBN 978-1-84150-693-7

Printed and bound by Cambrian Printers, Aberystwyth, Wales.

DIRECTORY OF WORLD CINEMA

LATIN AMERICA

ACKNOWLEDGEMENTS

This volume about contemporary Latin American cinema(s) is another volume of the Directory of World Cinema series, and another result of the commitment of a number of different contributors. The backgrounds and approaches of the writers are again quite diverse, as one can see in the articles, and one should also take into consideration the wide, wide field of this volume dealing with such a huge subcontinent. Like the other volumes, this one is not intended to be a conventional film guide, as the overall aim is mainly to discuss Latin American cultural life and history as expressed through the medium of film. Therefore, I am most grateful to all contributors for embracing this assignment and fully engaging with Latin American cinema(s) through their preferred method of analysis, be it socio-political, aesthetic or genre-based.

The *Directory of World Cinema: Latin America* would also not have been possible without the proofreading of Frederic Bartlett, Anthony Santoro, and in particular Annika Klein with her meticulous and professional care. Thank you! In addition, I would like to especially thank May Yao and Melanie Marshall from Intellect and my dear colleagues Maribel Cedeño and Christian von Tschilschke. Finally thank you very much to everyone who has contributed to this volume and supported me throughout what has been an immensely rewarding process – especially to film enthusiast Isabella Dumancic. I hope every reader will enjoy this volume and benefit from it.

INTRODUCTION
BY THE EDITOR

Already the label 'Latin American cinema' is problematic due to the danger of reducing a cinema that comprises such a wide range of different countries and nations, with their own histories and cultures and their own popular, artistic and experimental films: in the north there is Mexico; in the centre Costa Rica, El Salvador, Guatemala, Honduras, Nicaragua and Panama; in the south Argentina, Bolivia, Brazil, Chile, Ecuador, Colombia, Paraguay, Peru, Uruguay and Venezuela; and in the Caribbean the Dominican Republic, Cuba and Puerto Rico. A related problem is the language potpourri of Spanish, Portuguese, Quechua in Peru, Aymara in Bolivia, Guaraní in Paraguay, Miskito in Nicaragua, Nahuatl in Mexico, and Mapudungun in Chile. Regarding the early film markets and the competition between the US-American and the Latin American cinema(s), difficulties arose very early, especially due to the introduction of sound, the subsequent dubbing and subtitling attempts, as well as international film projects that included the production of Spanish-language films.

As the volume deals with contemporary cinema since the 1980s and due to the predetermined format of the *Directory of World Cinema* series, other important aspects could not have been taken into consideration, such as historical overviews and films from the silent area to the present, single characteristics, individualities, and special genres of the single countries in Latin America and their rich and turbulent histories with regards to cinematic, cultural and historical issues. Mexico with its Golden Era (1937–49) offered, for example, its typical *cine lacrimógeno* (tear jerker films), *Rumberas*, *Rancheras* and *Mariachi Films*. In Argentina flourished the tango films, and Fernando Solanas and Octavio Getino created a cinema of liberation called the Third Cinema in the 1950s and 1960s, to put a distance between the First Cinema (the Hollywood commercial cinema) and the Second Cinema (the European Author's Cinema). Glauber Rocha with the 'Aesthetics of Hunger' in 1965, created among others the *Cinema Novo* in Brazil where the *Cinema do lixo* (Rubbish Cinema), the *Chanchadas*, the *Porno-Chanchadas* and the *Tropicália* movement, based on the cultural concept of anthropophagy, the 'Manifesto Antropófago' (Cannibal Manifesto) by Oswald de Andrade in 1928, dominated the scene. Carlos Mayolo, Luís Ospina and Andrés Caicedo founded the so-called Caliwood in Colombia, and Cuba made a large profit from the successful Cuban Revolution (1953–59), founding for example the Instituto Cubano del Arte e Industria Cinematografica (ICAIC) in March 1959. Most of the

countries suffered military dictatorships, such as Chile, Uruguay and Argentina between 1973 and 1983 that resulted in a crisis in the film industry. These and many other aspects may be the material for another volume.

In this sense, as it is neither easy to capture nor to impart all the single facets of the cinema(s) of the subcontinent, the contributions of this volume try to throw light on the following aspects.

The first article 'Festival Focus' by Verena Teissl includes the very important focus on festivals as 'microcosms subject to their own rules, as traffic junctions, crossroads, or, in the diction of cultural theory, 'site passages', cultural spaces that temporarily attach importance to films and at the same time nurture their own reputations'.

Jorge Sanjinés: *Bolivia-la nación clandestina*, 1989 © Trigon Films.

The 'Industry Spotlight' by Roberto Herrera presents the solid present and the bright future of the contemporary Latin American film industry that is still establishing itself via the improvement of legislation and the utilization of public sector funds, which are available for annual projects as selected by national film agencies. This establishment is mainly made possible by the significant participation of national governments, which act as the main promoters and founders of the industry.

The next essay about interculturality by Beatrice Schuchardt focuses on other important tendencies such as globalization, co-productions, alliances and interculturality, as the equally antagonistic and productive negotiations between cultures that differ from one another. 'Negotiations of this kind can include both the various cultures within Latin America and its countries, and the cultural encounters and frictions between, for example, Latin America and the United States, Latin America and Europe, or Latin America and Asia.' This also means both the conscious and direct thematic handling of intercultural conflicts in films and their indirect cinematic treatment, for example, through focusing on – largely marginalized – indigenous or other ethnic communities within Latin American societies.

'Latin American Animation Films' by Dietmar Frenz pays tribute to the tendency of our digital age to computer-generated imagery (CGI), reflected, for example, in various newly founded festivals such as the 'ANIMA Festival' in Córdoba, Argentina, and the 'Anima Mundi Festival' of São Paulo and Rio de Janeiro, Brazil.

Gael García Bernal was chosen to represent 'bright stardom' and the 'Latino Boom' along with very well-known Latinos (or people who descend from Latinos) from many artistic areas, such as Christina Aguilera, Joan Baez, Benicio del Toro, Gloria Estefan, Andy García, Salma Hayek, Eva Longoria, Jennifer Lopez, Ricky Martin, Eva Mendes or Carlos Santana.

The essay by Victoria Kearley considers the significance of Bernal's star persona as a political figure, an actor, and author of images, as well as a representation of Latin sexuality being a contemporary Latin American cinematic image.

As 'Film of the Year' 2011 serves the comedy *Un cuento chino/Chinese Take-Away* by Sebastián Borensztein – 'the story of an Argentinean and a Chinese united by a cow fallen from the sky' – and as 'Scoring Cinema' serves *El viaje* (1992) by Fernando E. Solanas, one of the most important and best-known directors and theoreticians.

The section on directors provides the opportunity for more detailed discussion of some fascinating film-makers with their oeuvres being analysed regarding their production methodology, thematic concerns, and cinematic legacies: Lisandro Alonso, Lucrecia Martel, and Carlos Sorín from Argentina; Andrés Wood from Chile; Guillermo del Toro and Alejandro González Iñárritu from Mexico; as well as Solveig Hoogesteijn from Venezuela. There could have been many more articles dedicated to other great directors such as María Bemberg and Fernando E. Solanas from Argentina; Fernando Meirelles (Brazil); Tomás Gutiérrez Alea (Cuba); Claudia Llosa (Peru); as well as Román Chalbaud (Venezuela); and from Mexico Luis Buñuel and Arturo Ripstein, who presented his last movie *Las razones del corazón* (2011) at the '26 Festival Internacional de Cine de Mar del Plata 2011' in Argentina.

After these specialized essays the reviews focus on contemporary films since the 1980s, and deal with traditional genres such as comedy, documentary, drama, romance, thriller, horror, and women cinema that sensitively reflect the Latin American society. A filmography of the reviewed films, works used in the essays and recommended reading, information related to women cinema,

'Latin American Cinema Resources and Online', a short quiz, and notes on the contributors round up this volume.

As with the other volumes in the *Directory of World Cinema* series, the *Directory of World Cinema: Latin America* is intended to be informative and entertaining rather than exhaustive, allowing contributors to adopt their preferred and very different analytical approaches. Instead of providing a general overview of Latin American cinema, past and present, through a conventional A–Z structure, this volume rather aims at familiarizing readers with this particular cinema and a more culture-specific insight into the films, directors and genres.

Isabel Maurer Queipo

Sebastián Borensztein: *Un cuento chino/Chinese Take-Away* © with kind permission of Oscar Alonso, Festivals and Subsidies Coordinator, LATIDO FILMS.

FILM OF THE YEAR
CHINESE TAKE-AWAY

Chinese Take-Away

Un cuento chino

Studio/Distributors

Walt Disney Studios Motion
Pictures
Alta Classics

Director

Sebastián Borensztein

Producers

Pablo Bossi
Juan Pablo Buscarini
Gerardo Herrero

Screenwriter

Sebastián Borensztein

Cinematographer

Rodrigo Pulpeiro

Art Directors

Valeria Ambrosio
Laura Musso

Editors

Pablo Barbieri Carrera
Fernando Pardo

Composer

Lucio Godoy

Duration

93 minutes

Genre

Comedy

Cast

Ricardo Darín
Muriel Santa Ana
Huang Sheng Huang
Enric Rodríguez
Iván Romanelli
Javier Pinto

Year

2011

Synopsis

Jun is about to propose to his girlfriend on a boat, when suddenly a cow falling from the sky kills her. Jun travels to Argentina to reunite with his only relative, an uncle, but he is robbed when he lands in Buenos Aires. He is rescued by Roberto, a grumpy and irritable hardware-store owner, who lives a lonely existence. Roberto at first tries to help Jun find his uncle, but he can barely tolerate living with him and constantly attempts to get rid of his new housemate unsuccessfully.

Critique

This is Sebastián Borensztein's third feature film after working for Argentinean TV during the 1990s, and his tentative and more uneven first two films, *La suerte está echada/The Die Is Cast* (2005) and *Sin memoria* (2010), which showed a fledging auteur trying to find equilibrium between a story and its underlying content. *Chinese Take-Away*, on the other hand, is a very notable film with several cleverly interlaced layers, where the tension between the human story and its subtext dissolves in a perfect fashion, the first ingredient becoming a perfect metaphorical vessel for the second. The film has been a box-office success in Argentina, and it has been sold and distributed internationally. It begins with the somewhat surrealist incident in which a Chinese peasant's girlfriend is killed by a cow fallen from the sky. This unfortunate individual, we will learn later, is Jun (Huang Sheng Huang), one of the two main characters of the story. Nevertheless, the film quickly shifts its focus and jumps across continents to introduce us to the other main character, Roberto (Ricardo Darín). He is the owner of a small hardware store, a solitary man burdened by his own past and by an almost obsessive devotion to his dead parents. Roberto is a man absolutely dedicated to his work, although there is something unhealthy about such dedication. He is depicted as a prototypical neurotic, who compulsively counts the nails in each box provided by his supplier and goes to bed at 11 p.m. every single day. He is always grumpy and behaves in a cantankerous fashion, having very little time for anything or anybody else. Roberto's exclusionary tactics also go against María (Muriel Santa Ana), a classy woman who is deeply in love with Roberto, admiring his nobility, empathizing with his inner pain, and even being fond of the way he looks.

Nevertheless, María cannot get through the thick psychological wall that Roberto has built around himself. Borensztein builds Roberto's character on small and subtle details, which are carefully combined and cleverly staged in order to achieve a powerful emotional impact. This is a common trait in recent Argentinean cinema, where several talented young directors seem more inclined to build narratives around 'historias mínimas' (intimate stories), as the title of Carol Sorín's landmark 2002 film explicitly states. Such minimal or intimate stories are better suited to convey the complexities of stories with a profound human touch and to offer something different from the standard Hollywood narrative to viewers, something less focused on bombastic action and external or stereotypical human drama, and centred in exploring the depths of the human soul. Thus, this type of cinema partly connects with current defenders of 'slow cinema', such as Bela Tarr, Carlos Reygadas and Tsai Ming-Liang. On the other hand, there are clear differences. In *Chinese Take-Away*, the focus on the minimal stories or details does not render the narrative pace slow, and the rhythm and tempo of mainstream cinema is preserved. This certainly makes the movie more viewer-friendly. For example, we watch the small details making up the building blocks of Roberto's existence with increasing attention: Roberto's visits to the cemetery, the press clippings that he painstakingly collects about the most unique and unbelievable stories, and his disdainful bursts of anger at self-centred customers, especially at a particularly obnoxious one ('boludos!' is his favorite expression).

Roberto has isolated himself from a painful past. His parents died when he was young and he served as a soldier in the Malvinas (Falkland Islands) war. He lives in a parallel universe of parental worship and imaginary occurrences taken from the daily newspaper. In his daydreams he re-enacts the surrealist stories from his paper clippings, and these reality-imbued fantasies are the few events that can make him smile. Roberto's monotonous but well-organized existence becomes shocked by the accidental arrival of Jun, the Chinese man who is in fact involved in one of the stories collected by Roberto, a fact that he is unaware of until the end of the movie. The title of the film, *Un cuento chino* (literally 'A Chinese tale') is a lexicalized expression that in Spanish means a tall tale or a story with unbelievable elements, a sense that is lost in the English translation of the film title for international distribution – using the stereotypical and reductionist expression 'Chinese takeaway' as a title actually betrays what the movie tries to convey.

Roberto becomes thus accidentally involved in Jun's story, as he first tries to find Jun's uncle and later attempts to get rid of him. Roberto and Jun become a genuine 'odd couple', always together but unable to communicate, since Jun does not speak or understand Spanish. There are no subtitles translating Jun's words, so the audience becomes as lost as Roberto, trying to understand not only what he says but also the mysteries surrounding his identity and even the basic fact of his presence in Argentina. Jun and Roberto also have diametrically opposed characters. Jun's sweetness, passivity, and his deep sense of family attachment contrast with Roberto's bad temper, hyperactivity and isolationist tendencies. The film relies heavily on Darín's shoulders and he certainly delivers, building a masterful portrait where nothing is to be missed: his looks, movements and body expressions, and most importantly the way in which he delivers carefully crafted laconic replies, etc. His silences are loaded with a deep sense of despair on the one hand, but also with a somewhat ironic allure. In sum, this is one of the best of a series of masterful performances by an actor who has become Argentina's most important thespian.

Borenzstein's script navigates the two souls of the story with delicacy. The poetic and magic side of the story is clearly inspired by Borges and the masters of Latin American magic realism. The absurdity of life is reflected in how chaos creates a concatenation of events, apparently unconnected, which are nonetheless ultimately rescued from the surrealist absurd and linked to a moral payoff. The realist and psychological component strongly reminds us of Roberto Arlt's writings.

Cinematically, the influence of the great Italian masters of post-war cinema and beyond is clear, including the neo-realist approach to Buenos Aires, and the use of several stylistic and thematic touches that are very similar to the style of Fellini or Tornatore, with their unique combination of reality and fantasy, of funny and sad moments, memory and illusion, etc. This influence bodes well for the story since Roberto is of Italian ancestry. The stories in Roberto's daydreaming are filmed in a style that also reminds us of Jean Pierre Jeunet's *Le fabuleux destin d'Amélie Poulain/Amelie* (2001), another tale of a fragile and isolated soul, living in a dream world. As in *Amelie*, the city is not just a neutral background, but rather an existential environment that becomes a critical player in the story. Technically, the film is superb. Rodrigo Pulpeiro's cinematography and Lucio Godoy's melancholic score deserve special mention in this respect. They both contribute decisively to the film's unique tone. Thematically, *Chinese Take-Away* can ultimately be read as a metaphoric cartography of the Argentinean soul, torn between a traumatic past – with its isolationist and nostalgic tendencies – and the need to confront an ultimately reinvigorating multicultural reality of a global nature. The moral of this unique tall tale or *cuento chino* is particularly relevant in our day and age: accepting or, better said, embracing the other, with his differences and peculiarities will have decisively redeeming qualities. In other words, opening up to others frees us from our inner demons.

Javier Gutiérrez-Rexach

Daniel Burman: *El Nido Vacio/Empty Nest*, 2008 © BD Cine/Classic Film /INCAA/Paradise Films.

INDUSTRY SPOTLIGHT

A solid present and bright future: a spotlight on the contemporary Latin American film industry

From the 1980s to today, despite chronic social crises, Latin America has experienced significant advances in economic and industrial development. In addition to the improvement of its industrial sectors, certain prosperous economic moments provided the beginnings for the establishment of the film industry. When we say beginnings, it is because the Latin American film industry is still establishing itself via the improvement of legislation and the utilization of public sector funds that are available for annual projects as selected by national film agencies. The most remarkable aspect of the Latin American film industry is the fact that film production nowadays is mainly made possible by the significant participation of national governments, which act as the main promoters and founders of the industry.

During the period between 1990 and 2003 countries like Brazil, Chile, Colombia, Uruguay, and others promoted economical advances to stabilize themselves, setting reforms aimed at removing restrictions on free enterprise, increasing competition, privatizing public enterprises, and boosting productivity. The film industry was clearly stimulated by those reforms in the sense of production, but at this moment, national distributors had to compete against American films. The unlimited presence of Hollywood mainstream films was responsible for the extreme lack of competitiveness of domestic films except in sporadic cases of national movies that earn high box-office returns. On the other hand, this issue justifies governmental action to protect the national cinema. According to experts and professionals, this issue is attached to the low number of inhabitants per theatre, and the high price for the vast majority of the population.

Removing restrictions on free enterprise, increasing competition, privatizing public enterprises and boosting productivity

The continent's extensive territory necessitates a complex analysis of data provided by official institutions, where the methodology of the analysis, applied by each country, differs greatly from one country to another. Argentina, Brazil, Mexico, Uruguay and Chile provide more detailed data, facilitating the work of the researcher interpreting the real context of the current markets. It is remarkable that these countries still work towards better access, searching for an ideal system to provide more intense movement of national film over the continent. This effort is represented by what is now called the Reunion Specialized in Cinema and Authorities Cinematographic and Audio-visuals MERCOSUR (RECAM), founder of the Observatory Mercosur of Audio-visuals (OMA), whose main objective is the unification of their information systems. This agency defines its purpose as 'contribut[ing] to productive development and the integration of the audio-visual industry and cultural region, with production of a basic information system of the evolution of regional film activities, for the remission to periodic regional coordinators of the OMA' (Observatorio del Mercosur Audiovisual [OMA], 'Latin American Cinema Resources and Online'). In other words, the OMA seeks to unify the methods of analysis of the continent's markets.

Data from the Agência Nacional do Cinema (ANCINE, National Agency of Cinema in Brazil) shows that as of December 2009, 527 projects were launched to produce feature films, while in the same period Brazil released 108 domestic films that were screened in 1,964 of their 2,110 cinemas (Agência Nacional do Cinema [ANCINE], 'Latin American Cinema Resources and Online'). The data confirms that most of the content produced does not reach a minimum diffusion within its own territory. Brazil, a country with a population of 180 million where the number of inhabitants per theatre is approximately 47,000, knows that the dilemma facing national cinema distribution is its capacity to extend its market potential, knowing it needs more theatres. Such data confirms that most of the content produced does not reach a minimum level needed to extend this territory. The situation is worse when it comes to distribution among the other countries of the continent. According to Gustavo Dahl, CEO of Ancine,

> it is clear that unequal distribution of wealth, limits the number of sessions and audience. For example, the Brazilians go to the cinema once every two years. But the research done by exhibitors confirms that, indeed, ten million Brazilians attend the sessions eight times a year. A cruel copy of concentration of wealth, the only advantage becomes that there is space for growing. (Agência Nacional do Cinema [ANCINE])

A remarkable phenomenon that occurred in Brazil was with *Tropa de Elite* (José Padilha). In both films (*Tropa de Elite 1/Elite Squad* [2007]) and *Tropa de Elite 2/Elite Squad:*

The Enemy Within [2010]) it is explained how a captain of the Special Operations Battalion of Rio de Janeiro (BOPE) becomes secretary of public security. The first part was awarded the Golden Bear at the 'Berlin International Film Festival' in 2008; the second was launched in 2010 and was the most-watched movie in the history of Brazilian cinema – with nearly 11 million viewers, the film grossed over US$60,000. This film was a milestone for the thriving industry in Brazil because its distribution was 100 per cent independent, managed by film producer Zazen Produções, and led by film-maker Marcos Prado and director José Padilha. Up to this point, a film like this was an unknown event in Brazil, because movies with these numbers were never before unlinked to the American majors. We will need to wait for the 2011 numbers to see whether the Brazilian films will compete, as in this case, on a footing equal to the Hollywood studios.

In Argentina in 2009, of the twenty most watched films, only one was a national film: *El secreto de sus ojos/The Secret in Their Eyes* (Juan José Campanella, 2009). Not only was this the most watched film of the year, it also won the 2010 Oscar for Best Foreign Film. This confirms that it is not only the national audience that is extremely receptive to national Argentinean cinema, but also the international public. Something similar had occurred before with *El nido vacio/Empty Nest* (Daniel Burman, 2008) that was also placed first in the list of most watched films of the year. In 2007, the most watched film was *La señal* (Ricardo Darín and Martín Hodara), a masterpiece starring popular actor Ricardo Darín. Except for these hits, however, the rest of the most watched movies are

Glauber Rocha: *Antônio das mortes*, 1969 © Trigon Films.

Tomás Gutiérrez Alea: *Memorias del subdesarollo/Memories of Underdevelopment*, 1968 © Trigon Films.

predominantly American. Furthermore, leaders of the domestic box office are usually linked to major American distributions, resulting in a clear monopoly in the market. A large proportion of domestic films do not find adequate distribution, which results in an inability to find a more significant audience due to the persistent competition from Hollywood studios. It turns out that in Argentina, as well as in some other countries, a so-called invisible cinema exists: when good movies are produced, they receive recognition from professional critics but do not find adequate space in the cinema agenda. A good example is *La sangre brota/Blood Appears* (2008) by the young director Pablo Fendrik.

The distribution and exhibition sector must deal with a couple of questions: how to schedule the relatively high number of films that the countries of South America have nowadays in their relatively few theatres? And, once it has found its place in the cinema agenda, how will it compete against the American films? It is clear that publicity is a key instrument in developing the audience that the local film industries seek. Because most governmental incentives go to cover production costs, little remains to cover promotion costs. Most national films, especially those with less famous names, find it difficult to promote themselves. One potential solution to this challenge could be addressing the clear need to increase the number of theatres. There are some projects heading in that direction, all trying to reach a virgin audience: in Latin America, a considerable number of people have never been to the movies.

Not unlike other continents, Latin American cinema suffers from the persistent competition of American movies as absolute market leaders. Because of this competition, governmental subsidies designed to encourage consumption of domestic films are justified by virtue of the necessity of protecting national cinematography from the massive presence of foreign capital in their domestic market. On the other hand, the social character of movies produced in Latin America has been compromised. By using federal money to produce film art, both the population and the government expect the investment to benefit their whole society in some way. The fact is, however, that while the state finances most film production, most films never reach a general audience. Justifying the existence of this industry relies almost exclusively on its own cultural character. In this way, Latin American cinema stands closer to the general film production of the European Union, where governments, or involved national agencies, also act as the main stimulus for the production and protection of their cinema against Hollywood.

Despite the challenges facing the growing film industries, there is no doubt that this favourable economic moment provides Latin American cinema with a great opportunity to build towards a promising future. The significant foundations that provide the existence of a regulated film industry are solid, particularly the strategies of many of the Latin American Agencies or National Film Organizations that implement these strategies and encourage this industry. Authorities today are interested in using cinema 'as a window to the world', promoting national culture and making the country more attractive for foreign community opinion. Since the 1960s generation, directors such as Glauber Rocha in Brazil, Thomas Gutierrez Alea in Cuba (and others), promoted the first movement on this direction – cinema committed to social issues – but especially in the Brazilian case the movement was annihilated by the 1990s government.

The past ten years have seen a remarkable growth in the quality and quantity of produced films. Films like *Diarios de motocicleta/The Motorcycle Diaries* (2004), *Y tu mamá también* (2001) and *Cidade de Deus/City of God* (2002), among many others, show the level of maturity that Latin American cinema has achieved. It is important to note that after ten years of hard work, opportunities for the new generation of film-makers have begun to open naturally; this development continues down the path previously improved with the efforts of past generations. Currently, Latin American cinema aspires to be a sustainable business – which today's national cinema is not – but even so, we will see very few films removed from the social characters of their countries. Usually, the so-called commercial films are always linked to major television channels. We can therefore say that governmental interest in financing national cinema begins with recognizing what these films can do to give expression to their cultures.

Roberto Herrera

Dr Venedey (on the left) Daniel Díaz Torres during the award of the Peace Prize, Forum Berlinale 1991.
© Ekko von Schwichow, Berlin.

FESTIVAL FOCUS

How and why film festivals contributed and contribute to the reception of the Latin American film

> By changing the parameters of evaluation from economic to cultural, the contours of a new type of culture industry were created by Film Festivals as the obligatory points of passages for critical praise. Film Festivals are, in short, sites passages that function as the gateways of cultural legitimation. (Marijke de Valck 2007: 38)

Film festivals are microcosms subject to their own rules. They are traffic junctions, crossroads, or, in the diction of cultural theory, 'site passages'; cultural spaces that temporarily attach importance to films and at the same time nurture their own reputations. Quite apart from the United States and Europe, Latin America, especially Mexico, has developed a rich and continuous film tradition since the 1940s, a tradition that historically has been and remains somewhat unpopular in Europe. Festivals have played and continue to play important roles in the dissemination and reception of Latin American films.

The case of *Alicia en el pueblo de maravillas/Alice in Wondertown* (Daniel Díaz Torres, 1991)

In 1991, the Cuban comedy *Alice in Wondertown* was screened at the 'Berlin International Film Festival', where it won the Peace Prize. With his revolutionary attitude – 'may you never get used to the absurd' – director Daniel Díaz Torres began in the late 1980s to craft a satirical fable on socialist Cuba: Alicia (Thais Valdéz) takes a job as a theatre director in Maravillas, a truly peculiar place whose everyday life is marked by futility and whose inhabitants suffer from a collective disease called 'authoritarianism'. Alicia self-confidently throws herself into battle, trying to fight against all evils. *Alice* is full of biting ironic metaphors on the absurd elements of Caribbean socialism.

The year 1991 was also the year that marked the beginning of the 'periodo especial' (special period) in Cuban history. The effects of the collapse of the Soviet Union reached the island in the form of food shortages and political isolation. These changes intensified critical readings of *Alice*, which is why the normally sovereign political authorities reacted nervously against the film institute ICAIC – a role model for Latin American film production in the service of identity production. In Cuba, the film was suppressed just days after its theatrical release, in the Cuban foreign countries it was not allowed to be performed again until 1993 and it was among others shown at the film festival in Chicago, and in some larger and smaller film festivals in Europe.

This integration defined the history, glory and reception of the film – and the world may never have noticed if *Alice* had not been screened for the first time at one of the world's most prominent film festivals, attracting both acclaim and journalistic attention. The fact that it was the 'Berlinale' that offered the ramp into the public is a cruel irony of cultural history. For its first two decades, the Berlinale, founded in 1951 by the US film officer Oscar Martay, served as a platform to strengthen the cultural values of western democracies. Eastern European films were excluded from participation because of their socialist origins, while at that time non-European countries were barely on the radar. This seemed to be a kind of marking when in 1961 the Berlin Wall was built and the Berlinale extensively supported the cinemas on the border with East Germany (cf. Valck 2007).

Daniel Díaz Torres has always regretted the way *Alice* was received, because it defused the film's polyvalent potential impact and turned it into a 'case'. This 'case' can be re-opened from a different point of view, however: the authoritarianism that is critically picked out as a central theme is not a disease limited to Cuba. Would there have been a more general interpretation in Europe? Does Cuban film have the authority to formulate social and political questions? Or do such films land in the 'perceptive ghetto', Latin America? Since Latin American films reach Europe with the help of festivals, expectations oscillate between political positioning towards cultural or economic hegemonic relations and Latin American joy of life and magical realism. Actually, *Alice* fulfills none of these expectations, particularly as the political criticism is directed at a state regarded rather fondly by European intellectuals following the solidarity movement. Further, instead of magical realism, Torres serves up bad jokes. This works in Terry Gilliam's *Brazil* – but in Daniel Díaz Torres' *Alice*?

Theoretical and methodological investigations of film festivals as institutions and the special effects and consequences have arisen only with the establishment of cultural studies and the cultural sciences. Dutch media theorist Marijke de Valck has provided the most fundamental contribution to this literature to date in *Film Festivals: From European Geopolitics to Worldwide Cinephilia* (2007), in which she analyses the big European festivals and how they function. Also, a postponement occurs in the understanding of 'reception': film is not only a mirror of a society, but also must be understood as a product of the spectator's activity as cultural practice embedded in 'sensory connections' that are culturally determined or constructed (Schenk 2010: 9).

Festivals and 'festival films'

Film festivals were and are the nicest and strongest parallel world in the film business, on all sides: they connect art and commerce, industry and art house; they generate an unusual situation of gaze accompanied by spectacle and are accompanied by worldwide media coverage (cf. Valck 2007). At the same time, festivals are bottlenecks for the viewing public and generate what sociologist Pierre Bourdieu calls 'symbolic capital', a prestige value for the festival and for the biography of the film. When Hollywood films missed out on honours from Cannes, for example, they began screening films there out of competition not only to mitigate the loss of prestige associated with losing a competition but also to capitalize on the opportunity to participate in the most important event in the film world (cf. Junge 2009).

Festivals are intervening authorities set apart from the commercial and subsidized rental companies that form part of the (national) film scenery, and thereby allow for reception as a cultural practice on a broader base. The local and temporal restrictions of festivals admit no similar situation. Rather, starting in the 1990s, since the so-called 'film festival circuit' started to grow as a thick worldwide network, film festivals offer a sort of alternative distribution structure. On the reception side, they generate processes of cultural production – in postcolonial terms, migration movements and globalizing 'processes of hybridization': the festivals create a global audience, a spectatorship scattered about the planet which, for better or worse, does not interact with the same intensity or with lower effects on national spirit. Instead, this hybrid audience reads a film from different cultural contexts. One thus speaks of the phenomenon of 'festival films' that draw, over a one- or two-year period, on the worldwide festival circuit: 700 spectators in Vienna, 800 in Pusan, 900 in Toronto, 150 in Paris, 500 in Cairo, and 1,000 in Havana, etc.

In media theory, one also speaks of the 'film public'; does this not function best, however, within a state/national territory, trickling into the collective identity and forming this film public within a national process? In this sense, festivals actually create exactly the opposite scenario – a cinema counter-public that functions worldwide and not – or not only – nationwide. In many cases, the success of a 'festival film' does not extend beyond the festival; festival films tend to draw low numbers of spectators without the attraction and the constructivist character of a festival. Mexican director Paul Leduc, whose films include *Reed – México insurgente* (1973) and *Frida – naturaleza viva/Frida* (1986), who presented several films at Cannes and many other smaller festivals, turned to other activities in the 1990s because he found it frustrating to produce 'only' for festivals (Paul Leduc, conversation with Verena Teissl in Mexico City, 1994).

Festivals provide a third perspective

At festivals, stars and trends are not only presented but are also produced. In this way, festivals act as gatekeepers – they are the 'trendsetters', as Valck (2007) argues. Besides, the curators and the selections committees possess a high degree of importance; they juggle between festival statutes, the will to discover, and the care of already 'discovered' and established cinéastes or film countries, as well as of the trademark of the festival's artistic management. In their interlinking and power film festivals are influential for trendsetting up to the creation of cinematic canons. These processes often lead to festivals having their own abstract way of life, particularly as canonized films, as well as many of those works that revive during a festival thanks to media coverage, are hardly seen beyond festival contexts, and can disappear again from public consciousness. In some cases, these films cannot even be easily seen by the general public during the respective festival. Nevertheless, in the annual running of the worldwide circuit this cinema counter-public is constantly established anew. In their combination of the mainstream and the art house, festivals create a kind of 'third perspective' on film, and they allow for the 'cinematographic state of emergency' as Hans Hurch, the artistic manager of the 'Viennale, used to call it.

This third perspective has also benefited the perception and distribution of Latin American cinema. In the first phase of the festival history – dating from the foundation of the festival in Venice in 1932 to roughly 1968, according to Marijke de Valck (2007) – and which was primarily motivated by a desire to strengthen the European film industry, festivals functioned as platforms of national showcases (Valck 2007: 19 ff.). In the 1960s, the presentation of Latin American films became a significant component in the re-orientation of film festivals. The protests of the representatives of the *nouvelle vague* against the mainstream adjustment of the festival in Cannes had favoured the foundation of the festival in Pesaro (among other alternative festivals) and in the long-term had initiated a fundamental reorganization: the creation of the curator's model. Festival leaders began to select according to thematic and aesthetic criteria instead of organizing the submissions with the help of state-owned or film-union institutions. 'Festival editions and sections became mechanisms for intervention, institutionalized ways of playing issues on the international cultural agenda and with the worldwide dissemination of the festival phenomenon, signboards for competing festival images' (Valck 2007: 28).

Jean-Luc Godard's demand to make film political was put into practice at Pesaro. 'Mostra internationale del nuovo cinema' was the first festival for documentary films and features 'of an experimental and invariable political nature' and offered an alternative 'to the First World established cinema of Hollywood and Western Europe' (Valck 2007: 28). In 1968 the film manifesto *La hora de los hornos/The Hour of the Furnaces* (1970) by Fernando Solanas and Octavio Getino, a film that seemed to have been created precisely for that time of intellectual awakening that was represented by Roland Barthes, Umberto Eco and Pier Paolo Pasolini, among others, received the Critic's Award.

If this development initiated the genesis of Latin American film production and genres – the *cine militante* (Fernando Solanas, Argentina), the *Cinema Novo* and the 'Aesthetics of the Hunger' (Glauber Rocha, Brazil), the 'Cinema of the Third Way' (Julio García Espinosa, Cuba), all radically aesthetic forms of expression with political character – Latin American cinema was nevertheless stigmatized for exactly that. The popular cinema – built up by the state in Mexico from the 1940s as an effective form of expression for the post-revolutionary and mainly illiterate society, in the process becoming a love affair between the audience and the film business – essentially never arrived in contemporary Europe. One exception was Emilio Fernández's 1946 film *María Candelaria*, which won the Grand Prix in Cannes and was highly praised by Georges Sadoul. *María Candelaria* may also be considered one of those works that belong to the abstract canon that perhaps would never have succeeded without participating in and winning recognition at Cannes. It is impossible to know, at the moment of selection, whether a festival film will have a lasting impact.

In essence, Cannes is obligated to foster the establishment of an artistic cinema with focus on the European author's cinema and independent films from the United States, while at the same time serving as a 'ramp' for Hollywood. From the beginning, however, Cannes has had significant effects on the reception of the Latin American film in Europe and in Latin America itself: the fact that in 1951 Luis Buñuel was honoured as Best Director for *Los olvidados/The Young and the Damned* made the acceptance of the film possible in Mexico, where it had been previously perceived as a national insult and had been rejected. This example shows that festivals are authorities and have an effect as institutions. Another example is Glauber Rocha. Rocha received his first award in 1962 at the 'Karlovy Vary International Film Festival', which was founded in 1946 and developed into a sort of a counterpart to the Berlinale for film productions from socialist countries or with an affinity for socialist ideologies.

During the Cold War, Rocha managed the jump onto the 'other' side only via his multiple appearances at Cannes – in 1964, with *Deus e o diabo na terra do sol/Black God White Devil* (nominated for *Golden Palm* but failed to win); in 1967, with *Terra em transe* (International Critic's Prize by the F.I.P.R.E.S.C.I.); and in 1969 with *Antônio das mortes* (award for Best Director). In 1977, Rocha cemented his legacy, receiving yet another award for his short film *Di Cavalcanti*. In 1980, *A idade da terra/The Age of the Earth* was screened for the first time – not in Cannes, but in Venice, where Rocha's charged and highly complicated symbolism and narration ran up against a wide lack of understanding (cf. Jossner 2003). Here the borders expressed themselves in the reception of different forms of aesthetics and also from European ignorance of Latin American culture and history, which can be important for different literacy versions.

To counteract these knowledge deficits, the Berlinale Forum began, with its founding in 1971, to perform pioneering work that for the first time offered comprehensive background materials to help viewers understand and meditate upon the films (Valck 2007: 68). Forum operators also were the first to consider preserving the festival's films, and tried annually to archive all the films that they showed. This allows for historical rerun and discovery, another task of the festivals in conjunction with film museums.

New geopolitical accents

Beside the A-list festivals – Cannes, Venice and Berlin, all of which arose in response to geopolitical interests – the smaller geopolitical film festivals developing from the late 1970s onwards were decisive in helping spread and garner recognition for Latin American films. These festivals were packed into a 'Third World' packet, often launched under the collective name 'Films from the South' and marketed with the slogan 'Window to the World'. Their programmes – consisting of films rejected by the A-list festivals (but not only) – produce a discourse that criticizes the Eurocentric attitude and creates their special cinema-counterpublic. The 'Festival de 3 continents', founded in 1979 in Nantes, France, and the 'Festival International de films de Fribourg', founded in 1986 in Fribourg, Switzerland, are good examples of the festivals on this circuit. Moreover, the 'Horizontes latinos' section of the A-list 'Festival de San Sebastian Donostia Zinemaldia' also has a geopolitical origin. The biggest challenge facing the markedly geopolitical festivals is avoiding a form of 'ghettoization' and reaching a larger audience than that which understands itself as fans of the 'Latin American film' per se.

In Latin America itself, Colombia's 'Festival Internacional de cine y T.V. de Cartagena de Indias' was founded in 1960. In 1978, the most prominent Latin American film festival – the 'Festival del nuevo cine latinoamericano' – was created in Havana. This festival has devoted itself to Latin American and Caribbean film culture and was long the most important platform in Latin America for the regions films and also for multipliers from around the world. In 1999, the 'Buenos Aires Festival Internacional de Cine Independiente' (BAFICI) was founded. This festival aims to bring 'innovative, fearless and engaged film creating' (cf. *BACIFI*, 'Latin American Cinema Resources and Online') to the world, and may shortly assert itself not only in Latin America, but also in the festival world more broadly. Changes in the external cinematic world and the changed needs for the festival market go hand in hand. BAFICI's arrival announces a new trend, one that will leave the geopolitical discourse behind.

Patricio Guzmán during the award of *Salvador Allende* in Cannes, 2004 © with kind permission of Renate Sachse, ATACAMA Productions France.

Turn with *Amores Perros* (Alejandro Iñárritu González, 2000): Aesthetic accents

The desire to promote politically agreeable films in a parallel world of politically positioned intellectuals did not end immediately with the Cold War. Rather, the geopolitical festivals in particular have promoted the reception of Latin American film in which the political conformity sometimes overruled aesthetic concerns – not always to the joy of the film-makers who did not want to see their works reduced to 'messages'. *Alice in Wondertown* toes the line marking the edge of the playing area, not only in Cuba, but also with regards to the movement of solidarity and the politically dominated film understanding in the European reception of Latin American films – and with that the cultural practice of the film reading. A turn came in 2000 with Alejandro Iñárritu González's *Amores Perros*. First screened at the 'Semaine de la Critique' in Cannes in 2000, where it won two prizes, *Amores Perros* was the first Latin American film to break through and generate widespread partial understanding within the European world. Film aesthetics and authenticity connected with provenance and cultural method were taken into consideration, and offered 'a subversive pleasure which is not anchored in an essentialistic sense, but plays with the ambiguity and inherent tension between cultural homo- and heterogeneity' (Winter and Nestler 2010: 107). In this case, the film monopolized the screen, bringing to the screen the dynamism of New Hollywood and the epic of the European author's cinema in the no-longer-kitschy form of the Mexican pathos. Love, passion, and biographic dead ends function as trans-cultural identifiers, while the location is specific, not interchangeable. Mexico City here receives a fitting film portrait; engaging and cruel, occidental and exotic; an abstract idea and at the same time a concrete depiction of life's struggles.

Amores Perros was not reduced to be a mere 'festival film' but did become a worldwide rental hit. It was not the first Mexican or Latin American film to utilize neither a mainstream aesthetic, as in the Mexican melodrama of the *cine de oro*, nor the political activism of the *cine militante*. Nevertheless, Latin American experimental cinema and avant-garde cinema did not found its way with the relative lastingness of the creation of Maya Deren or the subversive cinema in the definition of Amos Vogel on the European festival market. *Amores Perros* is located aesthetically between the local and the worldwide; it is a film of its time, the age of globalization and 'glocalization'. The film also turns to an audience for whom the epoch of the Cold War and its ideologies belong already to the past.

The big European A-list festivals – Venice, Cannes and Berlin – remain the centres of the European film festival business. The ritual of the festivals, and with it the 'bed' of this cultural practice, feeds from the expectation of the not-routine: presentations in the presence of the film teams increase the power of the films; the media echo transmits the spectacle; and the myth of the premiere and the award mark the works and expectations. What has changed is the new lastingness that is created by the festival circuit, even if the film is presented 'only' for a global festival audience. This has extended the radius of the parallel 'world festivals' and has encouraged a new meaning. New computer-driven modes of communication, such as the blogosphere and social media platforms, offer journalists new tools, which also affects the festival universe: these new tools permit an exchange between and among global audiences. These new tools also serve as venues within which fans can discuss broader topics, such as the threat digital distribution poses to the place of 'cinema' as such. What concerns the New Latin American film creating one speaks for example of the *Nuevo Cine Argentino* that is primarily a festival phenomenon, like much of the new Latin American cinema used to be, including works by Fernando Birri through Patricio Guzmán to Fernando Solanas.

Fernando Birri.

Fernando Birri

The new Argentine cinema, however, with widely different representatives like Lucrecia Martel, Pablo Trapero and Mariano Llinás, differs from the broader new Latin American cinema in an essential aspect: it is far more aesthetically driven than politically. This aesthetic offer is a connector linking the social practice of film reading throughout the world. These aesthetics are also helping film find a new way politically – through its language rather than its content. Fernando Birri, doyen of Latin American film and a figurehead of the political essay as well as of magical realism, is persuaded that film is universally understandable. We know that a diachronic reading of films in different times and contexts creates new interpretations over and over again. The stress on the aesthetics thus also can be, at minimum, a challenging innovation for the reception of the Latin American film as a cultural practice. With its intellectual as well as playful aesthetics, the new Argentine film is an inspiring 'ambassador' for the fact that film as an art form can invent itself over and over again. What, if not film festivals with their effectiveness, can take up and promote such developments?

Verena Teissl

CULTURAL CROSSOVER:
INTERCULTURALITY

Interculturality has not only been a hallmark of Latin American cultures since the age of colonial expansion and globalization. Beyond the philosophical-political interpretation of the concept of interculturality in the context of the so-called Latin American 'liberation philosophy', which has been part of the academic debates on the cultural specifics of Latin America since roughly the middle of the 1990s and the research of Raúl Fornet-Bétancourt, the phenomenon of interculturality is also rooted in the history of Latin American cinema before 1990. If interculturality is understood in the sense of the cultural studies perspective of Nestor García Canclini, as most recently formulated in his 2004 *Diferentes, Desiguales y Desconectados. Mapas de la interculturalidad*, this means the equally antagonistic and productive negotiations between cultures that differ from one another. Negotiations of this kind can include both the various cultures within Latin America and its countries and the cultural encounters and frictions between, for example, Latin America and the United States, Latin America and Europe, or Latin America and Asia.

Transferred to the area of cinematography, this also means both the conscious and direct thematic handling of intercultural conflicts in films and their indirect cinematic treatment, for example, through a focusing on – largely marginalized – indigenous or other ethnic communities within Latin American societies.

Interculturality may also manifest itself through the phenomenon of the co-production, which is often found in the age of film industry globalization. As shown by the example of the US-Mexican co-production *Frida* (Julie Taymor, 2002), a biopic based on Hayden Herrera's *Frida: A Biography of Frida Kahlo* (2002), an intentional examination of the subject matter of interculturality is not necessarily required here. Instead, *Frida* – primarily at an unconscious level of the cinematic sub-discourse – illustrates the palimpsest-like superimposition and antagonistic friction between a Hollywood aesthetic directed towards attractiveness and entertainment on the one hand, and the ambivalence of indigenous Mexican cultural symbols in the context of Frida Kahlo's pictorial art on the other. An example of this can be seen in the *calaveras* – the skeletons and death's heads – that constitute recurrent motifs in Kahlo's paintings. If these cultural symbols in the context of the cinematic discourse of *Frida* are to be found primarily in those spaces that are to be assigned to the (sinister and suppressed) unconscious – delirium, dream, hallucination – it becomes clear how these symbols, threatening stereotypes of a Mexico understood as wild and archaic, still haunt the cultural consciousness of American identity today.

A further example of interculturality in the area of co-productions can be found in Miguel Pereiras *Verónico Cruz* (Argentina/United Kingdom, 1987), a fictional account of the life and death of a country boy from the Andes. In the area of documentary film and also in the context of co-productions, Lourdes Portillo's *La Ofrenda: The Days of the Dead* (Mexico/United States, 1988) – a documentary on the death-cult of the Mexican *Día de los Muertos* (Day of the Dead) – is an example of an intercultural perspective on Latin American culture in the medium of film.

Yet films with intercultural-production dimensions can also be found in Latin American film productions beyond the area of co-productions and before the emergence of the scientific interculturalism debate in the 1990s. Examples of this begin around the time of the Brazilian feature film production *Carnaval Atlântida* (José Carlos Burle and Carlos Manga, 1952), which ironically deals with the cliché of the hot-blooded dancing Latina that had become cemented primarily through the American musicals of the 1940s such as *That Night in Rio* (Irving Cummings, 1941), as represented above all by Carmen Miranda in her over-the-top *Baiana* costumes. A further early example of the intercultural aspects in Latin American films is Carlo Hugo Christensen's *La balandra Isabel llegó esta tarde/The Yacht Isabel Arrived This Afternoon* (Venezuela, 1949), in which elements of African-rooted folklore and their contrast to Venezuela's bourgeois culture are addressed as aspects of an internal otherness within national identity.

Interculturality, however, also manifests itself in Latin American films through the examination of indigenous cultures and their specifics, in, for example, ethnological short films such as Jorge Ruiz's *Vuelve Sebastiana* (Bolivia, 1953) and *Ukamau/And So It Is* (Bolivia, Jorge Sanjinés, 1966), as well as *Yawar Mallku/Blood of the Condor* (Bolivia, 1968) also by Jorge Sanjinés and the Ukamau-groups. In a more nuanced form, Antonio Eguino's *Chuquiago* (Bolivia, 1977) deals with the linkage of social stratification and ethnic origin.

More recent examples of intercultural negotiations in Latin American productions and co-productions can be found principally in the genre of road movies, in which the protagonists' odyssey turns out to be a search for an individual national and cultural identity – an identity which, in the context of the cultural and intercultural encounters that arise during the journey, is always newly defined and constantly changes. This, for instance, is the case in Fernando Solana's *El viaje/The Journey* (Argentina, 1992), in which the teenager Martín tours through the Latin American continent on his bike, but also in Alfonso Cuaróns *Y tu mamá también* (Mexico, 2001), in which, during a trip to the south of Mexico, two young Mexicans simultaneously embark on a search for their own cultural and sexual identity. Of a significantly darker character is the co-production *Sin nombre* (Mexico/United States, 2009), directed by the Swedish-Japanese film-maker Cary Fukunaga, which tells the story of a journey through Mexico by the teenagers Casper and Sayra and is marked by experiences of violence and life on the run.

Beatrice Schuchardt

Jairo Eduardo Carello: *Pequeñas voces/Little Voices*, 2004 © Cinecolor Films.

LATIN AMERICAN ANIMATION FILMS

From its beginnings in the 1920s, Latin American animation has reflected rather than set aesthetic and technical trends in worldwide animation. Production, with some notable exceptions, has been scarce, discontinuous, and artistically epigonic. Nevertheless, the foreign has been appropriated in interesting ways, and even an animated commercial or jingle can be a Proustian madeleine. During the theatrical era, while only a handful of shorts and features found their way to the silver screen – most of these were lost or have yet to be restored – television and limited animation allowed for countless children's series and programmes to be developed, even in the smaller countries. The possibilities of secondary exploitation of video eventually brought back, or made possible for the first time, feature films in Brazil, Chile, Argentina and Mexico. Currently, computer-generated imagery (CGI) is the state of the art in studio animation, while personal and independent animation also continues to use traditional animation techniques. These personal and independent productions today find showcases both on the Internet and in the festival circuit: the 'Festival Internacional del Nuevo Cine Latinoamericano' in Havana, Cuba, permanently offers a variety of animation; also the 'ANIMA Festival' in Córdoba, Argentina, and the 'Anima Mundi Festival' of São Paulo and Rio de Janeiro, Brazil, have specialized in animation for the last twenty years, while recently the 'Animarte Animation Festival' is touring various cities from Mexico down to the Cono Sur.

The beginnings of cinematic animation are scarcely documented, but are marked by the influence of mainstream American animation on the silent and early sound eras: comic strip adaptations, anthropomorphic animal funnies and picturesque images set to an orchestral tune dominated the field. Chilean animation pioneer Alfredo Serey may be an exception with his political satire *La Trasmisión del Mando Presidencial* in 1921, which, like so much early material, is now lost. His compatriot Carlos Borcosque adapted the Chilean version of George McManus' comic strip *Bringing up Father* in *Vida y Milagros de Don Fausto* as early as 1924. The era's preference for a live-action/animation mix is attested by Jorge 'Coke' Delano's *La calle del ensueño* (1929). Alfonso Vergara Andrade created anthropomorphized parrots Paco and Catita for what may be the first surviving short in Mexico, *Paco Perico en premier* (1935), and its sequel, *El Tesoro de Moctezuma* (1936). Myth, history and nature quickly became established as recurrent motifs in Latin American animation. Vergara's studio AVA continued until 1940 and released its first colour cartoon in 1937 – *Los cinco cabritos y el lobo*, a Grimm Brothers fairy tale – following another fashion of the time.

Even today, the most popular animated characters representing Latin America are most likely Disney's José 'Zé' Carioca and Warner Brothers' Speedy Gonzales, immediately recognizable to children all over the world thanks to television reruns. The first appearances of the little Brazilian parrot – in the 1942 package film *Saludos Amigos* – and the fastest mouse of Mexico – 1953 in the 'Merrie Melodies' short *Cat-Tails for Two* also roughly mark the beginning of a period of more ambitious works. In 1942, Chileans Carlos Trupp and Jaime Escudero released *15.000 dibujos*, a black-and-white starring the anthropomorphic condor named Copuchita. Although the film, which Walt Disney himself saw on a visit to Chile in the early 1940s, is lost today, the images that remain of Copuchita identify him as one of the models – along with the characters of *Saludos Amigos* – for Condorito, the most famous comic strip character in Chile. Created by Pepo in 1949 and continuing to the present, Condorito, like his ancestor, represents the typical Chilean day labourer. After a failed 1962 attempt to spin the comic off into a television series, a Spanish/Chilean co-production successfully turned the strip into a television series in the 1980s, with a Coca Cola spot in the 1990s. Brazilian animator Anélio Latini released his 75-minute feature *Sinfonia Amazônica/Brazil Symphony* in 1953 after years of pioneering work with his elder brother Mario. This was his first, and, for a long time, the last feature film in Brazil. The *Symphony*, set to an original orchestral score, tells seven etiological myths of the Amazonian fauna and flora, connected by the charming adventures of a little Indian boy.

The most systematic and enduring attempt at Latin American animation to date is the animation department of the Instituto Cubano del Arte e Industria Cinematográficos (ICAIC). Founded in 1959, shortly after the Cuban revolution, it continues producing films and training animators today, although production quality suffered a significant drop in the 1990s. Ever since its first short, *El Maná* (Jesús de Armas, 1960), ICAIC's often simplistic and ingenuous political, educational and entertainment films, clearly reflect international fashions: the then-dominant United Productions of America (UPA) style, with its psychological use of colour and extremely stylized and flattened characters and backgrounds – which had affected even Disney's realism – clearly marked its beginnings. Only in the late 1960s did the brilliant blend of pictorial and modelling techniques characteristic of Eastern European animation take over, as in Tulio Raggi's 1967 short *El poeta y la muñeca*. Today, limited animation with Japanese anime influences prevails – as in the *Filminutos* series – but other productions, such as Edwin Fernandez's *La marcha de las vocales* (2006), have incorporated surrealist elements into their narratives and styles. One of ICAIC's most brilliant shorts, Reinaldo Alfonso's *Marinero quiero ser* (1970), already praised by Gianni Rondolino, belongs to a series illustrating popular songs. The short features a small model ship and uses principally cutout technique to depict its dreamy voyage across a sea cleverly suggested by rotating disks. The boat encounters marvellous sea animals, withstands a night storm, and returns to its secure port: another outstanding example, Mario Rivas' *El pececito sin color* (1976), playfully links two stages of the animation process into a myth: a setting moon and a rising sun form and give colour to the body and fins of an initially transparent fish. Rivas later experimented with mixed techniques and abstract narrative in *En la tierra de Changó* (1997). In the late 1970s and early 1980s, Juan Padrón directed ICAIC's first feature films: *Elpídio Valdés* (1979), *Elpídio Valdés contra Dólar y Cañón* (1983) and *Vampiros en la Havana* (1985). While Elpídio Valdés, the fictitious soldier in Cuba's nineteenth century independence struggles, retains a strong political resonance, the 1985 mock vampire story offers some exaggerated genre parodies aimed for the international market.

Educational programmes were popular in other Latin American countries as well. Argentine caricaturist Manuel García Ferré, for example, used an enchanting mix of live action, puppets, and hand-drawn animation for *El Libro Gordo de Petete* (since 1972); the little penguin Petete, as a framing device, even starred in Ferré's feature film *Trapito* (1975), the adventure story of a young scarecrow, with an initial, sumptuous multiplane sequence. Another of Ferré's characters, Calculín, originally a puppet like Petete, was relaunched in a hand-drawn version in the 1980s programme *Saber más con Calculín*, partnered with a token of times to come: Piripi, a computer.

Comic book adaptations have flourished since the 1960s, when Mexican-born Bill Meléndez remade *Peanuts* for television in the United States. *Hijitus*, a mock super hero series by García Ferré starring a baby with a magic sombrero, was broadcast by Argentine television from 1967 to 1974 and caught audiences in Paraguay and Uruguay as well; a compilation of the series was later released in cinemas. García Ferré also animates other writers's characters, like María Elena Walsh's *Manuelita* (1999). The successful *Supermachos* by Mexican comic artist Rius were the pretext for a short in the late 1970s. Former Hanna-Barbera animator Álvaro Arce, who did the *Condorito* series, adapted Renzo's *Lukas* (1982) in Chile. Maria da Sousa's comic book characters from *A turma da Mônica*, published since 1959 and familiar to any Brazilian child, were recreated into television episodes and were mingled with live-action sequences in package movies. Most famous of all however is *Mafalda*, a kind of Bonarense *Peanuts*. Quito's comic strip lasted from 1964 to 1973 in various Argentine newspapers; his 1973 feature *El mundo de Mafalda* collected some of the previously produced television episodes for the big screen, showcasing some beautiful moments of the 1970s' motley style. The 1970s and 1980s, mostly in Brazil, also saw some experimental films that were obviously inspired by works of the National Film Board of Canada.

The year that CGI made its entrance into animation history with the first feature film shot fully in CGI, Pixar's *Toy Story* (John Lasseter, 1995), Brazil Clóvis Vieira released *Cassiopéia* in Brazil, a fully CGI movie about a space adventure; the foreign creatures and setting allowed for a basic geometrical design, reminiscent of Pixar's first film, *The Adventures of André & Wally B.* (Alvy Ray Smith, 1984). *O Grilo Feliz/The Happy Cricket from the Amazon* (Walbercy Ribas, 2001) and its sequel *O Grilo Feliz e os Insetos Gigantes* (Walbercy Ribas and Rafael Ribas, 2009) play with the ideas of Pixar's *A Bug's Life* (John Lasseter and Andrew Stanton, 1998) and DreamWorks's *Antz* (Eric Darnell and Tim Johnson, 1998); the 2009 version of the feature presents a 3D sequence, ahead of subsequent global blockbusters featuring the same. Chilean animation studio Cine Animadores has produced a number of recent feature films, including *La Araucana* (Julio Coll, 2010), which is based on the sixteenth century colonial epic by Spanish poet Alonso Ercilla y Zuñiga. Mexico launched the *Huevos* series (*Una película de huevos*, 2006, *Otra película de huevos y un pollo*, 2009, both by Rodolfo and Gabriel Riva Palacio Alatriste), while Peru contributed *El delfín/The dolphin* (Eduardo Schuldt, 2009) to the race for viewers. Overall, we can argue that the most intriguing works come from personal and independent animation. José Angel Garcia Moreno's *Largo es el Camino al Cielo* (Mexico, 1998), for example, is a Bill Plympton-like surreal pencil animation; Emilio Ramos blends different techniques into a poetic tale in his debut short *Niebla* (Mexico/Spain, 2006), a piece reminiscent of Norstein's work. *Até o sol raiá* (Brazil, 2007) by Fernando Jorge and Leanndro Amorim retell the evergreen Northeastern myth of Lampião and Cangaço using computer-generated images imitating claymation. Jairo Eduardo Carrello presents with *Pequeñas voces/Little Voices* (Colombia, 2010) a successful animated documentary. These last examples show recent Latin American animation at its best.

Dietmar Frenz

Gael García Bernal, *Babel*, 2006 © Anonymous Content/
Dune Films/ The Kobal Collection.

LATIN AMERICAN STARDOM
GAEL GARCÍA BERNAL

Since his breakthrough performance in *Amores Perros* (Mexico, Alejandro González Iñárritu, 2000), Gael García Bernal has become the most commercially and critically successful Mexican film star of his generation. An iconic figure of the Latin American New Wave, he has constructed himself, through his performances and in interviews, as a symbol of a changing Mexican and more widely Latin American cultural consciousness.

This short essay will consider the significance of Bernal's star persona as a contemporary Latin American cinematic image. It begins with a short introduction that gives a broad overview of Bernal's significant performances within Latin American cinema and beyond and the significance of these performances in the construction of his image as a symbol of national identity. Then the focus lies on what could be characterized as the key facets of his star persona, briefly discussing Bernal as a political figure, an actor, and author of images, as well as a representation of Latin sexuality, before concluding with a final word on his significance in the broader context of Latin American cinema.

An introduction to Gael García Bernal's star persona

Jethro Soutar, in his introduction to *Gael García Bernal and the Latin American New Wave*, a biography of the star published in 2008, aptly describes the moment in which Bernal became a Latin American star:

> the endeavours of many filmmakers went into forcing Latin American cinema onto the global consciousness but it was the charisma, the screen presence and devilish good looks of the man behind the wheel, Gael García Bernal, in that seminal sequence that ensured that the movement's star was born.

The sequence to which Soutar refers opens *Amores Perros*. In this film Bernal plays Octavio, a man who while speeding and under armed pursuit is involved in a traffic accident that connects the film's interlocking stories, which take place within different strata of Mexican society. As Octavio, Bernal embodies an image of trapped, underprivileged Mexican youth drawn into dog fighting in pursuit of his tragic love for his pregnant teenaged sister-in-law. Bernal's Octavio became a lightning rod for discussions of Mexican society and its cinematic New Wave. Since then, he has taken on a diverse range of contrasting roles on screen within Latin American cinema, playing a promiscuous and privileged Mexican teen on a journey of self-discovery in Alfonso Cuarón's *Y tu mamá también* (Mexico, 2001); the titular Catholic priest who succumbs to political and sexual temptation in *El crimen del padre Amaro/The Crime of Father Amaro* (Mexico, Carlos Carrera, 2002), the highest grossing domestic film in Mexican history; and burgeoning revolutionary Ernesto 'Che' Guevara in *Diarios de motocicleta/Motorcycle Diaries* (Walter Salles, Argentina, 2004).

What unites these somewhat disparate roles into a cohesive star persona is the way in which they combine to present Bernal as a metonym for Mexico, or for Latin America more broadly. Indeed, while he has portrayed very different characters, each of them can be seen as acting out issues of national consciousness on screen. In an interview with *The Guardian*, Bernal commented that 'here in Latin America our countries are [...] very young. They were born out of political and colonial caprice' (Charlotte Higgins). On screen, Bernal portrays young Latin American men searching for their own sense of identity, characters that reflect young nations and their New Wave of cinema seeking to make their mark in a global cinematic context politically and artistically. Off-screen, in interviews promoting his performances and his burgeoning career as a director and producer, Bernal has successfully cultivated an image of himself not as a celebrity but as a serious actor and an author and as a mediator of socially conscious images of Latin American identity. We should note, however, that aside from its nationalistic implications, Bernal's promotion of his star persona in the media can also be seen as an attempt to resist the potential trivialization and sexual objectification of the smouldering Latin sexuality that forms a key part of his persona. Having introduced the key facets of Bernal's image as a Latin American star, these central aspects of his persona and the ways in which they could potentially inform conceptions of Latin American identity and cinema will now be considered in more detail.

Bernal as serious actor and political pin-up

Bernal is somewhat difficult to characterize in terms of traditional conceptions of stardom. Aside from their national relevance, his screen performances do not really present us with a cohesive 'star image' – at least not one that fits into longstanding Hollywood archetypes for the leading man. Bernal is neither a romantic nor an action hero, and describing him as a rebel or anti-hero would be similarly inappropriate, though his image is certainly oppositional. Indeed, media promotion and reception of Bernal presents him as a serious actor with artistic integrity rather than as a celebrity. A profile in the *Edinburgh Evening News*, which describes him as 'arguably the best actor of his generation' who 'defies all the usual stereotypes of a major movie star', is an example of this uncertainty. So too are the countless articles that make reference to his time spent studying at the Central School of Speech and Drama in London, with such telling headlines as 'My Love is for Acting Not Money' as in the *Edmonton Journal*, or which describe the actor as 'saving his homeland from the "poison" of celebrity' as in the *Sunday Telegraph*. In general, we could characterize Bernal as what Christine Gledhill called the 'star-as-performer':

> In this [...] category [...] attention is deliberately drawn to the work of acting, so that, in a reversal of the celebrity category, it is performance and work which are emphasized, not leisure and the private sphere. [...] As a response to the proliferation of celebrity [...] there has been quite a pronounced shift towards performance as a mark of stardom and the concept of star-as-performer has become a way of re-establishing film-star status through a route which makes its claim through the film text rather than appearances in the newspapers.

Bernal's stardom fits this characterization, especially considering the diversity of his roles and the way in which he views himself as a central part of the cultural work performed by Latin American New Wave cinema. In transposing this idea of stardom in a new cinematic context, however, the typology is insufficient, since Bernal arguably presents himself as a serious actor in order to enhance the cultural cache of Latin American New Wave cinema, in opposition to Hollywood, rather than to reaffirm the importance of stardom.

Indeed, since he has repeatedly presented himself in the media as a vanguard for the Latin American New Wave and its political ideals, Bernal's claim to integrity is nationalistically political rather than simply artistic. Bernal best articulated his attitude towards the social responsibility of Latin American film-making and his role within that process in an interview in *The Guardian* at the National Film Theatre in October 2006: 'It is truly impossible to take politics out of any story made in Latin America or Mexico. The place demands that you involve its history. It would be very disappointing not to use that'. Not without reason, the Washington Office in Latin America (WOLA) honoured Bernal with the WOLA's 2011 Human Rights Award for 'fostering deeper understanding and visibility of migrant issues'.

His presentation of himself as a politically motivated 'star-as-performer', however, can also be seen as a defence against the commodification of his Latin sexuality. In constructing his star persona as discussed, and in largely resisting the commercial lure of Hollywood, Bernal also resists being stereotyped and dismissed as a 'Latin Lover' type. Yet it is impossible to ignore Bernal's Latin sexuality as an attraction to his performances, as much as the quality of his acting; despite his best efforts, he is still frequently described as a Latin 'heart-throb' as in the *New York Daily News* and in the *Screen International* and 'pin-up' as in *The Times* and *The Guardian*. What sets Bernal apart is the way in which he uses his appealing sexuality to question issues of national identity within his screen performances; his performance as Father Amaro in *The Crime of Father Amaro* uses his sexuality to question the power and sanctity of the Catholic church, while in his roles as Julio and Octavio, Bernal depicts sex as a means to reaffirm masculinity and escape societal constraints.

In the last decade, Gael García Bernal has had a significant impact on Latin American cinematic culture, acting as an iconic representative and champion of the continents' New Wave cinema and its political and artistic integrity, both domestically and globally. He has moved beyond Latin American cinema, working with such international directors as Michel Gondry and Pedro Almodóvar, and taking roles in US films, most notably in *The King* (James Marsh, 2005) and *Babel* (Alejandro González Iñárritu, 2007). In both films, his characters force the viewers to question the perception of Mexicans and Mexican Americans with US society. At the time of this writing, his star shows no signs of waning, and while he will always primarily be associated with Latin America's twenty-first century cinematic re-birth, Bernal looks set to remain an influential figure in world-film culture for years to come.

Victoria Kearley

Fernando E. Solanas: *El viaje/The Journey*, 1992 © Trigon Films.

SCORING CINEMA
THE JOURNEY

The Journey

El viaje

Studio/Distributors:

Cinesur
Les Films du Sud

Director:

Fernando E. Solanas

Producer:

Fernando E. Solanas

Screenwriter:

Fernando E. Solanas

Cinematographer:

Félix Monti

Art Director:

Fernando E. Solanas

Editors:

Jacqueline Meppiel
Alberto Borello
Jacques Gaillard

Composers:

E. Gismonti
Ástor Piazolla
Fernando E. Solanas

Duration:

140 minutes

Genres:

Drama
History

Cast:

Walter Quiroz
Dominique Sanda
Atilio Veronelli
Fito Páez

Year:

1992

Synopsis

In Solanas' film *The Journey*, the story is determined almost exclusively by Martín, the film's protagonist. In the first part of the film, titled 'En el culo del mundo' ('Out in the sticks'), the seventeen-year-old Argentine lives together with his mother, his younger sister and his stepfather, Raúl, in Ushuaia, the southernmost city of the Tierra del Fuego at the southern tip of Argentina and the end of the habitable world. Aside from his best friend Pablo, a rock musician, Martín's only reason to stay in Ushuaia is his girlfriend Violeta, who gets pregnant but has do undergo an abortion. This will cause a lot of different problems and irritations in the life of the young man. After another fight with his stepfather, he finally decides to leave. And find his biological father Nicolás, who is supposed to be working as a geologist in Brazil. The journey becomes a voyage of discovery for Martín through the entire immensity of the Latin American continent. The second part of the film begins with his departure and is titled 'Hacia Buenos Aires'/'On the way to Buenos Aires'. The second part of the film ends with Martín's departure from Argentina, and the story's third and final chapter, titled 'A través de Indoamérica'/'Across Indo-America'. The journey leads Martín further to Mexico, his last station, where he believes he will finally find his father.

Critique

Martín does not really see any future for his dreams and projects in his 'deserted' hometown and is not just dissatisfied with the bigoted school lessons at the 'Colegio Nacional Modelo' in Ushuaia; he also has to suffer the persistent accusations of the school director, Garrido, who constantly forces the pupils to follow the rules and wear the hated school uniforms. In addition to the dire economic conditions, represented primarily by the dilapidated schoolhouse which resembles a demolished prison going to rack and ruin, Martín is desperate about the situation at home. He cannot come to terms with his stepfather, who is financially responsible for the family yet has absolutely no understanding for Martín's worries and problems. He is just about to finish school, has no idea what he is going to do with his life and is not sure of himself.

He catches a glimpse of a possible way out of this hopeless future when Violeta announces one day that she is pregnant. He is very happy about the expected child and is ready to start a family with her. Unfortunately, the couple's joy is short-lived; Violeta's father is against the pregnancy and pressures her to undergo an abortion without telling Martín. After this painful incident, Violeta's father forbids her to see Martín, who falls into depression and reminisces about his father, Nicolás, a former comic-strip artist, who left the boy a picture story that introduces him to the history of his country and continent and whose main characters he will encounter on his later travels. Together with the letters that he has received in past years from his biological father, Martín crafts a fictional world whose icons are those of his father. The desire to leave his hometown, find Nicolás and discover his own identity slowly grows in Martín's heart.

The individual stations of the journey are crafted in a deeply contrasting manner, clearly illustrating the continent's diversity to both Martín and the audience. The audience is introduced to the absurd, dilettantish, criminal politics of Dr Rana (translated to English: Dr Frog), who heads the government in Argentina's capital city where people live in contaminated water up to their navels because of incessant flooding. Here, in the grotesquely rural and underdeveloped sphere of the cosmopolitan Buenos Aires, the boy meets his grandmother. Despite her scarcely tenable living conditions, she does not want to leave her hometown and scorns both the government and her brother, whom she insults as a traitor and pollywog (!) because he profits from the misery and does business with Dr Rana's regime.

Travelling through the Amazon, Martín reaches Peru, where he tries to buy food at the market. Yet, grotesquely, only single matches or grains of salt are offered for sale; no other wares are sold. His bicycle is stolen in the Inca capital city of Cuzco. An Indio girl helps him to protect his luggage from theft and provides him with shelter. He discovers that the girl is pregnant with the child of her señora's wealthy son, who raped her, of all places, within the walls of what was once the holiest temple in the Inca kingdom. With the aid of an itinerant preacher and a small acrobatic boy, both of whom he meets on a train journey, Martín overcomes his problems with the Brazilian border officials and enters the country in which he assumes his father lives. Martín is beside himself with joy to have made it this far. Yet after a short time, he discovers that Nicolás has again left the country and is now apparently working as a geologist in Mexico. Before the boy can continue his travels, though, he must earn the money he needs for his journey by working in a gold mine. He works hard, but cannot keep up with the tempo of the Brazilian miners. The mine supervisor blames this on Martín's nationality, saying, 'Martín has fallen down. He has fallen down because he is not a Brazilian!'

On the continued journey to Mexico, Martín crosses through Venezuela and later the Caribbean coast with Américo Inconcluso, a blind yet humorous driver who repeatedly saves Martín from dangerous situations and tells him about the Caribbean and its sad history. In Panama, Martín witnesses a summit meeting of the Organización de los Países Arrodillados (OPA), or 'the organization of kneeling countries'. In accordance with the group's name, all of the members of the organization and – for a time – their guests, such as the presidential couple from the United States, must crawl on their knees through the conference room. The journey leads Martín further to Mexico, his last station, where he believes he will find his father. Yet Nicolás has already moved on, and he has only left a few letters and drawings behind which one of his friends wants to publish. In Mexico, Martín speaks with the publisher at length about his father. He discovers the final details necessary to render the myth of his father into the figure of a real father. Martín continues to be inspired by his father, even if he has become so real and familiar to him that Martín no longer really needs to meet him to be able to understand him and his behaviour. Serene and yet touched by the events of his travels, the boy sits in Américo Inconcluso's truck and feels ready to go out into a world that is no longer so unfamiliar, into a future that is no longer so uncertain. Martín knows that he found his father long ago. His journey ends here.

In view of the celebrations organized in 1992 to commemorate the discovery of America, which facilitated the revival of an astonishing number of clichés, idealizations, and long-forgotten, concealed hegemonic discourses, Solanas' epic film offers a highly critical presentation of the consequences of the *conquista*. At the same time, the film is a declaration of love for a diverse and yet unified continent that has been suppressed, exploited and robbed for over 500 years. In this regard, Solanas' film is an indictment of the First World's constant invasion of Latin American countries, the destruction of thousand-year-old cultures, and the use of debt to cripple these states. As a proponent of pan-Latin American unity, Solanas takes up Latin America's past and present from his *poly*-perspective approach in which he uses metaphorically rich images. This style recalls the third phase of the *Cinema Novo* (independent Brazilian cinema), in which the allegorical language of film reached its apogee; using comics and popular songs to reconstruct the historical cultural heritage of Latin America.

The tension and interconnections between political engagement (an allusion to Solanas' own discourse in the *Cine Liberación*) and critical distance between myth and irony appears to be paradigmatic for *The Journey*. The self-reflexive toying with the constructability and deconstruction of myths begins in the first part of the film with the title, 'En el culo del mundo'. Solanas' characteristic intermediality is revealed in the embedding of three 'chapter headings' that divide the film's chronicle into three parts and structure it like a Romanesque discourse. The deconstructive play with the iconography of Argentinean society and media culture begins with the selection of the protagonist's name. Martín is an explicit allusion to *Martín Fierro*, a gaucho figure and hero of a national epic that is central to the production of Argentinean identity. The same applies to the representation of Martín's surroundings: the powerful, the authoritarian and the exploitative are all caricatured in a scornful way. Thus the school in Tierra del Fuego is situated in a wrecked prison, where literally everything is stolen. The school director – his face unflatteringly distorted with a wide-angle lens – struts about like a 'pompous' opera singer through the battered school, where the images of Argentine *próceres de la patria/national heros*, such as Domingo Faustino Sarmiento, fall in rows from the walls. Snow falls into the classrooms, and the patriotic monument to the father of Argentine independence, José de San Martín, actually flies through the air during the unveiling ceremony.

Martín (played by Walter Quiroz in the main role) and his schoolmates personify Argentina's post-dictatorship youth, who can scarcely identify with the icons of their history and overwhelmingly find escape – as well as an expression of their discontent – in the music scene. Among them, for example, is Martín's best friend Pablo, who wants nothing other than to become an Argentinean pop star in Buenos Aires. Solanas recruited the musician and actor Fito Páez to play the role; Páez played with Charly García in the *rock nacional* (or 'electric tango') movement of the 1980s. With his 'electric tango', Páez assumes the same prominent function as the tango singer Carlos Gardel in the film *Tangos: El Exilio De Gardel/Tango: The Exile of Gardel* (Fernando E. Solanas, 1985). Solanas' characteristic inter-generic style and heterotopia is comprised first of dedicating *The Journey* to the disappointed Argentinean youth of the post-dictatorship period, and second to integrate the transgressive element of the *rockero* subculture in his film.

Martín's search for his father is revealed as an entire generation's search for their heritage and identity. *The Journey* is therefore Solanas' answer to the questions of the 'fatherless', betrayed and marginalized post-dictatorship generation.

Nevertheless, Solanas manages to make these young people laugh when the risibility of the heroes of history and the authorities of the present are made clear. In this way, he inspires the young audience to reflect critically on the past and present of Latin America – a prerequisite for the active co-formation of the continent's future. Solanas' style is characterized primarily by short, calm takes. The movement and rhythm of the film are attained through cutting and editing. The comic sequences represent a noteworthy exception; zoom effects and camera movements – also around the optical axis to suggest the dynamism and liveliness of the comic figures – imbue these static scenes with lively vitality. Although telephoto shots, such as those for flattering close-ups of the protagonists, do occur, the wide-angle perspective is without question predominant. Not only does it distort the faces of the powerful and authoritarian figures into grimaces, it also allows people to seem extremely small and helpless before an over-powerful nature – an effect also increased by the selection of total and a static camera, or by shots taken from a worm's eye view. Furthermore, the dimmed wide-angle optics, due to the great possible depth of field, achieve an equally sharp image of object and background, particularly with regard to the human within the environment that shapes him – a central theme of *The Journey*. In the second part of the film, 'Hacia Buenos Aires' ('To Buenos Aires'), as he is underway on his bicycle across the south cape of the Americas, Martín reminds us of another icon of the medial culture of Argentina and Latin America: Ernesto 'Ché' Guevara, who also travelled across Latin America during the 1950s on a bicycle that he built himself. Like Guevara, Martín meets the victims of exploitation, who remember shattered pre-Columbian culture (Inca and Maya) and show him the way forward. During his station in the flooded capital city of Buenos Aires, we follow Solanas' camera and its focus on Martín's uncomprehending face as he takes in the operetta-like, demagogic speech of the Argentine president, Dr Rana, who comes out of the government building in Buenos Aires, wearing flippers on his feet. This is a city in which the citizens have resigned themselves in apathy to this natural catastrophe: even the coffins that float by in the heavily contaminated water are perceived as a normal state of affairs. Dr Rana's name is no accident either, as the terms 'frog' and 'pollywog' are associated with the Argentinean flooding catastrophe as well as the politics of treachery, fraud and exploitation pursued during this period. Martín's friend Pablo also sings about the frogs, pollywogs, traitors, and swindlers who 'burrow about in the ground [in Argentina]', an inescapable presence due to their ubiquity and their desire to gain advantage from the catastrophe. Dr Rana's flippers also seem to symbolically refer to this. He and his followers – like frogs – are able to continue moving about in this 'swamp', while the people are rendered helpless in the water.

On one hand, the boundless, hyperbolic flooding functions as Solanas' metaphor of the Latin American periphery as a symbolic rubbish heap of cultural centres; on the other hand, it also serves as an auto-referential allusion to the film *Los Inundados/Flooded Out* (Argentina, 1962), a film characteristic of the agitated atmosphere of the 1960s and directed by Solanas' friend and colleague Fernando Birri. But while Birri films with a simple technique à la Cesare Zavattini, Solanas' style is distinguished by its opulent series of images, its hyperbole, and a surreal kind of narrative that suggests strong affinities with the gigantism of Gabriel García Márquez.

The third part of the film, titled 'A través de Indoamérica' ('Through Indoamerica'), clearly illustrates Solanas' sympathy for the exploited and for the native Latin Americans whose narrative perspective now dominates the film. While Solanas captures the Inca city of Cuzco and the breathtaking terraces of Machu Picchu, the narration is performed from the 'visión de los vencidos' (the indigenous perspective) in Quechua (in voice-over). Another example for the 'vision de los vencidos' is the Indio girl who provides lodging to Martín and tells him about how she was raped by her mistress's wealthy son. Solanas' reflexive intermediality and post-surrealist technique is revealed here by the amalgamation of *chronicles* from the indigenous perspective and the *comics* beloved by young people.

Martín encounters collective figures with whom he is already familiar from his father's comic books. These characters allegorically represent a 500-year-old history of oppression and exploitation, and also sometimes assume the narrative perspective. The comics were created by Héctor G. Oesterfeld, an illustrator famous in the 1960s who was kidnapped and tortured by the Argentinean military and to whom Solanas dedicated the film. Various characters, somewhat like parents, take over the role of supervising the boy, above all Américo Inconcluso (the Incomplete One), whose name carries the symbolism of the entire incomplete continent. Just as Américo is incomplete because of his blindness, the continent also lacks personal responsibility, self-determination, economic stability and the autonomy of completeness. Américo personifies the *chronicler* of Latin America who tells Martín and the audience about the enslavement of the blacks in the Caribbean at the hands of the European conquerors. He has experienced all of the events himself on the Latin American continent: 'There is no route that I have not travelled, there is no people that I have not visited'. Despite his role not remain a serious or realistic figure; instead, he is effervescent, radiating charm, a love of life and humour à la *Buena Vista Social Club* (Wim Wenders, 1999).

The polyphonic narrative technique of *The Journey* is reinforced by the appearance of Tito El Esperanzador (the Beacon of Hope), an incarnation of the orthodox leftist masculine doctrine of the 1960s who fights for solidarity and human rights; Solanas quotes his Third World discourse in the film. Tito El Esperanzador's 'massive' drum, which he uses to imitate the heartbeat of the Argentinean people, is meant to convey hope and the strength to endure to the (young) people. The echo of the drumbeat is meant to be equated with the solidarity of an entire continent in the face of oppression and exploitation. Tito El Esperanzador meticulously ensures that the beat of the drum, which according to his words represents the heartbeat of Argentina, does not stop; otherwise, the Argentinean people would also cease to live. El Predicador (the Itinerant Preacher), who preaches to the travellers on the road to Paraíso, later presents the inhabitants of Latin America to the confused, wealthy gringo tourists, as if they were at a slave market in the Brazilian metropolis. All of the residents in the Brazilian capital city wear monstrous belts – gigantism à la Gabriel García Márquez and according to the *Cinema Novo* style – that are meant to fight 'inflation' as an austerity measure. The Brazilian people 'must tighten their belts' in the truest sense of the word, which denotes salary cuts and other financial cutbacks by the government to fight the economic crisis. Solanas clearly refers here to the *medium of television* and its advertising aesthetic in order to accentuate its deconstructive discourse: two television news commentators dressed in one outfit – in accordance with the austerity measures – enumerate the advantages of the new belt model in different variations, and people are interviewed as if on a *reality show*.

Lastly, there is the scene at the conference of the 'Organización de los Países Arrodillados' (OPA, which in colloquial Argentinean Spanish means 'stupid'). Like the organization's name, members only move forward on their knees. Dr Rana delivers an 'impressive' speech about the advantages of the kneeling life, for example about dangerous situations in which, according to Dr Rana, being on one's knees is 'the only reasonable position' to protect oneself. The OPA plays on the acronym of the OEA, the Organization of the American States, which is shown to be a collection of kneeling 'beggars' that prostrate themselves before the First World, represented by the great shareholder from the United States. The sequence in which the tennis match between the US president and Dr Rana (a bootlicker in the truest sense of the word), illustrates the continent's subaltern, marginal position. The audience also smirks here because both grown men are revealed as completely laughable. Solanas' cynical perspective becomes bitterly serious when Dr Rana loses the match. Once more, the United States depart victorious from the pitch, and once more a Third World country stays on its knees while the great power lifts itself up and is able to lord over the others.

Martín's difficult path finally leads him to Mexico and back. At the end of his journey of self-discovery, the seventeen-year-old Martín is an adult. The insecurity of the beginning, such as the question of what he is supposed to do after his school years, has disappeared, replaced by a calm certainty of his own identity and a sense of belonging to the wider continent.

Claudia Cabezón Doty

DIRECTORS
LISANDRO ALONSO

Alonso, Lisandro (Argentina) © courtesy of Samantha Baudier –
Slot Machine Zentropa International France.

Argentinean Lisandro Alonso, born in 1975, is one of the world's most idiosyncratic and uncompromising contemporary film-makers. His first feature film, *La Libertad/ Freedom* (2001), is characterized by a very distinct aesthetic, based on minimalism on all levels. Alonso's debut film depicts a day in the life of a lumberjack in the Argentine Pampas. The protagonist is played by Misael Saavedra, who essentially acts as himself. In the course of the film, the activities of his working day are shown in long, calm takes: Misael looks for trees and cuts them down, eats, rests and listens to the radio, delivers the wood, buys food at a service station, makes a phone call and returns to the forest, where he hunts an armadillo, which he roasts over the fire and then eats. Characteristic of Alonso's films, the chores are shown in great detail and without any dramatic effects. As in his subsequent films, *Freedom* has very distinct stylistic traits: it features only amateur actors; narrative and dramaturgic developments are extremely reduced; the action unfolds only in the present; long takes predominate; extradiegetic music is heard only during the credits; and dialogue is sparse. By reducing plot elements, the traits of the places and the basic activities of daily living come to the fore. Alonso steers clear of providing the spectator any interpretational guidance, though. Nor do his films provide psychological, sociological or ethnographical explanations. Instead of an explicit articulation of social issues, micropolitical dimensions of his films are revealed through bodily expressions and simple interactions.

Alonso's second film, *Los muertos* (2004), again deals with a taciturn loner and has a simple plot with little action: Vargas, played by Argentino Vargas, is released from prison and voyages into the wilderness of the Río Paraná in northern Argentina to find his daughter. Typically for Alonso, questions are raised but no answers are provided. The film's beginning is especially enigmatic: in a long, stylized sequence shot with little depth of field the camera meanders through the woods. Suddenly, bloodstained bodies of children appear on the forest floor, and then the camera registers the lower body of a passing man with a machete. After a long fade-out to green, a shot of the sleeping protagonist follows. Although Vargas is imprisoned for murdering his brothers, the reasons for his crime are not explained. He is not characterized as a bad person, and the film does not follow genre patterns that correspond with the bloodshed, i.e. the conventions of a prison film or a thriller. As a result of the first sequence, however, an uncanny touch emanates from the representation of nature, which dominates the film. Like the preceding film, the complex relation of nature and society is explored in regard to a marginalized man. Alonso never casts an appraising look at the people he depicts. Instead, the camera takes on the role of an observer, shooting from a distant angle and at times autonomously swerving away, leaving the protagonist behind to explore nature on his own. Again, Alonso observes his protagonist rather than telling a story. His films transcend the borders of fiction and documentary. The original locations and lay actors combine with the observing mode and result in a documentary feel. At the same time, a subtle fictionalization of the documentary images takes place.

Alonso's first two films are brought together in the meta-film *Fantasma/Phantom* (2006), which explicitly plays with the representational modes of fiction and documentary. The protagonists from *Freedom* and *Los muertos*, Misael Saavedra und Argentino Vargas, have come to the cultural centre Teatro San Martín in Buenos Aires to attend a screening of Alonso's films. In long takes they both – separately – wander through deserted, labyrinthine corridors and hallways. Vargas finally enters the cinema hall and watches his own performance in *Los muertos*. Ironically, he is his only viewer, except for one staff member, who apparently leaves before the film ends. This is Alonso's commentary on the fact that *Los muertos* was only screened in one theatre in Argentina – the very one shown in *Phantom*. Besides this ironic acknowledgement of his status as a non-mainstream film-maker, Alonso also reflects on the particular perspective he occupies in his movies. By confronting rural settings and characters with the urban space of the cultural centre, and with the cinematic apparatus in particular, he can depict the tensions and contradictions between these realms.

The disclosure of these contradictions is also characteristic of *Freedom* and *Los muertos*. Despite their documentary touch, both films steer clear of an allegedly immediate view of the 'primordial traits' of nature and of men. Repeatedly, autonomous camera movements transgress this observing view, thereby raising questions about the perspective on the action. At the same time, the apparent transparency of the cinematographic image is revealed to be a representational mode based on realist conventions. Furthermore, Alonso points to his urban cultural background, which greatly differs from the rural settings of both films. The credit sequences do not function as a transition into or out of the film's fictional world, as most credits sequences do. On the contrary, the credits are clearly separated from the rest of the film by highly contrasting music: the electronic beats in *Freedom* and the dark rock in *Los muertos* apparently are not part of the world represented in the films – which do not otherwise contain any non-diegetic sounds – but rather refer to the film-maker and the production background.

Where *Phantom*, with its explicit self-reflexivity, stands out in Alonso's oeuvre, his most recent film to date, *Liverpool* (2008), follows a pattern similar to *Freedom* and *Los muertos*. Again a taciturn loner is depicted in an isolated place on the periphery of Argentina. Farrel, played by Juan Fernandez, a worker on a container ship, disembarks in Tierra del Fuego to visit his childhood village after having been gone for years. In the village he encounters his sick old mother, his father and, allegedly, his daughter. Typical for Alonso, no dramatic incident occurs. The characters largely remain silent, and the communication between Farrel and his family is reduced to a minimum. Instead, their gestures and their relation to the surroundings come to the fore, as well as the passing of time which is made palpable in long takes with minimal action. With four feature films to date, Lisandro Alonso created a very consistent oeuvre, which might be called a cinema of gestures due to its focus on daily routines and on the interplay of bodies in cinematic space and time, without subordinating them to a plot.

Peter W. Schulze

DIRECTORS
GUILLERMO DEL TORO

Born in 1964 in Guadalajara (Mexico), Guillermo del Toro belongs to a new generation of Mexican film-makers who, influenced by the ideological and cultural changes of the late 1980s and the 1990s, have contributed to a renaissance of the Mexican film by exploring new directions in film-making. Whereas in the 1960s and 1970s, the icons of Mexican cinema such as Arturo Ripstein or Felipe Cazal were strongly committed to the concept of Cinema Auteur and the French *nouvelle vague*, thus seeking to create purely artistic or political films, their descendants were exposed to completely different influences. Television, advertising, globalization, and the constantly advancing process of Americanization during the 1980s have left their mark on today's productions. And it is above all due to the American distribution network and the slick marketing campaigns that Mexican films have become successful internationally. Accused of commercialization and a loss of identity by the elders, yet acclaimed by their much younger viewers, this new generation of film-makers is more liberal and progressive in that it does not necessarily see any contradiction between national heritage and international success, between the film industry and high-quality films.

The reinvention of the Mexican film can be witnessed time and again. Probably its best known advertisement, at least with regard to Hollywood, is Salma Hayek. At the turn of the twenty-first century, a great number of Mexican directors came into the spotlight. Suddenly the world became aware of films such as *Amores Perros* (Alejandro Gonzáles Iñárritu, 2001), *Y tu mamá también* (Alfonso Cuarón, 2001) or *El crimen del padre Amaro/The Crime of Father Amaro* (Carlos Carrera, 2002). Mexican directors have been gaining ground for many years and Guillermo del Toro is no exception.

Del Toro's oeuvre is broad and diverse. Not only is he committed to directing, he also works as a producer, screenwriter, novelist, and author for film magazines including *Sight and Sound* and *Village Voice*. His fascination for film stems back to his early childhood. At the age of seven he shot his first film with a Super 8 camera. In 1983, he made his first short film, *Matilde*. To date, del Toro's directional work includes twelve films: *Doña Lupe* (short, 1985), *Geometria* (short, 1987), *Hora Marcada* (TV series, 1986–89), *Cronos* (1993), *Mimic* (1997), *El espinazo del Diablo/The Devil's Backbone* (2001), *Blade II* (2002), *Hellboy* (2004), *El laberinto del Fauno/Pan's Labyrinth* (2006), and *Hellboy II: The Golden Army* (2008). Before working as a professional director, however, del Toro was the assistant producer of several films, amongst others *El corazón de la noche* (1983) and *Doña Herlinda y su hijo/Dona Herlinda and Her Son* (1984) by Jaime Humberto Hermosillo. In 1985, he left for New York to study special effects. His teacher was none other than Dick Smith, the make-up and special effects artist in films such as *The Godfather* (1972) and *The Exorcist* (1973).

Back in Mexico, del Toro worked as an artistic designer for *Cabeza de Vaca* (1993) by Nicolás Echevarría. It was in the same year that he made his breakthrough with his first full-length film *Cronos*. Set in Mexico City in 1997, *Cronos* is a modern vampire tale.

According to an old legend, the Cronos device was created by a Spanish alchemist. In the form of a scarab beetle, this little, bloodthirsty device is able to render men immortal with a single bite. Centuries later, the device ends up in the possession of an old antiques dealer, triggering a series of misfortunes.

The production of *Cronos* was a lengthy process. The design of the scarab beetle alone took more than a year. In the end thirteen beetles were made, all of which were stolen once the film had been shot. Del Toro was not only the director; he was also in charge of the special effects. It was for this reason that he founded his own company called Necropia. In total, the production costs of the film amounted to US$2 million, making *Cronos* the second-highest budgeted Mexican production of its time after *Como agua para chocolate/Like Water for Chocolate* (Alfonso Arau, 1993). Despite all the difficulties, the film was worth the trouble. Contrary to the predictions of the IMCINE (Instituto Mexicano de Cinematografía), *Cronos* was extremely successful at the box office. The film was awarded nine Ariels in Mexico and won 25 international prizes, including the Grand Prize during Critic's Week in Cannes.

Both the storyline and the themes occurring in *Cronos* are evidence of del Toro's predilection for fantasy and horror, elements he has made use of in his work ever since. The preference for the dark and the mysterious is deeply rooted in del Toro's childhood. It was his strict Catholic grandmother who nourished the future director's imagination. And it was the violence on the streets of Mexico which made del Toro an unwilling witness to blood and brutality. All of his films are reminiscent of magical creatures, of comics and horror movies. They can also be considered an homage to Francisco de Goya, Alfred Hitchcock and Luis Buñuel, as well as to E.T.A. Hoffmann.

Since the production of *Cronos* turned out to be very expensive, causing del Toro severe financial problems, it was not until 1997 that he was able to develop his next project: *Mimic*. The film was made for Miramax Studios and the cooperation between del Toro and his American employer was difficult for both sides in that they had differing ideas on what the film should be like. Today del Toro admits that shooting *Mimic* was a profound experience, making him realize that there are always two films being shot by the director: the first film corresponding to the screenplay, with the second reflecting the director's personal ideas. In the end, del Toro proposed a classical horror movie dealing with mutant insects threatening the city of New York. Despite the troubles between director and film studio, *Mimic* became del Toro's first Hollywood success and further blockbusters were soon to follow.

In 2001, he shot *The Devil's Backbone*. The story is set in the Spanish Civil War and is told from the point of view of a young boy. It definitely paved the way to Hollywood for del Toro. Just one year later, *Blade II* was released, followed by *Hellboy*, *Pan's Labyrinth* and *Hellboy II: The Golden Army*. With the exception of *Pan's Labyrinth*, which is thematically related to *The Devil's Backbone* since it focuses on a child's experiences during the Franco Regime in Spain, all his previous films are comic adaptations. Blade is a creature from Marvel Comics, half human, half vampire seeking to avenge his mother's death – she was fatally bitten by a vampire while pregnant with Blade. Based on the graphic comic by Mike Mignola, *Hellboy* is a red-skinned demon raised by Professor Trevor Buttenholm, his surrogate father, after being conjured by and rescued from the Nazis. He works for the Bureau for Paranormal Research and Defense (BPRD) and fights against dark forces. The *Hellboy* sequel is del Toro's latest film to date. His future projects include the completion of his novel trilogy and the release of a computer game. However manifold his plans may be, it has to be assumed that they will have one crucial thing in common: del Toro's love for the cruel and the fantastic.

Justyna Cempel

DIRECTORS
ALEJANDRO GONZÁLEZ IÑÁRRITU

Alejandro González Iñárritu is a director, producer and writer. Born in Mexico City, Mexico, in 1963, he began his career working as a DJ for the radio station WFM. He then dedicated himself to the world of movies, studying film-making and theatre. By 1990, he was one of the youngest producers in the famous Mexican company Televisa. Later, he created his own company called Zeta Films, where he began producing advertisements for Mexican TV. Evaluating his early productions, particularly his tendency to constantly recycle his earlier work in his later, we can see González Iñárritu as a postmodern director. He used many of his early commercials within, for example, his magnificent film *Amores Perros* (2000). Describing the structure of that film in an interview for BBC Home, he said that they 'originally planned to make 11 short films to show the contradictory nature of Mexico City, but they ended up settling on three and expanding them'. In the 1990s, before the enormous success of *Amores Perros*, González Iñárritu studied film-making in Maine and Los Angeles under the Polish director Ludwik Margules. During this period, he created the film *Detrás del dinero* (1995) with Spanish star Miguel Bosé in the lead role. This movie was a project proposed to Televisa, and was supposed to have been the first Mexican TV series totally to have been created as films first. After the first episode, 'El timbre', some problems arose between Televisa and Warner Bros. and the project was halted.

The collaboration between González Iñárritu and Guillermo Arriaga was undoubtedly one of the finest combinations of directors and screenwriters. Together, they created the fascinating 'Death's Trilogy' that consisted of *Amores Perros*, *21 gramos/21 Grams* (2003) and *Babel* (2006). *Amores Perros*, the first volume of this trilogy, won numerous awards, including eleven Ariels from the Mexican Art Academy for Best Director and Best Actor, among others. The film received a British Academy of Film and Television Arts (BAFTA) award for Best Film Not in the English Language, as well as a Critics award at the 'Cannes Film Festival' (Semaine de la Critique). The film also received an Academy Award nomination for Best Foreign Language Film. In Mexico, *Amores Perros* was acclaimed as the best Mexican film of the twentieth century. The second volume in the trilogy, *21 Grams*, like *Amores Perros*, is composed of a mixture of many plots organizing themselves around a dramatic car accident. This stylistic device sees González Iñárritu continuing to recycle within his films and presenting a reality structured as a puzzle made by many pieces that are oriented towards a pre-determined 'meeting point'. Here the causality is chance. The third film of this trilogy, *Babel*, is built in a very similar way. The difference is that now we do not have a puzzle that is territorially reduced; the fate of the characters in this film touches the whole world, from Mexico to Morocco to Japan. The destiny of some of them – the metaphor of 'us' – is mysteriously interconnected even though these characters had never met.

All of González Iñárritu's films after *Amores Perros* were made in Hollywood. The director explains this change by stating that in the United States he finds more possibilities for experimentation and more economic possibilities than in Mexico. He notes that this is not because Hollywood is more advanced in film-making, but that 'they have their well-known formulas same as always but he finds this not to be renewable'.

Despite the fact that many critics associate his name with Quentin Tarantino, Alejandro González Iñárritu's admits his admiration for, and perhaps influence from, Akira Kurosawa, David Lynch and Christopher Nolan. We can see that Alejandro González Iñárritu's style has changed by observing his most recent film, *Biutiful* (2010). This production is a story with a more conventional formula. In this film he returns to a story about a man exposed in a lineal temporality. The style is very 'realistic' in the sense of 'old-fashioned' social realism. The characters in this film represent a very special part of society, the more marginal side of Barcelona. In this way, the film's title and its spelling hints at its great irony, because we do not see the tourist's Barcelona, but rather its social borders and problems. The illegality of immigrants, their struggle to survive, their living conditions, etc., are themes presented in this film. The movie reveals a great evolution on the part of González Iñárritu, who here seems to show more preoccupation with the humanity of the story than the composition or the effects of the composition, which is constructed in a form of realism very near the one that a Ken Loach might express. The reasons for the stylistic change are not clear, but it may relate to the fact that it is González Iñárritu's first film that he did not make in collaboration with the famous screenwriter Guillermo Arriaga, with whom he collaborated on the 'Death's Trilogy'. The relationship between Arriaga and González Iñárritu ended badly because of a disagreement over the copyright for the script of *21 Grams*. Both men have been very discrete in their comments on the subject.

Although González Iñárritu's latest film is quite different from his previous productions, it was nominated for two Academy Awards (Best Actor and Best Foreign Language Film). Finally, Javier Bardem won the 2010 Cannes Best Actor award for his role in *Biutiful*. At the '22nd Stockholm International Film Festival' (9–20 November 2011) Iñárritu will be awarded with a prize for his work as visual creator, and will receive the Visionary Award as did Luc Besson, Gus Van Sant and Terry Gilliam before him.

Claudio Aldunate-Cifuentes

Solveig Hoogesteijn (Venezuela)
© courtesy of Alexander Gonschior,
www.agowebworks.de/
www.tuebingen-bilder.de.

DIRECTORS
SOLVEIG HOOGESTEIJN

Swedish-born Venezuelan film-maker Solveig Hoogesteijn (b.1946) studied philosophy and literature at the Universidad Central de Venezuela as well as sculpture and drawing at the Escuela de Artes Plásticas Cristóbal Rojas. She studied film and television documentary at the University of Television and Film in Munich, Germany.

Hoogesteijn's film-making debut was the documentary *Vasilis* (1970). After moving on to mid-length films, *Profesor Galetzki* (1971) and *La casa de campo* (1972), she directed her first full-length film, a documentary called *Puerto Colombia* (1975). While studying in Germany, Hoogesteijn gradually became aware that the stories that she as a film-maker wanted to tell were predominantly set in Venezula, so she sought permission to shoot *Puerto Colombia* in Venezuela.

Following *Puerto Colombia*, Hoogesteijn wrote, directed and produced *El Mar del Tiempo Perdido/The Sea of Lost Time* (1977). This film, a German-Venezuelan co-production based on a short story of the same title written by Gabriel García Márquez, won the Second Coral Award at the 'Havana Film Festival' in 1981.

In 1979, she directed *Manoa*, another German-Venezuelan co-production. This film delves into the search for identity inspired by Alejo Carpentier's novel *Los pasos perdidos/The Last Steps* (1953). Screened in 1980 in the Parallel Section of the 'Cannes Film Festival', the film won awards in other international film festivals, such as Cartagena and Biarritz. She next wrote and directed *Alemania puede ser muy bella, a veces/Germany can be very beautiful, sometimes* (1982).

Hoogesteijn's lasting fame stemmed from *Macu, la mujer del policía/Macu, the Policeman's Wife* (1987). A police drama based on a real murder – the so-called 'Mamera Case'. This film is the most responsible for turning her work into a subject of study both in and beyond Venezuela. This film broke box office records and amassed over 1.3 million viewers at a time when Venezuela's total population was 17 million.

Macu, the Policeman's Wife, tells the story of María Inmaculada (María Luisa Mosquera), an 11-year-old girl who marries Ismael (Daniel Alvarado), a policeman much older than her. By the time she is fifteen, she has already had two children. In her adolescence, Macu falls in love with Simón (Frank Hernández), a boy her age. Crazed with jealousy, Ismael kills his wife's lover and covers it up until the truth inevitably comes out.

A number of social problems are confronted in this film, including the unacceptable living conditions in slums, female illiteracy and the consequent economic dependence of women on men, early pregnancy, domestic violence, machismo, and police corruption and abuse of power. Religious syncretism is revealed in Macu's home through an altar with flowers, candles and prints of divers virgins and saints showing a mix of pagan objects and different elements belonging to divers religions and rites (Christian, Afro-Caribbean, indigenous).

Macu was shot inside a slum, or barrio, following realist aesthetic practices. The mixture of professional actors with real slum dwellers who speak the language of the barrio stresses authenticity and makes the audience forget they are watching a piece of fiction. Salsa music also plays an important role, since it transports the spectator right into the middle of Caracas. This is the music you hear in every corner of the city, even while travelling by bus.

In 1994, Hoogesteijn directed *Santera*, a Venezuelan-Cuban-Spanish co-production partly shot in Chuao, an isolated town on the Venezuelan coast with a high concentration of African descendants. Paula (Laura del Sol), a Spanish doctor who works for Amnesty International, is investigating conditions in Venezuelan women's prisons. She meets Soledad (Irma Salcedo), a taciturn mulatto woman accused of murdering her brother-in-law and his daughter by means of black magic rites. Paula decides to find out whether Soledad is guilty. After paying a visit to Soledad's family in Choroní and going to Chuao to meet Eulogio (Víctor Cuica), Soledad's spiritual godfather, Paula confronts Soledad and demands her to tell her the truth. Once Paula is convinced of Soledad's innocence, she helps prove it.

As in *Macu*, this film is defined by realist aesthetics. It graphically depicts the main problems in Venezuelan women's prisons: overcrowding, violence, bribery and injustice. The morgue, where Paula also works, is full of corpses that nobody else seems to notice. New corpses are constantly brought in and thrown indifferently to the ground, an indirect criticism of the prevailing indolence in an inhuman and violent city like Caracas.

Drum music, associated with black people in Venezuela, takes the spectator acoustically from Maracay to Choroní. Once there, both the conflict between Catholicism and santeria becomes evident, as does complementary character. Racism is indirectly thematized through the commentaries from Ms Medina, a white lady who refuses to rent her house to Soledad because she would not ever tolerate black rites being held in there.

Almost a decade later, Hoogesteijn returned to Caracas' slums with the melodrama *Maroa* (2005), a Spanish-Venezuelan co-production about the eponymous 11-year-old orphan girl living in a rancho with her deceitful grandmother Brígida (Elba Escobar). Maroa (Yorlis Domínguez) learns from an early age to survive by cheating, begging, stealing, as well as selling prints of saints and porno magazines on the streets. Domestic violence, drugs and criminality are part of the everyday environment surrounding *Maroa*. This situation changes when she meets the Spanish music teacher Joaquín (Tristán Ulloa), who gives her the opportunity to play the clarinet in a youth orchestra, a clear reference to the documentary *El sistema* (Paul Smaczny/Maria Stodtmeier, 2008).

Everyday violence in Caracas plays a key role in the recreation of reality in this film. In her struggle for survival, *Maroa* moves all over Caracas and lets the audience witness the daily acoustic violence she experiences through deafening traffic noise, as well as in chaotic bus terminals where vendors announce their goods at the top of their voice and the sounds of salsa music and *technomerengue* do not seem to delight but rather to hurt. There is a clear contrast between this aggressive outside world and the quiet inside world of the orchestra. Classical music, especially Mozart's clarinet concert KV 622, reveals to *Maroa* the power of music and enables her later to leave the violent and hopeless environment she comes from for good.

Religious syncretism and police abuse are recurrent in Hoogesteijn's film work. As in *Macu*'s home, there is an altar full of prints and statues of different virgins and saints in *Maroa*'s rancho. Ezequiel (Luke Grande), the policeman, like *Macu*'s Ismael, personifies police corruption and abuse of power.

Since 2002, Hoogesteijn has directed the Trasnocho Cultural Center, a centre run without governmental subsidies that offers a wide range of cultural activities including theatre and cinema.

Maribel Cedeño Rojas

Lucrecia Martel, 2008 © Aquafilms/
The Kobal Collection.

DIRECTORS
LUCRECIA MARTEL

The Argentine film-maker Lucrecia Martel belongs to the few internationally renowned women directors of the Latin American film scene and she has, to date, released three masterpieces that have been recognized as outstanding works of the national and international film history. Her film work is part of the *Nuevo Cine Argentino* (New Argentine Cinema) to which also belong film-makers such as Anna Katz, Adrian Caetano, Albertina Carri and Martin Rejtman, through an anti-conventional basic attitude (in Bertolt Brechtian terms), a primacy of the local over the global, and a contextualization in the aesthetic of the new cinema as conceptualized by Gilles Deleuze.

Martel's three feature films – *La ciénaga/The Swamp* (2001), *La niña santa/The Holy Girl* (2004) and *La mujer sin cabeza/The Headless Woman* (2008) – have been awarded numerous distinctions and her oeuvre distinguishes itself through a unique sensual and haptic quality. The central interest of her work lies not in the narrative but is directed essentially towards the intensive focus on sensorial perception (sight, touch, taste, smell and hearing) and thus integrates itself in the tradition of modern cinema.

In particular, with her first film *The Swamp*, which premiered worldwide at the 'Berlinale' in 2001 and was awarded the Alfred-Bauer prize, Lucrecia Martel has become a world-renowned woman film-maker. One of the most well-known readings of *The*

Swamp, which reveals the decline of the Argentine middle class in the province La Salta, is highly relevant, in particular for contemporary spectators. Even though the film contains no direct references to the corruption of the political class during the Menem era, the title of the movie, *The Swamp*, with its semantic connotations of mud, swamp and decay, still suggests the degeneration and corruption of the Argentine political system. Protagonists' remarks such as 'here everything decomposes and rots' serve the same purpose as implicit references to the economic decline of the Argentine bourgeoisie. The subtlety of the film lies in the close linking of implicit political codes to the perceptual-aesthetical, epistemological and anthropological signs of the movie, so that an aesthetics of politics, in Jacques Rancière's terms, is visible. Closely linked to the political reading of the film is also a mythological interpretation, which reads the movie as a post-Catholic redemption cinema that deconstructs the latent expectations of all the family members to witness a Virgin Mary apparition at the end of the movie through the last sentence of the youngest daughter in the family: 'I have gone where the vision of Maria should be. I didn't see anything.'

With her second feature movie (*The Holy Girl*), the Argentine film-maker has yet again produced a masterwork. The title of the movie can be read as an ironic play on words. The movie screens more the erotic desires of the youngest daughter than her mystical aspirations, even though the beginning of the film frames the latter in a virtuosic manner. The opening sequence shows a group of teenagers during a religious education class while they recite the mystical poetry of Saint Teresa of Avila and during the confession of religious experiences. Therefore, as in *The Swamp*, a post-Catholic, 'deconstructivist basic attitude' (again in Brechtian terms) dominates the narrative. After the realization of the two adolescent girls that every form of religious and mystical experience is impossible, they focus on their own and reciprocal erotic desires. As previously seen in *The Swamp*, Martel uses an aesthetic practice of modern cinema, as conceptualized by Deleuze, which focuses not on action but on the sensual experience of the protagonist. The primacy of the haptic sense can be understood as a decoding of the classical hierarchy of senses. Sensual bodies in water, extensive hair combing, the tender contacts between the two friends, as well as the perverse touch of a hotel guest who reveals himself to be a hypocrite patriarch, are highlights of haptic experiences, which also actively involve the spectator. Martel uses here a refined *mise en abyme* of the voyeur situation, through which she places the spectator as the voyeur of the voyeur and confronts the spectator to the perpetuator's perspective.

The third film of the film-maker, *The Headless Woman*, released in 2008, confronts us with the perspective of a woman again of the Argentine middle class from the province La Salta. Accident, hit-and-run, crime and effacement of the crime construct the filmic matrix of the movie, which tells the story of a neurotic female protagonist of the Argentinean bourgeoisie who runs over a living being at the very beginning of the movie. Using the patterns of the classic thriller, the film unfolds revealing that the victim was an indigenous boy. While the female protagonist falls into a state of torpor, the male members of the family begin to efface the criminal act so efficiently, that in the end she seems to acquire a new identity. Quoting filmic references from Alfred Hitchcock, Michelangelo Antonioni and David Lynch, the nervous breakdown of the protagonist is skillfully constructed. Close-ups reflecting the subjective perspective, the chromatic composition of the costumes and the focus on the emotional vacuum of the protagonist constitute the main features of the filmic construction. In *The Headless Woman*, the film-maker succeeds yet again in rendering visible the political subtext in the aesthetics of the film as well as in drawing a critical portrayal of the corruption of the Argentine middle class.

Uta Felten

DIRECTORS
CARLOS SORÍN

When Carlos Sorín (b.1944) won several internationally acclaimed awards for his debut film, *La película del rey/A King and His Movie* (1986), including the 'Venice Film Festival''s Silver Lion, he immediately attracted the attention of a wide international audience. Since his debut, Sorín has directed five other feature films: *Eversmile New Jersey* (1989), *Historias mínimas/Intimate Stories* (2002), *Bombón: El Perro* (2004), *El camino de San Diego/The Road to San Diego* (2006) and *La ventana/The Window* (2008).

A King and His Movie, based on Jorge Goldenberg and Juan Frésan's unfinished 1972 film project entitled *La nueva Francia*, was an homage not only to its uncompleted precursor, but also to cinematography itself: it is a meta-film that stages the hardship of its own realization.

Here a young director tries to depict the 'true' story of a French adventurer who declared himself King of Araucania and Patagonia in the nineteenth century. Sorín's fictional self in his first feature film leaves no doubt about his cinematic self-conception, and the western historiography of film treats him accordingly, as an aware and audacious director. From the very beginning of his career, Sorín displays his fascination with Italian neo-realist visions of reality, and his similar interest in characters reminiscent of Werner Herzog or Federico Fellini. Later, he displays his affection for episodic formats often compared to Robert Altman's *Short Cuts* (1993) and elements of road movies such as David Lynch's *The Straight Story* (1999). Ingmar Bergman's *Smultronstället/Wild Strawberries* (1957) discernibly influenced Sorín's *La ventana/The Window* (2008).

Sorín stands for a stylistically and thematically coherent cinema, one that balances between a specific Argentinean point of view and cinema traditions from Europe and the United States. Sorín's well-received films are characterized by certain key words, such as 'Patagonia', the 'road movie', 'amateur actors' and a silent 'entertainment cinema'.

Within Sorín's filmography of six feature films, the 1990s are a blank page, which may be significant for his position within the *Nuevo Cine Argentino*. The late 1990s belonged to a different generation in Argentinean cinema. Within this creative environment, Sorín later created an episode of the collective documentary *18-j* in 2004 and one of 25 perspectives on Argentinean history with his short *Argentina del Bicentenario. Las voces y los silencios* (2010).

After his debut feature Sorín made his comeback to the movies in 2002 with *Intimate Stories*, which repeated the festival success of *A King and His Movie*. In a sense, there seemed to be a direct line between the two festival successes, even though Sorín made with *Eversmile New Jersey* a hardly known and commercially unsuccessful film in 1989 with Daniel Day-Lewis in the leading role, playing a nomadic Irish dentist. It is a critically underrated film that profits from the energetic presence of its main actor and that leaves a delightfully ironic aftertaste compared with the charming innocence of Sorín's popular successes of the 2000s. In one of the first scenes we see Daniel Day-Lewis on the passenger seat of a pickup truck after an accident, next to his obviously concerned rescuer, who may or may not be surprised if his smiling lunatic of a passenger bit his ear off. Such a powerful moment of suspense later recurs just once, in a nearly identical camera angle focusing on Lechien, the huge Argentinean mastiff in *Bombón* seated next to his new owner in his pickup. Apart from this, the two films are worlds apart – at least as far as Patagonia, crossed in all directions.

Indeed, Patagonia is a leitmotif in all of Sorín's films except *El camino de San Diego/ The Road to Sand Diego* (2006). The wide horizon, the endless roads, the omnipresent wind, and the desert-like landscape oblige a camera smitten with panoramic views but sap the energy of soaring dreams and thoughts and leave its people modest and content, defending their little piece of happiness with brave optimism.

It is these people that the director privileges in his recent films. Nothing is more alien to this landscape than pathos, which is always an external import as in his first two films, *A King* and *Eversmile*, whether it arrives in the shape of a French utopian or of an Irish dental-missionary. Both are quixotic characters struggling for and against an enervating environment that is hard to overcome. In these films, Patagonia is portrayed as both promise and stress test, a tranquilizer for unusual projects, high aims or characters demanding more space. Their 'projects', which are somewhere between megalomania and vocation, are not depicted as either a happy or a tragic end. Tragedies, success stories and Bildungsromane are genres inadequate to the task of revealing Patagonia.

Rather, road movies structure the increasingly intimate stories. The long walks, trips and journeys of the protagonists, played by amateur actors particularly from *Intimate Stories*, lead them on long distances, to, after all replaceable destinations and back. The journey is the reward and sometimes achieves the level of a salvation path, a secular pilgrimage as developed in *The Road to Sand Diego* where a young unemployed lumberjack hits the road to bring a wooden statue to Diego Maradona's bedside. In fact it is the 'profane sacred', the 'marvelous' of the ordinary life, for which Sorín has an eye and that retrospectively unites the three road movies from 2002, 2004 and 2006 into a trilogy.

Such a profane myth of everyday life is also typified by television as a kind of an existential assurance of most of the portrayed anti-heroes in *Intimate Stories*, *Bombón* and *The Road to Sand Diego*. We see there a small and widespread 'society of the spectacle' consuming the promises of a tele-visionary 'second life'. Sorín knows well what he is telling; while working in the television and advertising industries earlier in his career, he was able to study the medium and its codes. In fact, he showed the mechanisms of the construction of reality in 1986 in his fictional television documentary *La era del ñandú*.

Sorín's *La ventana/The Window*, is a path of life that comes to an end. Following the immortality of the media idol Diego Maradona, the director alludes to the mortality of an aging writer, played by Antonio Larreta. This film is exceptional within Sorín's filmography in several ways. The end of a life is explored in close circles: a bed, a chamber, a garden; before, on a last walk, we once again encounter Patagonia, which appears this time – in its north – greener and fresher and more human than ever before. Perhaps after the lineal courses of the three previous films, a new branch has begun to diverge in Sorín's oeuvre. His most recent feature film to date, the thriller *El gato desaparece/The Cat Vanishes* (2011), can help to answer this question.

Kerstin Küchler

DIRECTORS
ANDRÉS WOOD

From his beginnings, Andrés Wood has shown to be a film-maker who looks for bridges; bridges between a personal and industrial cinema, between the Chilean cinema of the preceding generation (first of all Aldo France) and the present one, between the 'great history' and the 'little fabula', between the film genres and poetry. We can say that he has the strange and unusual prestige in Chile to be a film-maker who has been able to continue his work since the mid-1990s – with *Historias de fútbol* (1997) – until the end of 2010 – he is currently completing a biography about Violeta Parra. In this way, he does not only sustain himself in a volatile industry, he also attracts a big public, but not only for commercial reasons.

Wood is a director of the collective and seeks to speak to the Chilean public from an imagery typical of the local conditions: his images take us into landscapes that form the territorial identity of the country and his characters have always been beings belonging to that territory; sticking to it, contrasting in it. This search for identity is one of the main elements in three of his films combined at the same time with the great issues of democratic transition: integration, grief and discomfort. Three films (*Historias de fútbol*, *Machuca* [2004] and *La Buena vida* [2008]) seem to have given a correlate to these three stages of transition as a mirror of the changes and anxieties of the recent Chile.

Historias de fútbol should be considered as a milestone in the sense of artistic and collective vocation: the film that started with very few copies in the city of Santiago made us at its time overcome the averseness to Chilean cinema that characterized this period. It attracted about 600,000 spectators and inaugurated a period in which the Chilean film would increase its number of premieres. *Historias de fútbol* is also an artistic manifesto, and presents an idea of what Andrés Wood believed to be a film-maker, namely a reporter of the people. The film presents three stories which are set in three key points of the narrow geography of Chile (central, north and south) and which complement a narrative tone that appears together with an anecdote – football. This serves to discuss themes such as bribery (in the first story interposed between the soccer passion of a worker and his boss), sacrifice (in the second story, set in the north, a child must sacrifice his ball to remedy the plight of his family) and acceptance of others (the third story, set in the south and in a comedic tone, tells of the sexual encounter between a student from Santiago and a woman from the countryside). Wood seems to capture with grace and sympathy certain local idiosyncrasies, namely overflowing optimism in the characterization of his characters. *Historias de fútbol* wants to offer an image of the collective. It is a portrait that seeks to be representative and popular, while poetic and sensitive, and that is in tune with a certain optimism that characterized the early years of democratic transition.

After exploring some topics inherited from the playwright Andrés Perez such as a vocation for the rural (*El desquite* [1999], based on a book with the same title by Roberto Parra), Machuca seems to create a sort of second 'time level' both in the work of Wood as well as in the social context in which it is inserted. In the context of the commemoration of the coup d'état in 1973, Chile opened for the first time in many years a dialogue on the political memory. This climate set the foundations for the premiere of Machuca. Machuca is again a look at the 'we' identity, and is also a sort of witness to the film-maker's own experience of the rise of Allende and the subsequent coup d'état. Located in the Chile of 1973, the film is set in a polarized country and told from the viewpoint of Gonzalo, a child of the upper class. In his high school there is a social integration project attended by children of the lower classes from villages and territorial seizures. This project is led by Father McEnroe, a faithful representative of the most social doctrine of the Catholic Church in vogue these days via the 'Theology of Liberation'. In this context Gonzalo establishes a friendship with Pedro Machuca. Despite their social differences, prejudices and suspicions, they manage to establish an affective bond that will lead Gonzalo to question his social and family life. Towards the end, the military coup takes place with violence, frustrating not only the project of Father McEnroe but also all the government's attempts by the Unidad Popular (the popular party) in search of a more just society. The friendship between Gonzalo and Machuca becomes impossible because of the change and new repressive climate that arises among the population. The last image of Machuca is a long shot of the mountain range from the narrative point of view of Gonzalo. It is a viewpoint that is itself symbolic regarding the division of a country and the remoteness of 'ones' and 'others' in a social project. The mourning of Wood is about a lost utopia and a forgotten community, the end of a 'we'.

La Buena Vida (2008) marks a third poetic and political stage of Wood. In this film there is a departure from the countryside and the big collective subjects (historical memory, soccer), but it still leans towards a 'we' singled out in the individualized experience of the city. Wood involves a group of characters 'belonging' to a determined territory and time in the form of a 'choral story' focused on seven characters that must deal with their individual conflicts. The group portrayed by Wood belongs to a fragmented middle class in their residences – from a professional sexologist who does not communicate with her daughter to a prostitute with HIV, from a musician who cannot find jobs in Chile to a cosmetologist who plans to open his own shop. All of them have a variety of topics in common related to psycho-social discomfort: the lack of opportunity (the musician rejected by the Philharmonic), the lack of communication (familiar in the case of the sexologist), and even marginalization and inequality (the case of the prostitute). All seem to be the opposite story to the great dream of democratic integration. In addition, at the basis of the story, there is an erosion of the narrative, a narrative of downtime, pauses, silences, and a certain wintry tone. If *Historias de fútbol* seemed to extend the dream of social integration to social and geographical landscapes of the country, Machuca was aware of the political mourning of the great political projects of the past. *La Buena vida* is a more pessimistic view on the present and on the great political stories of democratic integration. It is a film of and about discomfort.

Andrés Wood is undoubtedly the film-maker of the transition. He has followed the hopes, sorrows and disappointments typical of this period and has been, without doubt, a film-maker who has known to give images to a Chile that, semi-hidden, is sensed in its daily living. Interesting, too, is that he has accompanied the processes of social charm and disenchantment with politics without being a strictly political film-maker. The reverse side of his image hides iconographic, visual and subjective motifs of a country and a historic moment. This trilogy of films has helped to X-ray these collective atmospheres.

Iván Pinto Veas

Friedrich Nietzsche defined 'comical' as transformation from present anxiety to a short moment of high spirits. In this respect, the decentralized human subject is temporarily able to banish the psychic pressures caused by an overpowering reality. If parts of this reality become ridiculous, the oppressed individual will bask in freedom for a few moments. Superiority over the formerly dominant political or social environment, won by laughter, produces a political system's or social class's comic heteronomy. As narrative has historically been understood as a medium that reflects reality, the Latin American comedic movie fought long and hard for acceptance in light of social, political and economic resistance. High quality comedy was established in the Latin American movie landscape only recently, and indeed has not yet been well received in some parts of the continent even today. Periods of economic instability, long dictatorships, revolutions and violent rivalries between competing political groups, such as the Colombian *violencia*, in numerous South American countries obstructed or suppressed the development of cinema, particularly of comedy films, several times in the last century.

While the fictional movie developed from documentary, narrative and dramatic genres, comedy evolved from three different generic models. The early slapstick burlesque comedy descended from late medieval popular farce traditions and early European and American film productions. Economically, Latin American silent cinema only made a profit from this successful genre because it did not have any of its own genuine national alternatives. A later incarnation of European operetta traditions – the Argentinean Tango Film – became the very first Latin American medium of self-identification, but even in its few ironic or comic features, this genre affirmed social and political escapism without raising problematic topics for the audience to laugh at. This escapism meant that only the third model, the trivial comedy, derived from nineteenth century boulevard pieces, flourished in the early talkie era of the late 1930s. During this short golden era of film comedy Argentineans Luís Slavasky, Francisco Mugica and Luís Cesar Amadori produced light film comedies steeped in Argentine middle-class ambiance. By using popular plots, Argentinean Manuel Romero's *Los muchachos de antes no usaban gomina/Yesterday's Boys Didn't Use Hair Fixers* (1937) followed the path of light bourgeois comedy. Antonio Delgado Gómez' *El rompimiento* (1939) was the first feature film in Venezuelan film history. A more innovative treatment of these genre features was offered by the Argentinean Leopoldo Torres Ríos – the father of the great director Leopoldo Torres Nilsson – with films such as *La vuelta al nido* (1938), where especially urban subjects were treated.

During World War II, a US embargo on film material and cinematographic equipment nearly stopped Latin American movie production. The first successful post-war comedies presented Argentinean actress Mirta Legrand in Benito Perojo's *La casta Susana/Chaste Susan* (1944) and Carlos Schliepper's *El retrato* (1947). Influenced by the comedy tradition evolved by Ernst Lubitsch, Billy Wilder and Howard Hawks, Schliepper created a softer kind of screwball comedy, the best example of which is *Cuando besa mi marido/When My Husband Kisses* (1950), one of the funniest film comedies ever directed in Latin America. Today nearly forgotten and more or less underestimated, Carlos Schliepper was the first Latin American director to understand the rules of the screwball genre by returning to the authentic old Spanish interpretation of perception. Like the plots of Lope de Vega's and Pedro Calderón de la Barca's comedies, Schliepper's screenplays deal with the simple Calderonian promise that reality never is what it seems to be. Schliepper adapts the classical happy ending for his inconspicuous heroes, who finally get the attractive ladies. At the same time, however, he uses a great deal of wit to analyse relations in the Argentine middle-class, often producing erotic ambiguity via linguistic irony.

Far from Schliepper's irresistibly charming highlight of the screwball tradition, directors in the 1950s preferred the more accepted genre of melodrama. When cinema's *enfant terrible*, Luis Buñuel, moved from Hollywood to Mexico, he created a handful of comedies drawing from both Mexican melodrama and surrealist ideology, such as the hero's adventurous bus journey in Manuel Altoaguirre's adaptation *La subida al cielo/Ascent to Heaven* (1952); the game of anarchy and fate in *La ilusión viaja en tranvísa/Illusion Travels by Streetcar* (1953); and the anti-bourgeois daydreams of the anti-hero in Buñuel's last Mexican comedy, *Ensayo de un crimen o La vida criminal de Archibaldo de la Cruz/The Criminal Life of Archibaldo de la Cruz* (1955). Some years later, Buñuel decided to produce movies in Spain and France.

Influenced by revolutionary movements in various Latin American states, cinema production became the preferred medium of contest for both sides. In post-revolutionary Cuba, internationally renowned director Tomás Gutiérrez Alea established a kind of comedy that was increasingly able to demonstrate the specific problems of the socialist system. His first screenplay, *Las doce sillas/The Twelve Chairs* (1962), adapted a well-known homonymous Russian novel written by two Soviet authors, Iliá Ilf and Yevgeni Petrov.

Staging the tale in contemporary Cuba, Gutiérrez Alea pokes fun at the hypocrisy of the former bourgeoisie and their efforts to cope with the revolution. He followed this film with *La muerte de un burócrata/Death of a Bureaucrat* (1966), which presents the difficulty of dying in Cuba's over-organized political system. The plot of *The Twelve Chairs* concentrated on the hunting of a rich lady's treasures hidden in twelve chairs; in *Death of a Bureaucrat*, the protagonist hunts only for a union membership card buried with a late worker whose widow needs this card to claim her pension.

The innovation of comedy coincided with a military dictatorship in Brazil during the 1970s when the accusatory power of the *Cinema Novo* had found a way to avoid censorship by inventing the 'Tropicalist Movement'. Tropicalists avoided direct confrontation with the political system by creating a metaphoric universe. Bruno Barreto's visually opulent movies – like 1976's *Dona Flor e Seus Dois Maridos/Dona Flor and Her Two Husbands* or 1983's *Gabriela cravo e canela/Gabriela* – hide their moderately critical moments within a camouflage of Brazilian clichés, such as the protagonist's exaggerated sexual appetites. Other Tropicalist productions deal with the national cliché of an Indian culture based on cannibalism, as in Nelson Pereira dos Santos's *Como era gostoso o meu Francês/How Tasty Was My Frenchman* (1971). In *Xica da Silva* (1976), Carlos Diegues brings colonial history to the screen, but at the same time, he reflects on the contemporary corruption and abuse of political power.

Although Gutiérrez Alea abandoned comedy for nearly thirty years, his international reputation grew in the years before his death in 1996 based on two comedies presenting painful subjects in Cuban society. In cooperation with Juan Carlos Tabío, he directed the gay comedy *Fresa y chocolate/Strawberry and Chocolate* (1994). His last comedy, *Guantanamera* (1995), satirizes daily Cuban life: through their dialogues, protagonists from different social groups discover that the human condition of different characters may not be as different as they had thought.

Continuing Gutiérrez's comedy efforts, his former co-director Juan Carlos Tabío released a handful of comedies such as *Se permute/House for Swap* (1984), *Demasiado miedo a la vida o Plaff/Too Afraid of Life or Splat* (1988) and *Aunque estés lejos/So Far Away* (2003). All of these deal with the absurd elements of life in Cuba. The run-down bus terminal in his comedy *La lista de espera/Waiting List* (2000), where busses pass without picking up the waiting passengers, may be seen as an ironic metaphor of Cuba's actual state of decadence.

In most of the region, democratization and improvements in production coincided with the spread of comedies discussing very different subjects. The range of comedic themes explored over the last two decades spans from Sergio Cabrera's take on the parallel world formed by a group of squatters (*La estrategia del caracol* [Colombia, 1993]) to María Luisa Bemberg's melodrama on the taboo subject of being handicapped (*De eso no se habla/I Don't Want To Talk About It* [Argentina, 1993]).

This development could be attributed to the growing political consciousness and to a broader media access. The expansion of mass media assists in presenting problems to an audience no longer encumbered by religious constraints. The discursive means used to showcase these problems extend from light irony to all kinds of verbal and visual ambiguity as used in the newly discovered screwball comedy. Latin American comedy no longer seeks public consensus by poking fun at normal society. Jorge Fernando's *Sexo, Amor e Traição* (2004), mocking sexual problems among Brazil's upper classes, is an example of this renewed comedy that is shown on the screen. Mexican director Jaime Humberto Hermosilla's *De noche vienes, Esmeralda* (1997) also derides traditional moral conventions by telling the story of the multiple adulteress Esmeralda, who is accused of having lived in bigamy with five husbands at the same time.

The greater the influence media has on society, the more media and art themselves become plot subjects. This media *turn* in comedy is influenced by the French *nouvelle vague* cinema and by the postmodern theory on self-referentiality of art. It is particularly prevalent in Brazil, Argentina, Mexico and in Peru, where Felipe Degregori's *Todos somos estrellas* (1993) makes fun of the would-be truthfulness of a reality TV soap. In Guilherme de Almeida Prado's *A Dama do Cine Shanghai* (1987), the sublime atmosphere of Hollywood's film noir is recalled with subversive irony by exhaustive quotation while the technical conditions in Sandra Werneck's *Pequeno Dicionário Amorosa/Dictionary of Love* (1996) are far away from Hollywood. Hermosilla, the great old man of Mexican cinema, also adjusted to the new self-referential movie with the intelligent comedy *La tarea/The Homework* (1990), an underhanded engagement with the mechanisms of seduction and voyeurism. The plot pretends to document the power of pornography, but at last the spectator must accept having been double-crossed by the supposed authenticity of the presentation, which is only a media effect. These final examples of highly intellectual reflections on media within movies hearken back to the old Hispanic idiosyncrasy that considers life as merely another form of dream. Nowadays, comedy is one of the most popular genres in Latin America.

Gerhard Wild

My Best Enemy

Mi mejor enemigo

Countries of Origin:

Argentina
Chile
Spain

Language:

Spanish

Studios/Distributors:

Alce Producciones
Matanza Cine
Wanda Visión

Director:

Alex Bowen

Producers:

Pablo Trapero
Alex Bowen

Screenwriters:

Julio Rojas
Paula del Fierro

Cinematographer:

José María Hermo

Art Director:

Verónica Astudillo

Editor:

Danielle Fillios

Composer:

Miguel Miranda

Duration:

100 minutes

Genre:

Drama

Cast:

Nicolás Saavedra
Erto Pantoja
Miguel Dedovich
Felipe Braun
Jorge Román

Year:

2005

Synopsis

Patagonia, 1978, at the height of the Beagle Conflict, the border conflict between Argentina and Chile over the possession of Picton, Lennox and the Nueva islands, Rodrigo from Santiago is fulfilling his military service in Punta Arenas when he is sent to the Pampa to defend the border between Chile and Argentina, together with four other young men. They cannot find the old fence that once marked the border, however, and the unchanging landscape hinders any orientation. When the men run into a group of Argentinean soldiers, both sides decide to mark a provisional border. Cautiously, they start to make contact with each other while at the same time constantly expecting an attack from the other side. Starting with the exchange of cigarettes, drugs and food, the men even end playing football together. The fragile friendship between Chileans and Argentineans culminates in a joint barbecue during which all soldiers drink, sing and dance together. Suddenly, the Argentinean sergeant Ocampo is informed about a forthcoming attack. He tries to convince his Chilean colleague Ferrer to leave together with his men, but the latter decides to stay. Eventually, a new tension replaces the burgeoning friendship between the camps. During the night, Ocampo hears about Pope John Paul II's interventions on behalf of peace on the radio.

Critique

The political conflict between Chile and Argentina over territorial claims and maritime rights in the Beagle Channel constitutes the historical background of Alex Bowen's tragicomedy. In 1977, a tribunal at the International Court of Justice in The Hague chaired by

Alex Bowen: *Mi mejor enemigo/My Best Enemy*, 2005 © Wanda Vision.

Queen Elizabeth II granted Chile the disputed Lennox, Picton and Nueva Islands. Argentina did not recognize the tribunal's decision and on 22 December of the same year threatened Chile with the military occupation of the islands. At the last minute, Pope John Paul II impeded the outbreak of a war by his diplomatic intervention.

My Best Enemy exposes the absurdity of the military conflict between the young reservists ironically and with a good sense of humour. It plays on the stereotypes of the Chilean and Argentinean national characters and makes an argument for overcoming prejudices and clichés. The film contrasts the military command structure, discipline and notions of duty with human solidarity, and shows that the similarities between the young men far outnumber their differences.

The film's title points out the ambivalent relationship between Chileans and Argentineans, who, over centuries, have been political enemies but on an individual level have lived together peacefully, especially in the transnational region of Patagonia. In this southern part of both countries, where history, culture and nature cannot be rigidly separated by nation states, the artificial separation of national territories becomes especially visible.

The camera illustrates the difficulties of defining a fixed borderline by using numerous wide-angle shots that dwell on the horizon and the monotonous, unchanging natural environment of the Patagonian Pampa. For the spectator, it is difficult to distinguish visually the different protagonists as they all blur with their uniforms in the ochre colours of the dry landscape and the military camp. In fact, while the film takes the perspective of the Chilean reservist Rodrigo (Nicolás Saavedra), who narrates his experience via voice-over, it does not fall into a nationalistic attitude. Rather, it underlines the similarities between the young men in both camps. As the characters are little explored, they all stand for more or less the same type of young man, with slight differences of origin or character – another way to underline the absurdities of the construction of political concepts of the enemy in national contexts.

Hence, the symbolically charged soccer match marks a point of culmination as it clearly proposes a peaceful alternative to military aggression. In a parallel metaphoric construction, the barbecue constitutes another solution of the political conflict on a personal level: both groups have found a lost single lamb but would not want to share it until they finally decide to have the barbecue together. While the film contrasts sequences of friendship like these to the military setting, *My Best Enemy* portrays the Argentinean-Chilean border region as a space that politically separates neighbours but at the same time opens up opportunities for cultural encounter and reconciliation.

Jenny Haase

Bombón

Bombón: El Perro

Countries of Origin:

Argentina
Spain

Language:

Spanish

Studios/Distributors:

Guacamole Films
OK Films S.A.
Wanda Visión

Director:

Carlos Sorín

Producer:

Oscar Kramer

Screenwriters:

Santiago Calori
Salvador Roselli
Carlos Sorín

Cinematographer:

Hugo Colace

Art Director:

Margarita Jusid

Editor:

Mohamed Rajid

Composer:

Nicolás Sorín

Duration:

97 minutes

Genre:

Drama

Cast:

Juan Villegas
Walter Donado
Rosa Valsecchi
Mariela Díaz
Gregorio (the dog)

Year:

2004

Synopsis

Juan Villegas, called Coco, tries to make a living by selling hand-crafted knifes. The 52-year-old auto mechanic has just lost his job at a gas station in vast Patagonia. He has not seen his wife in twenty years and lives with his daughter and her family. He is looking for work when one day he helps a young woman whose car has broken down. She takes him back home to her mother. As a reward for helping her daughter the mother offers Coco a gift: 'Le Chien' (The Dog), an Argentine Dogo, a pedigree, with which the late husband of the farm owner, a Frenchman, wanted to start breeding. Coco's daughter does not want the dog in the house, so he and his pet leave home. Coco and 'Le Chien' (his real name is 'Bombón' [which means sweet/chocolate/treat] as Coco finds out later) get a job as a guard and they meet a bank manager who himself is a fan of the breed. He sends them to the dog trainer Walter Donado who is sure that 'Le Chien' can win a dog show. He wins the third prize, at least. The two men agree to let 'Le Chien' inseminate a bitch on heat and make some money out of it – but the dog is a non-performer. Coco and Walter split up, Walter takes 'Le Chien' back to his home. When Coco returns later to fetch the dog, Walter's wife tells him that the dog has run away. Coco finds Bombón in a brick factory where he is mating with a stray bitch. Coco takes the dog with him in his car. They pick up two young hitchhikers as they drive into their future.

Critique

Most striking about *Bombón: El Perro* is that Argentinean director Carlos Sorín mainly worked again – as in *Historias mínimas/Intimate Stories* (2002) – with 'real' people, not actors. Shooting with these 'simple characters', as he calls his cast, gives him the opportunity

Carlos Sorín: *Bombón: El Perro/Bombon*,
2004 © Guacamole Films/OK Films.

to 'diminish the manipulation and deception that cinema inevitably involves'. Sorín's story is fictional, of course, but told in an almost documentary way. Finding Juan Villegas, who 'was' Juan Coco Villegas, rather than 'playing' him was the best of luck – for the director as well as for the audience. The main character is a sweet, soft, patient, quiet man who takes life as it comes, and it is not going very well in the beginning. There is a strong wind blowing in Patagonia.

With Bombón Coco's life changes a lot. Not taking the dog with him is out of the question, and suddenly things pick up. Coco gets a job offer, stumbles into the dog show, receives warm applause from 400 onlookers for his impressive big white dog, and has a lovely evening (and an almost imperceptible flirtation) with the singer Susana. Juan Villegas does not comment explicitly on anything that happens to him, it's all in his eyes, which are difficult to forget.

Bombón: El Perro is a road movie indeed – and the roads are long in inhospitable Patagonia. The takes of the landscape are beautifully shot in natural light but not overwhelming. It is more the people in this deserted landscape we are interested in. They are all so immensely friendly; nothing bad happens to Coco, although one is expecting someone to cheat him all the time. The open ending leaves the audience confident that the two of them will make it – whatever that means.

The pace of the film is slow, which does not mean that there is nothing happening. There is no real comedy and no real tragedy in the film, it simply narrates laconically a life that is sometimes beautiful, sometimes sad, and sometimes just is. *Bombón: El Perro* might say: 'Don't push the river, don't force it, nature will have it's way' – and that is not only true for dogs. To non-Spanish speakers the film could be the translation for 'tranquilo'.

Regine Wenzel

Duck Season

Temporada de patos

Country of Origin:

Mexico

Language:

Spanish

Studios/Distributors:

CinePantera
Esperanto
Filmoj

Director:

Fernando Eimbcke

Synopsis

Finally alone at home, Moko and Flama are happy to play their videogame, to drink as much Coca Cola as possible, and to do whatever they please. When 16-year-old neighbour Rita interrupts them, they let her use the stove, but do not pay much attention to her. But then the power goes out and they succeed in finding new means to defeat their boredom. The guy who delivers the pizza too late decides to stay, Rita shares her hash brownies with them, and the blackout ends up shedding light on latent issues that had been buried by everyday routines and diversions. Rita baked the brownies because nobody had remembered her birthday, the pizza man suffers from depression, Flama is very much distressed by the divorce of his parents, and Moko is trying to sort out his feelings for his best friend.

Critique

What seems to be a simple story in black and white is actually more complex than it seems. The mainly static camera witnesses what

Producers:

Jaime Bernardo Ramos
Frida Torresblanco
Christian Valdelièvre

Screenwriters:

Fernando Eimbcke
Paula Markovitch

Cinematographer:

Alexis Zabe

Art Director:

Amellali González

Editor:

Mariana Rodríguez

Composer:

Alejandro Rosso

Duration:

85 minutes

Genre:

Comedy

Cast:

Daniel Miranda
Diego Cataño
Danny Perea
Enrique Arreola
Carolina Politi

Year:

2004

Fernando Eimbcke: *Temporada de patos/Duck Seasc*
2004 © Cinepantera/Lulu/Tita

happens on a normal Sunday afternoon in long sequences and wide-angle medium shots. The significance of time is at the core of this film and is explored in several ways. Moko (Diego Cataño) and Flama (Daniel Miranda) cannot wait until they are alone. Finally free to shoot each other in their videogame, they are interrupted by Rita (Danny Perea). When they want to continue playing, the blackout stops them. Not knowing what else to do, they order pizza. The company promises to deliver within 30 minutes or the pizzas are for free. We see then how Ulises (Enrique Arreola), the pizza guy, races through the streets of Mexico City and how he has to run up eight flights of stairs because the elevator is not working. When he arrives, Moko announces that he is 11 seconds late and does not want to pay him. Ulises protests and threatens with a sit-in. The kids do not care and Ulises ends up playing a soccer videogame with them when the electricity is back on. While the men are having fun, Rita is killing time, looking out of the window and opening all the kitchen cabinets, the camera staring at her from within the cabinets. Then there is another blackout, and the dripping tap water seems to count the very long seconds of boredom. Whereas Moko helps Rita to bake her cake and gets his first kiss, Ulises tries to speak to Flama who has locked himself up in the bathroom. He tells him that he hates his current job, but that he is haunted by the memories of his former job as an executioner at a dog pound. Only when he slides his lucky coin under the door does Flama open up.

There are many references to ducks in this film. Apart from the title, the credits deliver the motto 'The ducks united will never be defeated'. However, the only ducks we see in the film are on a quite ugly painting. Despite having passed all of Flama's life in a closet, it has become a fiercely contested object in his parents' divorce. Ulises tries to comfort Flama by telling him that some ducks have to migrate, that it is in their nature. When the four get high after eating Rita's birthday brownies, the painting seems fascinating to all of them. Ulises explains the aerodynamic significance of the V-formation of migrating ducks and how they thus assist each other. With the help of very original camera angles, subtle details and humour, Eimbcke shows us how this group of four are somehow able to console each other.

Heidi Denzel de Tirado

Intimate Stories

Historias mínimas

Country of Origin:

Argentina

Language:

Spanish

Studios/Distributors:

Guacamole Films
Nirvana Films S.A.
Wanda Visión S.A.

Director:

Carlos Sorín

Producers:

Martin Bardi
Leticia Cristi
José María Morales

Screenwriter:

Pablo Solarz

Cinematographer:

Hugo Colace

Art Director:

Margarita Jusid

Editor:

Mohamed Rajid

Composer:

Nicolás Sorín

Duration:

87 minutes

Genres:

Comedy
Drama

Synopsis

For three very different reasons, three people journey 200 miles from the small town of Fitz Roy in Argentina's southern region of Patagonia to the district capital of San Julián. Don Justo is told by a friend that his dog Malacara, which has been missing for three years, has been spotted on the outskirts of San Julián. Travelling salesman Roberto is planning to surprise a widow whom he intends to woo with a birthday cake for her child René, although he has forgotten whether the child is a boy or a girl. The third traveller, the impoverished María, journeys with her baby to participate as a contestant on the game show 'Multicolour Casino' in the hopes of winning the grand prize and a possible trip to Brazil.

Critique

Intimate Stories contains three loosely connecting narratives that chart the journey of three of Fitz Roy's inhabitants as they journey to the port of San Julián. Don Justo (Antonio Benedicti) lives with his son and daughter-in-law, who run the local grocery store, but their relationship is strained. The son is condescending and impatient with his aged father, whom he views as senile: 'He's not weird; he's just crazy,' he says. When Don Justo learns from a friend, González, that his dog Malacara has been spotted in San Julián, he tells his son he wishes to retrieve him, but his son replies scornfully, 'How will you get to San Julián when you cannot get to the toilet?' Nevertheless, he leaves at sunrise with a thermos of water for his friend and a new pair of mountaineering boots donated by some Dutchmen passing through Fitz Roy. Don Justo's journey, which is perhaps the most touching of the three shown in the film, is in some ways redemptive as he seeks the forgiveness of his dog; he left it lying in the road after hitting it with his car. Given his advanced age and his poor eyesight, this journey may well be his last, thus the quest to assuage his guilt and salve his conscience takes on an almost mythic quality.

Roberto (Javier Lombardo) is a travelling salesman who extols the virtues of a 'life-changing book' on body language and positive thinking. 'Selling is a science,' he tells fellow salesman García. 'Never consider a failure as a failure, but as an opportunity to change direction.' Roberto is journeying to San Julián with a birthday cake for

Carlos Sorín: *Historias mínimas/Intimate Stories*, 2002 © Trigon Films.

Cast:

Javier Lombardo
Antonio Benedicti
Javiera Bravo
Julia Solomonoff
Laura Vagnoni

Year:

2002

René, the young child of a widow whom Roberto intends to woo, yet he cannot remember what sex the child is. In an attempt to create a unisex cake, he has the original football cake converted into a smiling turtle by the mother-in-law of a local police officer. While visiting the doctor Roberto recognizes Don Justo, who was taken there for low blood pressure. Fearing that his son might discover his whereabouts, Don Justo pretends not to know Roberto until they meet later in a cafe, where Roberto offers to drive Don Justo the rest of the way. The third and least-developed of the narratives is that of María Flores (Javiera Bravo), a rather simple and innocent young mother, who is journeying to San Julián after her application to be a contestant on a game show had been accepted. We never see María travelling to San Julián; it is only when Roberto returns to a motel room and watches TV that we see María on the gaudy, low-budget game show, 'Multicolor Casino'.

Intimate Stories, as the title suggests, is full of small, everyday moments; a narrative of simple hopes and dreams constructed on a cumulative series of minimal scenes: from Don Justo wiggling his ears for a group of giggling children to the smile of María winning a food processor on TV. There are no grand gestures, no heroic deeds; just simple folk from a small town in the southern region of Patagonia engaging with one another. The only element of grandeur is that of the vast Patagonian landscape (as it was in Sorín's early film *La película del rey/A King and His Movie* [1986]), which is beautifully captured by cinematographer Hugo Colace (who also filmed Carlos Sorín's *Bombón: El Perro* [2004]). This vast and harsh landscape, with its dusty roads disappearing over the horizon, contrasts with the simplicity and relative unimportance of the region's inhabitants, whose parochial existence in a largely desolate and undeveloped region is slowly being encroached upon by modernity and the capitalist consumer culture. Sorín has imbued *Intimate Stories* with a poetic sense of desolation through the region's isolated and windswept topography: the spiritual desolation of consumer society and the acquisition of useless items, the physical desolation of Don Justo (who is going blind and is almost deaf) and also economic desolation, perhaps a reflection on Argentina's recent financial crises. In spite of the prevalence of desolation, Sorín's film is not bereft of hope, but is rather sustained by a life-affirming appreciation of little joys.

Zachariah Rush

Lost Embrace

El abrazo partido

Country of Origin:

Argentina

Language:

Spanish

Studios/Distributor:

BD Cine

Director:

Daniel Burman

Producers:

Daniel Burman
Diego Dubcovsky

Screenwriters:

Marcelo Birmajer
Daniel Burman

Cinematographer:

Ramiro Civita

Art Director:

Maria Eugenia Sueiro

Editor:

Alejandro Brodersohn

Composer:

César Lerner

Duration:

100 minutes

Synopsis

Ariel Makaroff is a young man of Polish-Jewish extraction who lives with his mother Sonia and his brother Joseph in a neighbourhood in Buenos Aires, Argentina. His father left in 1973, when Ariel was a child, in order to go to Israel and fight in the Yom Kippur War. Rita, an older woman, runs a lingerie shop in a commercial gallery, a shop in which the film is largely set. The film focuses on the lives of Ariel's family and of the shopkeepers in the local gallery. Ariel, the narrator, is a man without any sense of direction. Apart of having an affair with Rita, he thinks of emigrating to Poland in order to become 'European' and to get some answers to his life. The fact that his father preferred fighting in the war instead of caring for his family leads to Ariel's permanent state of dissatisfaction. He thus asks his grandmother for some documents that should help him receive Polish citizenship. This forces his grandmother to remember experiences with the Holocaust in Poland. Later, Rita confesses to Ariel that his father left because she had an affair with Osvaldo, one of the other shopkeepers. In the end, Ariel gets to know his father's side of the story.

Critique

Daniel Burman's *Lost Embrace* forms part of a loose trilogy of films depicting the life of a young Jew in contemporary Buenos Aires. It deals with the multiculturalism of Argentinean society while showing Ariel's (Daniel Hendler) identity crisis; throughout the film he is constantly searching for his personal and cultural identity. Burman himself has both Argentinean and Polish citizenship; this film thus can be described as largely autobiographical. Although many of Burman's films have been featured in festivals around the world, *Lost Embrace* is his most successful film. It received numerous award nominations and won several prestigious prizes, including the Grand Jury Prize at the 'Berlin International Film Festival' and a Best Actor award for Daniel Hendler, famous for his portrayal of Ariel.

Daniel Burman: *Abrazo partido/Lost embrace*, 2004 © Trigon Films.

Genre:

Comedy

Cast:

Daniel Hendler
Adriana Aizemberg
Sergio Boris
Silvina Bosco
Rosita Londner
Isaac Fajm

Year:

2004

The specific topic of a multiethnic group living far away from its country of origin is a very current one in today's global world. Ariel's individual fate thus reflects an authentic situation, which helps viewers identify with him. Throughout the film we follow Ariel's attempts to find answers to questions that prevent him from living in tranquility. He cannot understand the fact that his father (Jorge D' Elía) left and why this does not seem to bother either his mother Sonia (Adriana Aizemberg) or his brother Joseph (Sergio Boris). The title also reflects his situation, since for many years the embrace between him and his father was lost. His situation leads his permanent insecurity and dissatisfaction with what he is doing, which we see in his decision to quit university to help his mother in the shop, although she is almost always working there instead of caring about his future. His insecurity is also reflected in his decision to leave his former girlfriend, Estela, with whom he had a relationship for many years; nevertheless, after leaving her, he constantly thinks about her.

The actors Burman chose are highly professional and act their parts in very fascinating ways. They combine with the most important place of the film – the gallery – to build the film's essential components. The 'gallery', that is to say the shopping mile, plays a significant role in its function as a microcosm in which everybody runs his own shop: Rita (Silvina Bosco), an Italian family, a quiet Japanese couple,

Mitelman and Osvaldo (Isaac Fajm), the solitary stationer. Burman uses stereotypes in order to depict the immigrants; the Italian family, for instance, is presented as 'typically' Italian – very loud, constantly engaged in discussion and consisting of many members. Further, Burman has created a film that is a mixture between comedy and drama. It is this combination of comedy together with some dramatic moments referring to Ariel's situation that makes the film incredibly engaging. Ariel's serious identity problem, explored through a variety of humorous situations, keeps the film from becoming stagnant. All of these elements keep the viewers interested, curious and exited: does Ariel really leave Argentina for Poland? Does he finally get to know his father? The film is hence not directed to one specific group of viewers but it offers a variety of aspects that will appeal to many people.

The humorous treatment of Ariel's problem in some scenes may lead some to find the film a bit too kitschy or not serious enough. Nevertheless, the film fulfills its promise: in the end, Ariel gets to know his father and the lost embrace is found again. It seems that he thus finds the balance that encourages him to go on.

Valentina Vazzano

Y tu mamá también

Country of Origin:

Mexico

Language:

Spanish

Studios/Distributors:

Producciones ANHELO
Twentieth Century Fox Film Corporation

Director:

Alfonso Cuarón

Producers:

Alfonso Cuarón
Jorge Vergara
Sergio Aguero
Amy Kaufman
David Linde

Screenwriters:

Alfonso Cuarón
Carlos Cuarón

Cinematographer:

Emmanuel Lubetzki

Art Director:

Gabriela Diaque

Synopsis

The tragicomedy relates the initially conventional coming-of-age story of two teenage friends from disparate socio-economic backgrounds, Tenoch and Julio. Diego Luna alias Tenoch Iturbide is the son of a well-respected politician and associate of the Mexican president. His character's name is a combination of the name of Mexico's first emperor Agustín de Iturbide and Tenochtitlan, the seat of the Aztec Empire, and emphasizes the protagonist's privileged lineage. The other teenager, Julio Zapata, played by Gael García Bernal, is named after the Mexican revolutionary Emiliano Zapata. Fittingly, in the film he is also the son of a single mother who works as a secretary. During the summer of 1999, while their girlfriends are away on a trip to Europe, Tenoch and Julio decide to embark on a trip of their own. At a wedding they meet 28-year-old Luisa Cortés from Spain, who is named after the conquistador Hernán Cortés and plays the wife of Tenoch's cousin, a writer. The two friends invite Luisa to join them on a trip to a beautiful imaginary beach. She decides to travel with them after learning that her husband has had an affair. Their journey takes them to the south of Mexico and, eventually, to a beach on the Pacific coast.

Critique

Mexican director Alfonso Cuarón's 2001 film, Y tu mamá también, on the surface, appears to depict the hedonistic world of Mexican youth. Through the adoption of an omniscient narrator and its enduring landscape shots the film not only tells the story of its adolescent protagonists but also comments on socio-historical aspects of modern-day life in Mexico. This tendency culminates in the film's concluding scenes.

Editors:

Alfonso Cuarón

Alex Rodríguez

Composers:

Annette Fradera

Liza Richardson

Susan Shufro

Duration:

101 minutes

Genre:

Drama

Cast:

Diego Luna

Gael García Bernal

Maribel Verdú

Year:

2001

Tenoch and Julío, one from a privileged and one from a poor background, appear to personify the class system in modern-day Mexico and, initially, overcome social class barriers. The movie's final scene, however, in which Tenoch and Julío meet by chance in a cafe after not having seen each other for some time, depicts something else. There are not many things that the two, now young adults, find to say to each other. This remains their last encounter. The class barrier that the film seeks to dissolve remains in place at the end of Y tu mamá también. In the end, the departure from their everyday teenage lives that their travels meant for them merely welds Tenoch and Julio more strongly to the social reality of their own environments.

The film can be interpreted as a road movie. It makes use of individual themes that characterize the road movie: these include love and friendship, but also revenge. Further, it includes such motifs as escape, odyssey and search for the holy grail, and structurally the vehicle serves as means of transportation from one scene to the next. Moreover, the journey by car delivers scenes that are essential to the movie. As in just about every road movie, in this film the vehicle carries not only people, but also their dreams of freedom and independence and especially their dreams of adulthood. This road movie, like others, conveys foremost a sense of contemporary life, in the form of the characters' hedonism.

And yet there are no speed scenes in this apparently conventional road movie. The adolescents travel in their car at a leisurely, slow pace. The way in which the three protagonists are depicted is of critical importance to this film. The reflective French cinema of the 1950s and 1960s, the nouvelle vague cinema, seems to have served as inspiration here. The influence of this cinematic movement is evident in the use of an ever omniscient off-screen narrator who figures in the numerous socially critical scenes in the movie. The multi-layered narration puts the characters at a considerable distance. Beyond what is spoken, the images also question in a critical way. It is as though the pictures of the journey are telling another story, one beyond that of Julío and Tenoch's sensual indulgences and in the midst of another, rural, exploited Mexico. The roaming camera, in the hands of Emmanuel Lubezki, never stands still during the movie; rather, it creates disturbances and irritations. These include a cross filmed from within the car, planted at the side of the road in remembrance of an accident victim, a police barricade that the adolescents successfully avoid, and a funeral cortège that only Luísa seems to notice through the windshield. These sometimes drastic images have the same effect as the off-screen commentary. They unsettle the viewer, keep the viewer alert and create a distance between the viewer and the ostensibly oblivious teenagers. For the two younger protagonists the surroundings are monotonous. The teenagers Julío and Tenoch – in contrast to Luísa – do not appear to reflect on these fleeting snapshots of life outside the car. In effect, according to the director and co-author of the script, the film is about 'the class system, the many different Mexicos that co-exist in time and place but appear unrelated to one another' (Isabella Reicher). This view of the landscape framed by the car windows and the comments of the off-screen narrator give this ostensibly conventional film its critical edge.

Marijana Erstic

Avellaneda's Moon

Luna de Avellaneda

Countries of Origin:

Argentina
Spain

Language:

Spanish

Studios/Distributors:

Pol-Ka Producciones
Tornasol Films
100 Bares
JEMPSA

Director:

Juan José Campanella

Producers:

Fernando Blanco
Gerardo Herero
Jorge Estrada Mora
Adrián Suar

Screenwriters:

Juan José Campanella
Fernando Castets
Juan Pablo Domenech

Cinematographer:

Daniel Shulman

Art Director:

Mercedes Alfonsín

Editor:

Camilo Antolini

Composer:

Ángel Illarramendi

Duration:

140 minutes

Synopsis

Settled in a working-class neighbourhood of Greater Buenos Aires, Luna de Avellaneda is a social club where in the good old days people used to gather, play sports and enjoy each other's presence. But now the number of members who pay their fees has dramatically collapsed and debts threaten its future. Román, who was literally born in the club, is trying to find a solution both for the club's and his marriage's crises. When an offer is made to turn the Luna de Avellaneda into a casino that would bring jobs and money to the impoverished area, its members have to vote whether they should accept the deal and start anew or be loyal to the original aims of the institution and remain a social and emotional support for those who live around. This tough decision will raise economic, ethical, political and even sentimental questions for everyone involved.

Critique

Campanella's fifth feature – third with co-writer Fernando Castets – is yet another example of his ability to combine different traditions and genres to create a product that successfully satisfies rather polarized desires in the viewer; something he had already proved with his former feature, the hugely successful *El hijo de la novia/Son of the Bride* (2001), and would once again achieve with his next one, Academy Award winner *El secreto de sus ojos/The Secret in Their Eyes* (2009). *Avellaneda's Moon* is a sparkling blend of those socially concerned issues that seem almost quintessential to Latin American cinema – Argentina's economic crisis around year 2000 – with a couple of very enjoyable – if not terribly original – sentimental plots and a generous portion of witty humour, including some uproarious lines; light-weighted features whose obvious origin lies in Hollywood's romantic comedy films. The result is not far from Frank Capra's *It's a Wonderful Life* (1946), Campanella's favourite movie to which he pays explicit homage here. The effective intertwining of comedy and drama, especially the way irony tones down romanticism in some climatic scenes, accounts partially for the charm of the film; but much more so the carefully conscious way in which writer and director treat their sensitive material. This can be clearly perceived in the way the characters themselves refer, in their dialogs, speeches and even in some stories-within-the-story, to their tendency to get entangled in fairy-tale romanticism or soapy clichés (as for instance in the hilarious review of Hans Christian Andersen's *The Little Match Girl*, which emphasizes the differences between corny fiction and the ugly surrounding reality). By predicting the sense of déjà vu so often felt in the presence of standard Hollywood products, the authors cleverly defuses in advance any accusation of sentimentality or kitsch;

Genres:

Comedy
Drama
Sport

Cast:

Ricardo Darín
Eduardo Blanco
Mercedes Morán
Valeria Bertuccelli
Silvia Kutika

Year:

2004

while still making his point perfectly clear when it comes to stressing the importance of fiction to make real life bearable, both within his picture and out of it. But this meta-filmic strategy, which is applied both to the love stories and to the social and moral question posed by the film, serves yet another purpose. It sets the focus on the distance (geographic, conceptual and emotional) that separates this Latin American film from their European and US models, therefore suggesting a possible way for Latin American cinema to preserve its identity – whatever that might be – while remaining appealing to mainstream audiences. (In this sense, the scene where a[n] [in]famous fast-food restaurant is ironically defined as an 'ethnic cuisine diner' suitable for a first date, besides a very funny gag, is a meaningful remark on the actual possibilities of the subaltern to speak – and even deride the metropolis – in a postcolonial world.) It must come as no surprise that Campanella reached maturity as a film-maker after returning to his homeland Argentina, following a technically helpful but artistically disappointing training period in the United States. It was only then, working with Argentinean actors – here with ever awesome Darín, movingly funny Blanco and the whole of an incredibly credible cast, especially the women – that he managed to develop a cultural product which wisely merged the best of his beloved classical Hollywood cinema with his own interests and concerns. In turn, the fact that these pictures gained him the recognition of Spanish speaking audiences worldwide, an Academy Award, and an Academy nomination while directing *House M.D.* (David Shore, 2004–) episodes, suggests that globalization can be a very fertile soil to work on, and postmodernism a useful tool to do so.

Daniel A. Verdú Schumann

Promedio rojo

Countries of Origin:

Chile
Spain

Studios/Distributors:

Aldea Films
Sobras.com Producciones
Amiguetes Entertainment

Director:

Nicolás López

Producers:

Miguel Asensio
Maria Luisa Gutiérrez
Cristina Ybarra

Screenwriters:

Nicolás López
Beatriz Santana

Synopsis

Roberto Rodríguez is an overweight high-school student who has to endure the scorn of his classmates while living in his own world of fantasy. This world will be transformed by the arrival of a new student from Spain, Cristina. Roberto tries to attract Cristina's attention, but he cannot compete with his good-looking classmate and rival Fele. Nevertheless, when Cristina becomes pregnant, only Roberto is able to rise to the occasion.

Critique

The title of the film refers to a failing average, the average characteristic of an underperforming student, in this case, the main character of the story, Roberto Rodríguez (Ariel Levy). Roberto is the prototypical freak/geek, avid reader, collector, and fan of comic-book series and films like *Star Wars*. He has clear difficulties in separating fiction and reality, or in just enduring the miseries of real life. Roberto wears thick glasses, is overweight, and has two friends who are also on the margins of their peer group: Condoro (Nicolás Martínez), who always manages to say the wrong thing at the wrong time, and the

Cinematographer:

Chechu Graf

Art Director:

Nelson Daniel

Editor:

Diego Macho

Composer:

Manuel Riveiro

Duration:

104 minutes

Genre:

Comedy

Cast:

Ariel Levy
Xenia Tostado
Benjamín Vicuña
Nicolás Martínez
Berta Muñiz

Year:

2004

mentally-challenged Papitas (Berta Muñiz). They represent the Chilean or Hispanic version of the freak/geek. In Spanish they would be called *frikkis*, a subgroup or tribe that this film portraits with a gentle, sometimes nostalgic, and always ironic touch. Roberto lives his life like a comic book, and sometimes the characters of the books he draws ('La enorme obesidad del ser'/'The incredible obesity of being') participate in his day-dreaming adventures. The movie at times interjects comic frames or vignettes as a narrative device, precisely to stress the parallels between life as a comic or the comic existence of our main character. Roberto's story would be that of a poorly adapted high-school student in any country, and there are very few references to the contemporary or past Chilean and Latin American society or problems, except in a vague way. Roberto and his classmates inhabit an indistinct middle-class landscape. Cristina (Xenia Tostado), the object of Roberto's attention, is a Spanish immigrant, and reference is made to the fact that she comes from *la madre patria* (mother land), but this is of interest to our characters only because it reminds them of porno films, which are normally dubbed into Peninsular Spanish. A sadistic physical education instructor is called Massera, and he is described as a Nazi, but no other parallels are found with the general of the militarist Argentinean junta bearing the same name. Nicolas López is clearly more interested in drawing a universal cartography of the adolescent state of mind, with its fortunes and misfortunes. References to comics and to other movies abound. From *Grease* (Randal Kleiser, 1978), to John Hughes' classics; from *Porky's* (Bob Clark, 1982) to *Animal House* (John Landis, 1978), all the paradigmatic titles of the adolescent film world of the 1970s/80s are condensed by implicit or explicit mention in the movie. Roberto acts like a young Tom Hanks; his rival and nemesis Fele is a Travolta surrogate, etc. Lopez adds a more sardonic and at times directly gross or obscene tone. References to masturbation and to body fluids are frequent. The general depiction of characters verges on the caricature or *esperpento*: Roberto's grandfather imparts his advice from his wheelchair and, once dead, as a surrogate Obi-Wan Kenobi; the school teacher lives a sadomasochistic relation with the nurse; Cristina's father was a former matador who was killed by a mechanical bull that he had installed at his bar; the Caribbean doctor, expert in abortions, is portrayed by Santiago Segura (also serving as film producer) with gusto, echoing a character straight from the successful Torrente films (Roberto has a poster from one of these films in his room). *Promedio rojo* is irregular at times, and some scenes are more successful than others. Nevertheless, the film originally crafts its own niche as a depiction of the experiential imagination of contemporary Latin American youth.

Javier Gutiérrez-Rexach

The Waiting List

Lista de Espera

Countries of Origin:

Cuba
Spain
France
Mexico
Germany

Studios/Distributors:

ICAIC
Tornasol Films S.A.
Tabasco Films

Director:

Juan Carlos Tabío

Producers:

Gerardo Herrero
Camilo Vives
Thierry Forte

Screenwriters:

Arturo Arango
Juan Carlos Tabío
Senel Paz

Cinematographer:

Hans Burman

Art Director:

Onelio Sarralde

Editor:

Carmen Frías

Composer:

José M. Vitier

Duration:

102 minutes

Genres:

Comedy
Drama
Romance

Cast:

Vladimir Cruz
Thaimí Alvariño
Jorge Perugorría
Noel García

Year:

2000

Synopsis

Cuba. In the middle of nowhere between Santiago and Havana, a diverse group of people are waiting for the bus to get to one of these cities. Each passenger is waiting for their turn according to the order of arrival, except the 'social cases', such as the blind man Rolando, who have priority, as Cuba is a socialist country. As the buses which arrive only have a very limited number of seats left, or none, the supervisor tries to fix the station's bus. When after the whole day of waiting the apparently fixed bus breaks down again, the manager wants to send everybody home. However, the passengers decide to stay and to fix the bus themselves. While the men are occupied with repairing the vehicle, the women prepare the station to make it more comfortable for the night – everybody according to their abilities. The men seem to be successful and decide to finish the next day – when there is sunlight to look for a missing spare part – and to take a rest first. The next day, most of the passengers participate in the search, while some prepare a simple meal for everyone. The story evolves, and the waiting time is long – a child gets lost, a cat is eaten, love stories come up, and all of a sudden some lobsters appear – a gift from heaven as the people are starving. Everybody contributes with what they have – some rice, some oil, some tomatoes – and together they prepare a wonderful meal and have a great time sharing their belongings and enjoying their social gathering. As a feeling of togetherness is coming up among the group, and the relations are getting closer, the passengers decide to make the station itself a better place. Thus it transforms from an unpleasant place of transition to a better place of living, as everyone contributes as best as possible to the well-being of the community. All seems now to be perfect.

Critique

The Waiting List is a comedy – at first sight. Realizing it is inspired by real life, it becomes much more than that. It becomes a reflection on everyday life and the living conditions in Cuba, which are determined by a shortage of (infra)structure and goods. The movie, based on the novel of the same title written by Arturo Arango, may be interpreted as an allegory to Cuba itself. Starting with the setting – a bus terminal – the story is situated in a place of transition, from which people want to travel or go back home, or at least want to have the theoretical possibility to do so. However, as a consequence of the political system and its failures when it comes to economic and infrastructural matters, they cannot. The movie reveals the problems and challenges Cubans have to face which extensively influence and lower their standard of living. Nevertheless it is quite a universal situation, as people all over the world need transportation and often have to deal with similar problems. Tabío plays with the current reality on the island combined with national stereotypes and myths and thus creates an amusing, slightly satiric and entertaining work, with just the right portion of subtle criticism. In the very beginning the question whether Cuba is a communist or a capitalist country arises, but Tabío does not give an explicit answer. Instead he stimulates the audience to come to a personal conclusion. Moreover, a small-scale example is given on how to build up a perfect community based on socialist ideals and structures, in which every member of the group gives their best. Thus it is demonstrated how the original idea of communism is supposed to be put into practice. Furthermore, the inadequacy of bureaucracy and the authority chain is criticized, as they rather obstacle than favour the progress of this ideal.

Summarized, *The Waiting List* is an entertaining movie and for those who have never been to Cuba it presents a slightly burlesque introduction to what it means to be a citizen there, how structures of a communist regime work and what the actual consequences for the people are.

Tabío himself does not claim his work to be political cinema but a reflection on an ever-contradictory reality from a humorous point of view.

Anna Paula Foltanska

Wind with the Gone

El viento se llevó lo que

Countries of Origin:

Argentina
Spain
France
Netherlands

Languages:

Spanish
French

Studio/Distributor:

DMVB Films

Director:

Alejandro Agresti

Producers:

Thierry Forte
Facundo Narducci
Alejandro Agresti
Antonio P. Pérez
Sarah Halloua
Julio Fernández

Screenwriter:

Alejandro Agresti

Synopsis

Argentina, 1970s: heading south from Buenos Aires without any specific destination, Soledad, a young, attractive taxi driver, ends up at an isolated village in the Argentinean territory of Patagonia. She stays at a rundown hotel owned by María, a sensual, lonesome Spaniard in her forties. Soledad slowly begins to integrate herself into the village community, where the locals, passionate film viewers, meet at the local cinema to watch movies. These films have suffered damage on their long travel down to Patagonia and their sequences have been pasted together again in the wrong order. Soledad falls in love with Pedro, an eccentric film critic who expresses himself nearly exclusively through cinematographic quotations and clichés. Unexpectedly, French actor Edgar Wexley appears and discovers that the villagers actually are his greatest fans. Soledad and Pedro get married; María and Edgar also become a couple. Their idyllic life is disrupted when the village's intellectual, the ingenious Antonio Tardini, returns from Buenos Aires and informs his friends about having been tortured by the military government because of his socialist ideas. Finally, technical progress takes over the Patagonian village as satellite TV is installed and eventually the importance of cinema and communicative social life decline. Soledad leaves the village together with her Patagonian husband and presumably returns to Buenos Aires.

Critique

With its title that clearly refers to Margaret Mitchell's romantic novel *Gone with the Wind* (1936) (Spanish: *Lo que el viento se llevó*) and its popular Hollywood adaptation by Victor Fleming (1939), *Wind with the Gone* exposes its main themes and ideas. First, the film is a passionate homage to the movies. While focusing on the

Alejandro Agresti: *El viento se llevo lo que/Wind With the Gone*, 1998 © Flax Films

Cinematographer:

Mauricio Rubenstein

Art Director:

Floris Vos

Editor:

Alejandro Brodersohn

Composer:

Paul Michael van Brugge

Duration:

83 minutes

Genres:

Drama

Comedy

Cast:

Vera Fogwill

Fabian Vena

Ángela Molina

Jean Rochefort

Year:

1998

importance of the movie theatre as a space of communication, sentimental education and desire and integrating numerous intermedia references, Agresti's film recalls Giuseppe Tornatore's *Cinema Paradiso* (1988). The syntactical inversion of the Hollywood classic underlines the playful attitude towards mainstream cinema that the film proposes and alludes to its eccentric characters, and the damaged celluloid rolls in the windy, isolated setting of southern Argentina.

Meta-cinematographic elements range from setting to storyline, characters, language and editing. For example, various black-and-white sequences are inserted into the generally coloured pictures and constitute a nostalgic tribute to the early years of cinema while they simultaneously mark the fluid border between cinematographic reality and the fantasies of the main characters. Soledad's (Vera Folgwill) voice-over comments continuously on ongoing events. In the opening sequence, for example, she states ironically that 'this is not a comedy'. Indeed, the film integrates other genres, as when it quotes the American road movie in the same sequence or when it gets tragic referring to the violent historic background of the last Argentinean military dictatorship.

Agresti narrates his story through Soledad's eyes in terms of a fictitious autobiographical documentary. Soledad presents her experiences through the distance of a metropolitan point of view and the camera especially focuses on her gestures to capture her initial confusion about the strange local characters. The camera's treatment of the villagers oscillates between distance and affectionate sympathy and the film plays with the clichés of centre and margin in an ironic, self-reflexive way. As they live isolated from modern telecommunication techniques and higher education, the strange inhabitants follow their own logic and exhibit signs of extreme creativity. In the end, the villagers decide to produce their own documentaries that mirror social reality beyond the filmic and cultural common places of the Argentinean plains. These short films within the film offer an alternative view of the Patagonian periphery, while the locals' own film productions may also be seen as a statement for an alternative cinema from the margins.

The camera captures Patagonia's wild, untouched nature with long, quiet shots that leave room for fantasies of peace and freedom. Metonymically, the film points to the country's political isolation and longing for democracy during the military regime.

Jenny Haase

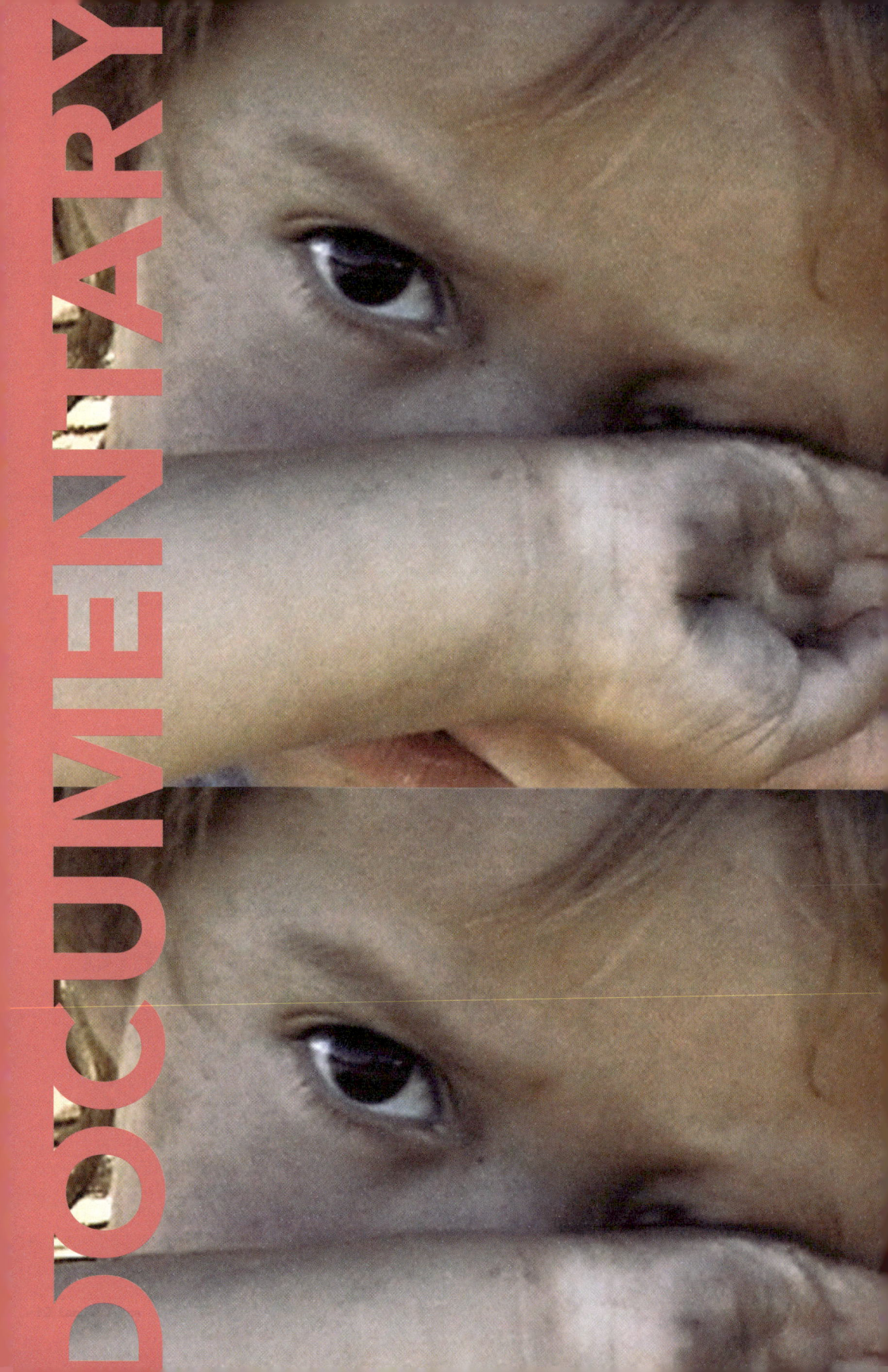

DOCUMENTARY

One of the most remarkable international cinematic trends observed since the mid-1990s has been the unexpected renaissance of the documentary film, as well as the reawakened interest in all forms of the documentary. Michael Moore's internationally successful films *Bowling for Colombine* (2002) and *Fahrenheit 9/11* (2004) have both triggered as well as served as symptoms of this development. In this wake, numerous other documentary films also made it into the movie theatres, from Nicolas Philibert's *Être et avoir/To Be and to Have* (2002) and Hubert Saupers' *Darwins' Nightmare* (2004) to *Man on Wire* (2008) by James Marsh, who won the Oscar for the best documentary film in 2009. At the same time there has been a rapprochement of fictional and documentary films, of fictional and factual cinematic forms that can be observed at the big film festivals of the world. In Cannes, for example, in 2008 the most important awards went to two docu-fictions: *Entre les murs/The Class* (Laurent Cantet, 2008) was awarded the Palme d'or and *Gomorra* (Matteo Garrone, 2008) the Grand Prix of the Jury.

In the past several years, the documentary film has also boomed in Latin America, although it had already played a decisive role there during the formation of the so-called *Nuevo Cine Latinoamericano* in the 1960s. In their widely known manifest *Hacia un tercer cine* (1969), for instance, Fernando 'Pino' Solanas and Octavio Getino had pleaded for a cinema that would engage itself politically and socially. Their monumental, three-part, four-hour documentary *La hora de los hornos/The Hour of the Furnaces* (1968) demonstrates this attitude. There are several reasons for today's growing interest in documentary films in Latin America. For example, suddenly, the digital revolution and easily available video cameras and desktop editing techniques have made it possible to produce films with minimum technical and financial input and to circulate films via DVD or over the Internet This has not only allowed for a new audience to form in spite of the grip and censorship of state-controlled media, but also to compensate partly for the absence of efficient distribution channels that have characterized the Latin American cinema long since. In the meantime, film producing companies have specialized in the production of documentary films, such as Cine Ojo in Argentina or Videofilms in Brazil. Today, there are also film festivals such as 'É Tudo Verdade' ('It's All True') in São Paulo and Rio de Janeiro, 'Forumdoc' in Belo Horizonte or the 'Festival Internacional de Cine Documental de la Ciudad de México' (DOCSDF) that have either entirely focused on

ernando E. Solanas: *Memoria del saqueo/ ocial Genocide*, 2004 © Trigon Films.

documentary films or at least devoted a section to this category, such as the 'Festival Internacional de Cine Independiente de Buenos Aires' (BAFICI) or the 'Festival Internacional de Cine en Guadalajara' (FICG).

Apart from the fundamentally altered conditions in terms of production, distribution, and reception of documentary films, it is mainly the political and social developments in Latin American countries; the end of military dictatorships, economic and social crises, the consequences of globalization, the emergence of new social movements as well as the rebirth of a new left-wing movement, that have provided for an environment favourable to the genre of the documentary. At the same time the field of documentary itself has become far more differentiated with regards to generational, formal and thematic aspects. In addition to still-active veterans of the *Nuevo Cine Latinoamericano*, such as the Argentinean Fernando Solanas and the Chilean Patricio Guzmán, a new generation of young film directors has formed. One of them is Eugenio Polgovsky, born in Mexico City in 1977, who had great international success with *Los herederos/The Inheritors* (2008), a poetical documentary essay on child labour in rural Mexico. Polgovsky's film is also representative, as it could only be implemented thanks to European grants. Many other documentary films are planned as international co-productions from the outset involving especially Spanish partners or depend on the support of NGOs. An

Fernando E. Solanas/Octavio Getino: *La hora de los hornos/ The Hour of the Furnaces*, 1968 © Trigon Films.

example for the latter case is *Tierra roja* (2006) by Ramiro Gómez (also born in 1977) which portrays the daily life of four peasant families at the heart of Paraguay and which was co-produced by the Swiss NGO Helvetas Paraguay.

Formally, documentary films of the classic observational type, which claims objectiveness and uses third-person narration and voice-over commentary, are still very common. However, more subjective, playful-experimental and hybrid forms have also started to gain ground. Examples include *La Televisión y yo* (2003) by the Argentinean Andrés Di Tella, who links the history of his own family to the history of television in Argentina, or the 'mockumentary' *Un día sin mexicanos/A Day without a Mexican* (2004) by the Mexican Sergio Arau, who shows what would happen if suddenly all Mexicans disappeared from California, as well as *Náufragos. Vengo de un avión que cayó en las montañas/Stranded: I've Come from a Plane That Crashed on the Mountains* (2007) by the Uruguayan Gonzalo Arijón featuring re-enacted memories of survivors of an airplane crash that happened in the Andes in 1972. The fact that the time of ideological agitation films that dominated Latin American cinema in the 1960s and 1970s ended at the latest with the collapse of the Soviet Union, is best demonstrated in more recent Cuban film productions. Emblematic in this respect are Fernando Pérez' *Suite Habana/Havana Suite* (2003), a film without dialogue describing everyday life in the Cuban capital in a melancholy romanticizing fashion, as well as Camila Guzmán's documentary *El telón de azúcar/ The Sugar Curtain* (2007), which oscillates between nostalgia and disillusion and asks, with regards to modern Cuba, what has become of the ideals of the Cuban revolution. This does not mean, however, that political cinema is generally on the retreat. On the contrary, there is a growing interest in political issues, social conflicts, and cultural and ethnic identities. In recent years the Latin American documentary film has gained significant momentum by popular movements and initiatives, such as the *Cine Imperfecto* and the *Cine Pobre* in Cuba or the *Video Indígena* and the *Cine Fronterizo* in Mexico and other countries that are deliberately avoiding traditional marketing strategies and the aesthetic and thematic patterns favoured by the film industry, looking for new forms of expression.

In this context, mention should also be made of the *Cine Piquetero* movement that formed in the wake of violent protests during the economic crisis in Argentina in December 2001, and the name of which originates from the Argentinean word for road blocks (*piquetes*). Young film directors spontaneously attended demonstrations and marched together with the angry crowd as the pot and pan brandishing *cacerolazos*. The videos taken during those events – with a hand-held camera and in direct sound, often with rock music in the background and ironically incorporated television and press images – were later sold in the streets and shown in factories and cafes, thereby challenging established media. Fernando Solanas welcomed the *Cine Piquetero* emphatically as the rebirth of the *Tercer Cine* and felt himself induced to return to didactical cinema after a 30-year absence. Starting with the street protest of the *cacerolazos* Solanas provides in *Memoria del saqueo/ Social Genocide* (2004), *La dignidad de los nadies/The Dignity of the Nobodies* (2005), and *Argentina latente* (2007) a polemical, slightly nationalistic description of the Argentinean Crisis, reconstructs its history, and undertakes an outlook into the potential future of the country. His films *Tierra sublevada-oro impuro (2009)* and *Tierra sublevada-oro negro* (2011) address the problem of environmental pollution caused by the exploitation of natural resources, an issue that is also dealt with in Francesco Taboada Tabone's film *13 Pueblos en defensa del agua, el aire y la tierra* (2008) about the fight of the indigenous population for the conservation of natural resources in the Mexican state of Morelos.

Another focus of Latin American documentary is the examination of the military dictatorships, especially in Argentina, Chile and Uruguay, generally referred to as *Cine Rescate*. Numerous films deal with the fate of the *desaperecidos*, including *Por esos ojos* (Gonzalo Arijón and Virginia Martínez, 1998), *Botín de Guerra/ Spoils of War* (David Blaustein, 1999), *(H) Historias cotidianas* (Andrés Habegger, 2000), as well as the more autobiographical films *Nietos (Identidad y memorial)* (Benjamín Ávila, 2003), *Los rubios/The Blonds* (Albertina Carri, 2003) and *M* (Nicolás Prividera, 2007). In *Papá Iván* (2000) María Inés Roqué confronts herself with the life of her father, the guerilla leader Juan Julio Roqué who was killed in Argentina in 1977. Patricio Guzmán, one of the key figures of Latin American documentary, also returned home to Chile after the dictatorship had ended. In *Chile, la memoria obstinada/Chile, the Obstinate Memory* (1997) he documents the reaction of the Chileans to his legendary four-and-a-half-hour documentary trilogy on the Allende era and the Pinochet coup La batalla de Chile (1972–79). Later in *El caso Pinochet/ The Pinochet Case* (2001) and *Salvador Allende* (2004) he once more returns to recent Chilean history.

In terms of the current political situation, it was particularly the triumph of the political left that has intrigued documentary film-makers. In *Entreatos* (2004) João Moreira Salles documents the presidential election campaign of Luíz Inácio Lula da Silva in Brazil in 2002, and in *Cocalero* (2006) Alejandro Landes accompanies Evo Morales on his way to becoming Bolivia's first indigenous head of state in 2005, an event that is also reflected in *Hartos Evos, aquí hay. Los cocaleros del Chapare* (Manuel Ruiz Montealegre and Héctor Ulloque Franco, 2006) and *El estado de las cosas* (Marcos Loayza, 2007). A wider view of the political changes that were taking place in Latin America – apart from Oliver Stone's *South of the Border* (2009) that largely limits itself to interviews with heads of governments – is given in *Ojos bien abiertos* (2009) by Gonzalo Arijón, who sets out for a trip through Latin America in the footsteps of Eduardo Galeano's famous book *Las venas abiertas de América Latina/The Open Veins of Latin America* (1971).

A likewise topical theme frequently presented in Brazilian documentaries is the omnipresent tangle of violence, poverty, the drugs trade and corruption. João Moreira Salles' and Kátia Lund's *Notícias de uma guerra particular/News from a Personal War* (1999) about life in the Favela Santa Marta close to Rio de Janeiro, as well as *Ônibus 174/Bus 174* (José Padilha, 2002) about the hijacking of a bus in Rio de Janeiro and its live coverage on TV, are particularly characteristic examples. The fact that Kátia Lund acted as co-director with Fernando Meirelles' fictional feature *Cidade de Deus/City of God* (2002) and that José Padilha took up the subject matter of *Bus 174* in his much-debated movies *Tropa de elite I/II/Elite Squad I/II* (2007/2010) shows once more that the boundary between documentary and fictional films has become increasingly blurred and is more permeable today than ever.

Christian von Tschilschke

Acta general de Chile

Countries of Origin:

Chile
Cuba
Spain

Language:

Spanish

Studios/Distributors:

Alfil Uno Cinematografica
Radio Television Española
(RTVE)

Director:

Miguel Littín

Producers:

Bernadette Cid
Luciano calducci
Fernando Quejido

Screenwriter:

Miguel Littín

Cinematographers:

Ugo Adilardi
Jean Ives
Tristan Bahuer
Pablo Martinez

Art Director:

Miguel Littín

Editor:

Carmen Frías

Composer:

Ángel Parra

Duration:

240 minutes

Genre:

Documentary

Year:

1986

Synopsis

Acta general de Chile is a documentary exposing the situation in Chile under Salvador Allende's government and the changes that occurred after the military putsch on 11 September 1973. It is told retrospectively, combining historical facts with personal stories of Chileans living an external or internal exile. After the United States-supported putsch against Allende's democratically elected government, Miguel Littín was forced to go into exile. Twelve years later he re-entered Chile clandestinely after having turned into a Uruguayan businessman, by changing his appearance, his accent, his way of moving and speaking. In order to be able to realize a documentary about life in Chile under a dictatorship, he arrived with a false wife – a member of the Chilean resistance movement – and under false pretences. The movie is divided into four parts:

Miguel Littín clandestinely in Chile
The movie begins in Santiago de Chile and gives the viewer an introduction to the Chile of 1985. Interviews with supporters and opponents of Pinochet are shown, including relatives of those Chileans who had disappeared, been murdered, tortured or illegally imprisoned. Interviewees include the former minister of justice as well as other political and military actors, such as a former member of Pinochet's torture crews. Interviewees further include marginalized citizens living in the slums around the big cities in Chile – especially Santiago – who are living in poverty due to the reigning regime.

Big North – When I went to the Pampa
The second part reveals the effects of the dictatorship. It focuses on Chileans who had been relegated to the country's wastelands, working in the saltpeter desert in the northern regions of Chile and living out an internal exile. In a certain sense, forgotten by the political system, their everyday life is determined by the poverty, misery and desolation that result directly from the imperialistic ideals of the fascist regime. Similarly, in the third part, the misery and the living conditions of the mineworkers in the south around Concepción are exposed, and thus too the exploitation of these workers subject to the 'free market'.

Miguel Littín: *Acta general de Chile*,
1986 © Trigon Films.

From the border to the interior
The third part demonstrates what the dictatorship meant for those Chileans who had been excluded – the exiled and their fight against the dictatorship from outside. The analogous internal battle – of the resistance movement and the students as well as the Chilean people in general – is also shown as they protest and demand a life under democratic and peaceful circumstances. All the fights and struggles, all the hopes and the feelings are concentrated and expressed though the memory of Pablo Neruda, a national poet and friend of Allende who died shortly after the putsch and became a symbol for the fight for social justice and peace. This third part also includes a number of interviews with the different persons mentioned above, declaring their motives and principles for fighting as well as their visions and understandings of politics, Pinochet and Allende. This part even includes an interview with the Frente Patriótico Manuel Rodríguez (FPMR), a militant underground resistance organization.

Allende
This last part is all about president Allende, his political personality and his last hours in the Palacio de La Moneda on the day of the coup – resisting until the end, until death. In order to reconstruct the events of 11 September 1973, friends, relatives, employees and admirers were interviewed, including Gabriel García Márquez, Fidel Castro, Hortensia Bussi (Allende's widow), Miria Contreras (Allende's secretary) and others. Their memories and reflections create an image of Allende's patriotic devotion to the people of Chile and the heroic idealism he was willing to die for. The situation at the end of the shooting was critical, since the secret police realized that Miguel Littín was inside Chile. He thus was compelled to get out of the country as soon as possible. Despite leaving under pressure, he still accomplished his project successfully: 32,000 million of filmed material had been brought to Spain, there to be edited into four-hour television and two-hour cinema versions, to show the world what Chile was like in 1985.

Critique

The documentary is a denunciation of the injustice of the political system and the social marginalization of those who would not sympathize with Pinochet's imperialistic regime.

Miguel Littín is one of the most recognized directors of the new Latin American cinema, and in his documentary he created a work that is an extraordinary representation of the Chilean cinema in exile. As admirer and supporter of former President Salvador Allende, Littín was forced to go into exile and leave his homeland after the military putsch in order to save his life. For this reason, this documentary is not only a cinematographic work – it is also rather a personal issue. For Littín, as for many other exiled Chilean directors, film is a way to understand and come to terms with what had happened in Chile in this period.

The Chilean cinema in exile deals with the persecution, imprisonment and repression of the Chilean people within the military regime as well as their lives in exile. In the early 1980s, attention turned to a new era of protest and public battles of resistance and opposition and the results of the dictatorship a decade on. Littín successfully reflects this changing situation of 1985 – from a Chile terrorized by the invisible hand of the system which would silence any kind of opposition, to a Chile slowly awakening and increasingly willing to fight for the rights of its people.

The filming was a collaboration of three European crews – from France, Italy and the Netherlands – and had the support of militant resistance groups, coordinated by Littín, both inside and outside of Chile. Viewers are shown different scenes of the country, from the slums in Santiago to Valparaíso, where Allende was born and where resistance was increasingly growing; to Isla Negra, where Pablo Neruda's house is; from the Pampas in the north then south to Concepción, where workers live in very poor conditions, living from hand to mouth. These scenes combine with the numerous interviews among different groups within the population from all over Chile – politicians, members of the resistance and the military, artists, and opponents as well as sympathizers of Pinochet – to provide a complete image of what it meant to be in Chile under a dictatorship.

The documentary had a number of objectives. It was intended as a call for attention, to make the world realize what is going on in Chile in those days. Further, by shooting these images of militarization and oppression from the inside, without being noticed by the secret police they were working next to all the time, Littín mocked Pinochet and his regime, using film as a medium of exposure. The film also intended to present an alternative to what would be proclaimed as the official history – with unimpeachable images and the camera as a witness, demonstrating that in these developed and modern cities, that on those bright and shiny avenues in Chile, there were people without faces, without any expressions, behind which everyday terror was hidden. Littín shows how the fear had become a permanent companion of people longing for a life in peace and with dignity.

Miguel Littín has created a work of perfect harmony between the pictures, dialogues, commentaries, images from the archives and interviews. These together are framed by the music, principally from Angel Parra, a representative of the *Nueva Canción* – a socially committed genre and movement. *Acta general de Chile* is a cinematographic work, a historical document, but more than this, it is a medium giving voice to those who lived in silence for so long – the Chilean people.

Anna Paula Foltanska

Che Guevara, donde nunca jamás se lo imaginan

Country of Origin:

Cuba

Language:

Spanish

Studio/Distributor:

Instituto Cubano de Arte e Industria Cinematográficos (ICAIC)

Director:

Manuel Pérez Paredes

Producers:

Juan Luis Galindo
Camilo Vives
Alberto Segura

Screenwriter:

Manuel Perez

Cinematographer:

Manuel Perez

Art Director:

Manuel Perez

Editor:

Pedro Suárez

Composers:

Edesio Alejandro
Ernesto Cisneros

Duration:

55 minutes

Genre:

Documentary

Cast:

Julio Acanda
Patricio Wood
Ernesto Guevara Lynch
Dr Roger Alvarez
Zdenka de Pesce
Dr Alberto Granado
Raul Castro
Fidel Castro
Salvador Vilaseca

Synopsis

Ernesto Rafael Guevara de la Serna, better known as 'Che', was one of the best-known revolutionary leaders in the world. The documentary *Che Guevara, donde nunca jamás se lo imaginan* tries to answer some fundamental questions about the background of this charismatic Argentine leader. It features interviews with his father and other contemporary witnesses such as the Castro brothers and an old woman from the leprosy station to which Che went. They speak about Che as a friend, a companion, a son and as a stranger. The photographs and archival footage of his trips through Latin America turn the documentary into a compilation film. The style of the narrator, underlined by music and revolutionary footage, can be seen as a hallmark of the film's producer, the Instituto Cubano de Arte e Industria Cinematográficos.

Critique

The director Manuel Pérez started his film career immediately after the founding of the Instituto Cubano de Arte e Industria Cinematográficos in 1959. He worked together with Tomas Gutièrrez Alea to realize the movie *Historias de la Revolucion* (1960), and made his first documentary, entitled *Cinco Pinos* in 1961. He is also one of the co-founders of the Committee of the Cineaste of Latin America, which was founded in Caracas, Venezuela in 1974. He teaches film in different organizations and cultural institutions.

The documentary is filmed entirely in black and white and starts with a musical collage. Pérez's movie follows Che's short life: his childhood in Argentina, his early interest in the Spanish Civil War, the motorcycle trip through Latin America, his revolutionary career, his political failures, and finally his execution in the Bolivian mountains in 1967. His last guerilla campaign was documented by Che in a diary. Then a clandestine copy of this diary was distributed by Fidel Castro for free all over Cuba arousing an outrageous interest among the Cubans. The execution of Che was a rude shock for all of his supporters. On 8 October 1968 at a place called 'Quebrada del Yuro', Che was injured and taken prisoner. The military took him to a farmhouse, where he was killed. After his death his body was taken to Vallegrande, a village in Santa Cruz, for everyone to see and Pérez makes clear that it was treated like an exhibition piece. Even if some people could not believe that he was dead; his exhibited body was the proof. The documentary then shows fragments of *Mi hijo el Che* (1985), a documentary by Fernando Birri, in which Che's father Ernesto Guevara Lynch talks about 'Ernestito'. The fascination for war and struggle and the roots for the revolutionary character of Che started at the age of ten when he heard from his father about the Spanish Civil War.

Che's experiences during his motorcycle trips with Alberto Granado, in particular the contact with the Chilean miners, made a very deep impression on him.

Manuel Pérez also mentions that Che was a man like any other. Che was not a politician who hid behind his paperwork. He always

Year:

2004

spent time with the workers, trying to find out what they needed and trying to right social injustices. This made him very special: a politician who spent time with the people, a hard-working man, a man who never did things for his own interest. He had many opponents, but this made him strong. The only things which might have been given too little attention in this documentary are Guevara's shortcomings and disputes with Castro. Besides, the dimension of executions is not mentioned at all in Pérez's documentary. His nomination to the Minister of Industry also created problems; Che did not know anything about the duties of this department. He had to start from the beginning. He made mistakes, his industrialization plan was ill-suited for Cuba, and he wasted resources on many unsustainable factories. Nonetheless, this documentary clearly reflects the status of Che Guevara in the twenty-first century: Che Guevara as one of the world's best-known heroes.

Silke Paulitsch

El círculo

Countries of Origin:

Uruguay
Alemania
Argentina
Chile

Language:

Spanish

Studio/Distributor:

SUR Films

Directors:

José Pedro Charlo Filipovich
Aldo Garay Dutrey

Producers:

José Pedro Charlo Filipovich
Yvonne Ruocco
Detlef Ziegert
Gonzalo Rodríguez Bubis
Pablo Salomón
Sergio Gándara

Screenwriters:

José Pedro Charlo Filipovich
Aldo Garay Dutrey

Cinematographer:

Diego Varela

Art Director:

Ozer Ami

Synopsis

The Uruguayan doctor and scientist Henry Engler, in the 1960s and 1970s one of the leading brains of the Uruguayan urban guerrilla organization MLN (Movimiento de Liberación Nacional), was a prisoner of the Uruguayan military dictatorship for thirteen years, from 1972 to 1985. In *El círculo* Engler, who currently lives in Sweden and is famous for his research on Alzheimer's disease, looks back on his eventful and unusual life full of inhuman cruelties. He travels back to Uruguay, visits the city where he grew up and the village where he spent jaunty holidays as a child, but also the places of his dreadful captivity. He meets some of his former friends, his former guards and cell mates. In doing so, he is capable of going on a second journey, a journey inside himself, and is able to reflect on the events of his past in a highly philosophical way. But the documentary does not only show Engler's perspective but also lets other people related to his life comment on his past, e.g. some of his relatives and former cell mates.

Critique

There are already several movies that cover the topic of military dictatorships in Argentina and Uruguay, as for example Marco Bechis' *Garage Olimpio* from the year 1999, or the movie *Kamtchaka*, released in 2002 and directed by Marcelo Piñeyros, but *El círculo*, an Uruguayan contribution to a possible handling of these difficult years in the history of the two countries, is not a repetition of the former movies at all, but manages to find a new and unique access to this challenging topic.

In *El Círculo*, factual knowledge and political statements play only a secondary role: what lies in the focus of the directors is mainly the personal experience of Henry Engler as a prisoner of the dictatorship. The movie wants to show his struggle for survival under inhuman conditions, including torture and solitary confinement,

Editor:

Federico La Rosa

Composer:

Daniel Yafalián

Duration:

92 minutes

Genre:

Documentary

Cast:

Henry Engler

Year:

2008

and his attempts and strategies to deal with the situation of his life. Engler, as well as all the other people who comment on the past, tell their personal stories and strategies to cope with what they have experienced. That is why the documentary does not need to follow the chronological course of events all the time, but can, for example, alternate images from Engler's present as a respected doctor and scientist in Sweden with images from times when he still was a member of the MLN.

The directors of the movie, Aldo Garay Dutrey and José Pedro Charlo Filipovich, both of whom have shot several documentaries before, manage to look back in a primarily serious, reflexive and sober way, without falling into sentimentalities. What they demonstrate is a fine feeling for tragic and touching situations, for example when Engler's sister narrates how their mother would wait patiently in snow and rain for hours in front of the prison where her son was held, only to see him for some minutes.

José Pedro Charlo and Aldo Garay: *El círculo/The Circle*, 2008 © guazú media, Montevideo. Photo courtesy of Ramiro Ozer Ami – with friendly authorization (www.elcirculo-doc.com).

A key sentence of the movie is articulated by Engler himself: he tells how, after his release from the prison in 1985, he tried to find the place where he had once, as a child, gone fishing with his grandfather: 'Lo que uno busca en el pasado no es tan fácil encontrarlo.' ('What you are searching for in the past is not so easy to find.') Nevertheless, the directors try to find at least some truths with the help of Engler's memories and the testimonies of his contemporaries.

Throughout the film, Henry Engler seems to be very authentic; his intelligent but emotional way of reflecting on his eventful life and his way of thinking about the thin line between insanity and sanity deeply impresses the viewer, creating a sense of admiration for this thoughtful man. However, the film also shows that not everyone has managed to distance themselves from the past and to regain their inner peace like Engler has.

In summary, this film is an extremely moving documentary which demonstrates that there are still new ways to explore the topic of the military dictatorship.

Kerstin Hörmann

Havana Kidz 2

Country of Origin:

United States

Languages:

Spanish
English

Studio/Distributor:

Quad Cinema

Director:

Alberto Gonzalez

Producer:

CubaRush
Alberto Gonzalez

Screenwriters:

Alberto Gonzalez
Adriana Alvarez

Cinematographer:

Ernesto Granados

Art Director:

Alberto Gonzalez

Editor:

Jesus Martínez

Duration:

43 minutes

Synopsis

With the documentary *Havana Kidz 2*, the Cuban-American director Alberto González enters into the lives of five teenagers in a musical band in Havana, Cuba. To become famous musicians is not that easy in a place like Havana, where lots of good musicians are born. It requires a lot of sacrifice and hard work. The director follows these boys in their attempt to become the next generation of Cuban musicians. Their funny way of acting and determination to achieve success glue the audience's attention to the screen. This musical documentary also shows the Havana of today in a realistic and natural way. Gonzáles did not try to sweep anything of the revolutionary Cuban lifestyle of the twenty-first century under the carpet.

Critique

González, born and raised in New York City, began his career as a radio and club DJ. His first contact with film was his contribution to the award-winning film *Anne B. Real* (Lisa France, 2003), a story about a Cuban-American female rapper whose source of inspiration is *The Diary of Anne Frank*. Gonzalez is also the co-producer of the feature-film *Love and Suicide* (Lisa France, 2005), a love story played in Havana.

The documentary starts with a black-and-white image collage, underlined with music and comments about the protagonists. The protagonists are five young Cuban musicians who are also known as Marea Azul. The undertone of the documentary is the hope of the musicians to achieve success one day, to 'gain popularity in Cuba' and to 'test their music in other countries'. As told in the film they are studying a career that requires a lot of sacrifice and are making music because they love it.

Genre:

Documentary

Cast:

Juan Carlos
Ernesto
Orlando
Renier (no surnames are given)

Year:

2008

The teens offer a unique insight into the spirit and soul of Havana, a city shaped of cultural diversity and political complexities. This complexity might not be easy to understand for a non-Cuban, but González has tried to paint a clear picture of the mystified Cuba. Through the representation of the unique stories, he is able to feature the lives of different families who struggle to raise their children here. This picture is fascinating and new, but at the same time universal. The director underlines that it reminds them, in these politically charged times, that despite their differences – be they religious, political, economic or ideological – they are all just trying to raise their kids the best way they can.

The climax of González' documentary is the scene on the roof terrace. The view is amazing and the impression is created that Marea Azul is a famous band already. The roof terrace is quasi the key scene of the documentary; it is the place where the band has its rehearsals and pep-talks and where they express their desire for a successful career outside their home country. Being internationally successful for a Cuban means that he can leave the country legally; a dream the vast majority of Cuban people (who are not allowed to travel at all) will probably never realize. Gonzalez was not scared to show this side of Cuba. That makes this documentary so special. By filming the unique and endearing personality of each kid, González creates a snapshot of Cuba itself. Quite different from an 'indigenous' Cuban film production in which the illusion of a perfect country is usually supported, he realistically reveals the economical woes and the anxiety about the future of the Cuban people.

The recordings on the streets provide a very close insight into the importance of music in Cuba that expresses a certain kind of Cuban spirit. But this spirit is not undersized at all. González follows the three youngest musicians of the band Mare Azul. They call themselves 'Los Rapperos' on the street. These scenes are an experience for the audience: the busy roads of Havana, the Malecón, and the typical Cuban extroverted behaviour makes you believe that you are in the middle of the city. The climax of the movie is at the end when the band presents their special song. The last part of the documentary is a music video; the first demo of Marea Azul. The fast editing and the Reggaeton sound bring the story of the charismatic, confident and savvy teens to an end. *Havana Kidz 2* is a must-see documentary not only for people interested in Cuba, but for anyone interested in music.

Silke Paulitsch

M

Country of Origin:

Argentina

Language:

Spanish

Studio/Distributor:

Trivial Media

Director:

Nicolás Prividera

Producers:

Nicolás Prividera
Pablo Ratto

Screenwriter:

Nicolás Prividera

Cinematographers:

Nicolás Prividera
Josefina Semilla
Carla Stella

Editor:

Malu Herdt

Duration:

150 minutes

Genre:

Documentary

Cast:

Guido Prividera
Nicolás Prividera

Year:

2007

Synopsis

On the verge turning 36, the age at which his mother, Marta Sierra, was kidnapped and made to disappear during the last military dictatorship in Argentina, Nicolás Prividera feels the need to find out what happened to her. Wrapped in his grey raincoat, Prividera plays the role of a suspicious, meticulous detective who is not willing to accept any objective facts or any apparently clear story. He confronts the witnesses in the film in an attempt to reveal their contradictions, their impressions and, at times, their base motives and veiled betrayals. Throughout his journey through 'official' and 'personal' memories, the young film-maker searches for evidence. He uses some of what he finds to answer the questions that have been haunting him ever since he was orphaned when he was only five years old, while other discoveries lead him to an even bigger puzzle: the liability of a whole community.

Critique

The first and only film to date by Nicolás Prividera, *M* is a feature film that questions the extent of civil liability concealed by the official history of the mechanical and bureaucratic Argentinean dictatorship. It is this history that the film-maker, the son of the missing Marta Sierra, redefines in his first-person investigation into the numerous and labyrinthine aspects of memory.

The complexity of levels and meanings revealed by Prividera's journey along the highways and byways of memory is evident from the very title of the film, a letter that might refer to her mother, Marta, Montoneros or memory. This 'M' announces, therefore, that for the two-and-a-half hours that the film lasts, Prividera will be travelling in the same guise through a variety of landscapes and using numerous points of view to search for a single object: the truth about the events before, during, and after his mother's disappearance.

A markedly subjective documentary, Prividera's voice and body reflect a critical and reflexive attitude as he responds to his findings with both curiosity and a certain distrust. Indeed, after his frustrated wanderings around organizations, institutions, and public spaces in search of any information whatsoever that might give him a clue to the final whereabouts of his mother, Prividera decides to listen to the testimony of Sierra's relatives, friends, former workmates and fellow political activists. However, many of these accounts are followed by an ironic refutation, a challenge or a shrewd comment from Prividera; he believes that the generation that lived through the revolution largely prefers silence to the embarrassment of accepting the old responsibilities that they have decided to ignore.

On a formal level, *M* is structured as a filmed diary and uses two types of material: the interviews he conducted in 2004 with his mother's workmates, fellow political activists and relatives, and fragments of home-made videos shot by his father before that fateful night when the soldiers took Sierra from her home. With this combination of audiovisual images, Prividera turns *M* into a sort of tapestry that, with its variety of textures, times and viewpoints,

Nicolás Prividera: *M*, 2007 © Trivial Media

subverts the expectations of the habitual testimonial documentary and at the same time uses the present to revaluate the legacy of the dictatorship, apparently so fixed and unchangeable. The recovery of his mother's pictures, the careful selection process, and the final composition at the end of the film, is somehow an examination of identity and an exploration of a memory that is no longer conceived as linear and closed but rather as a complex structure of reminiscences and inventions under continuous transformation.

Laia Quílez Esteve

Una foto recorre el mundo

Countries of Origin:

Cuba
Chile

Synopsis

The most famous picture of Che Guvara has a long and dramatic history. It was taken during the funeral of the victims of the explosion of the Belgian freighter 'La Coubre' in 1960, an attack some people claim to have been orchestrated by William Alexander Morgan, who was acting on orders from the Central Intelligence Agency. It was during this funeral, which was held on 4 March 1960, that the important quote 'Patria o muerte! Venceremos!' ('Fatherland or death, we shall overcome!') was first uttered by the revolutionaries.

Language:

Spanish

Studio/Distributor:

Distribuidora Internacional de Películas ICAIC

Director:

Pedro Chaskel

Producer:

ICAIC – Instituto Cubano de Arte e Industria Cinematográficos

Screenwriter:

Pedro Chaskel

Cinematographer:

Pedro Chaskel

Art Director:

Pedro Chaskel

Editor:

Caita Villalon

Composers:

Juan Marcos Blanco
Juan Márquez

Duration:

15 minutes

Genre:

Documentary

Year:

1981

The documentary tells the history of the famous photograph taken by Alberto Korda which travelled around the world and became synonymous for freedom, justice and protest. Korda recounts especially his feeling, his nervousness and excitement at the moment when he shot the picture of Che in an interview that gives the viewer an impression of how important the charismatic revolutionary has been.

Critique

Una foto recorre el mundo is a short documentary which was directed in 1981 by Pedro Chaskel, born in Germany in 1932. When Chaskel was seven years old his family migrated to Chile and in 1955 he established there the *Cine Club Universitario*. Chaskel is the director of numerous documentaries and feature films and edited the popular film *La batalla de Chile I-II-III* directed by Patricio Guzmán (1979). His short documentary *Una foto recorre el mundo* is a tribute to Ernesto Che Guevara. The movie starts with the dramatic attack on the freighter La Coubre in the harbour of Havana. The attack marked the beginning of a long-lasting battle between the United States and the Cuban Republic. The next scene shows the victims' funeral, which was attended by a huge number of people.

Then we hear the voice of Fidel Castro speaking the most famous sentence of the Cuban revolution, 'Patria o muerte! Venceremos!' The passion and the significance of these words are emphasized in scenes which show protesters all over the world: protesters who keep the image of Che held high, protesters who associate the revolutionary with freedom, justice and the fight against poverty, exploitation and imperialism. After the ninth minute the documentary turns into a musical collage: the poetic song 'Yo te nombro' by Gian Franco Pagliaro stresses also how important it is to fight for freedom. During the song, Chaskel shows us the diverse versions of the single photo. The picture can be seen in pop art, in black and white, as a painting or as a mural, and is found on T-shirts, bags, coffee cups, energy drinks, cigarettes, etc. In short, it is probably one of the most commercialized images in the world.

Chaskel's film was made during a period in which the Cuban Republic was bankrupt. The economic downturn of the 1980s led Cuba to be dependant on the USSR. This decision was not the best for the economic development of Cuba, as we know since the fall of the Berlin wall in 1989. The documentary seems to be a sort of *pronunciamento* during these economically hard times. It can also be seen as a revitalization of the original ideas of the Cuban revolution and the national heroism underlined with the song text from Pagliaro:

> Por las tierras invadidas, por los pueblos conquistados, por la gente sometida, por los hombres explotados [...] por el héroe asesinado, por los fuegos apagados – Yo te nombro Libertad. (For the invaded lands, for the conquered people, for the oppressed people, for the exploited men [....] for the assassinated hero, for the extinguished fires – I speak your name liberty.)

The narrative form of this documentary is a very poetic manner of representation that is found in many Cuban documentaries as well as in those of other parts of the Caribbean.

Silke Paulitsch

Havana Suite

Suite Habana

Country of Origin:

Cuba

Language:

Spanish

Studios/Distributors:

Wanda Visión S.A.
Instituto Cubano del Arte e Industrias Cinematográficos (ICAIC)
Cinema Tropical

Director:

Fernando Pérez

Producers:

Jose Maria Morales
Camilo Vives

Screenwriter:

Fernando Pérez

Cinematographer:

Raúl Pérez Ureta

Art Director:

Fernando Pérez

Composer:

Edesio Alejandro

Editors:

Pedro Oscar Pérez
Julia Yip

Duration:

80 minutes

Genre:

Documentary

Synopsis

The documentary *Havana Suite*, written and directed by Fernando Pérez in 2003, is an intimate portrayal of the capital of Cuba. It could be described as a film-poem, a confession of love to Pérez's sweet Havana. It is a well-rounded snapshot of the city and its inhabitants, from dawn until night. The film shows people and their everyday life. Pérez focuses on the dreams of every person depicted in the film. The film's stars are Havanans who do not stop to dream while living under difficult conditions. They try to live their lives in dignity. Step by step, each person is introduced with a short biographical insertion, including name and age.

Five plots cross in the documentary. Francisquito, a handicapped 10-year-old, buys peanuts from Amanda, a doctor, who works a second job as a clown on children's birthdays. Francisquito says goodbye to his brother who is living in the United States and on the way to the airport we get to know other characters of the documentary. After work the city's rhythm rises: people enjoy the nightlife, where they begin to flourish. Unexpected aspects of the people depicted come to light after dark. The film ends with descriptions of each person's dreams.

Critique

Havana Suite is a documentary to make people smile. The characters are real people who have lives full of difficulties, but they are all characters who dream. What is really special about the documentary is the fact that it is a film without words. Sometimes pictures and images truly are worth a thousand words. The only language used is the language the documentary speaks. The director composes a visual and musical suite with images, sounds, music, faces, noises, gestures and rhythms. *Havana Suite* is full of everyday sounds and voices, but these are the voices of people we cannot understand. Sometimes there is piano and jazz music. The mosaics of sounds and images substitute for the missing conversations.

The dream of Francisco, Francisquito, is that he will always take care of his son. Waldo's dream is to live a healthy life. Iván really wants to be part of a glamorous life and Heriberto wants to be a musician in an orchestra. All of these dreams are attainable. They are neither fanciful nor completely baseless. This illustrates the plainness of the people's lives. Peréz does not spoil the situation in Havana: these are just sketches of some normal lives. Nor is the cast unrealistic: they are neither particularly pretty nor particularly special.

Fernando Pérez: *Suite Habana/Havana Suite*, 2003 © Trigon Films.

Cast:

Francisquito Cardet
Francisco Cardet
Norma Pérez
Waldo Morales
Ivan Carbonell

Year:

2003

Even the background consists of everyday life. If a car happened to drive through the scene as it was being shot, it remained in the scene. Conversely, some sounds, especially the sounds of the street, are unnaturally amplified. Often they are even composed into a special rhythm, giving it the impression of a musical score composed with day-to-day sounds like car horns and pneumatic hammers and other construction tools. This device stresses the urban style of the capital, a metropolis that is home to two million people. Sometimes sounds or colours are arranged in a disturbing manner that might remind the audience of life's imperfections. Towards the end the music contains lyrics that fit the scenes.

The film lives on the special arrangement of people, sounds and colours, and offers a special otherness inviting the audience to focus on the numerous peculiarities of La Havana.

Esther Marie Stienen and Marlene Christine Sommer

La Vida Loca

Countries of Origin:

France
El Salvador

Language:

Spanish

Studios/Distributors:

Aquelarre Servicios
Cinematográficos
El Caimán
La Femme Endormie

Director:

Christián Poveda

Producers:

Carole Solive
Luis Gellaba
Emilio Maillé
Gustavo Angel

Screenwriter:

Christián Poveda

Cinematographer:

Christián Poveda

Art Director:

Mercedes Alted López

Composers:

Sébastien Rocca
Yuri Buenaventura
El Fugitivo
Big Boy

Editor:

Mercedes Alted López

Duration:

90 minutes

Genre:

Documentary

Cast:

'El Bambam'
'La Liro'
'La Chucky'
'La Wizard'
'Little Crazy'
'Little Scrappy'
'El Moreno'
'Spider' (all pseudonyms of
gang members)

Synopsis

The documentary *La Vida Loca* is about the *maras*, street gangs especially in El Salvador, Guatemala and Honduras. It addresses anyone interested in learning how these groups of criminals live and rule the small country El Salvador.

Central American immigrants initially formed these gangs in the suburbs of Los Angeles, later returning to El Salvador as rival gangs who continue to fight against each other. Poveda was interested in young Salvadorans who are members of either of the two local gangs in El Salvador, the Mara Salvatrucha (MS 13) and the 18th Street Gang (MS 18). He documents and displays their lives, which are full of bloody crime, battles, brutality, drugs, injuries, funerals, rivalry and tattoos. He portrays how they live in cult-like communities, with their special rituals and symbols. The film exposes the methods with which members are initiated into the gang, how they struggle to survive, how they plan their next steps, how they celebrate birthdays and give birth to children, and how they undergo medical examinations after being shot or badly wounded.

Critique

La Vida Loca was written and directed by Christian Poveda, a Hispanic-French photojournalist and film director who worked and lived with these people for approximately sixteen months, finally completing the documentary in 2008. The title – *La Vida Loca*, which means 'The crazy life' in English – reflects the gang member's motto; it is also a popular song, whose rhythm accompanies their daily lives in San Salvador (El Salvador).

Because nothing in this movie is staged, it has a very authentic story line with a strikingly realistic appearance. Everyone and everything is real. Poveda shot all scenes while accompanying the gangs in their daily life. Working with a hand-held camera, he puts the viewer in a situation where he seems to be part of the action.

Opinions differ on this point, however. On the one hand, the film is a successful documentary because Poveda had the courage to work with members of the gangs, even though this act represents an extraordinary threat – he risked and ultimately lost his life in this work. This courage is the reason *La Vida Loca* is so real and so successful. On the other hand, the documentary intends to present the daily life of the 'normal' Salvadorans. The gangs are chiefly located in the capital of San Salvador. The documentary merely portrays the lives of members of the *maras* and must not be seen as a reproach to El Salvador. If people want to visit El Salvador and watch the film prior to that they might change their mind and not go – apart from people who are not weary of life and put themselves at risk. One must understand that the film does not portray the whole country.

The documentary shows a lot of funerals, dead bodies and crying people mourning the loss of relatives and friends. At the same time, however, it is not Poveda's intention with *La Vida Loca* that viewers become frightened of the country or even of Central America. The point is what the viewer takes out of it. It is indispensable for the

Year:

2008

viewer to be critical and to distinguish between the gangs and El Salvador; the gangs are a part of the country but not El Salvador in itself. It is easy to dramatize, generalize and form a hasty opinion about El Salvador. Organized gang crime is a significant menace and dangerous, in contrast to nice people, peaceful places and beautiful landscapes.

La Vida Loca deals with dreams, hopes and yearnings, but also with death and imprisonment, and hateful and despairing people. Poveda's socially committed documentary is far from a moral rush to judgement. It is gratifying to see someone who wanted to experience the mystery of the *maras* first-hand and tried to present them fairly. In a way, the documentary is a political film that reveals political instability, unequal balances of power, injustice and a collapse of civil society, aspects that help explain why those gangs exist. Moreover, nothing in the film is obviously dramatized or romanticized. This is, after all, a documentary, one from which the viewer is expected to take realistic information and experience, rather than dramatization.

Undoubtedly, the MS 18 is one of the most brutal and dangerous youth gangs in Latin America. Nevertheless, Poveda tried to see something different in them. He was conscious of all the social problems that still exist in Central America. Victims of a generation full of political irregularities, they never had a chance to integrate into the larger society. In this situation it is quite normal to search for something that may give you some support and solidarity. Some Salvadorans found this support in the gangs, and this is the scenario Poveda wanted to shoot a film about.

Members of these organized gangs are cold-blooded killers, but are also human beings; fathers, dreamers, bakers, or just friends. Poveda wanted to come closer to the individual human beings inside the gangs and did not want to judge anything prematurely. He tried to give them the chances and humanity that they had lost some time ago. Transparency and communication play a main role for Poveda. He did not shoot this documentary only to show how bad and dangerous these gangs are; he simply wanted to portray their lives. This approach and intention makes the documentary so unique and important.

In 2008, the documentary was presented at the 'San Sebastián International Film Festival', the 'Morelia Film Festival' and the 'San Luis Cine International Festival'. In 2009, it was shown at the 'Berlinale European Film Market'. Tragically, Poveda paid for his research and film with his life: he was shot dead in 2009 and did not live to witness *La Vida Loca* being released in the cinemas.

Esther Marie Stienen

DRAMA

The classical drama is based on Greek theatre, tragedy and comedy, though it originated in ancient Greek religious rituals and ceremonies that became increasingly elaborated and performative. One of the best-known rituals is mentioned in the myth of Dionysus (or Bacchus), the God of wine and ecstasy, and is called the 'Dionysian Mysteries'.

According to the demands of classical theatre, drama has to be linear-chronological, causal-chronological and plausible. It refers to the French concepts of the 'classic doctrine', though being based on theories of Aristotle such as verisimilitude, propriety, the three units of time, place and action, as well as on imitation.

This is connected with the composition of a classical drama with its three acts: exposition – climax   solution. All these elements serve to dramatize the story for the entertainment of the audience and were adopted for the media of film and cinema and their new technological possibilities.

Drama is highly focused on human emotions and on the human drama of life in general, and is characterized by its seriousness. It indicates the performance of a fictional narrative and is to be understood to mean the staging and enactment of fictional events in a historically and socially credible frame for an audience. This performing aspect of the filmic drama is underlined by the name of the cinema auditoriums as movie *theatres*. In this sense, many of the Latin American directors studied also theatre and drama, such as Román Chalbaud, Alejandro González Iñárritu and Fernando Ezequiel Solanas, regaining experiences on the important dramaturgical fields. Dramaturgy is the most important aspect of the performative and purposeful character of a filmic drama.

In general it is always difficult to categorize genres as a specific narrative sample because they are mostly based on a wide variety of meanings and applications, and especially on the endless number of cultural and national differences and characteristics. In particular the difficulty of defining filmic drama is its wide and inflationary use. In this sense, even most of the fiction films are categorized as drama. Besides, there is a great variety of mixed genres and subgenres such as the historical, sentimental and psychological drama, the melodrama and the dramatic comedy. The social drama plays an outstanding role in Latin America. One should take into consideration the great number of country-specific differences concerning special dramas, such as the German

Ciro Guerra: *Los Viajes de Viento/The Wind Journeys*,
2009 © Arte/Cine Ojo/ ZDF.

sentimental films in a regional setting, Lederhosen films and Holocaust-dramas, the Japanese Samurai, Yakuza film and Pinku eiga films, author films, Tibet-films, French swashbuckler films, catastrophe dramas, Italian Giallo and Commedia all'italiana, Indian Gore and docu-drama. The drama as one of the hybrid genres has experienced in Latin America since the 1980s important historical changes and shifts that underline the cultural differences to the Hollywood mainstream and the joy for filmic experiments with the genre. Actually, in view of the new tendencies of interculturality, globalization and co-productions, the categorizations in general had to be renewed corresponding to the different countries.

In Latin America there are interesting combinations with other genres as elaborated in the following articles in this volume about the single countries: in Colombia, the first feature film was the 'romantic drama' *María* (1922) by Máximo Calvo and Alfredo del Diestro. The 'psychological drama' *La gran obsesión* (1955) by Guillermo Ribón Alba was the first Colombian feature film shot in colour, and another of the first Colombian films was the 'social drama' *El milagro de sal* (1958) by Luis Moya Sarmiento, that was shown at an international film festival, namely at the 'Festival de Cine de San Sebastián'. In Mexico the 'rural drama' *Flor silvestre* (1943) was released, in Cuba there is for example Sergio Cabrera's *La estrategia del caracol* (1993), a 'comedy-drama' about impoverished neighbours who are evicted from their house, and Víctor Gaviria's *La vendedora de rosas* (1998), which deals with the harsh living conditions of children involved with drugs in Medellín. In Mexico Mariana Chenillo creates with *Cinco dias sin Nora/Nora's Will* (2009) another comedy-drama, and Guillermo del Toro established his unique visual and visceral style in the 'ghost drama' *El espinazo del diablo/The Devil's Backbone* (2001). Brazilian film-maker Fernando Meirelles had his breakthrough with 2002's *Cidade de Deus/City of God*, a 'crime drama' about drug war in a *favela* in Rio de Janeiro which became an

Mariana Chenillo: *Cinco dias sin Nora/Nora's Will*, 2009. © Trigon Films.

Sergio Cabrera: *La estrategia del caracol*, 1993 © Trigon Films.

international box-office hit and garnered much critical acclaim. In Venezuela, Solveig Hoogesteijn sticks out with *Macu, la Mujer del Policía/Macu, the Policeman's Wife* (1987), a 'police drama' based on a real murder – the so-called 'Mamera Case'. There has also been an increase in the number of 'historical' and 'biographical dramas', including *El Caracazo* (2005) and *Zamora, tierra y hombres libres* (2010), both by Román Chalbaud, and an innovative commercial cinema presenting 'social dramas' using a fast-paced montage technique in which shots are not linked with each other continuously but rather collide with each other. Directors such as Walter Salles, Hector Babenco, Helvécio Ratón Fernando Meirelles and Sérgio de Rezende have created subgenres like 'jail' or 'township drama'.

Another important variation of drama is the 'psychological' one as a virtual drama of the soul about interpersonal and intra-psychic conflict. It is a sort of externalization of the inner world of characters on the screen. We find many psychological dramas in Latin American films due to the tendency of trying to find the identity of the single country in general, but also the increasing feminine self-confidence. The focus lies on different aspects of the persons often reflecting the social situation as shown in *El beso de la mujer araña/Kiss of the Spider Woman* (Hector Babenco, 1985), which is about the approximation of two prisoners, a journalist and a homosexual windows dresser; in *La frontera* (Ricardo Larraín, 1991), where the protagonist crosses his own inner frontiers; in *Danzón* (Maria Novaro, 1991), which is about a trip of the female figure to find her own feminine identity; and in *En tu casa a las 8/Eight O'Clock, at Your Place* (Christine Lucas, 1995), about a love triangle. It is also presented in the films *Gringuito* (Sergio Castilla, 1998), about an uprooted boy; *Corações Desertos* (Cristiano Burlan, 2006), about a couple during the last night of their relationship; *Glue* (Alexis dos Santos, 2006), a coming-of-age drama about a teenager in boring Patagonia; *La Misma Luna/Under the Same Moon* (Patricia Riggen, 2007) about a nine-year-old boy searching his mother; and *La nana/The Maid* (Sebastián Silva, 2009), about a maid who rediscovers herself.

Another aspect to be underlined is the mentioned origin in Dionysian rituals with sex, orgies and masquerade. These themes can nowadays often be found in Latin American ('social') dramas where sex and violence become dominating as in *La luna en el espejo/The Moon in the Mirror* (Silvio Caiozzi, 1990); *Garage Olimpo* (Marco Bechis, 1999), the story of a kidnapped and tortured woman under the dictatorship in Argentina; *Amores Perros* (Alejandro González Iñárritu, 2000), about the hard living conditions and fatality in Mexico; *Babel* (Alejandro González Iñárritu, 2006), about the intricate and cross-linked story of four groups of people; and in *Gigante* (Adrián Biniez, 2009), about a supermarket security guard secretly obsessed with a cleaning woman.

Josué Méndez: *Dioses/Gods*, 2008 © Trigon Film

The drama is often concentrated around one story so that the audience can focus on one person, on the main theme and on the dramatic situation connected mostly with a conflict or problem. The drama plays with the central dramatic aims and its expectations of creating suspense, tension and curiosity. The spectator is curious to know who the murderer is and he is full of tension to know whether he is captured. Moreover, the technological aspects support the content to emotionalize and involve the spectator.

At last there is either a happy ending à la Hollywood creating dreams, or a tragic ending as is often shown in Latin American drama, reflecting reality. In this sense, as drama refers to events of high emotional intensity, such as war, famine, crime, political scandal, terrorism and disaster. It is important for each single country to have a special connection and possibility of identification with the dramatic story. In Latin America this sort of naturalistic or even hyper-realistic tendency can be seen: the social and political problems are reinforced, as shown in *La Nube/Clouds* (Fernando Solanas, 1998), where an Argentinean group tries to save its theatre before it is sold, and in *Bolivia* (Adrián Caetano, 2001), about an illegally working immigrant and his discrimination. It can also be observed in *Madeinusa* (Claudia Llosa, 2006), where a woman wants to escape from the cruel microcosm of her village, and in *Dioses* (Josué Méndez, 2008), a story of an aristocratic and decadent family in Peru.

Finally, the filmic drama is concentrated with in-depth character studies, developments and interactions, as well as serious and emotional issues. An important goal of a well-made drama is that the audience identifies with the protagonists and their environment, developments and feelings, and sympathizes with and understands the process and feelings. Filmic dramas can provide greater understanding of cultural characteristics, stereotypical, and controversial issues by addressing the problem on a more personal and complex level.

Isabel Maurer Queipo

Babel

Country of Origin:

Mexico

Language:

Spanish

Studios/Distributors:

Dune Films
Zeta Film
Anonymous Content

Director:

Alejandro González Iñárritu

Producers:

Steve Golin
Alejandro Gozález Iñárritu
Jon Kilik

Screenwriters:

Guillermo Arriaga
Alejandro González Iñárritu

Cinematographer:

Rodrigo Prieto

Art Director:

Rika Nakanishi

Editors:

Douglas Crise
Stephen Mirrione

Composer:

Gustavo Santaolalla

Duration:

142 minutes

Genre:

Drama

Cast:

Brad Pitt
Cate Blanchett
Rinko Kikuchi
Adriana Barraza
Gael García Bernal

Year:

2006

Synopsis

A Japanese man who went hunting in Morocco gave his rifle as a gift to the guide who accompanied him. The guide sold the rifle to a peasant who bought it so that his children could take care of the family's cattle and defend them from jackals. One day while the children were playing they shot the rifle. The bullet hits a tourist bus and seriously – potentially fatally – injures an American tourist. Her husband is desperate; he thinks of their two small children who are alone in the United States with their Mexican nanny in a town near the Mexican border. The scene then changes to the United States, where we meet the maid, an illegal immigrant. Left alone with the children, she takes a chance and takes them with her to Mexico in order to attend her son's wedding. Her nephew, who also works illegally in the United States, drives them in his taxi. After the wedding, they try to return to the United States but encounter difficulties at the border. They choose to flee the police across the frontier desert. The nephew abandons the nanny and the children during the night and flees across the desert in order to avoid compromising his aunt and the children. The woman is not able to find her way through the desert and is lost with the children. The next morning, she decides to leave the children for a moment in order to find her way. She cannot find the way, however, and consequently loses the children as well until a border patrol agent finds her and helps her recover the children. The police take the children to the United States but the nanny is not allowed to return with them.

The movie constantly changes scenes – from Morocco to the United States and back, and from Morocco to Japan, where the police investigating whether the shooting was a terrorist attack on American tourists have found the weapon's previous owner: the Japanese businessman who had used it on his hunt. The police in Tokyo search the businessman's apartment but find only his deaf daughter who was on the verge of committing suicide. While an officer waited for her father she tried – unsuccessfully – to seduce him. In this movie, as with others directed by Alejandro González Iñárritu, we have a concatenation that seems to be independent stories but which is woven together with very fine but conspicuous ties, where Mexico is just a small piece of the overall mosaic.

Critique

The most modern films in Mexico are sets of stories that tell us to what degree we are interdependent beyond any geographic or linguistic border. Anything that happens in the world can affect our ordinariness. In this film the world itself – Babel – can be seen as a component of a project, the simple human project of 'living'. In this paradigm nothing should be indifferent to us because any 'you' can be 'me' and any 'yours' can be 'ours'. The signs sent from Mexico in its latest and most important film production are oriented towards locating Mexico as one more place inside the globalization and the interdependence into which we are inserted.

The subjects in the stories we see in *Babel* are fragmented by ignorance because they ignore the global view that the director proposes, that being the phenomenon of concatenation. The simple fact of turning a corner can change my or anyone's life. In this film, and others by González Iñárritu, we could speak of a cross aesthetic. The story begins with one – the nanny and the American children in Mexico – and goes on to another – children shooting in the Moroccan desert. Here we have national and supranational 'everydaynesses' that are fragmented but nevertheless joined. This film offers an aesthetic that takes different stories of many individuals; the film's project is to interrogate these individuals to show their mutual indifference towards each other while at the same time interrogating the viewers, because we could be showing the same portrait.

González Iñárritu's national and supranational mosaic continues with the theme of pain, but it is a pain that touches the characters' intimate and existential spheres. They are victims of their circumstances – always violent circumstances – but they are not shown as identity features, rather as confirmations that existence is a complex and hazardous phenomenon that has an inherent violence. This violence is no longer a piece of 'typical/folkloristic data' but a causality that can surprise us independent of time and place. *Babel* shows stories of 'random places' that could have been any place, and therefore the stories are 'similar' or 'connected' by definition, because the film proposes that our own story could be connected with a similar story.

Claudio Aldunate-Cifuentes

Biutiful

Countries of Origin:

Mexico
Spain

Language:

Spanish

Studios/Distributors:

Mod Producciones
Ikiru Films
Menage Atroz S. DE R.L. DE
C.V.

Director:

Alejandro González Iñárritu

Producers:

Alejandro González Iñárritu
Fernando Bovaira
John Kilik

Screenwriters:

Alejandro González Iñárritu
Armando Bo
Nicolás Giacobone

Synopsis

The film starts and ends at the same point: Uxbal and his daughter, Ana, talk about a ring lying in bed. What happens in the middle of the story is, therefore, a great flashback, which really begins at a hospital where Uxbal passes a medical examination and is diagnosed with a terminal cancer. He is an unlucky and desperate father, separated with two young children, and married to Marambra, who suffers from bipolar disorder.

To give their children a good start in life, he runs business in the only way he knows, in Barcelona's underworld of drugs and the trafficking of illegal immigrants. In addition, Uxbal, as a spiritualist who has the ability to speak with the dead. But the most important thing for him now, before dying, is to order his dark life.

Critique

Biutiful is the first feature film Gonzalez Iñárritu made without Guillermo Arriaga, his usual screenwriter. The director himself began writing the script and subsequently, he was attended by the Argentines Armando Bo and Nicolas Giacobone. If Arriaga's narratives were dislocated, *Biutiful*'s story is linear, except, as noted above, that most of the film is a great flashback. As a result, since it is the only violence over the narrative, it should be given special consideration because therein lies perhaps the key to Uxbal's

Cinematographer:

Rodrigo Prieto

Art Directors:

Marina Pozanco
Sylvia Steinbrecht

Editor:

Stephen Mirrione

Composer:

Gustavo Santaolalla

Duration:

150 minutes

Genre:

Drama

Cast:

Javier Bardem
Maricel Álvarez
Diaryatou Daff
Cheng Tai Shen

Year:

2010

character: a cog in a globalized world that is finally not working.

Precisely one of Iñárritu's highest virtues is his ability to combine a number of narrative and aesthetic keys to provide a work that is addressed to a global audience, pointing out the contradictions of globalization without falling into demagoguery. In fact, when Iñárritu first came to Barcelona in 1981 he experienced its brutal contradiction: a global world and, simultaneously, closed nationalism. Hence, perhaps, at the same time, this feature is often the target of the biggest criticisms against Iñárritu cinema, as his work would seem to fall into cultural relativism.

Probably never has Barcelona been represented in a more raw and dreamy way at the same time, far from the county town of tourists, or Woody Allen's *Vicky Cristina Barcelona* (2008). That is, you do not find Gaudi's Barcelona – although it still appears beautiful, but here it is rather 'biutiful' – and, above all, you do not get a Sagrada Familia postcard: when Uxbal stares out of the window of the treatment room hospital, he gets to see it with a ghostly panorama-shot in the distance, still under construction. Barcelona's symbolic temple is precisely what Uxbal seems to long for in his wanderings through the streets, that is, a law that will guide his decisions.

And, therefore, the story of his father, whom he could not know, becomes the secret key of the film, especially when he allows his daughter to say goodbye to him through a ring, and through the promise that might be enclosed in it. So it makes sense that the film is framed by that sequence, as a prologue and epilogue, with its derivative in the snow dream in which his father shows him a way out off-field.

There is thus the spiritual evolution of a protagonist who furrows in a dirty realism landscape as a descent into hell – like the Chinese illegal immigrants who die in a basement poisoned by gas – reminding Iñárritu's first film, *Amores Perros* (2000). But a magical and supernatural space emerges: we see these black butterflies emerging from the ceiling in the most desperate and reflective moments of the main character. In these moments – like in the stones he gives to his children – we also find the aesthetic pointed at by the title 'biutiful': not an imaginary beauty but a transcendent one. See, for example, the tremendous Barcelona sky streaked with black birds, which has been used in the movie trailer. All of this is helped by the fantastic Rodrigo Prieto, who has been the director of photography for all Iñárritu's films – as well as for *Brokeback Mountain* (Ang Lee, 2005), among others.

This rarefied aesthetic crystallizes in the protagonist's name: Uxbal is a strange name, as strange as that morning when Iñárritu and his sons were preparing breakfast, listening to the piano concerto in G major by Maurice Ravel which made them mourn: that very same morning that a character named Uxbal came knocking at the door of the director's imagination.

Although this may not be the most powerful Iñárritu's film, it shows a new path in Iñárritu's filmography, more universal and reflexive. And there is no doubt that this is, perhaps, the best Javier Bardem performance.

Lorenzo Javier Torres Hortelano

Clouds

La nube

Country of Origin:

Argentina

Language:

Spanish

Studios/Distributors:

Cinesur
Les Films du Sud
Continent Film

Director:

Fernando E. Solanas

Producers:

Fernando E. Solanas
Daniel H. Samyn

Screenwriters:

Eduardo Pavlovsky
Fernando E. Solanas

Cinematographer:

Juan Diego Solanas

Art Director:

At Hoang

Editor:

Luis César D'Angiolillo

Composer:

Gerardo Gandini

Duration:

112 minutes

Genre :

Drama

Cast:

Eduardo Pavlovsky
Laura Novoa
Angela Correa
Cristophe Malavoy
Bernard Le Coq

Year:

1998

Synopsis

During a prolonged and unrelenting rainy season in Buenos Aires, referred to as the 'Age of the Cloud', a small theatre troupe faces eviction. The troupe tries to prevent their theatre building from being demolished and turned into a shopping mall by appealing to the Ministry of Culture, but to no avail. Each member of the troupe also has their own personal difficulties to deal with: Max is visited by his estranged daughter, Cholo pursues a TV comedy career, Fulo faces a return to Rio because she can no longer afford to bring her daughter to Argentina, and retired teacher and poet Enrique is forced to sell his belongings while waiting to receive his state pension. In an effort to save the theatre building, the troupe makes one last stand by broadcasting their final performance over an independent radio station.

Critique

Clouds opens with a series of shots of a rain-soaked Buenos Aires as traffic and pedestrians move backwards through the streets. Similar shots frequently punctuate the film; a recurrent visual trope employed by director Fernando E. Solanas (perhaps implying what Solanas views as Argentina's artistic and cultural regression). Co-written by playwright Eduardo Pavlovsky, the narrative of *Clouds* follows the plight of the small Espejo theatre group, led by Max (Eduardo Pavlovsky), whose dwindling audiences (most of whom are over retirement age) place them in dire financial straits, leaving them unable to pay the electricity bills and under threat of eviction. In 'El Espejo' ('The Mirror'), the first of ten tableaux into which the film is divided, a performance by Globos Rojos must be cancelled when the electricity is suddenly shut off mid-performance, much to the chagrin of the spectators. As well as the theatre's threatened future, the small group of actors must also cope with everyday problems such as difficult familial relationships, financial hardship, loneliness and injustice, among other things.

The Teatro Espejo is just one of many small independent theatres in Buenos Aires that have been threatened by modernization throughout the years. Despite Max and his group's attempts to save the building, the prevailing bureaucracy insist that the land the theatre stands on is unproductive and would be better used to serve the people, who had after all voted on it, by installing a shopping mall. Max and poet Enrique (Franklin Caicedo) appeal to the Minister of Culture in an attempt to prevent the demolition of their theatre space, but to no avail. In the tableau 'Modernidad' ('Modernity'), which opens portentously with a shot of construction vehicles shovelling debris, Max and Cholo (Christophe Malavoy) are told bluntly that 'subsidizing culture is a thing of the past', and are shown a model of the city's development plan, which includes the demolition of their theatre, and the possibility of a supermarket in its place. Max and Cholo later meet with Enrique in a cafe where Cholo laments a growing culture of philistinism: 'Culture now means TV, whatever can be digested fast like hamburgers', to which Enrique

Fernando E. Solanas: *La Nube/Clouds*, 1998 © Trigon Films.

can only respond cynically, 'If Descartes were alive today he would no longer say "I think, therefore I exist", but, "I am on TV, therefore I exist".'

Despite the pessimistic tone, the endless rain, and the oppressive presence of 'The Cloud', there are moments of surreal humour in *Clouds*. For example, in the tableau 'Vida Llovida' ('Raining Life'), Cachito (Carlos Paez) walks numerous dogs to raise money. At one point he loses his grip on the leashes and the dogs run away, then the film is run in fast-forward, creating a slapstick effect as Cachito falls on his face and then chases the dogs through the park at high speed. In the tableau 'Ajuste' ('Adjustment'), the group sits and reminisces about Cachito's first lesson in Max's drama school. Max tells Cachito: 'You must believe you are the best; the most talented, the only one – God himself. I am God.' Then Max levitates, ascending into the air with arms outstretched. Later in 'Modernidad', when Cachito is admiring Fulo (Andrea Correa) in her underwear, he says to himself, 'I just feel like melting,' then he literally disappears, leaving a puddle of water in his place.

At the heart of *Clouds* is a critique of culture and of policy, and their relationship to the arts in Argentina. Both Max and Enrique, whose heyday was the 1960s and 1970s, express nostalgia for the days when the avant-garde was a vivifying and revolutionary form of political protest and progressive ideology; but the relationship between politics and art is now irremediably severed. There can no longer be any integration between the two spheres, and the encroaching market forces of modernization threaten to eliminate or commodify any remaining vestige of culture and high art. Max, who threatens to commit suicide if his theatre is demolished, gives a final performance on the roof of the building. Although the performance inspires the crowd below to begin pelting the demolition crew with stones, the fate of the theatre – just as the fate of art and culture in Solanas' Argentina – remains undecided.

Zachariah Rush

La gata borracha

Country of Origin:

Venezuela

Language:

Spanish

Studio/Distributor:

Gente de Cine C.A.

Director:

Román Chalbaud

Producer:

Miguel Ángel Landa

Screenwriter:

Salvador Garmendia

Cinematographer:

Arthur Albert

Art Director:

Ariel Severino

Editor:

José Alcalde

Composer:

Jesús Aquiles Vásquez

Duration:

100 minutes

Genres:

Drama

Synopsis

Víctor Mendoza, a working-class bank employee and apparently perfect father and husband, falls madly in love with Rosario, a prostitute working at a brothel located in the Venezuelan port city of La Guaira called La gata borracha (the drunk cat). Rosario arrives there fleeing a turbulent past in Maracaibo, a city in western Venezuela. The brothel's owner, La Gata, rents rooms to girls in order for them to meet their 'boyfriends'. She also deals with drugs and makes some other shady deals with the consent of the police. When Rosa Elena, Víctor's wife, discovers her husband's extramarital affair with this street woman, she initiates a face-to-face conversation with Rosario.

Critique

This film has a circular structure. The opening sequence shows a carnival party in which the guests dance to the song 'La gata borracha', played by the band Billo's Caracas Boys, a very well-known Venezuelan band whose music could be heard at almost every party during the 1980s. Soon afterwards, two children dressed as Zorro and Superman find Rosario's (Alba Roversi) corpse. Once the body is discovered, the police start an investigation to reconstruct the story of the deceased young woman's final moments up until shortly before Víctor (Miguel Ángel Landa) murdered her, a reconstruction made possible by La Gata (América Alonso) and a friend and colleague of Víctor's.

As in his other films, Román Chalbaud here focuses on the excluded. This film thematizes, albeit superficially, problems and characteristics of Venezuelan society such as prostitution, domestic violence, infidelity, male chauvinism, hidden homosexuality, peddling of political favours, bribery, police corruption, religious syncretism, racism, and the hypocrisy of the bourgeoisie. Prostitution and domestic violence are shown through the conflict between Rosario and her husband Atilio (Daniel Alvarado), who hits her for being a prostitute. Infidelity and sexual frustration resulting from a frozen

Cast:

Miguel Ángel Landa
Alba Roversi
Bárbara Teyde
América Alonso

Year:

1983

relationship are considered through Víctor's affair with Rosario. A *maracucho*, the Venezuelan macho prototype, who works in the brothel and is shown in bed with a naked woman after a night of supposed wild sex, suggests both verbally and through body language that he will sexually abuse La Gata's stepchild the moment the boy is alone and helpless in his room. As for peddling for political favours, police corruption and bribery – the law of the jungle – we see that at first La Gata does not take her detention by the chief police inspector seriously. Rather, she treats policemen as if they were her friends and offers them a glass of brandy from a bottle that a certain Colonel Otaiza, an influential friend of hers, brought her from France. However, as well as in Chalbaud's movie *Cangrejo/Crab* (1982), the police inspector leading the investigation turns out to be honest and committed to his work. With regards to racism and social classes, while Víctor's wife is an upper-class white woman, Víctor is a working-class mestizo. Religious syncretism is shown through references to María Lionza, prints of José Gregorio Hernández, patron of the sick, and elements of Santería – Afro-Caribbean religious rituals and practices involving such items as candles, altars and cigars. Clairvoyants and card readers complete the picture. Not coincidentally, the story reaches its climax during carnival festivities and ends on Ash Wednesday. At the end of the film Víctor, a symbol of the striving bourgeois society, takes off his mask. He has showed what he was capable of, even though, according to La Gata, 'he seemed to be a correct person'.

Although this film is neither particularly innovative nor especially surprising aesthetically or in terms of its plot, it is important to note the central role popular music plays in the narrative. The opening song, 'La gata borracha', anticipates the protagonist's death. She is like a mouse that is eaten by a drunken cat that in this case is a man caught in the maelstrom of his own instincts. It also alludes to the eponymous brothel where the protagonist works and which apparently saved her from her violent husband but, at the end of the day, is a trap from which she cannot escape. Moreover, it refers to La Gata, the brothel's owner. This is a woman who, among other things, has an ambiguous relationship with her German stepson, a disabled young man. She sometimes speaks to him in German and calls him 'Mausi', which in German literally means 'little mouse' and can be used both to express familial and carnal love. We should also note, finally, that 'mouse' in Venezuelan Spanish means 'hangover'. When she drinks more than usual, the cat 'catches' a mouse: 'La gata coge un ratón.'

Maribel Cedeño Rojas

Extraordinary Stories

Historias extraordinarias

Country of Origin:

Argentina

Language:

Spanish

Studio/Distributor:

Independiente

Director:

Mariano Llinás

Producer:

Laura Citarella

Screenwriter:

Mariano Llinás

Cinematographer:

Agustín Mendilaharzu

Art Director:

Laura Caligiuri

Editors:

Alejo Moguillansky
Agustín Rolandelli

Composer:

Gabriel Chwojnik

Duration:

245 minutes

Genres:

Drama

Cast:

Walter Jacob
Agustín Mendilaharzu
Mariano Llinás

Year:

2008

Synopsis

Extraordinary Stories essentially follows the strange, adventurous trips taken by three men referred to as X, Z and H. Although the stories are interwoven, the men's quests never intersect. X is involved in an assassination and escapes with a mysterious suitcase from the scene of the crime. Hiding in a hotel room he tries to understand what has happened. He stumbles into a conspiracy, the unfathomable clues of which ensnare him in an exhausting and paranoiac game of imaginative, historical reconstruction. Z accepts a dull job in an isolated office. Soon he discovers that his predecessor, who held the position until he died, led a mysterious life behind the facade of a cautious and shy person. Z becomes obsessed by the idea of retracing the dead man's steps and tries to reveal his secrets. In the third story, H is hired by an engineer, a member of a secret society, for a very unusual job. He has to locate monoliths situated on the shore of a river. Instead of finding them he meets another man contracted by a competitor for a similar (but actually opposite) search and gets involved in an unexpected odyssey. These are the starting points from which the three main stories are split into eighteen chapters and several secondary stories told by three different narrators who are not the characters in the film. There are no dialogues; a perpetual voice-over covers almost every inch of the footage. The idea seems to break the rules against redundancy that have been stressed in film courses since day one, but there is a crucial catch: sound and image are consistently separated, but while the image overlaps with the text, it does not do so perfectly. In some cases the story anticipates the image and in others trails behind it; sometimes the voice from the off tells what might be seen and what will not be seen, or describes characters. The consistent sarcastic tone in the narration maintains the disbelief keeping up the suspense and captivating the audience at every moment of the 245 minutes of running time.

Critique

In the year 1995 a group of young film students who had won a short film competition of the INCAA (National Institute of Cinema and Audiovisual Arts) decided to premiere their works in the cinemas as an anthology film entitled *Historias breves*. Some of these students soon became the main characters of a new wave of Argentine films. Many of their movies are low-budget productions shot in a neo-realistic style. Titles like *Historias mínimas/Minimal Stories* (Carlos Sorín, 2002) and *Historias cotidianas/Everyday Stories* (Andrés Habegger, 2001) are no coincident. More than a decade and five editions of *Historias breves*-anthologies later, another new generation of the *Nuevo Cine Argentino* film-makers has appeared. Director, producer, writer, editor, actor and teacher at the University of Cine of Buenos Aires, Mariano Llinás (b.1975), won with the jury's special prize at the 2009 edition of the 'Buenos Aires International Film Festival' (BAFICI) for his film *Extraordinary Stories*. The BAFICI is the main forum for independent Latin-American film-makers. As the title indicates, this indeed extraordinary film differs from previous productions. The usual Argentine film locations such as the inner city or the desert-like southern Patagonia are left behind. In contrast, *Extraordinary Stories* takes place in the vast plains and little towns of Buenos Aires province and the Pampa. Instead of short stories, Llinás made an epic film which neither looks nor feels like any representative Argentine film that one might have seen at international festivals in the last few years. Instead of minimal, everyday stories, there is an overabundance of anecdotes, a constant free flow of ideas. Instead of contemplation, there is one adventure after another.

Extraordinary Stories is an experimental movie that renews the proof of our unlimited thirst for thrilling adventure stories. It is a unique film that covers an unexplored space not only in Argentina, but in international cinema. Despite its uniqueness, influences on Llinás' style can be found: one can sense traces of Orson Welles, David Lynch, Jacques Rivette and the young Jean-Luc Godard. Sources of inspiration can also be found in literature: authors such as Robert Louis Stevenson, Jules Vernes, José Hernández and Jorge Luis Borges have influenced his work. Sometimes it seems that ideas of nineteenth century storytelling are brought back with modern techniques; the parody-like tone is 'Borgesian' to the bone, the construction of the stories is a 'garden of forking paths' – to quote the title of a short story by Borges – or a labyrinth without a centre.

Extraordinary Stories, a film at once excessive, eccentric, extravagant, dreamlike and utopian, is the renewal of the promise made by the first generation of the Nuevo Cine Argentino: the promise to innovate Argentine cinema.

Sven Pötting

Frida

Frida, naturaleza viva

Country of Origin:
Mexico

Languages:
Spanish
Russian
French
German

Studio/Distributor:
Clasa Films Mundiales

Director:
Paul Leduc

Producers:
Manuel Barbachano Ponce
Dulce Kuri

Synopsis

On her deathbed Frida Kahlo evokes memories of her life. Images of her childhood, her streetcar accident, and her physical pain are interspersed with memories of her marriage to Diego Rivera, her political activism, and her relationship with Trotsky and fellow painter Siqueiros, a Stalinist. A collage of several long sequences conveying a selection of important incidents and paintings of her life, *Frida* presents itself as a vivid portrait of Mexico's famous cultural icon.

Critique

The scarcity of dialogue and the focus on the visual are intriguing in Leduc's biopic of the artist. The film begins in Mexico City's Palace of Fine Arts and gives the viewer the impression of visiting an exposition of Frida Kahlo's self-portraits. The title *Frida, naturaleza viva* refers to 'naturaleza muerta', the Spanish term for 'still-life', and even as we learn that Frida (Ofelia Medina) is already dead, she seems to be very much alive.

We see eight sequences of *tableaux vivants* from Kahlo's life, presented by the prologue title card as her own memories, 'fragmented and disconnected… as her own thoughts'. Not

Screenwriters:

José Joaquín Blanco
Paul Leduc

Cinematographer:

Ángel Goded

Art Director:

Alejandro Luna

Editor:

Rafael Castanedo

Composers/Sound Recordists:

Ernesto 'Cato' Estrada
Penélope Simpson

Duration:

108 minutes

Genres:

Biography
Drama

Cast:

Ofelia Medina
Juan José Gurrola
Max Kerlow

Year:

1986

surprisingly there is no linear story, no obvious plot development; the film rather feels like a surrealist's stream of consciousness. At a very slow pace, the camera contemplates revealing images of Frida's life, strolling back and forth, travelling through time and space like the visitor of an exposition. We see images of pain: Frida after her accident, Frida watching the nurses preparing the amputation of her leg, a wheelchair. Her famous painting, *La columna rota/The Broken Column* (1944), is revisited twice, consciously accentuating Frida's self-description as a 'broken' and not as a 'sick' person, and celebrating her life-embracing will and vital strength.

Apart from her political activism, the film concentrates mainly on her intimate and private life in her Coyoacan home and studio. It is not the international, liberal, bisexual Frida Kahlo who is presented in this biopic, it is the Frida of the Mexican people. Clearly visualized through her traditional dress, suggesting a mestizo identity and her participation in popular customs like ceremonies of the Día de los Muertos, her *mexicanidad* is also accentuated through the importance of the blend of political and popular songs from Latin America.

Referring only twice to the Trotsky-Stalin opposition in the form of discussions (involving Rivera [Juan José Gurrola] and Trotsky [Max Kerlow]), Frida's political activism and her perseverance in the leftist cause make another tableau. Leduc does not elaborate on the nuances of Kahlo's political standing and prefers to put her in the context of world history. Consequently, we do not only see media images of the Spanish Civil War, of H-bomb tests, Stalinist assassins attacking Trotsky, Mexican troops firing on Mexican dissidents, we also watch Frida scolding a man who applauds Hitler during a cinema newsreel, Frida participating in Pro-Zapatista and anti-imperialist demonstrations, and Frida marching for peace. The prologue informs us that Kahlo was 'always near to Marx, Zapata and the Mexican Revolution, always moving away from the iron will of Stalin'. Meaningfully, the final image of the film shows Frida joining a protest against the CIA intervention in Guatemala, only ten days before her death. The combination of images of her private, public, political and artistic life leaves us with the impression of a highly intelligent, gifted and socially involved woman who chose to live and not to succumb to the manifold physical ailments that tormented her all her life.

Heidi Denzel de Tirado

Gringuito

Country of Origin:

Chile

Language:

Spanish

Studio/Distributor:

Amor en el Sur Ltda.

Synopsis

Eight-year-old Iván, the eponymous diminutive gringo, has to move with his mother and father (who are expecting another child) from New York to Santiago de Chile, his parents' home city, leaving behind his friends and the New York Opera. His parents try to make the arrival as pleasant as possible for the youngster, but Iván cannot get accustomed to his new home. One morning, he slips out of the door to discover the city by himself. When he does not find his way back, he is not only forced to finally speak Spanish, but also to get

Director:

Sergio Castilla

Producer:

Abdullah Ommidvar

Screenwriters:

Sergio Castilla

J. B. Miller

Cinematographer:

Chuy Chávez

Art Director:

Alejandra Egana

Editor:

Danielle Fillios

Composer:

Jaime Lawrence

Duration:

100 minutes

Genre:

Drama

Cast:

Sebastián Pérez

Mateo Iribarren

Catalina Guerra

Alejandro Goic

Kevin Dean

Year:

1998

to know the *santaguinos*. Iván gains the friendship of the fruit seller, Flaco, who first cheats the boy of his belongings, but then assumes responsibility for Iván and finally takes him back home.

Critique

Gringuito is neither only a children's film nor merely a 'Santiago film' that portrays the boy's odyssey through Chile's capital, but is also a document of the political polarization that marks modern Chile. Whereas Iván's parents – obviously due to his father's political attitudes – have lived many years in exile and are now returning to the Andean country, his maternal grandparents can be regarded as right-wing citizens. The different political cultures clash several times during the film; however, Castilla tries to seek reconciliation between the two through filmic devices. When the family arrives at the airport, Iván's father, Jorge, seems paralyzed when looking at a police officer. Young Iván follows his father's gaze and sees the officer's gun holster, a symbol of the military power which apparently brings back all the sad memories of Jorge's past. However, instead of cutting and assembling these two shots directly, the film uses a dissolve to connect them: for a very brief moment, we can see both the policeman and the startled Jorge in the same frame.

Another scene displaying the reconciliation of political opposites can be found in the conflict between Jorge and his mother-in-law, Teté. As a consequence of holding very different political views they have a rather frosty relationship. In their argument, the continuing divisions within Chilean society become manifest. At the beginning of their argument the two characters are shown in different frames. When Jorge tries to calm her down and apologizes, the characters are presented together in one medium close-up shot, but they are still separated from each other physically and visually by a carefully arranged *mise-en-scène*, putting a dark, thick line between them. Later in the film, however, we see that Jorge and his mother-in-

Sergio Castilla: *Gringuito*, 1998 © Amor en el Sur Ltda.

law have been reconciled when they walk home together arm in arm. Again, it is the *mise-en-scène* that emphasizes the newfound proximity, since there is neither a visual line nor any physical space separating the characters. Instead, they are touching each other.

Gringuito focuses on the boy's perspective and reveals Chile's political status quo as well as the beauty of its capital through the gaze of the child's eyes. It is one of the many Chilean films which paint a fond portrait of Santiago de Chile: the camera moves through the streets of the metropolis and documents the city centre, the suburbs, as well as the bars and brothels of Santiago's nightlife. Like a travelogue, the film presents the main sights of the city such as the Santa Lucía Hill. It registers the daily routines of the La Vega market as well as the upper-class neighbourhoods. And because it covers so many different parts of Santiago, it represents the most detailed portrait of the city in contemporary Chilean cinema. Not only does it offer foreign viewers a detailed visual impression of the city, it also presents the citizens of Santiago with an opportunity to recognize their capital anew and, moreover, to discover new parts of it.

Verena Schmöller

Hitting Bottom

En la puta calle

Countries of Origin:

Spain
Argentina

Studios/Distributors:

ATPIP Producciones
Trastorno Films

Director:

Enrique Gabriel

Producers:

Enrique Gabriel
Didier Haudepin
Piluca Vaquero
Tomás Cimadevilla

Screenwriter:

Enrique Gabriel

Cinematographer:

Raul Pérez Cubero

Art Director:

Angel Sarrion

Editor:

Julio Peña

Synopsis

Juan is an electrician whose life is shattered when he suddenly becomes unemployed. He leaves his family and goes alone to Madrid. He struggles to adapt to the big city and find any kind of employment. He accepts an offer for underpaid construction work and befriends Caribbean mulatto Andy, an illegal immigrant. When the construction job is complete, he barely gets money to pay his overdue rent. His landlady Margarita suggests sex for his rent, but he declines. Juan is reduced to sleeping in the streets. He stays in touch with Andy, who helps him survive and tries to convince him to become partners, something Juan refuses. Juan and Andy save junkie Beatriz, a wealthy businessman's daughter. They continue their descent into the numbing world of unemployment, but at the same time they are both able to maintain their dignity and develop a meaningful friendship.

Critique

This is the second feature by Argentinean-born film-maker Enrique Gabriel Lipschutz, after his promising debut *Krapatchouk* (1993). *Hitting Bottom* explores the dramatic consequences of unemployment and immigration, in a mixture of drama and comedy, which will become one of the director's most salient traits. The picture begins almost like a silent movie, offering us a glimpse of a desolated industrial landscape, the abandoned factories and collapsing industries that brought endemic high unemployment in the Spain of the late 1980s and early- to mid-1990s. We move to the individual drama of Juan Gutiérrez, an unemployed electrician, portrayed by character actor Ramón Barea, with sober and minimalist dignity. We

Composer:

Caco Senante

Duration:

95 minutes

Genre:

Drama

Cast:

Ramón Barea
Luis Alberto García
Sergi Calleja
Marga Escudero
Patricia García Méndez

Year:

1997

witness Juan as he leaves his house and small town and moves to the big city, and his struggle to adapt to a new, unfamiliar environment like a fish out of water. Gabriel adopts a purely behaviouristic approach, showing us Juan's gestures, his moves, his desperation, with barely any dialogue, echoing the approach of Jean-Pierre Melville in *Le Samouraï* (1967).

The film was shot during the last socialist government of the 1990s (1993–96), and specifically criticizes the social situation of that time; in fact, a character representing a contractor states: 'It's not my fault that my name is Felipe González, but at least I offer employment'. Nevertheless, the director is not only interested in the individual tragedy of unemployment but more so on the effects of immigration on society, and on the difficult mix of unemployed citizens with the new waves of immigrants; the Old World and the New World, meeting and clashing again in a totally different scenario.

The character of Andy Cardoso (Luis Alberto García) plays a pivotal role, as portrayed by Luis Alberto García in a powerful but playful performance. Andy's relaxed demeanour works as a contrast and complement to Juan's rigidity and bad temper. Like Don Quixote and Sancho, they are a unit of opposite personalities, backgrounds, cultures and attitudes, but they learn a lot from each other. Juan clearly represents Spain, the 'madre patria' full of racial stereotypes against people of Latin American origin (*sudacas*) and those of different colour, even if in the end Spanish citizens are not in better shape than those immigrants that they despise and ridicule. On the other hand, Andy represents an idealized immigrant, pragmatic in his approach to means and strategies, but with a solid ethical core. He is always ready to help Juan when he is in need; he shares with him whatever resources he has, and offers the other cheek to his jabs and temper tantrums.

The second half of the film focuses more squarely on the relationship between Juan and Andy. The film clearly benefits from it, becoming a superb mixture of dramatic moments and light comedic touches, mostly contributed by Andy's ingenuity and ability to draw a positive message from any situation. The film turns more dramatic at the end, touching on other topics such as the problem of drugs, violence or deportation. Nevertheless, it never loses its balance and we get the feeling that Juan has become a better human being, less rigid and more accepting of human diversity. The movie was screened at the 'San Sebastián Film Festival'. It also received the Best Actor award for Barea at the 'Iberoamerican Film Festival' (Huelva), and the Best Performance award for its two leading actors at the 'Amiens Film Festival'.

Javier Gutiérrez-Rexach

Machuca

Countries of Origin:

Chile
Spain
United Kingdom
France

Language:

Spanish

Studio/Distributor:

Wood Producciones et al.

Director:

Andrés Wood

Producers:

Mamoun Hassan
Gerardo Herrero
Andrés Wood

Screenwriters:

Eliseo Altunaga
Roberto Brodsky
Mamoun Hassan
Andrés Wood

Cinematographer:

Miguel Ioann Littin Menz

Art Director:

María Eugenia Hederra

Editors:

Fernando Pardo
Soledad Salfate

Composers:

José Miguel Miranda
José Miguel Tobar

Duration:

121 minutes

Genres:

Biography
Drama

Cast:

Matías Quer
Ariel Mateluna
Manuela Martelli
Aline Küppenheim
Ernesto Malbran

Year:

2004

Synopsis

Pedro Machuca is one of a handful of young boys from a Santiago de Chile suburb who is admitted to visit the renowned private school Saint Patrick. Its director, Father McEnroe, welcomes the group of poor men's sons in order to integrate the different parts of Chilean society into his school. While many of the pupils from privileged backgrounds do not mingle with the newcomers, the middle-class boy Gonzalo Infante makes friends with Pedro, and the two boys get to know each others' homes: Gonzalo is warmly welcomed by Pedro's mother, attracted by Pedro's older friend Silvana, but appalled by the family's living conditions. Pedro, in contrast, experiences bourgeois wealth and luxury.

Critique

The coup, as well as the Pinochet regime, is a common topic of Chilean cinema of the 1990s. Films of that decade which deal with recent history point at the dictatorship indirectly by using symbols and allegories, while films that were produced after the turn of the century address the incidents under Pinochet more overtly. In particular, documentaries such as *Estadio Nacional* (Carmen Luz Parot, 2001) or *El caso Pinochet/The Pinochet Case* (Patricio Guzmán, 2001) opened discussions about what had happened during the Pinochet era. *Machuca* can be regarded as the first feature film of this new 'phase of memory'.

Set during the last weeks and days of the Salvador Allende government, the film deals with the collapse of Chilean society in the 1970s and its climax: the Chilean military's *coup d'état*. A good example of Chile's political tension can be found in the scene that pictures a parent-teacher conference. Not only do the oppositional political factions clash, but also different classes of society, the poor and the rich: Gonzalo's mother wants to know what is the idea of mixing pears with apples, and expresses in this way her displeasure

Andrés Wood: *Machuca*, 2004 © Wood Producciones et al.

regarding the social mixture in Saint Patrick School. Pedro's mother however, stands up against the various accusations against the newcomers.

Moreover, the film portrays the concrete events of 1973 and their significance for Chile's history, as seen through the eyes of two teenage boys from different parts of society. In contrast to many other film-makers, Wood does not give only the victim's viewpoint, but also focuses on the 12-year-old Gonzalo, the son of a middle-class family which does not support the Allende regime although increasingly fearful of the growing socialist movement, and his conflict between his social background and his new-found friendship. After the military has taken over the country, Gonzalo accidentally observes a soldier shooting Silvana. Shocked by her sudden death, he cannot stand up for his friends when he is caught by another officer, and betrays their friendship in order to escape.

It is certainly this point of view that accounts for the film's national and international success. And it is this focus that makes *Machuca* an important and groundbreaking milestone for other films that are committed to dealing with Chile's recent past and to reconciling the still existing gaps in Chilean society.

Verena Schmöller

The Maid

La nana

Country of Origin:

Chile

Language:

Spanish

Studios/Distributors:

Forastero Ltda.
Tiburón Filmes
Puntoguiónpunto

Director:

Sebastián Silva

Producer:

Gregorio González

Screenwriters:

Pedro Peirano
Sebastián Silva

Cinematographer:

Sergio Armstrong

Art Director:

Pablo González

Synopsis

Raquel has served as the maid of a wealthy Chilean family for many years. She is very dedicated to her work and loyal to the family she works for in spite of the problems that arise with the family's daughter, Camila. One day, the family decides to engage a new maid to help Raquel. Raquel, however, protects her domain and shows very clearly that she will not permit anybody to impinge on her power. She has managed to get rid of several other maids who have tried to enter her territory right up to the moment in which the experienced Sonia imposes herself as Raquel's companion in the job.

Critique

We could classify *The Maid* as a psychological film, one that is entirely constructed from the maid's point of view. We do not receive any explanations; we see only the unforeseen and irrational reactions of the maid. Meanwhile, in the background, the double moral standards of the social class for which she works are on display. *The Maid* is a social film as well, as it shows the maid's engagement and identification with positive and negative aspects of life in a family. The maid has no life of her own; she helps the other members of the family to have and to construct their life. She gives her energy and her youth to a family that does not always include her as a member. Their relationships with Raquel are confined to the home, and for her this means that apart from work there is only loneliness.

The film accurately shows the elements that place the maid in a space that is not really hers. The luxury in which she lives – the

Editor:

Danielle Fillios

Composer:

Pedro Subercaseaux

Duration:

95 minutes

Genre:

Drama

Cast:

Catylina Saavera
Claudia Celedón
Mariana Loyola
Agustín Silva
Alejandro Goic
Andrea García-Huidobro

Year:

2009

garden, the quality of the furniture, the meals, etc. – is not hers. Her occupation construes an illusion of belonging to the same class that she works for, but she knows that this is not the case. When she goes home to her room, the simplicity and the poverty become evident. The villa as a kind of paradise disappears, and then life itself appears as a kind of prison, which has another prison inside: her room.

Indeed, this film is about something more than differences and struggles between social classes, as some critics have pointed out. The social differences constitute the framework within which loneliness appears in a mixture of psychological and sociological tones. As such, the story of the maid underscores abnegation and misidentification about working for a family that is not hers, but which nevertheless is the only family she has. This family is her only source of income as well as the only source of a sense of belonging. Moreover, as time passes, even their home becomes – in her imagination – a sort of property – her property – to which no other maid should try to gain access.

At the beginning of the movie, it is certainly difficult to sympathize with Raquel, who never strives to gain our sympathy. Beginning to understand her life, however, her loneliness, the emptiness and frustration she experiences, we begin to sympathize with her. Here another element comes to the fore: Raquel is being transformed, bit by bit, due to the inevitable hiring of another maid who is intelligent and seductive. At the end, the new maid can be regarded as a cause of Raquel's release from her own prison.

The reality in which the story unfolds is characterized by a huge economic and social gap between Raquel and the family she works for. More cruelly, her hard work is rewarded only with indifference and coldness from the family. It is the kind of family in which the husband escapes in infidelity, and in which the adolescents – who once upon a time were 'the children' – have changed their mind regarding their maid: she should not be a person closely related to them; the closeness she once enjoyed is now considered a social error. As a matter of course, the maid loses the sincerity and transparency of the people who once upon a time were children without prejudices towards her. Now, the adolescents have a private life, so the doors of their rooms are locked, and it is not possible for the maid to come in at any moment, as she used to. The link between Raquel and the 'kids' is now broken, and this is just the beginning of a collapsing reality.

Undoubtedly, Sebastián Silva (Director) and Catylina Saavedra (Raquel) deserve the national and international recognition they have received for their excellent film.

Claudio Cifuentes-Aldunate

Martin (Hache)

Martín (Hache)

Countries of Origin:

Argentina
Spain

Studio/Distributor:

Tornasol Films

Director:

Adolfo Aristaráin

Producers:

Adolfo Aristaráin
Gerardo Herrero

Screenwriters:

Adolfo Aristaráin
Kathy Saavedra

Cinematographer:

Porfirio Enríquez

Art Director:

Abel Facello

Editor:

Fernando Pardo

Composer:

Fito Páez

Duration:

130 minutes

Genre:

Drama

Cast:

Federico Luppi
Juan Diego Botto
Eusebio Porcela
Cecilia Roth
Sancho Gracia
Ana María Picchio

Year:

1997

Synopsis

Martin is a divorced Argentinean film-maker who works and lives in Spain, separated from his family and feelings. When his son Hache has a near-fatal drug overdose, Martin travels back to Argentina and brings his estranged son back to Madrid with him. Hache is a teenager who refuses to go to school and is fascinated by drugs. Martin has a hard time adapting to living with his son, and Hache becomes fascinated with the two other individuals in Martin's life, his on-and-off girlfriend Alicia, and his best friend, Dante, a talented actor who is completely open about his bisexuality and experimental drug use.

Critique

Aristaráin wrote *Martin (Hache)* while he was resting in bed for two months after suffering an accident at home. When an Argentinean production company backed down from the project, Aristaráin himself co-produced the film with Gerardo Herrero (Tornasol Films). The film was presented at the 'San Sebastián Film Festival' in September 1997, and it won the Concha de Plata for Federico Luppi's performance as Martin. Cecilia Roth (Alicia) was awarded the Goya for Best Leading Female Performance, and Eusebio Poncela (Dante) also received a prize for his performance at the 'Biarritz Film Festival'. Such critical recognition to the film's central performances is not casual, since *Martin (Hache)* rests on the shoulders of its four leading actors, the above-mentioned three plus Juan Diego Botto (Hache), all engaged in an emotional tour de force lasting more than two hours. Aristaráin, well known for supporting his stories in traditional narrative conventions, audaciously moves this time in the opposite direction.

The film is almost a chamber piece in which narrative development relies entirely on a series of masterfully assembled, precise, intense and poignant dialogues. Nevertheless, it never feels theatrical or stale. The spectator is completely absorbed and engaged in the interactions and confrontations of four human beings, and in the raw intensity of the feelings and emotions portrayed. As Martin states, taking a quote from *Un lugar en el mundo/A Place in the World* (Adolfo Aristarain, 1992), the 'best psychoanalyst would be a barman'; in other words, it is through casual conversation and dialogue that we get to know and understand a human being. And there is a lot of psychological dissection here.

Martin represents the forces of the superego, a repressed and ill-tempered film director who has been unable to exteriorize his feelings about those surrounding him and who uses criticism and demeaning words as a way of remaining detached from what surrounds him: his own country ('The only home country is your neighbourhood, you are only attached to your friends and that only remains so long'), his estranged wife and son, and his lover Alicia. He is highly judgemental of everyone and everything around him but, tragically, he fails to see that his acerbic comments are so damaging that they will bring tragic consequences. Alicia, the woman who stands by Martin despite his distancing strategies, will succumb to his cruel words and to her own

Adolfo Aristaráin: *Martín (Hache)*, 1997 © Trigon Films.

demons, including drug addiction. She commits suicide in the most devastating scene of the film. On the other hand, Dante represents the forces of the id, an epicurean free spirit who is able to use drugs as a freeing experience and lives his sexuality as a form of intimacy ('I don't fuck bodies, I fuck brains').

The film is also the story of Hache, which stands for the letter H in Spanish, the initial of *hijo* (son). Hache is not just Martin's son, an imperfect and inadequate byproduct who will never reach his father's ideal. He is a teenager transitioning from adolescence to maturity, not feeling at home anywhere, but with sufficient insight to understand what goes around him. Hache obviously loves his condescending father but finds more support in Alicia and Dante.

In the end, his stay in Madrid will teach him that he has to become his own man and that he is more at home where he does not have to prove himself. He will also teach Martin and Dante that he is not as lost as they thought. The final scene is another tour de force, as we watch Hache's taped farewell and Martin and Dante's reactions.

Aristaráin stages every scene around his actors and the camera often captures their emotions in powerful close-ups. This film marks a breaking point in Aristaráin's career, transitioning from the ethical and ideological concerns of previous films into a more intimate territory, focusing on issues such as family relationships, friendship, work, sex and drugs.

Javier Gutiérrez-Rexach

The Moon in the Mirror

La luna en el espejo

Country of Origin:

Chile

Language:

Spanish

Studio/Distributor:

García y Calozzi Ltda.

Director:

Silvio Caiozzi

Producer:

Andrea Films

Screenwriters:

Silvio Caiozzi
José Donoso

Cinematographer:

Nelson Fuentes

Art Director:

Guadalupe Bornand

Editors:

Álvaro Ramírez
Silvio Caiozzi

Composer:

Mario Díaz

Duration:

71 minutes

Genre:

Drama

Cast:

Gloria Munchmayer
Ernesto Bearle
Rafael Benavente
María Castiglione
Mónica Echeverría

Synopsis

This film is about the life of El Gordo ('The Fat'), a bachelor who lives with his alcoholic father, a retired captain in the Chilean navy. The father is sick and is bedridden. This situation makes El Gordo's life a real prison, because his father requires his constant attention. The only contact he has with the world is with the beautiful widow Lucrecia, a neighbour who helps him with his purchases. El Gordo's house (prison) is constructed in such a manner that he cannot move around without being controlled by the father's eyes (Don Armando's). This occurs as the father orders El Gordo to construct a system of many mirrors in the house, in order to control where he is and what he is doing at all times. Within the 'panopticon' there is a very small area of the flat that is not covered by the mirror system and is therefore out of the father's control. It is precisely in this secret angle that El Gordo receives visits from Lucrecia and where they have their 'murmured dialogues'. The father does not permit anything that could leave him without the protection and service of the son. For that reason the son can have neither a relationship nor speak with anyone. As a consequence, the film is spoken in whispers for roughly 90 per cent of its duration. El Gordo, who can neither move nor do anything, is an obese man who spends his time baking and selling enormous cakes. When the cakes do not sell, El Gordo assumes the responsibility of eating them.

To celebrate New Year's Eve, El Gordo and Lucrecia organize a small party just for themselves when the father has drunkenly passed out. During the party El Gordo tells Lucrecia that his father became an alcoholic because being paralysed and bedridden after having been a national hero was very humiliating for him. He tells her that his father keeps a box under his bed with all the medals he was awarded during his service in the navy. Lucrecia, who is a little drunk, becomes curious and during this whispered 'party' discovers that the moon is reflected in many mirrors, and she shows this phenomenon to El Gordo. Minutes later, she enters the father's room and looks under the bed to search for the sacred box of medals while El Gordo is terrified by the idea that the father could wake up.

Critique

Silvio Caiozzi has created a fantastic and disgusting universe in this film, one that shows a take on life. There is the tyranny of the father (Rafael Benavente) who, in a symbolic sense, castrates his son (Ernesto Bearle), because he prevents him from forming any relationships or having a personal life. The real shock in this film occurs at the end, when we learn that El Gordo's father is not really ill

Silvio Caiozzi: *La luna en el espejo/The Moon in the Mirror*, 1990 © with kind permission of Andrea Films.

Year:

1990

and that he constructed this sad life for his son capriciously, because he wanted a kind of slave for himself.

This film's themes are loneliness and repressed psychological evolution. El Gordo's confinement in his own home and the lack of any possibility to realize himself by love, the 'absence of a name', and the fact that he was constantly addressed by his nickname (El Gordo) all combine to goad El Gordo to transgress his father's law. These transgressions consist of inviting Lucrecia (Gloria Münchmeyer) to the home, which gives El Gordo the possibility of having a kind of love and the possibility to experience poetry: to see – close to her – the moon in the mirror – freedom, the exterior world – and the moon itself, as a symbol of love.

Caiozzi's film is a tribute to the magnificent and poetic city of Valparaíso. The few external captures of the city in the movie represent all the beauty that El Gordo is missing during the long confinement planned by his father. When the moon comes to his mirrors it is the exterior visiting El Gordo, and this phenomenon gives him the light to experience love with Lucrecia. Summarized, in this movie we have an exciting mixture of loneliness, tyranny, prohibited desire (castration), rebellion against the father's confinement and, finally, freedom.

Claudio Cifuentes-Aldunate

The Motorcycle Diaries

Diarios de motocicleta

Countries of Origin:

Brazil
United States
Spain
Argentina

Language:

Spanish

Studios/Distributors:

Film Four
South Fork Pictures
Tu Vas Voir Productions

Director:

Walter Salles

Producers:

Daniel Burman
Diego Dubcovsky
Mónica Lima
Michael Nozik
Robert Redford
Edgard Tenenbaum
Karen Tenkhoff
Paul Webster
Rebecca Yeldham

Screenwriter:

Jose Rivera

Cinematographer:

Eric Gautier

Art Director:

Coco Oderigo

Editor:

Daniel Rezende

Synopsis

The year is 1952. The young medical student Ernesto Guevara de la Serna, who would later become the revolutionary 'Che', and a biochemist named Alberto Granada embark on an 8,000 km-long motorcycle trip across Latin America. Based on the real-life diaries of the two men, the film follows their ambitious plan to cross the Andes, travel along the coast of Chile, across the Atacama Desert, and into the Peruvian Amazon and reach Venezuela in time for Alberto's 30th birthday. The two friends embark on their journey for the simple pleasures of seeing as much of Latin America and seducing as many of its women as their time and fortunes will allow them. As they traverse the continent, however, these pursuits give way to more serious, political concerns, and we witness Guevara's awakening to the social inequality that exists across these nations as he bears witness to the sufferings of the many people they encounter. The film ends with an impassioned speech by Guevara, in which he declares that he has been fundamentally changed by his experiences and advocates the ideological unification of the Latin American continent.

Critique

A truly pan-Latin American film, The Motorcycle Diaries is as much an exploration of the continent itself as it is the story of the political awakening of one of its most enduring icons. Indeed, the film is immensely effective in the way in which it humanizes Guevara, presenting him not as the iconic figure that he would become, but as an empathetic mediator through which the audience can gain a new understanding of Latin America and its people. The tagline for the film reads: 'Before he changed the world, the world changed him', which is an accurate description of the way in which this dialectic film aims to portray the evolving relationship between the future revolutionary and his continent.

The film is undeniably successful in achieving this aim, capturing stark and often beautiful contrasts of the Latin American landscape and its population and rendering them in their minute detail and grand scale. The film's stunning cinematography takes its audience on a visual journal across the continent; we are exposed to images of dense forests and arid desserts, are invited inside lavish mansions and humble shacks, and see the ancient and the contemporary-modern placed side by side. However, The Motorcycle Diaries is most successful in portraying the diverse Latin Americans that the men meet on their travels, allowing the audience to feel as if they are viewing them through the eyes of Guevara himself. As the film's journey ends

Composers:

Gustavo Santaolalla
Laurent Ott
Maria Eugenia Sueiro

Duration:

126 minutes

Genres:

Adventure
Biography
Drama

Cast:

Gael García Bernal
Rodrigo De la Serna
Mercedes Morán

Year:

2004

we are presented with snapshots of the many people that have been encountered in the course of the narrative; these images are like still-life portraits in black and white, yet the small movements within them constantly remind us that these people are vividly alive in the mind's eye of Guevara the narrator. These images are exemplary of the way in which *The Motorcycle Diaries* encourages us to view Latin America as an evolving nation and to see the continuing relevance of the idea of a united, continental consciousness.

Indeed, *The Motorcycle Diaries* as a cinematic production in itself also advocates pan-Latin American collaboration through its consummate employment of artistic talents from across the Americas, in front of and behind the camera. A key film of the Latin American New Wave, it is exemplary of the way in which the idea of a Latin American cinema is fostered, benefitting from the humanity of Salles' Brazilian direction, the redemptive warmth of Argentinean Rodrigo Del la Serna as Alberto Granada, and the presence of Gael García Bernal, a native Mexican whose understated performance and star charisma imbues Guevara with the combination of gravitas and human frailty that is needed to achieve the film's aims.

Ultimately, *The Motorcycle Diaries* is about the unifying of a continent. This was profoundly expressed by the film's director in an interview with Geoff Andrews at the National Film Theatre in 2004 when he stated that he was in doubt about whether such a thing as Latin American unity truly could exist, could be thought of, or even imagined. But the more they went into the continent, the more they thought, 'Yes, it exists'. The film encourages its audience to be convinced by the idea of Latin American unity and is a testament the potential of Latin American cinema to capture a continental consciousness.

Victoria Kearley

A Place in the World

Un lugar en el mundo

Countries of Origin:

Argentina
Spain

Studio/Distributor:

Cooperativa de Trabajo La Colmena

Director:

Adolfo Aristaráin

Producers:

Adolfo Aristaráin
Osvaldo Papaleo

Synopsis

Mario and Ana are two left-leaning professionals, a teacher and a doctor, who left Argentina for Spain to escape the military dictatorship. After returning to their country, they choose to forgo a middle-class existence in Buenos Aires and move with their son Ernesto to a distant agricultural valley. With their friend Nelda, a progressive nun, they establish a school, a clinic, and a wool cooperative. Conflicts with Andrada, the main landowner in the area, are constant. Their existence is disrupted by the arrival of Hans, a Spanish geological engineer, who claims to be hired by Andrada to look for oil but in reality works for a Spanish company developing plans to build a dam in the valley.

Critique

After the Spanish TV series *Las aventuras de pepe Carvalho* (1983–85) and the American production *The Stranger* (1987), two failed incursions in mainstream media production, Aristaráin returns to his roots and delivers what is arguably his most significant, beautiful

Adolfo Aristaráin: *En un lugar en el mundo/A Place in the World*, 1992 © Trigon Films.

Screenwriters:

Adolfo Aristaráin
Alberto Lecchi

Cinematographer:

Ricardo De Angelis

Art Director:

Abel Facello

Editor:

Eduardo López

Composer:

Emilio Kauderer

Duration:

120 minutes

Genre:

Drama

and powerful film. The production was not without problems, after Spanish TV decided to withdraw, and the film was shot in 1991 within a cooperative regime, in which the cast and crew renounced their salaries. Released in 1992, it received the Goya award for Best Spanish Language Foreign Film, and the Concha de Oro and audience awards at the 'San Sebastián Film Festival'. It was also nominated for an Academy Award for Best Foreign Language Film. Unfortunately, it was disqualified and removed from the ballot because it was presented as Uruguay's official entry when it was mostly an Argentinean production.

Whereas in previous films Aristaráin explored his concerns within the framework of the narrative structure of the thriller, in this case he used several narrative and visual conventions from the western. The story depicts the struggle of small peasants and cattle owners against the powerful land baron. In this fight, they are helped by a sceptical loner of ambiguous motivations, whose appearance will serve as a catalyst and trigger for several conflicts, and who will side with the peasants and leave town after helping them in their struggle. George Stevens'

Cast:

José Sacristán
Federico Luppi
Leonor Benedetto
Cecilia Roth
Rodolfo Ranni
Hugo Arana
Gastón Batyi

Year:

1992

classic western *Shane* seems to serve as inspiration here. A horse-riding competition acquires special significance, as in *The Quiet Man* (John Ford, 1952), and the semi desert-like landscape of the San Luis valley plays an essential role, almost as one more character in the drama.

Aristaráin seamlessly works most of his thematic constants in this story: the conflict between ideals and reality, the ethical commitment to one's principles and to other individuals, the omnipresent role of a powerful corporation (once again named Tulsaco), the importance of education and literacy as freedom agents, etc. Mario Dominici (Federico Luppi) is the quintessential Aristaráin hero, who gives up a comfortable existence in Buenos Aires to pursue the idealistic goal of building a cooperative ('We might have lost the war but we can still win a battle,' he confesses), but will be driven to questionable behaviour. In a masterfully-shot nocturnal scene, he sets on fire the barn containing all the peasants' wool to prevent any defections ('I am not crazy […] now they will have to start from scratch,' he concludes).

Nevertheless, as a sign of maturation and transitioning to a new phase in his career, Aristaráin is more interested in building a choral story, in which other characters are equally important. Hans (José Sacristán), the Spanish geologist who comes from a wealthy family, acts as the more practical and skeptical counterpoint to Mario. Interacting with Mario and his family will change him forever. He gets involved in teaching, he confronts Andrada (Rodolfo Ranni), and reveals the true nature of his geological work in the valley. We also witness the increased romantic tension between Hans and Ana (Cecilia Roth), a tension that never materializes but is subtly shown in look exchanges, minimal gestures, etc. This is also the coming of age story of Ernesto (Gastón Batyi), who tells the story in a flashback. He learns about life, loss and love, and in one of the most delicate scenes, he teaches the girl he is in love with to read using Jack London's *Call of the Wild* (1903). Technically, the film is one of the purest examples of cinematic classicism of the last thirty years. Two elements deserve special mention: the masterful use of the classical 1:33 aspect ratio in carefully-composed shots, and Emilio Kauderer's nostalgic and elegiac music.

Javier Gutiérrez-Rexach

Time for Revenge

Tiempo de revancha

Country of Origin:

Argentina

Studio/Distributor:

Aries Cinematográfica
Argentina

Synopsis

Pedro Bengoa, a former anarchist and union leader, hides his past in order to be hired as a demolition engineer at a copper mine owned by the Tulsaco corporation. He travels to the mine's location in Patagonia with his wife Amanda. Among the mine workers, he finds an old friend from his anarchist past, Bruno. Bruno proposes Pedro an elaborate plan to scam 300,000 dollars from the company, but Pedro sees it as too risky. Disgusted by the working and safety conditions at the mine and affected by his father's death, Pedro changes his mind and agrees to stage an accident. Pedro contacts Larsen, who arranges a meeting with Tulsaco's owner, Don Guido. Back in touch with his old

Director:

Adolfo Aristaráin

Producers:

Héctor Olivera
Luis O. Repetto

Screenwriter:

Adolfo Aristaráin

Cinematographer:

Horacio Maira

Art Director:

Abel Facello

Editor:

Eduardo López

Composer:

Emilio Kauderer

Duration:

112 minutes

Genre:

Drama

Cast:

Federico Luppi
Haydee Padilla
Julio De Grazia
Ulises Dumont
Joffre Soares

Year:

1981

ideals, Pedro rejects any settlement offer and decides to go to trial against the company, unaware of the cost and consequences of this move.

Critique

Aristaráin's fourth film is one of the best Argentinean films of the 1980s. It was made in haste due to the fact that Luppi had been banned by the military Junta controlling the country. The film was very successful in Argentina and abroad, and it was the first one in which Aristaráin received unanimous international critical appraisal and several awards at international film festivals (Biarritz, Montreal, Cartagena de Indias). Aristaráin managed to escape censorship despite the obvious references to the current political and social situation, probably because the film has several layers of complexity and cannot be read just as sociopolitical commentary. Federico Luppi is superb as Pedro Bengoa, the aging anarchist, a man who has lost his ideals and only wants to survive and make a decent living. In order to be hired, he has to falsify his credentials and lie about his past, overtly proclaiming his disdain for union struggles before being hired by the powerful mining company Tulsaco. This attitude disgusts his father Aitor, an idealist until the end, who challenges his son to look at himself in the mirror to see whether he can still recognize himself.

Bengoa's attempts to remain unnoticed are undermined by chance. Bruno (Ulises Dumont), an old friend and comrade from past struggles is also working at the remote copper mine. Bruno has moved away from his ideals too, but has a plan to escape from everything: an elaborate plot to become injured in an explosion and collect compensation for damages. The film carefully narrates the full-circle transformation of Bengoa, from his initial anarchist past to a jaded engineer, to a reluctant accomplice in the plan to extort the wealthy capitalist enterprise to, in a surprise twist, a new man who gives up half a million dollars for the possibility of exposing the inner workings of the mining company in court.

Pedro has to pretend to be completely mute, as a psychological injury from the accident. This plot device acquires symbolic undertones in Aristaráin's carefully crafted script. It is clearly a symbol of the anarchist heroes prosecuted by the dictatorship, struggling to remain silent under torture. Nevertheless, remaining silent allows Pedro not only to take revenge on the company but also to collect a compensation for his disability. He will pay a hefty prize. His wife (Haydée Padilla) abandons him, frustrated by his silence. His lawyer (Julio De Grazia) also abandons him, irritated by an idealism of unclear origin ('a hard-headed Basque cannot change history'). Finally, he also pays a personal price: the company follows his every move to expose him; he has to remain in hiding in his father's old apartment, and he periodically gets tape players with anonymous recordings. The reference to Francis Ford Coppola's *The Conversation* (1974) is clear here: an agonizing hero trapped and driven to madness by his own plot and by the clever use of technology by a powerful enemy, in this case the capitalist empire owned by Don Guido, a man who 'never loses, always wins'.

Aristaráin skillfully manages to keep the story moving at a fast pace, treating it like a pseudo-Hitchcockian thriller, and keeping the audience intrigued by the fate of the main character, who is silent for half of the film. At the core, we find some of Aristaráin's thematic concerns, which will become more salient in later films: aging and its effects on ideals, the struggle to remain ethical in a corrupted environment, and the interplay of personal and general interests in social struggles.

Javier Gutiérrez-Rexach

The Wind Journeys

Los viajes del viento

Country of Origin:

Colombia

Language:

Spanish

Studio/Distributor:

Elle Driver

Director:

Ciro Guerra

Producers:

Cristina Gallego
Diana Bustamante

Screenwriter:

Ciro Guerra

Cinematographer:

Paulo Andrés Pérez

Art Directors:

Angél
ica Perea

Editor:

Iván Wild

Composer:

Iván Ocampo

Duration:

117 minutes

Genres:

Drama
Music

Synopsis

Ignacio Carrillo is an elderly accordionist leaving his home town on a donkey after the death of his wife. After vowing never to play again, he embarks on one last journey in order to return his accursed black accordion decorated with two bull's horns to its owner who, according to legend, won it in a duel with the devil. On the way, the taciturn troubadour is followed by Fermín Morales, an obstinate teenager who wants to learn to play the instrument and to become Ignacio's apprentice. At first, the musician rejects him, but when the youngster manages to breach Ignacio's solitude and overcome a number of obstacles (such as recovering the accordion after it is stolen by bandits), he finally accepts Fermín as a companion, although not without trying to spare him the disadvantages of life as a travelling musician. Together they traverse the mountains, valleys, swamplands and deserts of the Caribbean coast of northern Colombia, experiencing a variety of encounters and adventures, and discovering not only themselves, but also the cultural diversity of their country on their way.

Critique

After his well-received debut with *The Wandering Shadows* (2004), *The Wind Journeys* is Ciro Guerra's second feature film. It is both a travelogue and a buddy movie, the latter being a cross-genre which blends elements of adventure film and drama. Exquisitely filmed in Cinemascope, this road trip across the picturesque Colombian landscape follows an old man and a young boy and their strong relationship which oscillates between father and son, maestro and disciple. Although both protagonists are heading in the same geographical direction, their spiritual and emotional background could not be more different. While Ignacio is fleeing from his profession, Fermín is looking for precisely the opposite. The youngster is in search of his future, the elderly musician trying to reconcile himself with the past.

The linear, episodic structure organizes the events narrated and is reinforced by an original soundtrack that combines a lack of dialogue, the use of several spoken languages other than Spanish, sound-effects from nature such as the wind, and the integration of the regional music, *Vallenato*. Furthermore, the continuity of the narration

Ciro Guerra: *Los viajes del viento/The Wind Journeys*, 2009 © Courtesy of Ciudad Lunar Producciones and Ciro Guerra.

Cast:

Marciano Martínez
Yull Núñez
Agustín Nieves
Erminia Martínez
José Luis Torres
Justo Valdéz

Year:

2009

is often maintained by sound bridges of diegetic and extradiegetic songs and music that represent the cultural diversity of Colombia's post-colonial heritage. In particular, the *Vallenato* reunites elements of African, European and indigenous culture, and the incidental encounters of the two protagonists with African drummers or Indian villagers also serve as a pictorial and audiovisual introduction to the multiculturalism of Colombia.

With universal, but at the same time innovative aesthetics for Colombian cinematography, Ciro Guerra has created a masterpiece of reflective and poetic cinema, following other directors like Andrei Tarkovski, Werner Herzog and Robert Bresson. Primarily addressing local audiences in order to introduce Colombian culture, myths, legends and geography, the variety of landscapes depicted in panorama perspectives and wide angles as well as the meticulous camera-work in relation to the use of shadows, natural light, backlighting and colour also makes this film attractive for an international public. Frequently showing the two protagonists as tiny figures in the middle of spectacular environments, the film offers a glimpse into a unique topography that integrates extremes, such as the snow-covered peaks of the Andes, fertile valleys covered with multicoloured flowers, or the whiteness of the salt mines of La Guajira.

With an interesting mix of reality (the cast consists mainly of locals and amateur actors), nature and fictional situations, Ciro Guerra's film strongly resembles other films of World Cinema in which priority is often given to the depiction of natural settings, such as the Middle Eastern and Maghrebian deserts of Nacer Khemir's trilogy *Wanderers of the Desert* (1986), *The Dove's Lost Necklace* (1991) and *Bab'Aziz* (2006), the breathtaking scenery of Eric Valli's *Himalaya* (1999) or the harsh steppes of Kazakhstan in Sergei Dvortsevoy's *Tulpan* (2008). Consequently, *The Wind Journeys* offers a sensitive portrait of the secret, but seductive sides of the Colombian hinterlands. It is certain that this film will predominantly attract an audience appreciative of contemplative cinema without much action, and who will respond to the ravishing beauty of a movie that tells a story about the human need for company 'on life's journey', even when it takes place on a donkey.

Verena Berger

The Window

La ventana

Country of Origin:

Argentina

Language:

Spanish

Studios/Distributors:

Guacamole Films
Wanda Visión S.A.

Director:

Carlos Sorín

Producer:

José María Morales

Screenwriter:

Carlos Sorín

Cinematographer:

Julián Apezteguia

Art Director:

Rafael Neville

Editor:

Mohamed Rajid

Synopsis

Don Antonio is a bedridden writer in his eighties. A heart attack has left him weak, requiring an intravenous drip and completely dependant upon his nurse, Emilse, and his housekeeper, María del Carmen. On this particular day he is awaiting the arrival of his estranged son Pablo, a world-famous concert pianist. Don Antonio ensures that the old piano is tuned, requests the best champagne to be ready and that his best blue jacket is pressed. In the afternoon, Don Antonio goes outside to inspect the vegetable gardens after the night's storm, and soon finds himself wandering among the vast acres of fields on his estate. After exerting himself too much, he collapses to the ground. Luckily he is discovered by cyclists who send for help, and is returned to bed in time for his son's visit.

Critique

At the centre of *The Window*'s minimalist narrative is Don Antonio (Antonio Larreta), an aged, bedridden writer, tethered to an intravenous drip after suffering a heart attack. Every aspect of Antonio's life is controlled by his nurse Emilse (Emilse Roldán) and his housekeeper María del Carmen (María del Carmen Jiménez). He is told what to eat, what to wear, how to sit, and when and how long to write. His bedroom window, like a cinematic frame, is the only view of the world beyond his confinement. At the very beginning of his film, writer and director Carlos Sorín seems to equate memory with cinema and its ability to reproduce images. Antonio dreams of a girl from eighty years ago. The dream sequence has the aesthetics of an old

Composer:

Nicolás Sorín

Duration:

77 minutes

Genre:

Drama

Cast:

Antonio Larreta
María Del Carmen Jiménez
Emilse Roldán
Roberto Rovina
Arturo Goetz

Year:

2008

silent movie as the sound of the projectors whirs in the background. When calling to mind the name of the girl in the dream, he thinks her name might have been Garber, or Garbo, perhaps confusing his memory with the iconic face of Greta Garbo. When Antonio's doctor arrives later in the day, the two discuss literature, including Adolfo Bioy Casares' novella *La invención de Morel/Morel's Invention* (1940), in which the eponymous inventor creates a machine to perpetually project the souls of his friends and of himself, so that their week of pleasure on an isolated island will exist forever, like the immortal images of movie stars. Antonio tells his doctor that the image of the girl comes and goes like the characters in Casares' novella.

The Window also explores the relationship between fiction and reality. Sorín blurs the lines by having his characters use the actors' real names. For example, Antonio is played by renowned Uruguayan writer Antonio Larreta, his nurse Emilse is played by Emilse Roldán, the housekeeper María del Carmen is played by María del Carmen Jiménez, and Roberto, the piano tuner, is played by Roberto Rovira.

Carlos Sorín: *La ventana/The Window*, 2008 © Wanda Vision

Sorín thus stresses an overlapping of reality and fiction, of the actor on set and the character within the film, of the fictional world created and the real location in which the film was shot. In this way Sorín both alludes to and utilizes the narrative device used in Casares' novel, i.e. that of different temporal dimensions.

One outstandingly beautiful sequence worthy of note is when Antonio slips out of the house, escaping the bondage of his bedroom and the fastidious pampering of his caretakers. Antonio walks through his vegetable garden, then wanders further out onto his estate, beautifully photographed by cinematographer Julián Apezteguia as a golden Elysian scene. Sorín delights in the simplicity and profundity of nature as he captures the rural panoramas of the Patagonian landscape. The sequence is shot almost entirely without dialogue and lasts close to ten minutes, yet it is never tiresome as the sequence unfolds like a melancholy poem, a visual meditation on the simple joys of life and the ever-present reality of death. Antonio is dwarfed by the immense landscape, an all too human reflection when faced with man's place within an infinite universe. Yet, there is a moment of understated glee on Antonio's face as he communes with nature, by urinating in the open air, perhaps an unconscious gesture of territoriality.

The Window is comparable in some ways to Ingmar Bergman's early masterpiece, *Smultronstället/Wild Strawberries* (1957); both narratives centre on an aged protagonist who, nearing death, is visited by remembrances of times past. For Antonio, he remembers for the first time in eighty years a precious memory of his first crush, the beautiful babysitter appointed by his mother. Within the duration of a single day, Antonio traverses time, evoking his first memory, which also proves to be his last. What Antonio first remembers is also that which he will last remember, thus completing the cycle, and at this point Antonio is ready to die. In the closing frames of the film we return to the dream sequence with its black-and-white aesthetics of old movies, and as Sorín's film ends, the old footage runs off the spools, and everything fades to black.

Zachariah Rush

ROMANCE

Most films contain a story of love or a special friendship and deal with emotions, but while here the love story is only a part of a subplot and normally plays a minor role, in romances it forms the main story. The love story – especially the love between the main (heterosexual) characters – is underlined by classical romantic elements with a focus on private happiness, longing and/or suffering that make love films different from the other genre of narrative cinema.

The most important elements of romances are based on the early nineteenth century artistic movement romanticism, which emphasized passion and liberation from artistic conventions as underlined by Gill Branston:

> 'Romantic' is now used in film and television studies to indicate a concentration on particular feelings and passions: those of intimate personal life, additionally often implying sexual feelings, and both a woman protagonist and a largely female audience. Debate rages about whether the form provides important escapist and compensatory outlets for women's dissatisfactions with the intimate emotional consequences of a patriarchal order, often via narratives involving nurturing males and yearnings dramatized by unhappy or unfulfilled outcomes. Or is it inherently masochistic and compliant with that order?

The romance is one of the most famous genres because of these traditional themes of love and friendship. Otherwise, because of this fact it is mostly considered as a 'feminine' genre following the classical attribution of women and emotions as well as women and the irrational on the one hand and men and the rational on the other hand. In this sense, these films often focus on women in society and their destiny mostly with a romantic happy ending. However, before the protagonist experiences such a happy ending, she has to confront problems, overcome obstacles and go through adventures. The focus lies on activities that make the fulfillment of the love difficult to reach. Dramaturgy serves clearly to underline such exciting love stories and allows the person in question to reach goals only with difficulty, creating more space for desire. The dramaturgy in particular of the melodrama as a special sort of romance, for example, intensifies the grief. It leaves the lovers united in order to emphasize the pain when they lose again.

The stories deal with eroticism, different sentimental relations, friendships and love stories which are sometimes forbidden and politically persecuted, and with pleasure focusing on the situation of women. Examples are *El* (Mexico, Luis Buñuel, 1953) which is a dramatic romance about the relation between obsessed Francisco and Gloria and the cruel changing of his character after getting married; *Bye, Bye Brasil* (Brazil, Carlos Diegues, 1979) which is about the tour of a group and its leader 'the Gypsy Lord', a magician and showman, in their 'Caravana Rolidei' (a misspelling of 'holiday') through Brazil; *Retrato de Teresa* (Cuba, Pastor Vega, 1979) about the emancipation of multi-tasking Teresa; *El beso de la mujer araña/Kiss of the Spider Woman* (Brazil, Héctor Babenco, 1985) about a homoerotic relationship; and *Central do Brasil/Central Station* (Brazil, Walter Salles, 1998) about the relation between a young boy and an older woman. *El mismo amor, la misma lluvia* (1999), *El hijo de la novia/Son of the Bride* (2001) and *El secreto de sus ojos/The Secret in Their Eyes* (2009) by Juan José Campanella; *Le temps retrouvé* (Raoul Ruiz, 1999); *Solo con tu pareja* (Alfonso Cuaron, 1991); *Como agua para chocolate/Like Water for Chocolate* (Alfonso Arau, 1992); and Sandra Gugliotta's *Las vidas posibles/Possible Lives* (2007) are other examples of different love stories. Eliseo Subiela's *El lado oscuro del corazón/The Dark Side of the Heart* (Argentina, 1992) and *El lado oscuro del corazón II* (Argentina, 2000) are about the young writer Oliveiro searching for a love that makes him fly and find 'the dark side of the heart'. In Part 1 he apparently finds it in the prostitute Ana who in the sequel film leaves for Barcelona so that his search goes on. *Fresa y chocolate/Strawberry and Chocolate* (Cuba, Tomás Gutiérrez Alea and Juan Carlos Tabío, 1994) is about the complicated and scheming gay relationship of two young men (Diego and David) during Castro's regime. *El callejón de los Milagros/Midaq Alley* (Mexico, Jorge Fons, 1995) is about the complex lives of some inhabitants of El Callejón de los Milagros ('the alley of the miracles') in Mexico City and especially the (sentimental) life of Don Ru and his son Chava who murders the gay lover of his father. *Guantanamera* (Cuba, Tomás Gutiérrez Alea and Juan Carlos Tabío, 1995) is a comedy-drama about the relations between some lorry drivers and the members of a funeral procession on their journey to Havana. *Profundo carmesí/Deep Crimson* (Mexico, Arturo Ripstein, 1996) is about the nurse Coral who falls obsessively in love with a swindler and turns into a criminal. *Plata quemada/Burnt Money* (Argentina, Marcelo Piñeyro, 2000), a mix between crime/drama and romance, is about a love between two men who plan with other gangsters a bank robbery that will be botched, so that the gang has to flee to Uruguay where the story ends tragically. *El crimen del padre Amaro/The Crime of Father Amaro* (Mexico, Carlos Carrera, 2001) is about 24-year-old Father Amaro and his new life in Los Reyes, Mexico, full of hypocrisy and corruption between the Church and the Military, and forbidden loves. *Japón* (Mexico, Carlos Reygadas, 2002) is about a suicidal painter getting to know and love an older religious woman; *Frida* (Julie Taymor, 2002) is about the artistic and sentimental life of Frida Kahlo; and *Batalla en el cielo/Battle in Heaven* (Carlos Reygadas, 2005) is about the tragic life of a poor couple full of sex and violence.

Sandra Gugliotta: *Las vidas posibles/Possible Lives*, 2007 © Trigon Films.

Contracorriente/Undertow (Javier Fuentes-León, 2009) is another 'unusual' love story about the married fisherman Miguel and his affair with another man.

Thus, one of the figures can fall ill or even die, or there can be a separation of the loving couple because of religious, cultural or family reasons. Mostly, these problems are solved in the end (as in a comedy), but sometimes the story takes a sad ending (as in a tragedy). In this sense, the Hollywood-like idea of a romance is not simply applicable to Latin America. Happy endings in Latin America can often turn into a tragic reflection of the society; the reality and its tragedies due to the turbulent and devastating histories of the single countries, the dictatorships, the race conflicts, the melting pots of different cultures and nationalities and, in relation to the women's history, the patriarchal structures and the machismo. There are still not so many alternative relationships in contrast to the heterosexual couple and harmonic family life shown on the screen due to these often conservative, old-fashioned mentalities and patriarchal structures of governments and the church.

Due to these emotionally turbocharged themes and the narrow relation with women, the romance is a genre that may comprise broadly the melodrama: its use has often been pejorative because of its tendency to manipulate on the emotional level and concentrate on old-fashioned feminine roles, though the melodrama derives from the Greek 'melos' which signifies song and 'drama' which signifies action. The pathetic aspects are the motor of this genre, and as a tear-jerker it contains trivial, portentous and emotional elements. The love story is often centred around a woman and has been used since the 1970s as a special form of romance to describe a type of romantic, sensational and affecting film. One outstanding romantic melodrama is for example the three-part film *Lucía* (Humberto Solas, 1968). It is about three women, three 'Lucías' at three different times: Lucía during the War of Independence (1895), Lucía during the dictatorship of Gerardo Machado (1933) and Lucía during the first days of the Cuban Revolution (1960). Solas visualizes a rather marginalized subject at that time, namely that of the sexes. Before, all conflicts between the sexes had been dominated by the struggle against colonialism, dictatorship or pseudo-democratic governance. In the part about 1960 the relationship between a man and a woman is in fact in the foreground.

In Latin America there are famous romantic precursor genres such as the so-called 'tissue films', the cinema of teardrops (*cine de lágrimas*) and the so-called 'rumberas'. Another very special relation with the melodrama is the special love for soap operas, the famous telenovelas with an outstanding economic and cultural impact. The first telenovela appeared with extraordinary success in Cuba with the radionovela *El derecho de nacer* ('The right to be born') by Félix B. Caignet in 1948 and was adapted for television in 1958.

Apart from *Cristal*, *Topacio*, *La usurpadora*, *Rosalinda*, *María la del barrio*, *Triunfo del amor* and *La fuerza del destino* there is to be mentioned *Betti la fea* based on the novel 'Yo soy Betty, la fea' ('I am Betty, the ugly') by Fernando Gaitán. This telenovela entered the *Guinness Book of Records* in 2010 as the most successful telenovela in the history of television.

They are all calculated to flee reality. This fact reinforces again the etiquette of women cinema. Another variation of romances is the 'romantic comedy' with a studio style and a star system, to increase the possibilities of identification. The melodrama is ideologically aligned with the conservative goal of preserving traditional values or to restore and highlight the central importance of family and the marital bond in a woman's life. Due to this, female directors do not often choose this genre.

Isabel Maurer Queipo

Battle in Heaven

Batalla en el cielo

Countries of Origin:

Mexico
France
Germany
Belgium

Language:

Spanish

Studios/Distributors:

Société Parisienne de
Production
Coproduction Office
Tarantula

Director:

Carlos Reygadas

Producers:

Philippe Bober
Susanne Marian
Carlos Reygadas
Jaime Romandia
Joseph Rouschop

Screenwriter:

Carlos Reygadas

Cinematographer:

Diego Martínez Vignatti

Art Directors:

Elsa Ruiz
Daniela Schneider

Editors:

Adoración G. Elipe
Benjamin Mirguet
Carlos Reygadas
Nicolas Schmerkin

Composer:

John Tavener

Duration:

98 minutes

Genre:

Drama

Synopsis

After the prologue of a very graphic scene of oral sex between the silently suffering Marcos and the silently crying Ana, Marcos is informed that the baby that he and his wife have kidnapped has died. Absent-minded, he drives Ana, the daughter of his boss, to the 'boutique', a place where rich girls prostitute themselves for fun. When Marcos tells Ana about the dead baby, she tries to convince him to go to the police, whereas his wife wants him to participate in a religious pilgrimage and to silence the boss's daughter. The next day Marcos sleeps with Ana, goes on a family excursion, and decides to turn himself in.

Critique

The most shocking and dominating theme of the film, the death of the kidnapped baby, is not shown and only mentioned at the beginning. But Marcos (Marcos Hernandéz) is ridden by guilt. As if there was a ghost haunting Marcos, the hand-held camera witnesses the whole story in real-time through extreme close-ups and angles. Sometimes it follows Marcos in long sequences as if somebody was pursuing him; sometimes it suddenly flies into the air and overlooks the scenery in long distance shots.

After Ana (Anapola Mushkadiz) tells Marcos that he should turn himself in, the sequences oscillate between carnal lust and the search for spiritual salvation. Arriving at home, Marcos makes love to his wife beneath the eyes of a suffering Jesus and a crying angel. The montage combines close-ups on parts of Christ's body, the bodies of the couple and the face of the crying angel echoing the crying Ana of the first scene.

The whole film feels like a *cinéma-vérité* documentary, using nearly exclusively intradiegetic sound; we hear music in only two sequences. The first time we hear it, Marcos is watching a religious procession at a gas station, which is playing a Bach concerto for their costumers. The concerto is cross-faded with the pilgrims singing, 'We all go to heaven.' Marcos is hypnotized by them but describes them as a 'flock of sheep'. The next day he makes love to Ana. When she tells him that he has to go, the camera makes them look like two corpses on a shroud, and the only extradiegetic sound of the whole film begins. It is the 'Saeta de la Virgen de la soledad', a Spanish march performed during religious processions, characterized through its mournful power and intense sorrow. The *saeta* goes on to the next sequence, in which Marcos is masturbating during a soccer game on TV. The repeated phrase 'eso no es la realidad' ('this is not the reality') seems to refer to the soccer game, but we understand that he could be speaking about the death of the baby as well. During an excursion with the family he disappears in a fog of light and reaches a few shots later the top of a mountain. Facing a cross, he covers his face in shame. Despite his decision to turn himself in, he kills Ana and holds her bleeding body in the posture of a reversed Pietà. The fact that he dies shortly afterwards in a religious procession makes it difficult to interpret the opening and ending scene of oral sex. If that were the 'Battle in Heaven', Ana and Marcos would have won it.

Cast:

Marcos Hernández
Anapola Mushkadiz
Bertha Ruiz

Year:

2005

Carancho

Country of Origin:

Argentina

Language:

Spanish

Studios/Distributors:

Fine Cut
matanzacine
Ibermedia

Director:

Pablo Trapero

Producers:

Alejandro Cacetta
Juan Pablo Galli
Felipe Braun
Gregory Gajos

Screenwriters:

Pablo Trapero
Alejandro Fadel
Martín Mauregui
Santiago Mitre

Cinematographer:

Julián Apezteguia

Art Director:

Mercedes Alfonsín

Editors:

Ezequiel Borovinsky
Pablo Trapero

Composer:

Lim Giong

Duration:

107 minutes

Genres:

Crime
Drama
Romance

Whereas some critics complain about the boring senselessness and crude pornography of the film, others are in raptures over its deep poetic realism which captures the fragility of life and death, body and soul, Heaven and Hell.

Heidi Denzel de Tirado

Synopsis

Sosa is an ambulance-chasing personal-injury lawyer who works for a shady attorney firm called 'the foundation', getting hefty settlements from insurance companies, of which his clients see only a small fraction. Luján is a doctor with a substance-abuse problem who works the night shift as an EMT. Sosa and Luján meet at an accident scene, and Sosa falls in love with her. They start dating and Sosa, seeing this as his opportunity for a new beginning, begins to reassess his priorities and tries to cut his ties to the foundation. Nevertheless, this will turn out to be an almost impossible task, and Sosa's actions will carry him and Lujan into a downward spiral of violence and crime.

Critique

A 'carancho' is a type of vulture common in Argentina, which feeds on dead or small animals and insects. The word also applies metaphorically to those individuals who prey on other people's weaknesses or needs. It is also applied to lawyers like Sosa (Ricardo Darín), who work for 'the foundation', a mafia-style company benefitting from the insurance settlements and payouts to the victims of the more than 8,000 yearly traffic accidents occurring in Argentina. The film (a mix between drama, thriller and romance) exposes the vast network of corruption in this flourishing and lucrative shady business, implicating not only the lawyers who con the victims and sometimes go as far as staging fake accidents to collect insurance money but also doctors, ambulance drivers, and police officers of the highest rank. All these facts are revealed to the viewer in a slow and fragmentary way, as we witness Sosa interacting with different layers of this enterprise.

One of the strongest points in Pablo Trapero's film is how he stresses the personal impact of this state of affairs on the lives of those involved, creating a bleak and nightmarish trap from which it is impossible to escape. Sosa, as embodied by Darín in a splendid but subdued performance, physically almost resembles a *carancho/* vulture, with his shaved head, deep dark circles under his eyes, avuncular nose, and a face ravaged by the scars of multiple brutal beatings, of which we see a few. Sosa is a man beaten down not only physically but also morally, as he takes part in all sorts of questionable dealings with the hope of saving enough money to get his practice license back and be able to escape from the foundation's tentacles. He sees meeting Luján (Trapero's wife, Martina Gusman) as a sign of good luck, as shown in the touching scene in which they go out on a date for the first time and he bets her that he will kiss her if he

Cast:

Ricardo Darín
Martina Gusman
Carlos Weber
José Luis Arias
Fabio Ronzano
Loren Acuña

Year:

2010

is right in predicting how many cars will cross an intersection before the traffic light changes to red. Luján, a quiet and intensely dedicated doctor, also faces her inner demons and battles anxiety with drugs. The relationship between these two troubled souls seems doomed from the start and the events unfold in a fateful manner towards the bleak ending.

Narratively, Trapero borrows from his previous films. As in *Leonera/ Lion's Den* (2008), he focuses on an individual trying to escape desperation and a doomed environment; as in *El bonaerense* (2002), the leading character is a prototypical anti-hero of dubious morality. Trapero intercuts scenes of romantic bliss between the two lovers with others of increasing violence and despair. This deliberately fragmented narrative is strengthened by well-thought stylistic choices. Most shots frame the actor's faces in tight close-ups. At times Trapero just frames body parts and events take place off-screen (for example, we only see Luján's foot as she injects drugs). The film was shot with a Red digital camera, allowing cinematographer Julián Apezteguia to seamlessly follow the characters in fluid hand-held moving shots.

Through an intelligent use of this dynamic narrative in service of a fatalistic violent thriller, Trapero refreshes and reinvents Scorsese's mold for similarly-themed films. *Carancho* succeeds in innovating such as a framework by centring on a fatalistic love story, in the spirit of the best film noir tradition.

Javier Gutiérrez-Rexach

Giant

Gigante

Country of Origin:

Uruguay

Language:

Spanish

Studio/Distributor:

Control Z Films

Director:

Adrián Biniez

Producer:

Fernando Epstein

Screenwriter:

Adrián Biniez

Cinematographer:

Arauco Hernández

Art Director:

Alejandro Castiglioni

Synopsis

The shy and taciturn Jara lives a monotonous life in Montevideo: by night he is a security man in a supermarket, during the day he is so tired that all he is able to do is turn on the TV and fall asleep while watching it. His social contacts are limited to the few words that he exchanges with his colleagues and the afternoons that he spends playing computer games with his nephew.

This situation suddenly changes one night, when he notices the new and pretty cleaning woman Julia on one of his monitoring screens and falls in love with her immediately. In trying to find out everything about her life, the previously constant and slow rhythm of Jara's plodding life accelerates bit by bit. He secretly starts to follow Julia not only on his computer screens at night, but also after working hours to places where she spends her leisure time: to her karate school, internet cafes, beaches, and even to a restaurant where Julia has a blind date. He becomes a kind of guardian angel for Julia, protecting her, for example from the anger of her boss, but always without presenting himself to her. The only demonstration of his affection is a cactus that he offers her by putting it anonymously on the floor of the supermarket.

But Jara cannot continue to observe her on his monitors forever; one day he gets suspended from his work. When he learns that Julia, too, has lost her job as a cleaning woman, he gives free rein to his anger and knocks down one of her bosses. After this unexpected

Editor:

Fernando Epstein

Composers:

Federico Billordo
Daniel Yafalián

Duration:

84 minutes

Genre:

Drama

Cast:

Horacio Camandulle
Leonor Svarcas
Fernando Alonso
Diego Artucio

Year:

2009

emotional release, he also manages to break out of his silent loneliness and finally starts to talk to Julia.

Critique

Gigante is the first feature-length film by director Adrián Biniez, who created this unusual and surprising love story, and especially his main character Jara, with much attention to detail. Although he mainly uses static shots and tells his story in a very slow rhythm, Biniez manages to captivate his spectators from the first minute to the last. This is also thanks to newcomer Horacio Camandull, who manages to portray a unique character who always walks the thin line between obsession and love, and that does not fulfill any characteristic trait that a spectator would expect from a protagonist: he is neither attractive, eloquent nor witty, and does not seem to have an opinion of his own. But the awkward way of dealing with his feelings for Julia (Leonor Svarcas) is what makes him more and more charming, so that he gradually gains the sympathy of the spectator, who starts to wonder if Jara will ever make the first move.

Gigante also offers an exciting and new point of view by never showing Julia's true feelings and only letting the spectator see what Jara sees in her. But the most outstanding quality of *Gigante* is probably its felicitous and refreshing mixture of genres: not only are there serious, dramatic scenes, but also ones that prove Biniez's distinctive sense of situation comedy. Thus the movie is in stark contrast to all the predictable and unoriginal romantic comedies made in Hollywood: it deals with the developing feelings of a man for a woman, but even at the end, the spectator surprisingly does not know if these feelings will ever be returned or not.

Adrián Biniez: *Gigante/Giant*,
2009 © CTRL Z Films.

Gigante is not only an unusual love story and a sensitive character study, but also a critique of capitalism: by situating the major action of his movie in a supermarket in which the employees are exploited and the genders strictly separated into female cleaning women and male guards, Biniez demonstrates that true love apparently can only be possible outside of a capitalistic and hierarchal system.

So *Gigante* can be seen as a debut film that treats surprisingly complex, profound topics, and hopefully will not be the last work of director Adrián Biniez.

Kerstin Hörmann

Like Water for Chocolate

Como agua para chocolate

Country of Origin:

Mexico

Studios/Distributors:

Arau Films Internacional

Aviacsa

Cinevista

Director:

Alfonso Arau

Producers:

Alfonso Arau

Óscar Castillo

Screenwriter:

Laura Esquivel

Cinematographers:

Steven Bernstein

Emmanuel Lubezki

Art Director:

Ricardo M. Kaplan

Editors:

Carlos Bolado

Francisco Chiu

Composers:

Leo Brouwer

Annette Fradera

Duration:

123 minutes

Synopsis

Tita and Pedro are passionately in love with each other. But according to family tradition, the youngest daughter must remain unmarried as the mother's caregiver. In order to be close to Tita, Pedro marries her older sister Rosaura and Tita has to suppress her feelings. However, the food she cooks becomes pervaded with her emotions, unconsciously affecting the people who eat it. Whereas all the guests start weeping at their first bite of the wedding cake Tita made, the quail with rose petal sauce, which she prepared for Pedro with all her love, makes the people who eat from it burn with ardent desire.

Critique

The cooperation between Laura Esquivel, the writer of the best-selling novel, and her husband Alfonso Arau, the director of the film, turned out to be a perfect combination. The film's flavour of magical realism, with a pinch of subversive food movie and nostalgic family saga, hit the 'taste' of the time and became an outrageous international success among critics and box offices. Transporting the viewers into the time of the Mexican Revolution, *Like Water for Chocolate* follows the typical pattern of Latin American magic realism and connects elements of magical Indian mentality with European rationality. On the day of her husband's death, Tita's mother declares that Tita, her youngest daughter, (Lumi Cavazos) will never marry and that she will help the Indian servant Nacha in the kitchen. Nacha becomes the Indian version of Cinderella's fairy godmother. She dies the day that Tita's heart is broken, and the wedding guests suffer from a 'collective vomiting' at the river. But Nacha keeps on protecting Tita and gives her advice even after her death. When Pedro (Marco Leonardi) offers Tita roses, it is Nacha who tells her to make a rose petal sauce instead of throwing the flowers away, as her mother summoned her to do. Whereas Rosaura (Yareli Arizmendi) feels sick immediately, all the others experience a sensual exaltation.

Rosaura cannot breastfeed her little son, but Tita's reflex to feed anybody who is hungry enables her virgin breasts to nurse her nephew. Her mother does not approve and sends Rosaura's family to Texas. When Tita hears that the baby has died because everything

Genres:

Drama
Romance

Cast:

Lumi Cavazos
Marco Leopardi
Regina Torné
Mario Iván Martínez

Year:

1992

he ate upset his stomach, she hides in the dovecote for several days. Esquivel refers here to Cinderella's doves, her comfort when her stepmother is castigating her, but it is also a reference to love and fertility, as doves are symbolically related to Venus and Aphrodite. Dr Brown rescues her, although it is not clear if it was his caring love for Tita or Chencha's soup that brings her back to sanity.

The film starts with Tita's grandniece crying while she prepares one of her recipes. She explains her sadness by telling the story of her family. Magical realism's cyclical dimension of time and its inherent repetition is present in the fact that Tita understands after her mother's death that Mama Elena also had to marry the man that her youngest sister had loved. When Rosaura announces that her only daughter has to remain unwed in order to care for her in her older days, Tita gets very angry.

Suspiciously Rosaura dies of fatal flatulence only three days after a controversy with her sister. Due to Rosaura's death, the cruel family tradition is not repeated and the story ends at the day of her daughter's wedding and Tita's and Pedro's fatal romantic final unification. Still crying, the grandniece keeps cutting onions, her mother and her grandaunt Tita watching benevolently over her.

Heidi Denzel de Tirado

Sólo con tu pareja

Country of Origin:

Mexico

Language:

Spanish

Studio/Distributor:

Sólo Películas

Director:

Alfonso Cuarón

Producers:

Alfonso Cuarón
Ignacio Durán Loera
Pedro Armendáriz
Rosalía Salazar

Screenwriters:

Alfonso Cuarón
Carlos Cuarón

Cinematographer:

Emmanuel Lubezki

Art Director:

Brigitte Broch

Synopsis

Womanizer Tomás Tomás is falsely diagnosed with AIDS by his nurse Silvia Silvia, with whom he has a one-night stand. While pondering how to die as quickly as possible, Tomás gets the chance to help his beautiful neighbour Clarisa enter her apartment without her key, which she has misplaced. When Clarisa then finds her fiancée cheating on her, she decides to commit suicide with Tomás.

Critique

Tomás (Daniel Giménez Cacho) is evidently a modern Don Juan. Just as Mozart did in his famous *opera buffa The Marriage of Figaro*, Cuarón blends comedy with melodramatic elements, portraying his main protagonist as being similar to his famous predecessor: an egocentric womanizer with no respect for real feelings. Whereas Don Juan only wants to make love to a bride on her wedding day, Tomás actually does it without the slightest remorse. The chaotic sex comedy has a calm and poetic counterbalance in the character of Clarisa (Claudia Ramírez). Tomás sees her the first time through her window when he has to commute between two women and two different apartments on a narrow window ledge outside of his apartment building. At the moment he sees her, we hear Mozart's third movement of the Serenade No. 10 in B flat major. Tomás is filled with an unknown feeling of longing, and even if he has to hurry between the two waiting women, he pauses and watches, fascinated by the stewardess Clarisa's choreography of instructions for an emergency landing. Every time he sees her, we hear Mozart's serenade and have

Editors:

Alfonso Cuarón

Luis Patlán

Composer:

Carlos Warman

Duration:

94 minutes

Genres:

Comedy

Romance

Cast:

Daniel Giménez Cacho

Claudia Ramírez

Luis de Icaza

Astrid Hadad

Dobrina Liubomirova

Isabel Benet

Year:

1991

to think of Salieri's comment about this Adagio in Forman's biopic *Amadeus* (1984) that it is like 'hearing the voice of God'.

Just like Doña Inés turns out to be Don Juan's salvation in José Zorrilla y Moral's version, Clarisa seems to be the only chance of peace and catharsis for Tomás. After he meets her, he vows that he wants to change his irresponsible behaviour and is – for the first time in his life – shy and clumsy in the presence of a woman. When he learns that he has AIDS, he makes a list of all the girls he ever had – thematically and musically a reference to Mozart's 'Madamina, il catalogo è questo' – and wants to commit suicide. Facing death, Clarisa appears and they decide to throw themselves from the Torre Latinoamericana, because Clarisa wants to be close to Heaven. Zorrilla's Doña Inés and Don Juan go to Heaven together and Don Juan is redeemed. Clarisa and Tomás are as close to Heaven as possible, on the very top of the highest building in the city of Mexico. They do not die but make love. When Tomás finds out that he does not have AIDS, he marries Clarisa and is therefore redeemed and bound to her eternally.

The fast-paced romantic comedy and funny coming of age story with great timing has nevertheless a slightly moralistic undertone and is divided into five moments. The different stages of maturity are introduced by title cards with quotations ranging from E. E. Cummings 'Mike likes all the girls (the fat ones, the lean ones, the mean kind dirty clean) all except the green ones' to Isaac Newton. His third rule, 'For every action there is an equal and opposite reaction,' is the motto for the last movement and leaves Tomás as a changed man who uses condoms (something that he had despised before). Whereas the film was not released in the United States until 2006 because of its use of AIDS as a comic plot device, *Sólo con tu pareja* has been adopted as the official slogan for the Mexican anti-AIDS campaign.

Heidi Denzel de Tirado

El mismo amor, la misma lluvia

Country of Origin:

Argentina

Language:

Spanish

Studio/Distributor:

Warner Bros.

Director:

Juan José Campanella

Producer:

Jorge Estrada Mora

Synopsis

In the late 1970s, Jorge Pellegrini is a writer of short stories who is regularly published by a small Buenos Aires magazine, making ends meet while staying out of the governing Junta's sights. He first catches a glimpse of Laura in a taxi, soaking up the rain with the windows rolled down; from this beautiful moment onwards, however, their story takes on a much more subdued and prosaic tone. Laura yields to Jorge's courtship and decides to forget about the boyfriend who, after travelling abroad, has never called or written. Jorge soon begins to grow disgruntled when Laura's passion for him threatens to interfere with his writing. They break up as the country moves from dictatorship to democracy, and from then on their recurrent meetings reflect the ebb and flow of a country trying to find itself.

Screenwriters:

Juan José Campanella
Fernando Castets

Cinematographer:

Daniel Shulman

Art Director:

Mará Julia Bertotto

Editor:

Camilo Antolini

Composer:

Emilio Kauderer

Duration:

113 minutes

Genres:

Comedy
Romance

Cast:

Ricardo Darín
Soledad Villamil
Ulises Dumont
Eduardo Blanco
Graciela Tenenbaum

Year:

1999

Critique

To describe Juan José Campanella's *El mismo amor, la misma lluvia* as a romantic comedy set against the backdrop of two decades of Argentinean history would be accurate, but the film is more than the 'Forrest Gump' of Latin American cinema. History, to Campanella, is not the wars you fight or the presidents you meet; it is rather the announcements that are on TV as you sit in your office, surrounded by friends and colleagues. Thus, at the heart of *El mismo amor, la misma lluvia* is the way in which the various social and political upheavals of the protagonist's home country in the period between 1980 and 1999 change and influence his romantic, platonic and professional relationships.

Soledad Villamil is a somber beauty whose large, friendly and eager eyes are offset by her stern features. Accordingly, she plays Laura as a person who takes childlike pleasure in the very fact of being an adult and all the activities this entails, like falling in and out of love, getting married, having children and, finally, growing up. Even so, she does not change, bringing the same serenity to her scenes set in the present day that she does to those of her youth. Ricardo Darín, whose crooked smile and crescent eyes perpetually mark him as an actor who should be playing characters on the edge of despair (or sanity) instead of romantic leads, is a perfect fit for the role of a writer who is never fully comfortable with happiness and unable to stand still. His character is haunted by the death of a former colleague who died jobless after being blacklisted by the government, but he also suffers, as Jorge's friend and boss Roberto (Eduardo Blanco) says, from a 'teenage thing, always going after something new'.

What holds the film together at its core, though, is its engaging cast of supporting actors. The aforementioned Blanco, for one, infuses the subplot in which his character unexpectedly finds his soul mate in Laura's ditsy friend Marita (Graciela Tenenbaum) with a genuinely youthful enthusiasm. This enthusiasm is in juxtaposition with the main romance, making Jorge's self-pitying romantic meanderings and the disillusioned marriage of prudence that Laura enters and then leaves seem foolish. The veteran character actor Ulises Dumont, meanwhile, plays Márquez, an ageing political journalist who finds happiness with the office wallflower. His dismissal by the *nouveau régime*, after he refuses to write a gossip column, triggers Jorge's bid for a late redemption. Throughout the film, Roberto and Márquez squabble over politics, as governments, relationships and decades come and go, and the office of their little magazine becomes a second home for Jorge, the one constant in his life.

Campanella addresses the weighty issues at stake in any discussion of history with due subtlety, emphasizing how they are cushioned into the actual rhythms of adult life, with its recurrent patterns of working to make ends meet and searching for love to make it all worthwhile, even as the past, private and public, tugs away at everyone. He foregoes cheap sentimentality by isolating the main characters on screen via close-ups in the great emotional scenes, evoking the loneliness and quiet despair that goes along with being delivered bad news.

In *El mismo amor, la misma lluvia*, the public is filtered through the private; it is not a change from dictatorship to democracy that will liberate a person from his or her personal prison, but the past can be overcome via a good deed done for a friend. The film moves swiftly and anecdotally through the decades, divided, book-like, into chapter titles and with narration by Jorge, paying tribute to both the corrosive and the healing qualities of passing time, and to the way in which people keep themselves from growing up, being finally pushed into adulthood by those who surround them. It is a comedy of togetherness in spite of a national history that is too much for one person to carry on his shoulders.

Paul Becker

The Secret in Their Eyes

El secreto de sus ojos

Country of Origin:

Argentina

Language:

Spanish

Studio/Distributor:

Sony Classics

Director:

Juan José Campanella

Producers:

Juan José Campanella
Gerardo Herrero
Mariela Besuievski
Vanessa Ragone
Axel Kuschevatzky

Screenwriters:

Eduardo Sacheri
Juan José Campanella

Cinematographer:

Félix Monti

Art Director:

Marcelo Pont Vergés

Editor:

Juan José Campanella

Composers:

Federico Jusid
Emilio Kauderer

Synopsis

Ricardo Darín plays Benjamin Esposito, a retired employee of one of the Buenos Aires courthouses charged with investigating the cases passed on by the police and compiling evidence for the prosecution. Facing the long days of the autumn of his life, he decides to write down the story that has irrevocably shaped his life: the case of the rape and murder of a beautiful young woman in the 1970s, in which he was the principal investigator. On a hunch, he made Isidoro Gómez (Javier Godino) his prime suspect. Soon, though, the story becomes more than just a simple case to be solved, since the question arises: what is in Esposito's own eyes when he looks at his new boss, the young and fetching Irene Menéndez Hastings (Soledad Villamil)? And what is in hers? As the case and its resolution are pushed further into the background by the intervention of some harsh political truths, the film turns into a somber meditation on missed opportunities and the powerful sway men are held in by their obsessions.

Critique

The Secret in Their Eyes, adapted from a novel by Eduardo Sacheri, is Juan José Campanella's most ambitious film to date. In only two hours it attempts to show no less than exactly what life is.

For a story with such obvious potential for melodrama, Campanella wisely chooses to downplay many of the crucial scenes: the moment in which Esposito first sees the evidence of the gruesome murder, for instance, comes at the end of a long take that follows the investigator, annoyed at having to deal with a case that should not even be his, through a maze of colleagues and on into the bedroom of the victim's house, where he stops short in sight of the beautiful, defiled body. Similarly, the first time he meets Irene, there are neither close-ups nor violins, merely the sight of Esposito, wide-eyed and speechless. Campanella emphasizes the matter-of-fact way in which stories and obsessions can enter a person's life from out of nowhere, turning it upside down as though it were the most natural thing in the world.

Duration:

127 minutes

Genres:

Drama
Mystery
Thriller

Cast:

Ricardo Darín
Soledad Villamil
Guillermo Francella,
Pablo Rago
Javier Godino

Year:

2009

The same technique also cleverly subverts some of the established gender roles in crime stories. The opening scene, in which Irene, in a flashback, desperately runs after the train that carries away Benjamin putting her hand against his with the window separating them, tugs at the heart. However, when she reads about the same scene in his manuscript decades later, she scoffs at the sentimentality of it. As in *El mismo amor, la misma lluvia* (1999), in which both actors had previously played lovers in a romance spanning half a lifetime, it is Villamil's matter-of-factness and steely determination that sets the tone: Darín's character is more likable here, his romanticism hardly concealed behind a gruff exterior, but he does not have any power in their relationship, neither to hurt her nor to protect her. In the end, it is Irene who is responsible for the breakthrough in the case: it is her superior social standing that protects him from the revenge of the people he has angered as the political climate changes for the worse – in short, the positive values connected with machismo, i.e. the regard for one's personal honour and that of women, now takes on a decidedly feminine connotation.

Elsewhere, though, the story is considerably more conservative. One of Campanella's key themes, male friendship, is given a more tragic turn in the form of Sandoval (Guillermo Francella), Esposito's subordinate, who happily drinks his life away in bars yet remains lucid enough to recognize what drives him, the murderer, Esposito, and by extension, all men everywhere. 'A man cannot change his passion,' he declares. The measure of a man, as evidenced by Sandoval's eventual redemption, lies in the outlet he gives his passion: murder, revenge, love, friendship.

The key theme of *The Secret in Their Eyes* is that such a passion, or in other words, love, lasts forever, continuing to define one's life even after everything else, such as jobs, marriages or friends, has washed away. It is a love story disguised as a drama about crime and punishment, set against the unstoppable passage of time. However, despite its many awards which include an Oscar as Best Foreign Language Film, it is perhaps not necessarily Campanella's greatest achievement. The director's formidable taste for melancholy is far better suited to small, character-driven stories, such as his films featuring the great Eduardo Blanco opposite Darín, than to crime dramas of this calibre. The somber mood and understated performances add up to an air of inevitability, which for all the beautiful symmetry of its thematic development, puts the film somewhere up in the clouds, smiling benevolently on all this folly, rather than fully confronting the occasional ugliness of human behaviour that is at the heart of this story.

Paul Becker

The Son of the Bride

El hijo de la novia

Countries of Origin:

Argentina
Spain

Language:

Spanish

Studio/Distributor:

Patagonik Film Group & Pol-ka

Director:

Juan José Campanella

Producer:

Adrián Suar

Screenwriters:

Juan José Campanella
Fernando Castets

Cinematographer:

Daniel Shulman

Art Director:

Mercedes Alfonsín

Editor:

Camilo Antolini

Composer:

Ángel Illaramendi

Duration:

121 minutes

Genres:

Comedy
Drama
Romance

Cast:

Ricardo Darín
Héctor Alterio
Norma Aleandro
Eduardo Blanco
Natalia Verbeke

Year:

2001

Synopsis

Juan José Campanella's *Son of the Bride* starts with a sepia-tinged childhood scene in which a group of mischievous boys are attacked by a mysterious stranger wearing a Zorro costume. The battle is a short one though, and soon our hero is retreating to the safety of his home, where the magisterial presence of his mother sees off his enemies and then soothes his nerves with cocoa and cookies, the boy's dark eyes glowing with adoration. The film then jumps forward 30 years, and we see the same eyes grown tired and weary, as the life of Rafael Belvedere has suffered the inevitable decline from a swashbuckling and risk-free childhood adventure to a never-ending battle with no prizes to be won, where the family is no longer a safe haven but one more problem to be dealt with as curtly as possible.

Rafael manages the restaurant built by his parents, but he runs it less like a family business than like a battleship: giving orders, shouting into his telephone and dealing, in exasperation, with his dimwitted aide, just to be able to continue to say 'no' to the corporate envoy who wants to buy the place and give it a good do-over in the name of efficiency. On the other side of the fence are a nagging ex-wife and a daughter he neglects, a ravishing girlfriend Nati, whom he treats with similar aloofness, and his parents: his father Nino, who lives out his days dreaming about the past glory of his restaurant, and his mother Norma, who has Alzheimer's disease and is confined to a nursing home. She has tragically become every bit the child that Rafael can no longer be.

Critique

In an inversion of the dynamics of Campanella's earlier film, *El mismo amor, la misma lluvia* (1999), in which the friends and (metaphorical) family that surround Darín's character are what keeps him afloat through decades of turbulent history, Rafael here feels their pull on him like a millstone around his neck. After a heart attack lands him in hospital, he thus confesses to Nati (Natalia Verbeke) somewhat cruelly, that the only dream he still has left is to 'drop out', i.e. go to Mexico and unwind, all by himself. Before he can take that step, however, he wants to help his father (Héctor Alterio), who after 44 years has decided to finally give Norma (Norma Aleandro), what his ideals had never allowed him to do when she was still healthy: a church wedding. At first, Rafael dismisses Nino's idea as pointless – 'she would not even notice,' he protests, and not without reason – but his heart attack, and the arrival of an old friend, Juan Carlos (Eduardo Blanco), slowly change his perspective. Having externalized his past, which for him exists only in the photos that hang on the walls of his restaurant and in the memories of his father, he embarks upon a spiritual journey to recover a life of his own in the midst of so many muddled relationships. This is made altogether more poignant by the fact that a huge part of his past – his troubled relationship with his mother – is lost in the fog of her disease. Where has the past gone? For whom do we really do the things we do for others? Should we live our life according to a romantic ideal of love, or let such questions

Juan José Campanella: *El hijo de la novia/The Son of the Bride*, 2001 © Patagonik Film Group & Pol-ka.

be drowned in the day-to-day? 'I do not watch Argentinean movies,' Rafael tells his actor friend Juan Carlos, who replies, 'I do not watch Argentinean reality.' *Son of the Bride* is a melancholy masterpiece, a family film and a film about family, bittersweet and meditative.

As in all of Campanella's films, much of the praise must go to the actors, in particular Norma Aleandro, who plays Norma with an affecting mixture of childlike wonder – her wide-open eyes tell you everything there is to know about the film – and old-person grumpiness, and who suggests that even as most of the details of a life may be lost in time, the important things yet remain. Eduardo Blanco, whose character is something of a device (his initials and tragic life story suggest that he is a prophet sent to Rafael to teach him about the importance of having a family), provides most of the comedy. However, typical for this film, his mixture of cartoonish behaviour and quiet, existential despair and a real need for companionship, is palpable and even believable. Lastly, Ricardo Darín, who without a doubt is modern Argentine cinema's leading lonely man, an actor whose piercing eyes and distinctly unromantic features would not be out of place in a Hollywood noir of the 1940s, is perfect as the aloof and lost hero embodying the universal struggle between the ideals of youth and the realities of adulthood, between hope and disillusionment, past and present, love and independence, peace and family.

Paul Becker

Marcel Proust's Time Regained

Le temps retrouvé, d'après l'oeuvre de Marcel Proust

Countries of Origin:

France
Italy
Portugal

Language:

French

Studios/Distributors:

Gemini Films
France 2 Cinéma
Les Films du Lendemain

Director:

Raúl Ruiz

Producer:

Paulo Branco

Screenwriters:

Raúl Ruiz
Gilles Taurand (writing credits: Marcel Proust)

Cinematographer:

Ricardo Aronovich

Art Director:

Bruno Beaugé

Editor:

Denise de Casabianca

Composer:

Jorge Arriagada

Duration:

169 minutes

Synopsis

Looking at photographs on his deathbed, moribund writer Marcel Proust meets acquaintances from throughout his life in a succession of flashbacks. The dreamlike images fluctuate between the writer's present and his childhood, youth and adulthood, taking him to the Rue Hamelin, Combray, Balbec, Venice and the Parisian salons. Once again he experiences episodes when he lived with the Baron de Charlus, Morel, Saint Loup, Albertine, Odette, Gilberte and Madame Verdurin, and the anxiety of their erotic relations. Time and space lose their contours when, in the dreamlike scenes of Marcel's childhood at Combray, signs of the World War I emerge, a conflict he did not observe until an adult from the very distant viewpoint of the glamorous soirées he attended. There, notably at the last ball of his strangely aged companions, the narrator faces the social changes – such as the marriage of Gilberte Swann and the noble Robert de Saint-Loup – that announce the end of an era.

Critique

This film seems like a concentrated version of the cinema of Raúl Ruiz: Keith Reader notices that as a 'Chilean expatriate with a background in leftist politics and experimental filmmaking' Ruiz has found a home in France where he lives, films, and teaches since he had fled the Pinochet regime in the 1970s. The film's *mise-en-scène* multiplies the styles of early cinema by citing magic (Georges Meliès) or Gothic darkness (Louis Feuillade), while the remarkable photography of Ricardo Aronovich alludes to impressionist and academic painting, surrealism and even cubism in composition, colour and light. In this way the film parallels Proust's wide-spread visual citations, which were limited neither temporally nor artistically. Yet, at the same time, the cinematic image becomes independent of the literary sub-text as well as of its own genre by undermining all verisimilitude and authenticity and by constantly pointing at the image itself as artificially made. What we see seems rather an experimental than a classical heritage film.

The following freeze frame shows, for instance, how Marcel as a child (Georges du Fresne) directs the projector onto us, while his adult self (Marcello Mazzarella) reads a letter from Gilberte about the war on a flying chair in a cinema. The screen behind him shows war images in black-and-white that seem to have their origin of projection from behind us as spectators. It is because of such sequences that Ruiz's adaptation of Proust can be called a success: he succeeds

Genres:

Drama
Romance
War

Cast:

Catherine Deneuve
Emmanuelle Béart
Vincent Perez
John Malkovich
Pacal Greggory

Year:

1999

in melting concepts of the literary model without denying his own medium. The scene shows us the written (letter), lets us hear the voice of Gilberte, who speaks from a distant place and time, and accompanies this content like background music with the projection of the news. The reading Marcel seems to be part of the spectators, part of the screen, yet at the same time completely detached from both, only committed to his attentive reading. Looking at him we grasp the dreamy space uniting distant places and distant times. Looking at his self as a child, we recognize the dual nature of the writer that Proust often pointed out in reflections of identity and memory. Via the trick of apparently projecting outside as well as inside the screen, the uncertainty of space extends to the viewer, who in Ruizan cinema never remains a passive entity, but rather takes part in constructing the film. Thus Ruiz visually comments on Proust's narrator's belief that a reader is always a reader of himself.

By pointing out complex cinematic time and spatial construction and by integrating elements of film history, Ruiz also comments ironically on his own medium, which Proust denigrated for its cinematographic – that is chronological – way of telling a story. Here Ruiz proves that film as a medium – with all its possible plays on time and space constructions – is very apt indeed to show how Proust's *Time Regained* meanders around multiple identities, parallel times and uncertain spaces.

Joanna Jaritz

THRILLER/HORROR

Although not every Latin American country has a vividly producing film industry, phenomena such as genre cinema are very well know to their film-makers and audiences. Thus every country has brought forth a variety of thrillers and horror-films over the decades, sometimes over a certain period of time or sporadically.

Thrillers

Latin American thrillers have enjoyed huge popularity in recent times. As to that, Juan José Campanella's celebrated Oscar winner *El secreto de sus ojos/The Secret in Their Eyes* (2009) is only just the tip of the iceberg. *The Secret in Their Eyes* draws on a long tradition of political thrillers from post-junta Argentina, starting after the arrival of democracy in 1983 with Juan José Jusid's *Asesinato en el senado de la nación argentina/Murder in the Senate* (1984) and including such current titles as Gaston Biraben's *Cautiva/Captive* (2004), Lucía Cedrón's *Cordero de Dios/Lamb of God* (2008) or Marcelo Piñeyro's *Las viudas de los jueves* (2009). Apart from this, there are also suspense thrillers like Murió Fabián Bielinsky's *Nueve reinas/Nine Queens* (2000) and *El aura/The Aura* (2005) or psychological thrillers such as Lucrecia Martel's *La Mujer Sin Cabeza/The Headless Woman* (2008).

In comparison, Colombian thrillers frequently are dominated by gritty urban stories about drug and gang violence. In Barbet Schroeder's *La virgen de los sicarios/Our Lady of the Assassins* (2000), José Antonio Dorado's *El rey* (2004), Andi Baiz's *Satanás* (2007), Carlos Moreno's *Perro come perro/Dog Eat Dog* (2008), and Jorge Nava's *La sangre y la lluvia/Blood and Rain* (2009) the influence of 1970's *pornomiseria* (porno-misery) cinema still can be detected, considering the high degree of poverty and human misery depicted on the screen.

Mexican thrillers often also deal with social problems responsible for street violence. Not considering any number of direct-to-video productions, with Rodrigo Plá's *La zona* (2007) and Amat Escalante's *Los Bastardos* (2008) there are strong examples of thrillers shaped by the caring ethics of the *Nuevo Cine Mexicano*. With these contemporary-set films on the one hand, on the other hand there is Francisco Vargas Quevedo's *El Violín/The Violin* (2005), a period picture set during the Mexican peasant revolts of the 1970s, telling the story of an aged patriarch developing a new method of smuggling ammunition unnoticed by the government troops. In Chilean, Uruguayan and Venezuelan cinema the thriller cannot count as a particularly popular genre, yet Gustavo Graef-Marino's crime thriller *Johnny cien pesos/Johnny One Hundred Pesos* (1994), Esteban Schroeder's political thriller *Matar a Todos/Kill Them All* (2007), and Jonathan Jakubowicz's kidnapping thriller *Secuestro Express* (2004) have to be named as significant exceptions.

Brazilian thrillers came to prominence with the enormous transnational success of José Padilha's socially conscious action diptychon *Tropa de Elite/Elite Squad* (2007) and *Tropa de Elite 2 – O Inimigo Agora é Outro/Elite Squad: The Enemy Within* (2010), however Brazil can look back at many interesting thrillers ranging from Roberto Farias' *Pra Frente, Brasil* (1982) up to Beto Brant's *O Invasor/The Tresspasser* (2002) and Bruno Barreto's *O Que e Isso, Companheiro/Four Days in September* (1997). Latin American cinema recently has also seen the return of Peruvian thriller auteur Luis Llosa, cousin of Nobel Prize-winning novelist Mario Vargas Llosa. Having debuted with *Mision En Los Andes/Hour of the Assassin* in 1987, Llosa quickly emigrated to the United States via Roger Corman, directing several highly sophisticated movies including *Crime Zone* (1989), *Sniper* (1993) and *The Specialist* (1994). Back to Latin America, Llosa adapted in 2005 his cousin's novel *La fiesta del chivo* (2000) into a complex political thriller. Shot on location in Santo Domingo de Guzmán, capital of the Dominican Republic, *La fiesta del chivo/The Feast of the Goat* (2005) stages several narrative levels into an epochal time-image.

Finally the tendency to create new forms of genres should be mentioned, such as the 'metaphysical thriller' *The Adventures of God/Las aventuras de Dios* (Eliseo Subiela, 2000), a combination of thriller, drama and fantasy.

Horror

Horror is one of the most universal genres in film history. Based on local traditions as well as popular myths every culture has produced certain images of fear which cumulate in horror-cinema. With the advent of sound in cinema different versions of a film were produced for different language markets. One of the most well-known examples is Tod Brownings *Dracula* (1931), of which a Spanish version was filmed by Enrique Tovar Ávalos and George Melford at night in the same sets. Not only was the language different, but also the level of eroticized wardrobe used for the female victim.

While horror-films occur frequently in Latin American cinema, there are certain film series which gained a world-wide cult following, such as the Brazilian 'Coffin Joe' series. José Mojica Marins directed and played this psychopathic and evil character always in search of a female to continue his bloodline. His distinctive outfit with black top hat, cape, and long, curled fingernails became a trademark of the character and appeared in books, comics and TV shows as well. Besides the sadistic original 'Coffin Joe' adventures, *À Meia-Noite Levarei Sua Alma/At Midnight I'll Take Your Soul* (1965), *Esta Noite Encarnarei no Teu Cadáver*

Eliseo Subiela: *Las aventuras de Dios/The Adventures of God*, Argentina 2001 © Trigon Films.

(1967) and *Encarnação do Demônio/Embodiment of Evil* (2008), Marins also directed other genre films, exploitative and erotic fare like *A Estranha hospedaria dos prazeres* (1967), *O Estranho Mundo de Zé do Caixão* (1968), *O Despertar da Besta: Ritual dos Sadicos* (1968), *Inferno Carnal* (1977) and the programmatic *Delirios de un Anormal* (1977). Still working today Marins is amongst the most famous Brazilian film-makers with a very explicit and playful style.

Around the same time in the late 1960s the Chile-born surrealist Alejandro Jodorowsky started making his nightmare-like phantasmagoria. While *Fando y Lis/Fando and Liz* (1967) is still a very dreamlike fairy tale, his later Mexican films (*El Topo* [1971], *Montana Sacra/ The Holy Mountain* [1975]) combine bizarre and surreal violent rituals with established genre elements (horror, western, science fiction). His Mexican production *Santa Sangre* (1989) tells the twisted story of an Oedipal psychopathic killer in expressive colour schemes and is the closest Jodorowsky ever came to making a generic horror film.

The Mexican film industry was always busy in adapting and copying marketable American concepts and combining them with local aspects. In the 1950s Mexican film-makers began to create a horror boom with awakened mummies (*La momia azteca*, *La momia azteca contra el robot humano*, *La maldición de la momia azteca*, all in 1957 by Rafael Portillo), the invisible man (*El hombre que logró ser invisible* [Alfredo B. Crevenna, 1958]) and other occult concepts (*Muñecos infernales* [Benito Alazraki, 1960]; *Espiritismo*, [Benito Alazraki, 1962]). Cult status was reserved for *Alucarda, la Hija de las Tinieblas/Sisters of Satan* (Juan López Moctezuma, 1978), the tragic and bizarre tale of a teenage girl destined to become a nun, seduced by a wicked sister and soon dedicating her life to satanism, vampirism and witchcraft. The most productive Mexican genre director was René Cardona, who started with genre mixes of wrestling and horror (*Las luchadoras contra la momia/Wrestling Women vs. the Aztec Mummy* [1964]; *Las luchadoras contra el médico asesino/Doctor of Doom* [1963]) and continued with several horror films which gained worldwide distribution: *La Horripilante bestia humana/Night of the Bloody Apes* (1969), *La Noche de los mil gatos/The Night of a Thousand Cats* (1972) and the mystical *Il Triangolo del Bermude/The Bermuda Triangle* (1978). His semi-remake of Steven Spielberg's *Jaws* (1975), *Tintorera* (1977), had international success. Cardona Jr also directed violent western and thrillers as well as comedies.

Most popular is Mexican director Guillermo del Toro who established his reputation as an original horror mastermind with the vampire film *Cronos* (1993). After his mainstream foray *Mimic* (1997) del Toro established his unique visual and visceral style in the ghost drama *El Espinazo del Diablo/The Devil's Backbone* (2001) and the coming-of-age-nightmare *El Laberinto del Fauno/Pan's Labyrinth* (2006). Many of his films effectively mingle historical terror (Francoism, national socialism) with fantastic horror – even his mainstream film *Hell Boy* (2004). In 2007 del Toro also produced the successful haunted house thriller *El orfanto/The Orphanage* by Juan Antonio Bayona.

Other Latin American countries like Argentina also have established genre film industries with classic horror director Emilio Vieyra (*Sangre de Virgenes* [1967]) up to recent productions like *Mala carne* (Fabián Forte, 2003), the gothic chiller *Jennifer's Shadow* (Daniel de la Vega and Pablo Parés, 2004) or the hyper-violent rape and revenge thriller *No Morire Sola/I'll Never Die Alone* (Adrian Garcia Bogliano, 2008). But other singular attempts also frequently hit the world market like the ghost film *Km 31: Kilómetro 31/Km 31: Kilometre 31* (2006) by Rigoberto Castañeda from Mexico or the rare visionary Colombian horror film *Al final del espectro/At the End of the Spectra* (Juan Felipe Orozco, 2006).

Latin American genre cinema is known for being more outrageous and daringly sexy than thrillers and horror films from the West. Thus, many of these films are mainly distributed directly to home media on the western market.

Ivo Ritzer and Marcus Stiglegger

The Aura

El aura

Countries of Origin:

Argentina
Spain
France

Language:

Spanish

Studios/Distributors:

Patagonik Film Group
Tornasol Films, S.A.
Davis Film Productions

Director:

Fabián Bielinsky

Producers:

Ariel Saul
Victor Hadida
Cecilia Bossi

Screenwriter:

Fabián Bielinsky

Cinematographer:

Checco Varese

Art Director:

Mercedes Alfonsín

Editors:

Alejandro Carrello
Penovi and Fernando Pardo

Composer:

Lucio Godoy

Duration:

127 minutes

Genres:

Crime
Drama
Thriller

Cast:

Ricardo Darín
Dolores Fonzi
Pablo Cedrón
Walter Reyno
Alejandro Awada

Year:

2005

Synopsis

As in *Nueve reinas/Nine Queens* (Murió Fabián Bielinsky, 2000), Ricardo Darín plays the lead, a taxidermist who in his free time likes to plan and execute the perfect crime in the safety and seclusion of his mind. When a colleague of his, as boisterous as the taxidermist is withdrawn, invites him along on a hunting trip deep in the Argentinean countryside, the atmosphere suddenly bristles with possibility: he chances upon a man who is plotting to hold up an armoured car, and when that man is incapacitated, the taxidermist is suddenly the only player in the game who is in a position to coordinate the heist. The only problem: the taxidermist is heavily epileptic.

Critique

At first glance, *The Aura*, the second and final film by Fabián Bielinsky, who died in 2006 at the age of 47, could not appear to be any more different from his debut, *Nine Queens* – the latter being a light-hearted caper with a moral, the former a moody existentialist melodrama with a heart of purest black. Look closer, though, and you will see that both works are blood relatives, father and son rather than brothers, with youthful exuberance giving way to world-weariness, the thrill of community devolving into the suspicion that people are as alone in their lives as they are in death.

The film's title refers to the sensations preceding his epileptic attacks, in which, as he tells it, 'a door opens in your head, and lets things in… sounds… music… voices… during those few seconds, you're free. There's no choice, no alternative, nothing for you to decide.' It is an experience that Bielinsky attempts to reproduce for the audience by clouding his protagonist in a fog of dreamy atmospheric music and draining the film of colour, which, together with the extraordinarily precise camerawork at hand, imbues every image with a sense of clarity and mystery – in a word, with an aura. It also serves to bring home the inevitability with which the plot unfolds, where the taxidermist, like an antihero in a Hollywood film noir, meets dark characters in chiaroscurist surroundings at night and manages to convince a number of these unsavoury characters that he is an underworld figure from Buenos Aires through sheer guilelessness.

The story Bielinsky tells, though, is not a sequel to *Nine Queens* in terms of plot. He is less interested in showing how the protagonist uses his photographic memory and extraordinary observational skills to manipulate a couple of hardened criminals and pull off the coup of a lifetime (despite never having committed any kind of crime in his life) than he is in exploring the psychological aspect of the story. *The Aura* is, in fact, possibly the only example of a thriller told, from start to finish, from the point of view of a semi-autistic mind. The taxidermist may see what goes on around him better than anyone, but he cannot communicate with the world. Darín plays him with hunched shoulders and a perpetually dazed expression; a man invisible to himself, perhaps, as much as to others. When he tells his hostess Diana (Dolores Fonzi) about his condition, his eyes wander, the camera circling him like an animal, completely shutting out the person he is talking to as though he were actually addressing something within himself.

In the climax, when gunfire unsurprisingly complicates his perfect plan, Bielinsky keeps the camera tightly focused on the taxidermist, bullets shredding the foliage around him with no more clues as to who is firing them and from where than one might guess. These scenes are grim and exciting, showing what happens when reality, as it were, comes crashing through the haze that surrounds the protagonist. In that segment of life which cannot be controlled by the taxidermist's plotting, people die – pointlessly, desperately and alone. Together with the protagonist, we are jolted out of the mesmeric atmosphere by a full stop in the soundtrack and by the camera scanning the woods for clues as to what is going on, no longer representing a viewpoint of perfect awareness. Forbidding nature is represented by a German shepherd, who looks at the taxidermist with jet-black eyes, with a bloodied muzzle, and runs alongside his car through the forest, knowing but unknowable.

Bielinsky thus strikes a beautiful balance between dreamlike, poetic sequences, such as that of the taxidermist observing a group of gangsters raiding a factory on the outskirts of a town from his car as

Murió Fabián Bielinsky: *El Aura/The Aura*, 2005 © Davis-Films.

if watching a western, and bafflingly realistic ones, like the opening, which finds him lying unconscious on the floor in front of an ATM following an epileptic fit, then getting up, taking his money, and leaving as though nothing had happened. *The Aura* is a study of loneliness in the guise of a neo-film noir, a requiem, an astounding achievement for a director's second feature but a perfectly realized final effort from one of Argentina's finest film-makers.

Paul Becker

Chronicles

Crónicas

Countries of Origin:

Ecuador
Mexico

Language:

Spanish

Studios/Distributors:

Cabezahueca
Tequila Gang
Producciones Anhelo

Director:

Sebastián Cordero

Producers:

Alfonso Cuarón
Guillermo del Toro
Isabel Dávalos
Berta Navarro

Screenwriter:

Sebastián Cordero

Cinematographer:

Enrique Chediak

Art Director:

Roberto Frisone

Editors:

Luis Carballar
Iván Mora Manzano

Composers:

Antonio Pinto
James David Goldmark

Duration:

98 minutes

Synopsis

While on a trip to Ecuador, Miami-based journalist Manolo Bonilla saves local man Vinicio Cepeda from being lynched by a furious mob after having unwillingly killed a boy with his truck. Once in prison, Vinicio tells Manolo he knows who the Monstruo de Babahoyo (Monster of Babahoyo), a serial killer of children, is, thinking that disclosing that information will help him out. Considering the impact the news could have in his career, the journalist agrees to interview him much against the opinion of Marisa, his producer and lover. However, suspecting Vinicio himself is in fact the serial killer, Manolo tries later to get him to confess while withholding the interview that would set him free. While he and his team try to put things straight, the police start wondering why Manolo knows so much about the murders. In the meantime, media have their own agenda, regardless of the consequences of their actions.

Critique

Produced by Hollywood-based Latin American directors Alfonso Cuarón (*Children of Men* [2006]) and Guillermo del Toro (*Cronos* [1993], *Hellboy* [2004]) and with a score by Brazilian Antonio Pinto (*Cidade de Deus/City of God* [Fernando Meirelles and Kátia Lund, 2002]), this is a powerful feature that skillfully combines the gripping plot, lively narrative, and effective film work of US psychological thrillers with the more socially and ethically concerned elements often found in Latin American dramas. The former is rather obvious from the very beginning of the picture, a violent and impressive sequence where a nervous hand-held camera places the viewer almost literally into a crowd that beats and tries to burn alive a scared-to-death man. The latter, on the other hand, is more subtly disguised. Although the plot revolves around a good number of commonplaces – the whodunnit itself that keeps the suspense high throughout the movie, a typical conflict of interest between ethics and professional success, a rather incidental low-key romance – some of which seem a rather unnecessary concession to Hollywood-fed audiences, the orthodox dichotomy between goodies and baddies does not apply here. Not because it is not known until the end whether Vinicio is the Monstruo de Babahoyo or not, but because of the distinction the film establishes between authorship and responsibility. Ultimately, the real gap exists between those who are part of a society that suffers and those who behold, enjoy, and exploit that suffering from the outside.

The humble origin of both suspect and victims and the limited resources of the police accurately portray the relative poverty and the local reality, while the self-assured, occasionally arrogant attitude of the US journalists and the yellow nature of their TV programme depict a media world more than ready to do anything for the audience or a promotion. Given that the TV station is set in Miami and that the journalists are American and the producer Spanish, it is not difficult to read this contrast in terms of modern colonialism, where Ecuadorian rural society becomes the object of voyeuristic consumption of once-Cuban upper-class US citizens fascinated by sordidness and foreign pain.

Alcázar's astonishingly nuanced performance, which makes Vinicio appear tenderly helpless and at the same time terribly creepy, not only helps sustain the tension but also underscores the ambiguous nature of the case. The same can be said about an ending that suitably departs from the usual happy end; even if not as much as the original one, quite more radical and daring in its depiction of the ultimate consequences of Manolo's behaviour, but finally sadly dropped. All these elements allow for an interpretation of crime and moral indigence not only in terms of common responsibility (if not guilt) and social failure, as opposed to the usual US films depicting serial killers, but also as the result of the economic, social and welfare gap between the First World and developing countries. The impact of this post-colonial approach, however, should not be extrapolated too much: while the film's contents are a sharp critique of the ugliest aspects of globalization – the consequences of the lack of morals of media corporations in an ever smaller world – the feature itself is, at the end of the day, a perfect example of its benefits – namely its co-production, international cast and successful festival career in Toronto and Cannes.

Daniel A. Verdú Schumann

Cronos

Country of Origin:

Mexico

Languages:

Spanish
English

Studios/Distributors:

CNCAIMC
Fondo de Fomento a la Calidad Cinematográfica
Grupo del Toro

Director:

Guillermo del Toro

Genres:

Crime
Drama
Thriller

Cast:

John Leguizamo
Damián Alcázar
Leonor Watling

Year:

2004

Synopsis

Together with her lovable grandfather Jesús Gris, who is an antique dealer, Aurora finds a golden mechanical device in an old statue of an archangel. Gris is intrigued and winds the clock-like, scarab-shaped device, which releases a needle that injects him with a slimy solution. Although Gris is miraculously rejuvenated, feeling more vigorous than ever, he discovers an inexplicable thirst for blood. Ángel de la Guardia harasses Jesús, because his uncle Dieter, a rich, dying businessman, knows that the Cronos-device gives eternal life and has been looking for it for several years. However, Jesús has become addicted to the rejuvenating effects of the Cronos and does not want to hand it over. After he is killed by Ángel, he is resurrected and hides in Aurora's toy box. Together with his granddaughter he manages to defeat the de la Guardias and destroy the Cronos-device at the moment when he is longing for Aurora's blood.

Producers:

Arthur Gorson
Bertha Navarro

Screenwriter:

Guillermo del Toro

Cinematographer:

Guillermo Navarro

Art Director:

Brigitte Broch

Editor:

Raúl Dávalos

Composer:

Javier Álvarez

Duration:

94 minutes

Genre:

Horror

Cast:

Federico Luppi
Ron Perlman
Claudio Brook
Margarita Isabel
Tamara Shanath
Daniel Giménez Cacho

Year:

1994

Critique

The film is full of references. The Italian alchemist invents the Cronos-device exactly at the same time as his legendary contemporary Johann Faust is supposed to have made a deal with the Devil (1536). Just as in Faust's case, it is more professional curiosity than the thirst for power and eternal life that brings Gris (Federico Luppi) into contact with evil, and it is the pure innocence of a girl that saves him from Hell.

After his 'fatal accident' Gris looks like Frankenstein, with grey skin and gruesome scars. Despite the obviously telling names of the characters, it is difficult to interpret *Cronos* as a religious allegory. Although Jesús Gris has a lot in common with the central figure of Christianity, rising from the dead and dying in redemptive self-sacrifice in order to save the world from evil, Ángel de la Guardia (Ron Perlman) is certainly more an egoistic killer than a guardian angel. The scenes in Dieter de la Guardia's industrial building give the impression of a black-and-white film, and the sepia toned monochrome environment of the de la Guardia Company reminds us of the black-and-white world of Wim Wenders' angels in *Wings of the Desire* (1987).

Del Toro wanted to avoid the typical gore-fest of vampires and people becoming ciphers. Whereas the plot follows the conventional horror movie plot in which idyllic peaceful life is terrorized by a monster but eventually restored at the end, the film delves mainly into human issues and plays with several genres and modes. Daniel Giménez Cacho's hilarious performance as Tito, the embalmer, brings perfectly timed comic relief to the story when we mourn for Jesús. Besides, Jesús Gris is less of a romantic, charismatic villain-vampire than an ignorant drug addict. The injections by the Cronos-device increase his energy as well as his feelings of competence and sexuality. Despite his knowledge that the Cronos must be dangerous, he gives in to the sensation of 'comedown' and becomes desperate for another shot. After the first injection he is not only physically rejuvenated, he also experiences drastic changes in his personality and shows erratic and aggressive behaviour when Ángel wants to get the Cronos-device. The two bathroom scenes, Jesús locking himself in to get an injection and the nose-bleeding in the men's bathroom, are typical drug-junkie scenes; it only gets creepy when Jesús wants to lick the blood from the sink. The finale on the top of the building of de la Guardias is again an allusion to Wenders. Whereas Wenders' angel tries to prevent a man from committing suicide, del Toro's Angel wants to kill Jesús, this time for real. Aurora's (Tamara Shanath) red raincoat represents the only colour in the last scenes. She represents life and light in contrast to the grey dying Dieter (Claudio Brook), and her already dead grandfather.

Heidi Denzel de Tirado

Deep Crimson

Profundo carmesí

Country of Origin:

Mexico

Language:

Spanish

Studios/Distributors:

Ivania Films
IMCINE

Director:

Arturo Ripstein

Producers:

Pablo Barbachano
Marin Karmitz
José María Morales
Miguel Necoechea

Screenwriter:

Paz Alicia Garciadiego

Cinematographer:

Guillermo Granillo

Art Director:

Mónica Chirinos

Editor:

Rafael Castanedo

Composer:

David Mansfield

Duration:

111 minutes

Genres:

Crime
Drama
Romance

Cast:

Regina Orozco
Daniel Giménez Cacho
Sherlyn, Giovanni Florido
Fernando Palavicini
Patricia Reyes Spíndola

Year:

1996

Synopsis

Coral Fabré is an overweight nurse who takes care of terminally-ill old patients and struggles to earn a living for herself and her two children. She lives in a world of fantasy, dreaming of a Charles Boyer lookalike – a French actor – who would take her out of her misery. That opportunity comes when she answers an ad in a magazine from an alleged Spanish gentleman looking for love. Nicolás Estrella is not a Spaniard and he is not a gentleman either. He makes a living preying on naïve ladies looking for a husband. In order to get together with Nicolás, Coral abandons her children at an orphanage. Together they begin an itinerating relationship, moving from place to place in order to take advantage of widows and wealthy lonely women. Due to Coral's jealousy, their swindling attempts always end in murder.

Critique

Arturo Ripstein is arguably the most prominent Mexican director in the last two decades of the twentieth century, and one of the few who has been able to maintain a constant output despite his independence of the big Hollywood machine, unlike emerging talents such as del Toro or González Iñárritu. He is also the one who has achieved the most prominent international recognition, especially in France and Spain. *Deep Crimson* marks the masterful culmination of his trajectory, integrating his thematic and stylistic constants. It continues his collaboration with screenwriter Alicia Garciadiego, a collaboration that started with *El imperio de la fortuna* (1984) and that has earned both worldwide accolades. The film is based on the true story of Martha Beck and Raymond Fernández, the 'Lonely Hearts Killers', a couple posing as brother and sister who killed several widows in the post-war United States. This story also inspired the cult classic, *The Honeymoon Killers* (Leonard Kastle, 1970), a modestly-budgeted black-and-white crime movie that did not fall into the trap of becoming another pale imitation of Bonnie and Clyde and relied on a gritty approach combined with black humour undertones.

   Ripstein's film is not a remake of Kastle's, since he had been interested in this story for a long time. With screenwriter Garciadediego, he carefully researched the true events but also took the story to a deeply personal territory, distancing it from a mere serial-killer narrative pattern. In several interviews he has highlighted that he sees this more as a twisted love story, about the excesses that can follow from an excessive ill-fated love, with the quintessential ingredients of *amour fou* as advocated by surrealist poets. It is at this intersection that the film clearly connects with the universe of the cinematic master of surrealism, Luis Buñuel. Ripstein served as an uncredited assistant to Buñuel in *El angel exterminador/The Exterminating Angel* (1962) and has always declared his admiration for the Spanish director. Connections with *Ensayo de un crimen/The Criminal Life of Archibaldo de la Cruz* (1955) and *Él* (1953) are obvious. These were two movies in which Buñuel explored the connections between erotic desire, perversion, madness and ultimately crime. Ripstein charts the same territory. Coral is presented from the very beginning not as a victim but as a woman with perverted desires (she fondles the old man she is taking care of, she does not care about her children taking a bath together completely naked, her admiration for Charles Boyer is clearly fetishistic). She is always the stronger member of the couple, carrying Nicolás' primitive swindles to a new level of depravity. Nicolás is shown to be a weak man, obsessed by a balding forehead that betrays his charming good looks and afflicted by debilitating migraines. After stealing her money during their first encounter, he surrenders to Coral's obsessive love, charmed by the fact that she abandons her children in order to follow him or that she does not care about his baldness, his lies about his Spanish background, and the possibility that he might have actually killed his former wife. None of this stops Coral in her mad love for Nicolás. Rather, it serves as a catalyst and propeller for her disturbing *pulsions*. When they meet their victims, Nicolás plays the role of a gigolo/seducer rather well. Nevertheless, this invariably triggers Coral's jealous rage, which ends with the victim's murder. The film's first half exhibits a predominant interest in the erotic and in the humoresque or absurdist side of the story, but it progressively gets into a darker and grislier territory and is not afraid of going where very few films dare to go. The last killing is especially harrowing: Coral performs a botched abortion attempt on the victim with the intent of letting her bleed to death and, since she is not successful, the killers brutally stab her. Afterwards, the victim's child will suffer the same fate.

From mad love, Ripstein concludes, we can easily get to true madness. The two leads in the cast are particularly convincing as the tormented lovers, and the supporting cast is uniformly strong, particularly Almodóvar's veteran Marisa Paredes. The rich cinematography by Guillermo Granillo mixes earthy and reddish tones in a dream-like glow. Finally, David Mansfield's piano riffs lend a melancholic and romantic tone to the story. The film received awards for its screenplay, music and set design at the 1996 'Venice Film Festival', and an honorary mention at the 'Sundance Film Festival'.

Javier Gutiérrez-Rexach

The Devil's Backbone

El espinazo del diablo

Country of Origin:
Mexico
Language:
Spanish

Synopsis

Spain in 1939: the Republicans are about to lose the civil war. The 10-year-old Carlos is sent to a remote orphanage and is intrigued by an unexploded bomb in its courtyard. However, the bomb is not the only danger lurking nearby: Carlos has to defend himself against the bullying of the other boys, especially against the harassments of Jaime and the ghost of a former orphan called Santi. The orphanage's caretaker Jacinto knows about a hidden stash of gold and does everything to find it. When the head of the orphanage, Carmen, and her faithful friend and colleague Dr Casares decide to leave as the Nationalists are approaching, Jacinto takes action and tries to blow

Studios/Distributors:

El Deseo S.A.
Tequila Gang
Anhelo Producciones

Director:

Guillermo del Toro

Producers:

Agustín Almodóvar
Bertha Navarro

Screenwriters:

Guillermo del Toro
Antonio Trashorras
David Muñoz

Cinematographer:

Guillermo Navarro

Art Director:

César Macarrón

Editor:

Luis de La Madrid

Composer:

Javier Navarrete

Duration:

106 minutes

Genres:

Drama
Horror

Cast:

Federico Luppi
Eduardo Noriega
Marisa Paredes
Fernando Tielve
Íñigo Garcés

Year:

2001

up the safe. The badly wounded Dr Casares promises the children that he will never leave them and that he will defend them against Jacinto.

Critique

'What is a ghost? A tragedy condemned to repeat itself time and again? An instant of pain, perhaps. Something dead which still seems to be alive. An emotion suspended in time. Like a blurred photograph. Like an insect trapped in amber.' These lines are spoken off-screen at the beginning and ending of the film. Ghosts play an important role *The Devil's Backbone*, but the story differs from conventional horror movies. It is not the ghosts who threaten the normal peaceful life of the living, it is the absurdity of war and violence. Like its sequel *Pan's Labyrinth*, *The Devil's Backbone* is a horror movie immersed in the context of the Spanish Civil War.

A fantastic war movie seems to be the obvious choice for del Toro, who thinks that all politics is fantasy, whereas all fantasies have a political standard. Just like a group of right-wing military generals attempted to topple the leftist government, Jacinto (Eduardo Noriega) and his friends try to overcome the directorate whose gold is dedicated to the cause of the republic. The ideals of compassion, love and sharing are attacked by egoistic greediness and violence. The omnipresent metaphor for the ongoing war is the not yet detonated bomb in the courtyard. But del Toro's supernatural melodrama is more than just a parable of the Civil War. The reflector figure of the story – Carlos (Fernando Tielve), 'a force of innocence' as del Toro describes him – represents optimism, curiosity and empathy. Due to Carlos' courage and loyalty to his friends, the children end up as comrades. Even Jaime (Íñigo Garcés), Carlos' former antagonist, teams up with the others in order to fight their common enemy, Jacinto, who finally is hunted down by the group with wooden spears just like the mammoth they have been studying in class at the beginning of the film. With the help of the ghosts of Santi and Dr Casares (Federico Luppi), Jacinto – the 'devil's backbone' – is defeated and the boys survive. While we do not get to see the ghost of Dr Casares, we see the hideously scary ghost of Santi, the orphan who was drowned by Jacinto in the orphanage's cellar. Santi's blood flows out of his waterlogged corpse and represents fear physically on the screen, a very important factor for del Toro for the genre and a detail that earned this film several nominations in the category Best Horror Movie (Academy of Science Fiction, Fantasy & Horror Films, USA).

Heidi Denzel de Tirado

Embodiment of Evil

A encarnação do demônio

Country of Origin:

Brazil

Studios/Distributors:

Olhos de Cão Produções
Cinematográficas
Gullane Filmes

Director:

José Mojica Marins

Producers:

Caio Gullane
Fabiano Gullane
Débora Ivanov
Paulo Sacramento

Screenwriters:

José Mojica Marins
Dennison Ramalho

Cinematographer:

José Roberto Eliezer

Art Director:

Cassio Amarante

Editor:

Paulo Sacramento

Composers:

André Abujamra
Marcio Nigro

Duration:

94 minutes

Genre:

Horror

Cast:

José Mojica Marins
Jece Valadão
Adriano Stuart
Milhem Cortaz
Cristina Aché

Year:

2008

Synopsis

After 40 years in prison, gravedigger Zé do Caixão is released on a legal technicality. Unrepentant of the countless atrocities he committed, Zé is joined by several loyal disciples and immediately plans to resume his old activities. While the streets of São Paulo have changed, his obsession is the same, and he is hell-bent on impregnating a woman to continue his lineage – granting the, 'continuation of the blood', as he puts it. But Zé must choose the right partner and kidnaps and tortures several women to test their worth. Angered by Zé's release from prison, the brutal Police Colonel Miro Pontes vows to capture him, but his assignment masks a desire for revenge after Zé blinded him in one eye years before. Miro is assisted by his equally sadistic brother and a deranged monk whose father Zé murdered. After beating Zé's defence lawyer, the Colonel finds his adversary's crypt lair and pursues him to a closed down amusement park.

Critique

'Here I am back in the world,' spits Zé do Caixão (aka Coffin Joe) into the camera. 'The time has come!' The resurrection of director, writer and actor José Mojica Marins' most famous creation has been a long time coming. Some forty years since Zé's last official outing (though in the interim he has appeared in TV programmes, spin offs and comic books) *Embodiment of Evil* marks the conclusion of an 'unholy trinity' of horror pictures Marins began in 1964. *À Meia-Noite Levarei Sua Alma/ At Midnight I'll Take Your Soul* (widely considered Brazil's first horror film) set the tone, while its 1967 sequel *Esta Noite Encarnarei no Teu Cadáver* continued to follow the atheist Zé as he murdered, taunted God and raved about the Nietzschean power of the will. *Embodiment* then is more of the same. But with a larger budget and more relaxed censor, Marins is finally allowed free expression (for better or worse) to attempt his ultimate Zé do Caixao film.

While in the 1960s Zé's distain for theology ('while you negotiate with your God, I look after my corpses!') was deemed controversial by a mostly Roman Catholic nation, Marins adhered to the strict censorship of Brazil's military government. At their request the ending of *Esta Noite Encarnarei* was altered to reinforce a positive message of faith and Zé was last seen sinking into a swamp begging God for forgiveness. Here Marins has no such restrictions (going as far as to reshoot *Esta Noite*'s ending to see Zé escape). Plot is abandoned, disregarded in favour of several characters that reinforce his distaste for religious hypocrisy. The men hunting Zé are zealot but each is just as depraved as their quarry. The monk (Milhem Cortaz) is a masochist (seen clamping electric prongs to his nipples) while military cop Miro (played with relish by Novo veteran Jece Valadão, who sadly died mid-production) savagely beats and murders anyone in his path to get answers. A statue of Saint Expendite seemingly justifies his actions.

The early stages of the film set up Zé as a sort of dark protagonist and when Miro's brother Oswaldo executes two children, an appalled Zé cuts him across the throat in retaliation. Here the film toys with the concept of fantasy horror (the archaic Zé and his minions) coming face to face with the horrors of the real world and being disgusted, but the film never rests there. Zé is still a monster and Marins seems to relish in torture for its own sake. The camera closes in as human flesh is desecrated – bodies are hung from hooks, lumps of skin are sliced off, naked bodies are branded, scarred and whipped. While these scenes may appease Marins' hardcore following, they undermine his central message. Here it is not just religious hegemony that is bad; it is a world of evil full stop, where even the virtuous are seen to be corrupt or perverse.

Aside from showcasing Kapel Furman's *vérité* special effects, these scenes of torture seem an attempt to make up for the lack of horror elsewhere. Stripped of the black-and-white Gothicism of the previous entries, Zé cuts a weird, anachronistic figure; his iconic black top hat, cloak and talon-like fingernails jarring against the passing *paulistanos* in jeans and T-shirts. The film is full of similar archetypal movie bogeymen, from Zé's hunchback assistant, to the blind old hags who practice witchcraft in the slums. These antiquated terrors are now the stuff of the spook house, and it is ironic that is where Zé himself winds up. As the central character, Marin has lost vitality, his beady eyes set in a puffy, worn out face. São Paulo, a towering metropolis, dwarfs him further and as he wanders the streets, dodging speeding cars and weird looks, he comes across more as a pathetic old man than the embodiment of evil.

Though his character now seems visually outdated, as a director it is visually where Marins triumphs. Zé is plagued by hallucinations of long dead victims and they appear (through some CGI trickery) with grey flesh and black tongues, as if they have literally crawled out of the black-and-white celluloid of Zé/Marins' past. In the film's opening, we are led through dark caverns, the walls red, alive and pulsating, a Bosch like vision of hell. But as the shot continues we realize we are in the human body, and it concludes with a close-up of a beating heart. Marins' films are prone to grandstanding, his character beating us into submission with speeches about 'the law that cannot be revoked – the law of the fittest!', but here he has created a pertinent metaphor of evil within. It is just a shame that the rest of the film cannot live up to this, let down by a muddled message and a reliance on shock tactics and brutality.

Tom Fallows

Highway Patrolman

El Patrullero

Countries of Origin:
United States
Mexico
Japan

Synopsis

After graduating from the academy with distinction, highway patrolman Pedro Rojas arrives on the Mexican roads determined to do good. Idealistic, Pedro refuses bribes, remaining honest despite the costs his job incurs. While out on the road he meets Griselda and they soon marry, but the pressures of family life lead Pedro to finally accept kickbacks. Guilty at his compromises, Pedro slides into despair and becomes involved with the prostitute Maribel. Things worsen when Pedro is shot and left with a damaged leg. His life becomes destructive, he insists on driving a beat up car and is unable to stop fellow patrolman Anibal from being killed. Pedro is given drugs for

Studios/Distributors:

Cable Hogue Co

Together Brothers Production Inc.

Ultra Films

Director:

Alex Cox

Producer:

Lorenzo O'Brien

Screenwriter:

Lorenzo O'Brien

Cinematographer:

Miguel Garzón

Art Directors:

Omero Espinoza

Bryce Perrin

Editor:

Carlos Puente

Composer:

Zander Schloss

Duration:

104 minutes

Genre:

Thriller

Cast:

Robert Sosa

Vanessa Bauche

Zaide Silvia Gutiérrez

Pedro Armendáriz Jr

Ernesto Gómez Cruz

Year:

1991

his depression and determines to save Maribel from herself and get revenge on the men who killed his friend. On the highway he routinely busts drug runners but keeps the evidence – giving money to his wife and drugs to Maribel. After killing a dealer, Pedro is suspended but instead resigns. But having sent Maribel back to her rural home without income, Pedro now has two families to support and is left wondering where he will find the money to look after them both.

Critique

Despite the critical and commercial failures of both his *Straight to Hell* (1987) and *Walker* (1987), Hollywood still saw a talented film-maker and thought it about time he stepped into the mainstream and did as he was told. The $14 million sci-fi sequel would have given him a chance, as they saw it, to reform. But Cox, with the same punk sensibilities that made *Repo Man* (1984) such a masterpiece of anarchic rebellion, was finding that he actually liked it on the fringes and *Highway Patrolman* – a low budget cop drama, shot in Mexico, entirely in Spanish – marginalized him further. Worse still Cox and screenwriter/producer Lorenzo O'Brien's movie pokes fun at US action movies, rejecting the triumphalism inherent in the genre. For the most part their story takes place in a doggedly real world, where the generic notion of 'one good cop standing alone' is repeatedly undermined or compromised.

Indeed Pedro Rojas (Roberto Sosa) is far from the typical masculine representation of a hero. Tiny and boyish, his enormous machine gun and tightly tucked in shirt make him look more like a kid playing at being a cop than the real thing (while his mirrored shades recall the fake-cool of Stallone in US actioner *Cobra* [George P. Cosmatos, 1986], the kind of ascendant hero that Pedro aspires to be). His initial dreams of being saviour of the roads are childlike and are eventually abandoned for the pragmatism of feeding his family and paying bills. 'Even stones bleed out here,' he is told and like many pious men when he falls, he falls hard – stealing from drug dealers and revelling in his guilt by drinking, fucking and popping pills. He looks for salvation in the job, but his attempts are seen as both pedantic and futile – like driving truant kids to school only to find them back on the streets come the film's close.

Pedro's heroic gestures are constantly attenuated. His rescue of Maribel from the whorehouse is devalued because the script continues past the moment of triumph (were most Hollywood pictures end) and sees Pedro naïvely set her up in a Casa Chica he cannot afford. Pedro's conduct is impotent and Cox emphasizes this by denying him (and the audience) action. The bulking police cars constantly arrive on the scene too late, finding only the aftermath of violent crashes and shootouts. The entire film is shot by cinematographer Miguel Garzón in *plano secuenca* (each scene composed of one long, moving master take) a technique that reinforces this lack of momentum. Rather than the kinetic editing of traditional action pictures, events are forced to play out in real time adding a sense of the mundane. The closest we get to conventional drama is when Pedro, in one long uninterrupted take, hobbles along the asphalt, machine gun in hand, desperate to save his friend from the drug runner's gunfire. Of course, he arrives too late.

By breaking each scene into master takes, Cox creates a series of short stories, hinging on the life of a highway patrolman, both on and off the road. While his desert post burns with inaction, Pedro's life becomes an urban melodrama. His wife (Zaide Silvia Gutiérrez) is nagging, bouncing between doey-eyed affection and knife wielding fits of rage – only placated by the kickbacks he brings back home. His scenes with Maribel also offer no relief. Shot matter-of-factly by Cox, he avoids romanticism and their first night together culminates with her alone in the bathroom wiping him from between her legs. That these two women come to dominate his life emphasizes Pedro's emasculation (made figurative in the limp, beat up car he is forced to drive) and his weakness again is parenthetical of the genre; by the end he is not even a cop, but a henpecked husband with two families.

Cox's presentation of ineffective masculinity adds a much needed realism to the cop genre, as if, in the reverse of John Ford, he has printed the truth, not the legend. But like his hero Buñuel (who also made a filmic pilgrimage to Mexico) Cox is a surrealist at heart and cannot resist moments of oddness to accentuate Pedro's deteriorating mental state. A psychiatrist's coffee table turns into a festering vision of death before our eyes and later Pedro is visited by an apparition of his dying father, who dismisses him as a, 'petty taker of bribes'. These moments of weirdness work in Cox's favour, and one cannot imagine Hollywood allowing him such whimsies. And Cox knows this. When Pedro is at his lowest he drunkenly stumbles home and stops for a moment to catch *Robocop 2* (Irvin Kershner, 1990) on TV. Here is a reminder for both character and director of what they might have been – the dream and the nightmare of Hollywood cinema rolled into one.

Tom Fallows

Hell's Highway: KM31

Km 31: Kilómetro 31

Countries of Origin:

Mexico
Spain

Studios/Distributors:

Lemon Films
Filmax
Salamandra Films

Director:

Rigoberto Castañeda

Synopsis

Catalina and Ágata Hameran are twin sisters with a traumatic past, the tragic death of their mother when they were children. Ágata is critically wounded in an accident at the 31 km-mark of a lonely road, and she falls into a coma. Catalina has to investigate the strange circumstances surrounding the accident, since moments before her death Ágata called reporting that she had run over a child, but there is no trace of anybody else being involved. She is helped by a Spanish friend, Nuño, who is secretly in love with her, and by Omar, Ágata's boyfriend. The three begin to uncover a mysterious series of accidents, all taking place at the same point in the road and involving the ghost of a boy and his mother. Catalina has to solve this mystery in order to help her sister, who is trapped between the realms of the living and the dead.

Producers:

Julio Fernández
Billy Rovzar
Fernando Rovzar

Screenwriters:

Rigoberto Castañeda
Ricardo Álvarez Canales

Cinematographer:

Alejandro Martínez

Art Director:

Rafael Mandujano

Editor:

Alberto De Toro

Composer:

Carles Cases

Duration:

103 minutes

Genre:

Horror
Mystery
Thriller

Cast:

Iliana Fox
Adrià Collado
Raúl Méndez
Luisa Huertas
Fernando Becerril

Year:

2006

Critique

The Mexican fantastique/horror genre languished during the 1980s and part of the 1990s before Guillermo del Toro almost single-handedly revived it with *Cronos* (1993). Del Toro's style and approach was far removed from traditional Mexican horror cinema, from endless variations on the vampire theme to the hybridization with the action/adventure narratives as represented by the Santo films. Castañeda's film is not related to this tradition or to del Toro's themes either, although one can find several parallelisms with the ghost story in *El espinazo del Diablo/The Devil's Backbone* (2001), and in the fusion of fictional elements with historical facts.

Km 31 cleverly integrates two very different sources. On the one hand, the traditional Mexican ghost story, the myth of La Llorona, a woman maligned during colonial times and whose spirit still haunts young women. There is also the universal prototype tale of 'the ghost of the road', a ghost that haunts a particular road stretch or curve where a deadly accident occurred in the past. In this case, the road is related to an old river where the tragic events from the colonial past took place. Thus, Castañeda roots the ghost story in traditional Mexican myths and universal archetypes.

Filmically, the inspiration also comes from several sources, mostly from the revival of Japanese horror cinema, as represented by *Ringu/The Ring* (Hideo Nakata, 1998), *The Grudge* (Takashi Shimizu, 2004) and *The Eye* (Oxide Pang Chun, Danny Pang, 2002), which have as a common link − the presence of an evil-child ghost who haunts the leading female. The popularity of *Ringu*, and its American remake (*The Ring* [Gore Verbinski, 2002]), coincided with a wave of high quality ghost and horror films in Spain, from *The Others* (Alejandro Amenábar, 2001) to those produced by Julio Fernández at the Fantastic Factory in Barcelona, most notably those directed by Jaume Balagueró (*Los sin nombre/The Nameless*, 1999, *Darkness 2002*) or Paco Plaza *Rec*, 2007/2009 together with Balagueró).

Km 31 is a Mexican-Spanish co-production, and the producer on the Spanish side is precisely Julio Fernández (Filmax). As expected, the film has a majority of the elements in a Fernández production: tight stories, excellent cinematography, the Hitchcockian score by Carles Cases, etc. Castañeda successfully integrates the revival of the Mexican story with the stylistic traits of the contemporary horror film, and in so doing he creates a worthy film, which only received mixed reviews when it was originally reviewed but has gained critical consideration more recently. The main character, Catalina (Iliana Fox), is connected to her twin sister Ágata by a special extra-sensorial link. Omar (Raúl Méndez) and Nuño (Adrià Collado), their respective boyfriends, are rivals, given that both sisters look very similar. Castañeda creates a few powerful surreal images: the twins' dead mother emerging from the bathtub (clearly inspired by Stanley Kubrick's *The Shining* [1980]), the final scene in the underground, the imagery in Catalina's dreams, the forest landscape around the road, etc. In sum, *Km 31* successfully navigates traditional horror conventions and integrates them in a powerful genuinely-Mexican ghost story.

Javier Gutiérrez-Rexach

The Victim's Last Days

Últimos días de la víctima

Country of Origin:

Argentina

Studio/Distributor:

Aries Cinematográfica
Argentina

Director:

Adolfo Aristaráin

Producers:

Héctor Olivera
Luis O. Repetto

Screenwriters:

Adolfo Aristaráin
José Pablo Feinmann

Cinematographer:

Horacio Maira

Art Director:

Abel Facello

Editors:

Eduardo López
Laura Bua

Composer:

Emilio Kauderer

Duration:

90 minutes

Genre:

Thriller

Cast:

Federico Luppi
Soledad Sylveira
Ulises Dumont
Arturo Maly
Julio De Grazia
Mónica Galán

Year:

1982

Synopsis

Raúl Mendizábal is a hit man, who always fulfills his assignments with methodic precision. After killing a corrupt financier, Carlos Ravenna, he receives the assignment of following and later killing Rodolfo Külpe, an apparently anonymous individual. Mendizábal starts following Külpe's every movement. He discovers that he is the lover of the wife of his former victim, Cecilia Ravenna. Intrigued and concerned by this coincidences and the lack of information he has received about the identity of his target and the reasons for killing him, he moves to an apartment closer to his victim and starts getting deeper and deeper in his pursuit, crossing certain boundaries. He enlists the help of his friend and guns supplier, Gato Funes. Fuentes is killed after inquiring about Külpe's identity. The powerful individuals who hired him cancel the contract, pay him, and instruct him to forget about his assignment and disappear, but Mendizábal is determined to finish the job.

Critique

Following the critical and box office success of *Tiempo de revancha/ Time for Revenge* (1981), Aristaráin adapted José Pablo Feinmann's novel *Útimos días de la víctima/The Victim's Last Days* (1978). Feinmann also worked on the screenplay. The film was released in 1982, during the Malvinas, and this fact probably explains why it was not as successful as his previous film. Nevertheless, it was well reviewed, and received the top award at the 'Huelva Film Festival'.

The film is an extraordinary exercise in pure narrative. The audience is never given the full details about what is going on, who Külpe (Arturo Maly) really is, what are the motives of the powerful corporation that targets him, or why he is the lover of Mendizábal's (Federico Luppi) last victim. In this respect, it fully adopts Mendizábal's point of view and dialogues are scarce. This behaviouristic approach to the day-to-day actions of a contract killer is clearly reminiscent of Jean-Pierre Melville's French polar films. Aristaráin is less contemplative, he knows how to build tension, create intriguing settings, and walk the fine line between unease and romanticism. Before starting his career as a film director, he worked as assistant director in several European co-productions directed by genre-film masters of the 1960s and 1970s: Mario Camus, Sergio Leone, Peter Collinson, Giorgio Stegani. He learned the mechanics of how to build a successful thriller and he also acquired a masterful dexterity as a pure story-teller.

The film starts on a high note. We see Mendizábal as he wanders through the apartment of his victim, the cold manner in which he confronts him when he arrives, and how he dispatches him with a clean shot in the head. Mendizábal is the prototype of the perfect hit man, carrying his assignments without remorse or questioning the motives of those who hire him: 'I am a weapon,' he tells Peña (Enrique Liporace), his contact with the organization. Mendizábal can cope with his role and his place in society, marginalized and despised by those who hire him. Peña's boss does not want to talk to him directly, and Peña repeatedly expresses his disgust about his actions. He is growing old, and his only soulmate and friend is Funes (Ulises Dumont). They are both lone wolfs, but Funes is changing and living with a prostitute, Vienna, a lucid and tender lady who sees both friends as what they really are ('Playing dominos is the only thing you need to look like true retirees, you have more than enough years'). Mendizábal has no family, no contacts, and no social life or hobbies. He devotes himself completely to his assignments, incessantly taking pictures of his target, and hanging them in his bedroom's walls. As in Michelangelo Antonioni's *Blow-Up* (1966), Mendizábal is trying to make sense of life through images, a puzzle as difficult to decipher as the Rubik's cube he plays with. He becomes obsessed, absorbing the life of a target the he ultimately has to finish off (or 'erase'). Külpe's sexual affair with Ravenna's widow, full of erotic games and drug addiction, fascinates him. This will be the trigger for Mendizábal's downfall. Trying to find more about Külpe, he meets his ex-wife and son, and he takes unnecessary risks. In the end, Mendizábal will learn that he has been pursuing one of his own, a mirror image of himself, and that the destiny that awaits him is what he often staged for others.

Javier Gutiérrez-Rexach

Nine Queens

Nueve Reinas

Country of Origin:

Argentina

Language:

Spanish

Studio/Distributor:

Patagonik Film Group

Director:

Fabián Bielinsky

Producers:

Cecilia Bossi
Pablo Bossi

Screenwriter:

Fabián Bielinsky

Cinematographer:

Marcelo Camorino

Art Director:

Marcelo Salvioli

Editor:

Sergio Zottola

Synopsis

A chance encounter in a gas station makes temporary colleagues out of two con men: Marcos (Ricardo Darín), a slightly older, less scrupulous, hawk-nosed professional who exudes an aura of contempt for everybody and everything, and Juan (Gastón Pauls), a young man with soft, friendly features and puppy-dog eyes. Marcos needs a partner, and Juan needs a lot of money, fast, to bail his father out of jail. What a stroke of luck, then, that the score of a lifetime is waiting just around the corner: the 'Nine Queens', a set of flawed and thus incredibly valuable stamps from the 1920s, which have been forged to perfection by a former colleague of Marcos' and only require a minimum of effort on the part of our heroes in order to be sold to a millionaire philatelist who is leaving the country forever the very next day…

Critique

Needless to say, nothing is as it seems. Over the 109 minutes of writer and director Fabián Bielinsky's debut feature, *Nine Queens*, identities and roles transform and blend together as it becomes clear that the Buenos Aires we observe is populated by two sorts of people only: the players and the played. Characters who are initially perceived as a threat, such as the detective who almost throws Juan and Marcos out of the hotel their target is staying at before they can even approach him, turn out to be part of the act the very second they leave the room. Curtains upon curtains are continually being drawn and redrawn upon the larger game Juan and Marcos are playing against time, and on the smaller games they play against each other to assert their dominance in the partnership.

Composer:

César Lerner

Duration:

109 minutes

Genre:

Thriller

Cast:

Ricardo Darín
Gastón Pauls
Leticia Brédice
Elsa Berenguer

Year:

2000

Onstage and backstage are the central motifs of this caper, where Juan and Marcos enter elegant and intimidating rooms, populated with colourful characters, as Humphrey Bogart did sixty years before in *The Maltese Falcon* (John Huston, 1941). In step with all this, the supporting characters are drawn almost as caricatures, at least in contrast to Darín and Pauls' more down-to-earth performances: our heroes are trying to con into buying the stamps, Gandolfo, the Spaniard, has his perennial whiskey glass; Berta, the old lady from whom the two must retrieve the stamps, wears crimson lipstick and keeps a young lover with comically bleached hair; and last but not least, Valeria (Leticia Brédice), who is Marcos' sister and is coincidentally employed in the very same hotel in which the majority of their business unfurls. Valeria has a stylized, almost 'super-modelish' elegance of bearing, hips swishing by about 45 degrees with each step she takes. All of this leads to the question: if Juan and Marcos know they are playing a game and everybody else acts as though they are playing a role, just who exactly is playing whom?

The plot thickens further as little glimpses of the leading characters' private lives are revealed beneath the protagonists' thick veneer of cool. Marcos, as it turns out, is a social predator, feeding mercilessly upon those in any way weaker than him – whether this means conning a kiosk operator out of today's newspaper or swindling his brother and sister out of their share of the family inheritance makes no difference to him whatsoever, as is evidenced by his string of grudge-bearing ex-business partners. Juan, on the other hand, is bad with money and far too kind-hearted to survive on the street, as Marcos laments, yet he has an incredible gift for improvising solutions to all sorts of problems. The question of 'honour among thieves' is a problematic one in view of such complications, but Bielinsky gives it a satisfactory twist in the end. 'I've never seen such goodwill for doing business,' says Gandolfo of the Argentineans as a people, qualifying them, one and all, as potential crooks. A fair assessment, it must be said, in a film titled *Nine Queens* – after all, with only four queens in a full set of cards, cheating goes with the territory.

Nine Queens is a balancing act between two worlds, as demonstrated in the juxtaposition between the principals' conversing in bustling Buenos Aires thoroughfares or by the harbour, with traffic and passers-by going about their business in the background, and the calm, focused and tense scenes set in hotels and luxury apartments. This tight little thriller is balanced with enough moments of bizarre comedy and beauty, elicited principally through character, and insights into the psyche of career criminals – *Criminal* being, appropriately, the title of the film's 2004 US remake by Gregory Jacobs – to transcend the limitations of a debut film, particularly a genre effort. Building on the groundwork laid by earlier and more famous examples of caper movies such as *The Sting* (George Roy Hill, 1973) or *House of Games* (David Mamet, 1987), Fabián Bielinsky has created a miniature masterpiece about the mechanics of acting and of being duped.

Paul Becker

Pan's Labyrinth

El laberinto del fauno

Countries of Origin:

Mexico

Spain

Language:

Spanish

Studios/Distributors:

Estudios Ricasso

Tequila Gang

Esperanto Films

Director:

Guillermo del Toro

Producers:

Guillermo del Toro

Bertha Navarro

Alfonso Cuarón

Frida Toresblanco

Alvaro Augustin

Screenwriter:

Guillermo del Toro

Cinematographer:

Guillermo Navarro

Art Director:

Eugenio Caballero

Editor:

Bernat Vilaplana

Composer:

Javier Navarrete

Duration:

119 minutes

Genre:

Thriller

Fantasy

Horror

Cast:

Sergi López

Maribel Verdú

Ivana Vaquero

Álex Angulo

Ariadnia Gil

Doug Jones

Synopsis

Fascist Spain, 1944. Ten-year-old Ofelia and her pregnant mother Carmen are on their way north to meet Ofelia's stepfather Vidal, a brutal and merciless captain in the Franco Regime who has decamped with his soldiers to an old mill to fight the remaining partisans hiding in the surrounding woodland. On her first night at the mill, Ofelia is awakened by a fairy who leads her to a labyrinth. It is there that she meets an old faun who tells her an amazing story: according to the creature's tale, Ofelia is actually a princess of a fairy kingdom. A long time ago, she left her home and ended up getting lost in the human realm, forgetting her true identity. To prove she is the legitimate heiress to the fairy throne and to return to her parents, Ofelia must complete three tasks before the next full moon. The smart yet dreamy girl willingly accepts the challenge and soon faces her first task. Her adventures and encounters with magical creatures contrast with the second storyline, the events unfolding against the backdrop of the Spanish military regime. As the violence and brutality towards the partisans intensifies, Ofelia increasingly seeks refuge in her imagination. But the more the story advances, the less certain we become about whether her adventures are purely imaginary, or whether there is more to them than meets the eye.

Critique

As far as awards are concerned, *Pan's Labyrinth* is del Toro's most successful film, winning him three academy awards and close to 30 prizes worldwide. Had the story not been set in post-Civil War Spain, based on the title of the film alone, one might think that *Pan's Labyrinth* is a fairy tale written for children. And this is what is so cunning about the film. In a manner which is typical of del Toro, two seemingly contradictory aspects are combined: the magical and the gruesome. We are invited to witness Ofelia's (Ivana Baquero) adventures in a colourful and innocent world, an invitation which turns out to be a trap; after our attention is caught, we are exposed without warning to the violence exercised by Vidal (Sergi López) and his soldiers. Such shocking strategies are reminiscent of the surrealist movement started up by André Breton shortly after World War I. One of the surrealists' central aims was to question and revolutionize human perception, an idea which is concretely and violently visualized in Salvador Dalí's and Luis Buñuel's silent film *Un chien andalou* (1929), in which a woman's eye is sliced open with a razor.

Pan's Labyrinth may therefore be considered a surrealist film in that it both seeks to shock its viewers while simultaneously promoting imagination and childhood. However, the crucial point is not the question of to what extent Ofelia's adventures are fictitious or not, or whether her death is real or nothing but a dream. The film's major concern is rather to convey the fact that horror and violence are all around us and that the best way to cope with this is to face it head on. What seems magical and tempting one moment turns out to be evil the next. It would be naive to believe that Ofelia's dream world is innocent, since she exposes herself to even greater dangers, in parallel

Guillermo del Toro: *El laberinto del fauno/Pan's Labyrinth*, 2006 © Photograph by Teresa Isasi. With kind permission of Tequila Gang and Telecinco Cinema.

Roger Casamajor
Federico Luppi
Year:
2006

with the persecution of the partisans. The same is true for the viewer who is constantly witnessing the horror and absurdity of violence. We have compassion for the young villager who Vidal kills with a broken bottle at the very beginning of the film, and we also suffer with Pedro, a stammering dissident who is tortured by the captain for an entire night. Watching such scenes is certainly not pleasant, but, as has already become clear in so many previous works by del Toro, what is even more dangerous than horror itself is to ignore it, thus rendering oneself vulnerable to the forces of the unknown.

Justyna Cempel

Phase 7

Fase 7

Country of Origin:

Argentina

Studios/Distributors:

Aeroplano Cine
INCAA
Telefe

Director:

Nicolás Goldbart

Producers:

Sebastián Aloi
Tomás Elio Cohen
Ricardo D'Amato

Screenwriter:

Nicolás Goldbart

Cinematographer:

Lucio Bonelli

Art Director:

Mariela Rípodas

Editors:

Pablo Barbieri
Nicolás Goldbart

Composer:

Guillermo Guareschi

Duration:

95 minutes

Genre:

Comedy
SciFi
Thriller

Cast:

Daniel Hendler
Jazmín Stuart
Yayo Guridi
Federico Luppi
Carlos Bermejo
Abian Bainstein

Year:

2011

Synopsis

A young couple is trapped in a quarantined building, as a deadly and highly contagious virus spreads across the world. Problems and tensions rise among the few other neighbours also imprisoned in their own homes, as the feeling of isolation and being abandoned begins to grow. The couple's fight for survival will include alliances with some of these neighbours and violent confrontations with others.

Critique

Phase 7 represents the first Argentinean post-apocalyptic film, very successful in its home country and sold across the world. The story is a variation on the pandemic/end of the world scenario. A killer virus propagates through several countries, including Argentina. The inhabitants of a building are quarantined because one of its residents is suspected to have the virus. Days go by and, as society collapses around them, the neighbours will have to fight for survival. Goldbart lets the story develop not just as a straight thriller/sci-fi narrative, but rather introducing comedy elements from the very beginning. In the first scene, we follow a couple, Coco (Daniel Hendler) and Pipi (Jazmín Stuart), as they buy groceries and argue about trivial matters during their shopping trip in the mall, unaware of the events that unfold around them and that give us (not them) a hint of what is going on: people running, sirens, police cars, etc. Only later they learn about the virus, but this awareness seems to do little to interrupt their continuous bickering. The other neighbours in the building are also depicted with ironic touches. Horacio (Yayo Guridi) is the survivalist who has been planning for an event of this sort for a long time. He takes Coco as his sidekick, giving him weapons, food and an insulating suit. Zanutto (Federico Luppi), the oldest neighbour, always with his cat, is a tender old man who will become a vigilante killing machine after he is threatened by two other neighbours: the calculating Guglierini and Lange, who are trying to get Zanutto's food supply with the excuse that he is sick.

The film is clearly based on similar recent horror films, which also play their thriller/horror ingredients with a fresh coating of comedy; one can easily think of *Shawn of the Dead* (Edgar Wright, 2004), *Zombieland* (Ruben Fleischer, 2009), *Stake Land* (Jim Mickle, 2010), and similar films. Other recent horror films explored the claustrophobic effects of a surrounded building under siege, for example, the French zombie film *La Horde/The Horde* (Yannick Dahan, Benjamin Rocher, 2009). A closer model seems to be the internationally successful *Rec* (Jaume Balagueró and Paco Plaza, 2007), in which a block is quarantined and its inhabitants have to fight for survival. Whereas *Rec* and similar films play the sci-fi and horror elements in a straight fashion, building tension in a traditional manner, *Phase 7*'s script has the confidence to never renounce its comedic undertones. Coco, our main character, remains a laid-back, reluctant, clumsy, and somewhat lazy hero. He loses his weapon several times, he triggers himself the bomb traps that Horacio sets for others, he continues to argue with his pregnant wife, etc. As the sequence of events progresses, the movie becomes a metaphor for the Hobbesian dog-eat-dog theme, since everyone ends up turning up against each other with predictable consequences. External help from local or national authorities is non-existent. After being quarantined, the neighbours are instructed to call a phone number if they need anything, but nobody answers when Coco calls.

The film has been made working from a low budget, but it substitutes ingenuity and technical craft for the lack of sophisticated special effects, which are not needed in this type of story. A brief clip shows Saul Bass' 1974 classic *Phase 4* on TV, paying homage to another low-budget cult classic. The electronic score strongly reminds of John Carpenter's music, and the theme of the group of individuals trapped in a closed, hostile environment is also reminiscent of Carpenter's classics such as *The Thing* (1982) or *Assault on Precinct 13* (2005). The cinematography is elegant, with bright colours and well-thought framing arrangements. Despite its technical competence, what ultimately makes the film a very successful endeavour is how it manages to find its niche in the post-apocalyptic subgenre, inserting a realistic and comedic backbone into the survival story representing a known narrative cliché from American cinema. This film will hopefully mark the beginning of a new trend in Argentinean cinema, which unlike Mexican cinema, lacks a tradition in the fantastique/horror genre.

Javier Gutiérrez-Rexach

Red Bear

Un oso rojo

Countries of origin:

Argentina
Spain
France

Language:

Spanish

Studios/Distributors:

Lita Stantic Producciones
TS Productions
Wanda Visión S.A.

Director:

Adrián Caetano

Producers:

Lita Stantic

Synopsis

After paying seven years in prison Oso is trying to make up for lost time. Although his wife Natalia is now living with Sergio and his 8-year-old daughter Alicia hardly remembers him, he is determined to be a good father. He finds a job as a chauffeur and much to Natalia's confusion visits her daughter relatively often; Alicia's original distrust will eventually become curiosity and somewhat joy. He even starts looking after loser Sergio, who drinks and gambles too much. However, Oso's past keeps haunting him. He contacts his old boss 'El Turco', who still owes him his share of the hold-up that got him in jail; but instead of paying him, 'El Turco' suggests Oso joins in a last robbery that will make them both rich. After initially rejecting the idea, Oso decides to enroll in the job when he realizes Natalia's financial difficulties.

Critique

Genre films have always been a perfect way to address both social issues and human psychology while keeping the audience entertained. *Red Bear* is not only a good example of this, but also an interesting translation of Hollywood generic conventions into Latin American reality. If the plot and situations clearly refer to crime movies, and particularly to its noir and heist versions, the characters

Screenwriters:

Adrián Caetano
Graciela Esperanza

Cinematographer:

Willi Behnisch

Art Director:

Graciela Oderigo

Editor:

Santiago Ricci

Composer:

Diego Grimblat

Duration:

95 minutes

Genres:

Crime
Drama
Thriller

and the *mise-en-scène* ultimately derive from western films. There is a fearless gunman with a dark past behind him and his own set of ethical rules, a saloon run by a patronizing old villain (charmingly played by real-life one-armed magician René Lavand), a pathetic drunkard who makes himself laughable, an attractive woman who has left our hero but remains uncertain about her feelings, and even a dusty, solitary, ghostly town setting with wooden two-storey houses and cars instead of horses, where events develop under a pitiless sun – the suburbs of Buenos Aires, explicitly referred to by Lavand's character as the 'Far West'.

Events, which, on the other hand, take us back to the realm of noir – turbulent pasts, pending issues, last jobs, wild violence. The same can be said of the film's dry but intense direction, which aptly transfers throughout the film the inner tension of the main character to the world around him, only to effectively release that tension in a violent but consistent ending. In the smoothly shot – with an ever moving camera, à la Robert Altman – and wisely edited robbery sequence, a cross-cut from Oso's daughter's class singing the Argentinean National Anthem takes the viewer to the beginning of the film's climax. That the resulting massacre takes place to the rhythm of a national song

Adrián Caetano: *Un oso rojo/Red Bear*, 2002 © Flax Films.

Cast:

Julio Chávez
Soledad Villamil
Luis Machín

Year:

2002

that celebrates freedom, glory, and sacrifice is obviously an ironic comment on the real success of the old civilizing dream exalted by the hymn: that promise of progress that permeates Latin American history – and particularly Argentina's from Sarmiento's Facundo onwards – up to our days. As for the protagonist, however, it must be noted that his reason to resort to extreme violence is paradoxically his desire to ensure the welfare of his daughter, who is not by chance shown escorting the Argentinean flag to the mast. In this light, the peculiar ethics of the leading role, who in spite of his past is neither a cynic nor a wicked man, must be read as an individual attempt to counterbalance the political, social and economic failure of that promise. It must therefore come as no surprise that the end of the film echoes the distinguished dignity of the ruthless pioneers responsible for the mythical foundation of both America, as told in western films, and Buenos Aires, as sung by Jorge Luis Borges, rather than the tragic destiny of most crime films' protagonists.

In spite of this intelligent rendition in local terms of two paradigmatic Hollywood genres, much of the credit for the movie's appeal must be given to Chávez's beautifully restrained performance, which allows the viewer to appreciate the powerful mixture of unconditional care, unbreakable determination, controlled rage, and diffident hope that explain his behaviour. It is ultimately his ability to make the audience empathize with Oso's care-taking mission that gives sense to the film's intellectual construction.

Daniel A. Verdú Schumann

No Return

Sin retorno

Countries of Origin:

Argentina
Spain

Studios/Distributors:

Castafiore Films
Haddock Films

Director:

Miguel Cohan

Producers:

Mariela Besuievski
Geardo Herrero
Vanessa Ragone

Screenwriter:

Miguel Cohan
Ana Cohan

Synopsis

The lives of three individuals are linked and dramatically affected by two accidents in Buenos Aires on a hot summer night. In the first one, Federico Samaniego runs over the bicycle of a young man. Shortly after, Matías Faustiniano runs over the same man and leaves the scene of the crime. With the help of his wealthy parents he will cover the traces of the hit-and-run accident. Víctor, the deceased young man's father, with the support of the media, demands that the person responsible for his son's death be hunted down and punished. By a series of unfortunate coincidences Federico is linked to the scene of the crime and he is eventually arrested, goes to trial and is sent to jail, where he spends almost four years. He leaves prison with his life in ruins but with a new determination to find the real killer.

Critique

Miguel Cohan's first feature is a terse, suspenseful thriller that methodically explores the consequences of a hit-and-run accident. Like two recent Latin American masterpieces, *Amores perros* (Alejandro González-Iñárritu, 2000) and *La mujer sin cabeza/The Headless Woman* (Lucrecia Martel, 2008), this film takes a traffic accident as a powerful metaphor for showing how random events can bring powerful social and psychological undercurrents to the

Cinematographer:

Hugo Colace

Art Director:

Federico Cambero

Editor:

Fernando Pardo

Composer:

Lucio Godoy

Duration:

104 minutes

Genres:

Drama

Thriller

Cast:

Leonardo Sbaraglia
Martin Slipak
Barbara Goenaga
Federico Luppi
Luis Machín
Ana Celentano

Year:

2010

surface, changing and even destroying lives forever. The film starts in González-Iñárritu's vein, tracing the parallel paths of the three lives that will converge at a random point: the deceased man, a tattoo artist with a strong bond with his father; Federico (Leonardo Sbaraglia), the man who will pay for a crime he does not commit, a stand up comedian and ventriloquist, full of ideals and love for his family, but somewhat resentful of needing the help of his wife's wealthy father; and finally, Matías (Martin Slipak), the adolescent university student who will leave a party with a friend looking for a cocktail blender and will get distracted and run over the cyclist.

Nevertheless, we quickly realize that Cohan's intentions are much closer to Martel's work. He is not interested in the stylistic and narrative game of changing perspectives and connecting lives and destinies. He prefers to explore a tragedy affecting lives that will probably be affected sooner or later by powerful social structures and constraints. The accident's deceased victim becomes just a pawn in the public-perception game, whose case will be ferociously pursued not because of his father insistence but because the media transforms it into a test of police and prosecutorial inefficiency. Federico, accused of a crime that he did not commit, is an idealistic middle-class man, trying to make a decent living by himself, pursuing personal and family dreams that can be swept away by a random accident. Matías, on the other hand, has all the required protection from his privileged environment to survive these events. His wealthy parents discourage him when he starts having thoughts of turning himself to the police, quiet away his remorse when he sees that an innocent man will be punished, and methodically eliminate all the evidence linking him to the crime. Cohen skillfully plays all the social and ethical cards without ignoring the mechanisms that build a traditionally structured thriller, with similarities to Hitchcock's 'wrong man' films. Unlike the perpetually passive Manny Ballestrero in *The Wrong Man* (Alfred Hitchcock, 1956), Federico will emerge from jail a changed man, and the final segment of the movie becomes a revenge story. Nevertheless, Cohan surprises us again. Refusing to follow the standard path, he confronts the audience with the ethical dilemma and the social inexorabilities of this drama.

Sin retorno uses traditional cinematic resources with extreme restraint and efficiency. Especially powerful are carefully placed temporal transitions that show how much of his life Federico loses. Most scenes are elegantly arranged, for example the death of Víctor's (Federico Luppi) son at the hospital or the tense interrogation of Matías by an insurance adjuster. Ultimately, *Sin retorno* pays a quiet homage to Juan Antonio Bardem's *Muerte de un Ciclista/Death of a Cyclist* (1955), the Spanish classic film that also explored the ethical dilemmas and consequences of the hit-and-run death of a cyclist on the lives of those involved. Cohen's film has achieved international recognition and received three awards at the 2010 edition of the 'Valladolid Film Festival': the top prize or *Espiga de oro*, the Best New Director award, and the FIPRESCI award from international critics.

Javier Gutiérrez-Rexach

The signal

La señal

Countries of Origin:

Argentina
Spain

Language:

Spanish

Studio/Distributor:

Buenavista International

Directors:

Ricardo Darín
Martín Hodara

Producer:

Pablo Bossi

Screenwriter:

Eduardo Mignogna

Cinematographer:

Marcelo Camorino

Art Director:

Margarita Jusid

Editor:

Alejandro Carrillo Penovi

Composer:

Juan Ponce de León

Duration:

95 minutes

Genres:

Crime
Drama
Mystery

Cast:

Ricardo Darín
Diego Peretti
Julieta Díaz

Year:

2007

Synopsis

Buenos Aires, 1952. Private detectives Santana and Corvalán live on small cases, like following unfaithful wives and solving small rip-offs. When former safe cracker Corvalán is hired by beautiful and mysterious Gloria to trace a man who is found killed a few days later, his partner encourages him to leave the case. But Corvalán, bored with his usual assignments, cheated by his girlfriend, and fascinated by her hirer, goes on to discover she is the wife of an important gangster entangled in a violent vendetta with another crime family. Events develop rapidly and inexorably: the gangster gets killed, Gloria asks Corvalán for protection, they become lovers, and together they face her husband's gunmen. Eventually she asks him to do a last job: open his husband's safe so they can split his fortune. But things never come out as planned…

Critique

Set in Argentina in the early 1950s, *La señal* copies rather literally the dark atmosphere, twisted plots, strained situations, strong characters (particularly the stereotypical femme fatale), laconic dialogs, chiaroscuro lighting, tense music, traditional editing, lavish art production and iconic visual style of the classical Hollywood noir films of the 1940s and 1950s, from *The Maltese Falcon* (John Huston, 1941) to *The Killing* (Stanley Kubrick, 1956), to name only two, while later movies such as *The Godfather* (Francis Ford Coppola, 1972) and *Chinatown* (Roman Polanski, 1974) also come to mind during certain sequences. The feature was initially intended to be directed by Eduardo Mignogna, writer of both the novel and the screenplay, but was eventually shot by star Ricardo Darín and assistant director Martín Hodara following Mignogna's death. It would have been interesting to see how the original author would had dealt with his own mimetic hardboiled material and turned his words into images.

This must by no means be understood as a criticism on the freshmen's direction: as a matter of fact, their respect for Mignogna's archetypical script runs parallel to their ability to imitate, to the point of obsession, the aesthetics of detective films. As a result, the clichés become so evident in terms of both narrative and look that the whole movie may seem at first glance an ultimately pointless effort. A closer reading, nevertheless, suggests all three film-makers are actually performing a rather remarkable operation. In fact, like most postmodern products, the film displays subtle strategies to emphasize the distance between the copy and the original. Santana's fondness for American actors and singers and his slightly over-the-top mimicking of US private eye's attitude (for instance through the constant use of English expressions) are probably the most obvious, but not the only ones.

The employ of Eva Perón's death throes as a background for the story suggests a parallelism between the often shady Peronist regime and a criminal world that evokes Chicago's violent Roaring Twenties, a feeling of displacement emphasized by the directors' preference for medium shots and close-ups over longer shots on location.

Meanwhile, however, tango music and River Plate Spanish remind the audience that action takes place in the Southern Hemisphere. This clash between audio and video is a good example of the tension that permeates the whole picture between the imported archetype and its local version. So, while the orthodoxy of the model is kept, the boldness of the translation and the originality of the final result are opportunely underlined. And despite the fact that it never gets to the level of irony, there is undoubtedly a certain tongue-in-chick attitude in this strategy.

This perfect example of what Fredric Jameson called nostalgia film becomes then, above all, a statement about the importability and flexibility of genre conventions and their possibilities as a means to capture the spirit and mood of different stories, eras and places. In front of such an unconventional product, one would be tempted to say that this is a feature that appeals to the academic rather than to the general public. But one would be wrong: *La señal* was a huge success in its home country. As Jameson himself noted, pastiche and retro are typical mass culture products.

Daniel A. Verdú Schumann

Without name

Sin nombre

Countries of Origin:

Mexico
United States

Language:

Spanish

Studio/Distributor:

Focus Features

Director:

Cary Joji Fukunaga

Producer:

Amy Kaufman

Screenwriter:

Cary Joji Fukunaga

Cinematographer:

Adriano Goldman

Art Director:

Carlos Benassini

Editors:

Luis Carballar
Craig McKay

Synopsis

The movie begins with two plots that meet at one point. One is about Willy, called 'El Casper', who is a member of the Mexican gang Mara Salvatrucha, also known as MS 13 and of which the initiation ritual is beating up the initiate for thirteen seconds.

Since Casper has trouble with his boss, Lil Mago, he himself has to undergo the ritual again as a punishment. After a tragic incident with the girlfriend of Caspare, he and a younger homeboy have to accompany Mago on a raid on the refugees fleeing north on the roof of a train. There Caspar meets Sayra, a Honduran emigrant trying to escape to New Jersey with her father and uncle. This is the second plot: the journey from Honduras to the Mexican train roof. Casper saves Sayra from Mago and together they find shelter at an old friend of Casper's and then try to head for the US border, not knowing that Casper's 'friend' Smiley had betrayed them. The movie ends with Sayra reaching the United States alone and calling her father's family in New Jersey.

Critique

The movie is an authentic depiction of the difficult journey Central American emigrants make and, in its subplot, of the everyday life of Central American *mara* gangs. Although there is a connection between the two protagonists, the plot is not spoiled by a sentimental love story; rather, it is to the audience to judge the relationship as love or friendship. In the scenes with the *mareros* a full range of brutality is shown, but, seemingly, only to display the violence used by the gangs and the danger surrounding them, without emphasizing

Cary Joji Fukunaga: *Sin nombre/Without Name*, 2009 © with kind permission of
Roni Lubliner (NBCUniversal).

Composer:

Marcelo Zarvos

Duration:

96 minutes

Genres:

Adventure
Crime
Drama

Cast:

Paulina Gaitan
Edgar Flores
Kristyan Ferrer
Tenoch Huerta Mejía
Diana Garcia
Luis Fernando Pena
Hector Jimenez

Year:

2009

it excessively. *Sin nombre* was rated R by the MPAA for violence, language and sexual content.

On the advertising poster and the DVD cover *Sin nombre* is written with a special S and M as a symbol for Mara Salvatrucha (MS). The Mara Salvatrucha is a real gang, which originated in the suburbs of Los Angeles and has now spread over the North and Central American continent. Their members are usually marked by large tattoos of MS13 or other symbols/names, even to the point of covering their whole faces or bodies.

The effort Cary Fukanaga has put into research is visible in the quality of the movie where he worked with real immigrants. He underlines that he did not intend to change the audience's opinion on immigration, but rather to show a snapshot of Mexican immigration. *Sin nombre* does not seem to colour the truth in pursuit of authenticity nor are the characters exaggerated. They look 'normal', without extremely pretty 'Hollywood faces'. The movie has earned many prizes, including the Sundance Film Festival Award 2009.

Marlene Christine Sommer

Tony Manero

Countries of Origin:

Chile

Brazil

Language:

Spanish

Studios/Distributors:

Fábula Producciones

Prodigital

Director:

Pablo Larraín

Producer:

Juan de Dios Larraín

Screenwriters:

Alfredo Castro

Mateo Iribarren

Pablo Larraín

Cinematographer:

Sergio Armstrong

Art Director:

Pablo Larraín

Editor:

Andrea Chignoli

Composers:

José Alfredo Fuentes

Juan Cristóbal Meza

Duration:

97 minutes

Genres:

Crime

Drama

Cast:

Alfredo Castro

Paola Lattus

Héctor Morales

Amparo Noguera

Year:

2008

Synopsis

Raúl Peralta is a Chilean cabaret dancer living under Pinochet's dictatorship. Peralta is in his fifties and adores *Saturday Night Fever*'s character Tony Manero (John Badham, 1977). He is portrayed by a near-focus photography whose point of view strictly avoids any psychological or social explanation of Peralta's behaviour, which is that of a criminal. We follow Peralta with Pablo Larraín's handheld camera and its ruthless lens across the empty streets of Santiago to the empty theatre where they show *Saturday Night Fever* and where he doubles the words spoken by his idol in his broken English. We watch him fabulously dancing, displaying his impressive moves alone in his room or with his group at an improvised nightclub in Santiago's suburbs. Peralta has no problem killing three people on his way to his crowning achievement, victory on the TV contest 'Who is the best Chilean Tony Manero?' – glory that ultimately is denied him.

Critique

One essential question that emerges from this piece of original and irreverent cinema is the following: where does the character of Peralta/Manero stand relative to Chile's dictatorship? Is it possible to imagine this figure in circumstances that are not those of the totalitarian structures in South America in the 1970s? The answer is yes and no. This ambiguity will be explained in the following: on the one hand, Larraín portrays a marginal Santiago in dialogue with contemporary literary production in Chile focusing on the same urban scene – with texts by Diamela Eltit and Pedro Lemebel, for example – full of allusions to the unbearable life under dictatorship of a part of the country's inhabitants, who we barely see in the film. Theirs was a world of conspiracy, persecution and suspicion between a completely divided population, more than half of which supported Pinochet for a long time; the persistence of this support among an important segment of society may be the most dramatic scandal of post-dictatorial Chile. The film and especially Peralta (Alfredo Castro) as a kind of urban lumpen, in this sense, is extremely Chilean. Because of the way he avoids communication, the way he adores and imitates neo-liberal idols created by Hollywood, his sexual breakdowns in an uptight and machismo-dominated society, some critics want to see in Peralta a miniature dictator who terrorizes his companions and the three women around him. In this context, his tendency to see no difference between killing and dancing to get to the top is not so astonishing. He is acting as unethically as others do, and these others are those who rule the country.

On the other hand, Peralta stands for a universal 'American Psycho' without being a 'real' serial killer. He is the product of a perverted life under late globalized capitalism: Chile begins to ride on the neo-liberal wave and places itself and its products on the world market during dictatorship, leaving behind the 'Chilean way of socialism' vindicated by Salvador Allende and abolished by Pinochet's *coup d'état*, executed with a little help from Pinochet's CIA friends (of course, this is only another example of the fact that totalitarian regimes and neo-liberal economic structures are not mutually exclusive and that their contiguity is convenient for many of their main actors). In this wider sense, Peralta is an outsider who obeys 'non-symbolic' structures, staying far away from social, ideological or discursive networks that would connect him to the world he lives in. For example, he is totally indifferent to the activities of printing fliers denouncing repression and crime in his country undertaken by his cohabitants; in another sequence, he does not kill but metaphorically knocks out his cabaret show partner, because Peralta's partner also wants to participate in the television contest. Peralta enters his partner's room and literally shits on the other's pristine white Tony Manero suit. This is another of the film's sarcastic details: the reason Peralta's partner does not participate turns out not to be the suit full of shit, but rather the visit of two agents of the DINA – Pinochet's intelligence services – who concentrate all the inhabitants in the dining room and let nobody leave the house; Peralta first hides and then escapes through the window. He is pure desire, motivated by illusory mechanisms of perverted obsession: 'I will make it; I am Chile's Tony Manero, no matter what it costs'.

Pablo Larraín: *Tony Manero*, 2008 © Prodigital.

Did he plan his first murder? From his window, he observes some street boys assault an old lady, then runs down, helps her get up and takes her home. They watch a TV programme together in which Pinochet appears while the lady talks about the dictator's blue eyes, so different from the eyes of all the useless Mapuche people around. Could that comment be a reason for him to kill her with his bare hands? Or is it simply the TV set that he needs to sell? The second and third murders are more obviously planned: to get some glass bricks used in the installation of his homemade disco floor to produce some special light effects while he dances without paying, he kills the man who sold him the bricks. When he brutally kills the cinema's owners and steals the celluloid roll containing *Saturday Night Fever*, he does so because the elderly couple changed the film for another one starring John Travolta: *Grease*. In Peralta's 'non-symbolic' logic, the couple 'killed' Tony Manero, his illusory identity, and has to die for that.

We have drawn closer to the point where the two given answers could converge. The explosive mixture of dictatorship and neo-liberal economic structures creates the perverse figure of Peralta. Nevertheless, the film does not demonstrate a leftist-oriented political correctness of the type that the old socialist warhorses Miguel Littín and Patricio Guzmán stand for. Rather, it is much more an unusual portrait of a catastrophic moment of Chilean and world history. The film is certainly exceptional in Chilean cinema in recent years and has the significance of rupture that characterizes the mythical *El chacal de Nahueltoro/Jackal of Nahueltoro*, filmed by Littín in 1969, another intense portrait of a criminal emerging from the social margins. On the other side, *Tony Manero* rigorously respects a disorientating and (post)modern aesthetics: the film is comprised of fragmented, dislocated, and blurred images without any established point of view – nobody fits the pieces together or tells a coherent story. Certainly, the TV competition is the film's grotesque showdown. It is the final choreography of Peralta's breakdown whose consequences we only can imagine. He comes in second, very closely beaten by a young dancer very similar to the John Travolta in *Saturday Night Fever*, and both take the same bus on their way home. The film ends with images of Peralta's empty and exhausted face.

Wolfgang Bongers

La zona

Country of Origin:

Mexico

Language:

Spanish

Studios/Distributors:

Lulú producciones
Memento films

Director:

Rodrigo Plá

Synopsis

La zona is an exclusive area of a large Mexican city where the upper-middle class lives apart from the lower classes. It is a kind of social island, physically separated from slum neighbourhoods by a long, high wall topped with barbed wire, which protects the inhabitants from 'the others'. During a thunderstorm, a power pylon falls down onto the wall, acting as a bridge – or as a door – between the two separate universes. Three young boys from 'the other side' come inside the zone to commit a theft. Things do not go according to plan, however; they kill an old lady and two of the boys are shot dead by the guardians of the community. Though the third boy, Miguel, manages to escape from the house, it is impossible for him to escape from the zone. The zone

Producers:

Alvaro Longoria (Morena Films)
Pilar Benito
Rafael Cuervo
Ricardo Fernández-Deu

Screenwriters:

Rodrigo Plá
Laura Santullo

Cinematographer:

Emiliano Villanueva

Art Director:

Antonio Muño-Hierro

Editors:

Quique Cañadas
Laura Sánchez
Marga Villalonga

Composer:

Fernando Velázquez

Duration:

97 minutes

Genres:

Drama
Thriller

Cast:

Daniel Giménez Cacho
Marivel Verdú
Alan Chávez
Daniel Tovar

Year:

2007

has its own security guard. The rest of the movie focuses on the pursuit of Miguel, with the residents of the zone participating in the chase. Only one of them, Alejandro – a young boy like Miguel – will be capable of empathizing with and trying to save Miguel, albeit without success.

Critique

La zona, as the title proposes, is a film where the central subject is space in general. More precisely, the film is concerned with social space. The term 'zone' indicates a parcel of land within a larger space, and this is precisely what the film shows: a divided society living in separate areas without any form of communication. It is only via transgression – coming inside this protected zone – that communication can take place, in this case, more for worse than for better. The transgressors must be executed; such is the unanimous opinion of the invaded. The topics that thus interlace here are based on ideas of transgression. The initial transgression of the story, made concrete by the crime, which is motivated by social differences; a second transgression occurs in the form of prohibited community justice, i.e. the execution of the offenders motivated by revenge. The third theme concerns corruption, i.e. the police turns a blind eye to the disappearance of the three boys in return for a sum of money. The fourth theme is more positive and refers to Alejandro's empathetic attitude towards Miguel, whom he supports and tries to save.

Formally, the movie clearly shows 'the order' within the zone. This is expressed in different ways, such as the geometrical disposition of the houses and streets with impeccable gardens and the children going to school with elegant uniforms, all in the same colour. By contrast, we find 'the other side of the wall' characterized by urban chaos – bad streets, rubbish and disorder, where people dress poorly, drive old cars, and are in continuous need. Dialogue between the two sides does not exist, and when it occasionally happens, it is by accident. A *dues ex machine* permits the connection, with the fatal outcome we already know.

The movie could be characterized as a mixed genre that we could call a social thriller. It is a remarkable first film by Uruguayan-born Mexican director Rodrigo Plá, a little masterpiece. *La zona* is without doubt a film that should be related to other films with a social vision about the non-integration of certain communities in big Latin American cities. The non-solution of economic polarization that produces 'separate worlds' with an aprioristic hate between them, is narrated in films from other Latin American countries. A brilliant example is *Machuca* (2004) by Chilean director Andrés Wood. In this film, we again have a casual meeting between two social classes separated by economics, education and a river, in this case contextualized in Santiago de Chile under the socialist government of Salvador Allende. During the process of acquaintance, two schoolboys, the film's protagonists, initially meet each other with distrust. A friendship develops but is finally disrupted violently in the chaos of Pinochet's coup and the persecution the military carried out in the poorer neighbourhoods. Although the political element is not explicit in *La zona*, these two stories share many features in common.

Claudio Cifuentes-Aldunate

WOMEN CINEMA

Women Cinema can be understood in three ways: as cinema for women like romances or melodramas, as cinema about women, and as cinema directed by women as female directors. It is the latter way which is basically meant here. Most Latin American societies are dominated by patriarchal structures. The film industry was and is dominated by men. As a consequence of emancipator tendencies, since the 1980s there has not only been the so-called New Latin American Cinema but also a new boom of Women Cinema. While in Europe and the United States the female pioneers had already founded Second Wave Feminism, in Latin America some few female directors began first with small attempts, such as the first feminist film group in Venezuela called the Grupo Feminista Miércoles (Feminist Group Wednesday) which wanted to investigate the situation of women in the country. In 1981 they produced *Yo, tu, Ismaelina/I, you, Ismaelina* (1981), a 35-minute documentary about the female potters in Táchira (Venezuela) addressed to Venezuelan women with the idea to identify with the characters in the film and then to focus on their own female condition. Peter Schumann declares correctly that this interview film is a damning testimony of the oppression of women by men, a centuries-old gender role which leaves the woman no possibility for her own development. He also states that it is a film about a lack of awareness and slow awakening which also tries to establish new formal qualities. Due to this background, the women try to enter the male domain.

While most of the occupations as producer, screenwriter, cinematographer, composer or editor rest in male hands, the art director has developed to be a typical female occupation as most of them are female. However, there have been more and more female directors who began to reflect the society in their critical films about the traditional and new roles of men and women, the (misogynic) middle-class values, the facade of domestic harmony, and the repression of female desire. This new generation of female directors hardly uses, for example, the genre of classic romance that can be two-edged, suggesting to be a women genre, but often pushes the woman subversively again into the traditional role. Apparently social and socio-critically compromised films turn out to be hidden patriarchal films.

There is, however, not only a preoccupation for social issues, marginalization, violence and injustice but also a desire for experiments and new styles on the aesthetic level. As Juan Francisco González Rodríguez explains in his article in

dia Llosa: *La Teta Asustada/The Milk of Sorrow*, © Oberon/Vela/Wanda.

one of the most important online forums for Latin American cinema – *Portal del cine latinoamericano y del Caribe* (http://www.cinelatinoamericano.org/index.aspx) – the old experts of the film industry declare that there are two things to be avoided by directors: working with children and with animals. Yet, for example, Paula Markovitch, the co-screenwriter of *Temporada de patos/Duck Season* (2004), does not pay any attention to those old rules as she showed in her first feature film *El premio* (2011) where a little girl lives hidden with her mother during the military dictatorship in Argentina.

Precursors of this new women's cinema, which aims at its own aesthetic, its own memory-culture, and frequently at a subversive affect and corporeal encoding, are among others Mexico's first female film-maker Mimí Derba (*La tigresa/The Tigress* [1917]) who founded Azteca Films together with Enrique Rosas and Margot Benacerraf, whose documentary *Araya* (1959) shared the Critics Prize at Cannes with the much more known Franco-Japanese co-production *Hiroshima, Mon Amour* (1959) by Alain Resnais. Because of its novelty and importance, in 1990 the movie was elected as one of the five most important films in the history of Latin American cinema (1930–88). The Mexican film-maker Maria Novaro (*Lavaderos* [1981], *Azul celeste* 1988, *Danzón* [1991], *Sin dejar huella/Leaving No Trace* [2000], *Las buenas hierbas/The Good Herbs* [2009]) supports a women's cinema of emotions, and the famous Argentine film-maker Maria Luisa Bemberg (1922–95) became known primarily through the screening of the life of the Sister Juana Inés de la Cruz in *Yo, la peor de todas/I, the Worst of All* (1990), but has been an active film-maker since the early 1970s. With the last film she seemed to focus on new themes apart from the emancipation of the woman as the general right to liberty and difference (Lucía Puenzo will continue this line).

Among the most important countries producing women's cinema are undoubtedly Argentina, Mexico and Brazil, which all possess an extensive film tradition. Peru and Chile add their own innovative women's cinema to this list as well. With three internationally known women film-makers such as Lucrecia Martel (*La ciénaga/The Swamp* [2001], *La niña santa/The Holy Girl* [2004], *Mujer sin cabeza/The Headless Woman* [2008]), Lucía Puenzo (*XXY* [2007], *El niño pez/The Fish Child* [2009]), and Albertina Carri (*Los rubios/The Blonds* [2003]), Argentina has taken a leading position.

The nomadic movie *The Blonds*, in which the film-maker launches the search for evidence of her disappeared parents during the military dictatorship, can be read as a filmic blueprint of a subjective memory-culture, developed in the form of a docufiction. In this movie, Carri employs a refined intermedial aesthetic, which establishes tensioned relationships between image and text. Therefore, the film mixes, for example, letters written to their daughter by her parents during the first months of their imprisonment and enables the active participation of the spectators to the memory quest and search for the vanished victims of the dictatorship. Through this technique, Carri's film and, in a similar manner, Lucretia Martel's films, which are internationally known, can be described as a search for a new aesthetic of the political in the film medium.

Lucrecia Martel's cinema can be understood as political post-Catholic, anti-redemption cinema, revealing the corruption and decadence of the Argentine middle class through a deconstructivist gesture. Her cinema is a way of remembering Argentina's political history on screen and as a consequence, particulary in *The Holy Girl* and *The Headless Woman*, the perspectives of the spectator and of the perpetrator merge. Martel's three masterworks will thus become an integral part of national and international film history. The search for identity and the culture of memory between indigenous, Christian, and profane corporeal performances construct the filmic matrix of her sensual cinema, which also develops the mentioned aesthetic of the political.

Lucía Puenzo's subversive cinema, which focuses on intimate communication in the family, addresses the search for a sexual identity that deliberately denies clear-cut judgments. In her film *XXY*, which focuses on the theme of hermaphroditism beyond the habitual norms, the film-maker asks for the right to a dual sexual identity from the perspective of the young Alex, who, against his parents' wishes, does not want to adopt a strictly defined sexual identity. In this context, Puenzo states in an interview with Viviana Rangil (2005) that what she finds most interesting about this story is the question, which a lot of hermaphrodites ask: why does the whole world wait for him to fit in its categories, why does not the world adapt to himself. Consequently, Puenzo's film refuses to adopt a clear-cut position on a singular sexual identity, and can be understood as a plea for the right to a hermaphrodite identity.

Among the most successful women directors of the contemporary Mexican film certainly are Dana Rotberg (*Intimidad/Intimacy* 1989, *Ángel del Fuego(Angel of Fire* 1991), Busi Cortés (*El secreto de Romelia/Romelia's Secret* 1988, *Serpientes y escaleras/Snakes and Ladders* 1991) and María Novaro (*Lola* 1989, *Danzón* 1991, *El jardín del Edén/The Garden of Eden* 1994). While Novaro produces a feminine cinema of emotions, which addresses the analysis and display of feminine vulnerability and focuses on the female condition in Mexico and the struggle of the woman for national survival, Rotberg focuses on a subversive construction of feminine pleasure invoking pornographic strategies, and displays a production of sexuality beyond the normalizing discourses of conventional cinema. Busi Cortés, on the other hand, situates herself in a classic feminist tradition and screens feminine complicity as the fundamental theme of her cinema.

An illustrative example of the new feminine cinema in Brazil is the film-maker Suzana (Tata) Amaral whose movies, such as *A hora da estrela /Hour of the Star* (1985) – based on the novel of Clarice Lispector (1977) –, *Através de janela/ Through the window* (2000), and *Antônia/Antonia* (2006) focus often on the feminine experience in São Paulo, screening diverse ethnic and social backgrounds from the favelas to the middle class. Poverty, violence and racism are the obstacles against which the protagonists from the favelas in *Antonia* fight and which they attempt to surpass through new identity constructions in media such as hip hop and rap.

Chile has also produced internationally known women directors, the youngest being those such as Elisa Eliash with her first feature film *Mami te amo/I Love You Mum* (2007) and Alicia Scherson. In her two movies *Play* (2005) and *Turistas/Tourists* (2009), Scherson develops a nomadic cinema, which screens the identity search of feminine figures coming from different social backgrounds.

The Peruvian woman film-maker Claudia Llosa (*Madeinusa* [2006], *La teta asustada/ The Milk of Sorrow* [2009]) provides an outstanding example for current discussions related to feminine memory-culture. Similar to Lucrecia Martel's *The Holy Girl*, Llosa's film *Madeinusa* constructs the intimate experience of a young girl trapped in the conflict between her own erotic desires and Catholic chastity vows during Easter week. As a conflict-laden negotiation between indigenous and Catholic strategies of discourse, the movie can subsequently be described using post-colonial theorems. Llosa has achieved her international breakthrough with *The Milk of Sorrow*, for which she was rewarded with a Golden Bear at the 'Berlinale'. Llosa uses here the filmic medium to screen Peruvian war and terrorism memories and shows how the traumatic experience of rape is inscribed in the body of female figures.

Some of the newest films of 2011 are *Asalto al cine* by Iria Gómez Concheiro, *El chico que miente* by Marité Ugás, *El lugar más pequeño* by Tatiana Huezo Sánchez, *Paraísos Artificiales* by Yulene Olaizola and *Trabalhar Cansa/Hard Labor* by Juliana Rojas/Marco Dutra.

Finally, the change in attitudes to gender relations is evidenced not only by the growing number of female directors. Even many male film-makers strive to offer

Alicia Scherson: *Turistas/Tourists*, 2009 © 20th Century Fox.

more differentiated images away from traditional stereotypes, such as whore and saint, defenseless victim or militant heroine. The questioning and shaking and chumming up of the stereotypes are not only valuable for the representation of women but also for the male image (cf. Bremme 2000).

The consciousness of the female situation was and is also expound in various films by male directors such as Paul Leduc, Jaime Humberto Hermosillo, Walter Salles, Iván Sanjinés and Humberto Solás (see the list of films related with women at the end of the manual). In conclusion, Women's Cinema in Latin America tests new forms of aesthetic perception and reveals through this very gesture film also as a medium of aesthetics of politics. The central renewal impulses of the film aesthetics stem nowadays from Latin American Women's Cinema.

Uta Felten and Isabel Maurer Queipo

The Blonds

Los Rubios

Country of Origin:

Argentina

Language:

Spanish

Studio/Distributor:

Barry Ellsworth

Director:

Albertina Carri

Producer:

Barry Ellsworth

Screenwriter:

Albertina Carri

Cinematographer:

Catalina Fernández

Editor:

Alejandra Almirón

Composers:

Charly García
Ryuchi Sakamoto
Gonzalo Córdoba

Duration:

89 minutes

Genre:

Documentary

Cast:

Analía Couceyro
Albertina Carri
Santiago Giralt
Jesica Suárez
Marcelo Zanelli

Year:

2003

Synopsis

On 24 February 1977, when political activists Roberto Carri and Ana María Caruso were kidnapped and then made to disappear by the military junta of General Jorge Rafael Videla, their daughter had only just turned three. From that moment on, Albertina Carri's life was affected by the irreparable absence of her parents. Twenty-five years later, Carri decided to make *The Blonds*, a documentary that focuses on this black period in the history of Argentina. The film is made from the point of view of a generation that had to cope with mourning, orphanage and uncertainty. Accompanied by the film's technical team, Carri travels around the province of Buenos Aires in search of information that might shed some light on the violent and suspicious disappearance of her parents. However, her relatives, her parents' former political colleagues and neighbours are unable to help. Her disappointment prompts Carri to use her imagination and creativity to reflect on the distortions of memory and the inevitable weight of obscurity in all reconstructions of the past. Carri's fractured universe consists of childhood fantasies recreated with Playmobil figures, an actress who plays her in some scenes and blond wigs that she uses to disguise herself.

Critique

The Blonds is Albertina Carri's (Buenos Aires, b.1973) second feature film and the one that has caused the most controversy among cinema critics both in Argentina and abroad. Indeed, while one sector of public opinion regarded the documentary as a new and vital look at the country's recent past, another branded it as a frivolous and irreverent treatment of the memory of the dictatorship. The reason for this divergence of opinion lies not only in the formal and narrative complexity of the film but also in the critical position that its director adopts with respect to witnesses and the possibility of determining the unambiguous truth about what happened at that time.

    The Blonds can be defined in many different ways: it is at once a political documentary, a recording of the process of filming a documentary, a cinematic self-portrait and a meta-documentary. What ever else it might be, Carri's film is undoubtedly a journey through various states of memory and a reflection on the difficulty of finding a uniform narrative about the past. Unlike other studies made of the dictatorship, Carri's documentary makes no attempt to paint a biographical portrait of those who laid down their lives for the revolutionary cause. Since she was so young when her parents were kidnapped, Carri has no real memory of them; this natural amnesia, in conjunction with her fantasies about her parents, leads her to focus the film not from their point of view but from her own. In this regard, the scenes featuring Playmobil figures are significant: filmed using the stop-motion technique, these fictionalized memories evoke events between the time Carri spent on her uncle and aunt's farm and her parents' kidnapping, the latter of which she portrays as if they had been abducted by extraterrestrials.

The documentary is structured around Carri's voice and her presence in front of the camera, but it also features Analía Couceyro, an actress who co-stars with the film-maker and who even plays her in some scenes. Couceyro, in her role as Carri, interviews most of the witnesses in the film and their words are subsequently shown on cold monitors, thus relativizing the significance that they might have in other contexts. The most fictional part of the film are the colour scenes in which Analía plays Carri. These are combined with other black-and-white scenes in which the real film-maker makes an appearance to give the actress instructions about how to play the role. Carri's intrusion into the inner space of her film not only shows that any attempt to record history involves a certain amount of pretence, but also that she has no intention of providing the absolute truth about her family's history. By falsifying reality by using actors as well as by disguise and animation with Playmobil figures, Carri manages to stage an impossibility, a failure, an absence. In other words, she calls on a tirelessly different identity: Albertina projects herself on Analía and Analía on Albertina, in a sort of masked dance over which hangs the long and tragic shadow of disappearance.

Laia Quílez Esteve

Danzón

Countries of Origin:

Mexico
Spain

Language:

Spanish

Studios/Distributors:

Fondo de Fomento a la Calidad
Cinematográfica
Gobierno del Estado de
Veracruz
IMCINE

Director:

María Novaro

Producers:

Jorge Sánchez
Dulce Kuri
Miguel Necoechea

Screenwriters:

Beatriz Novaro
María Novaro

Cinematographer:

Rodrigo García

Art Director:

Marissa Pecanins

Synopsis

Julia Solórzano, a telephone operator and middle-aged single mother living in Mexico City, relishes her weekly routine of danzón in the 'Salon Colonia'. For the last six years she has always danced with the same dance partner, Carmelo, whom she barely knows despite the many awards they have won together. When Carmelo mysteriously disappears, Julia decides to look for him. Her quest leads her to Veracruz, where she makes friends with a motherly hotel manager, a prostitute and the drag queen Suzy. After Suzy's advice to 'feminize' her appearance, Julia becomes more self-confident and has an affair with a much younger man. Although she does not find Carmelo during her journey, she ends up finding a new self. Back in Mexico City, she returns to the 'Salon', where Carmelo asks her for a dance.

Critique

Julia's (María Rojo) life in Mexico City echoes Novaro's early documentaries about the lives of working-class women, when she was part of the feminist film-making group 'Cine Mujer'. Made by a woman, featuring mainly women and for a predominantly female audience, Danzón has often been described as a 'feminist film'. Julia seems to avoid men of her age and most of her contacts are women. The three men that appear are somehow no 'threat'. The transvestite Suzy, refers to herself as a woman and Julia seems to see her as such, her young lover could be her son (she is actually older than his mother) and Carmelo (Daniel Regis) could be her father. However, many feminists criticize the conventional plot. The danzón, in which 'the man seduces' and 'the woman shines', is a metaphor of the past and of a patriarchal order. The fact that the film ends where it

Editors:

María Novaro
Nelson Rodríguez
Sigfrido Barjau

Composers:

Felipe Pérez
Pepe Luis
Agustín Lara
Consuelo Velázquez

Duration:

120 minutes

Genre:

Drama

Cast:

María Rojo
Carmen Salinas
Tito Vasconcelos

Year:

1991

began could be seen as a return to rigid social boundaries, a failed coming-of-age story. An alternative reading focuses on Julia's change in behaviour. While she was passive and timid in the beginning, she smiles and flirts with Carmelo after her trip to Veracruz. In addition, the band dedicates the last song of the film to her; she is singled out and opens the dance. Whereas the camera was focused on the feet in the opening scenes, it concentrates on the faces, e.g. on Carmelo's smile and Julia's tender gaze, in the closing scenes, as if the dance had suddenly changed from a rigid choreography to something more personal, intimate and sensual. Romy Sutherland calls Novaro's style a 'rhetoric of ambiguity' and refers to the ideological complexity of her characters, the construction of images and the plot development. Despite the misleading title, *Danzón* is not a typical dance film; it plays with several genres and has lengthy sequences of very long shots. This film is slow and linear, just like the dance itself, an homage to the past and to local music, reminiscent of older popular Mexican movies. Most of the dancers are in their sixties or older and the atmosphere is non-sexual and respectful. In Veracruz, the camera dwells upon lush panoramas, the harbour with its fresh sea air and other similar places, somehow foreshadowing Julia's blossoming and self-discovery. Nevertheless, Novaro does not change her slow rhythm when Julia breaks free from social conventions, her maternal and professional roles; the editing does not become faster despite her new interesting, mostly younger acquaintances. An homage to the past, to national folklore, and to several film classics of Mexican cinema, *Danzón* is a film that seems to resist modernization.

Heidi Denzel de Tirado

The Fish Child

El niño pez

Country of Origin:

Argentina

Language:

Spanish

Studios/Distributors:

Historias Cinematográficas, S.A.
Wanda Visión, S.A.
MK2 Productions

Director:

Lucía Puenzo

Producers:

Luis Puenzo
José María Morales

Synopsis

'The Fish Child' tells the love story between Lala, the young upper-class daughter of Judge Brönte, and Guayi, the Paraguayan maid of twenty years who has worked in the house since she was a child. Both women have been stealing for some time the paintings and the jewels of the family in order to raise enough money to allow them to escape to the town where Guayi comes from and where they plan to live in a home of their own next to the lagoon Ypoá. But the relationship that unites the two women is torn apart when Lala discovers that her father takes advantage of Guayi – occasionally raping her. Desperately jealous, she decides to commit suicide, but it is her own father who ends up drinking the glass of poisoned milk. After being a passive witness to the death of her father, Lala heads to Paraguay where she wants to wait for her lover. There she will discover, however, another story of legend and crime. Guayi's father, the famous soap opera star Socrates Espina, made his daughter pregnant when she was just 13 years old. Not knowing what to do with the baby, she drowned it in the lagoon and then escaped to Buenos Aires. In Paraguay Lala receives the notice that Guayi has been accused of the murder of her father, so she decides to return to give herself up to the police. After a visit to the women's correctional facility where Guayi is kept, she

Screenwriter:

Lucía Puenzo

Cinematographer:

Rodrigo Pulpeiro

Art Director:

Mercedes Alfonsín

Editor:

Hugo Primero

Composers:

Andrés Goldstein
Daniel Tarrab
Laura Zisman

Duration:

96 minutes

Genres:

Drama
Romance
Thriller

Cast:

Inés Efron
Emme
Pep Munné
Arnaldo André
Carlos Bardem

Year:

2009

suspects something strange is going on. Together with Guayi´s friend, Vasco, they discover that the young women are prostituted overnight at private parties organized by the commissioner Pulido and together decide on a rescue operation.

Critique

In the latest film since her debut as screenwriter and director in XXY (2007) where she tells the tragedy of Alex, an intersexual teenager (Goya Award, 2008), Lucía Puenzo once again demonstrates a highly transgressive affinity in her choice of subject. In The Fish Child, based on her own novel of the same name, Puenzo passes from an idea of androgyny to that of lesbian love. But in this latest film it is not only the transgression of generic taboos that might scandalize the more conservative in Argentina, but the love between two social classes that are at odds: Lala (Inés Efron), a private school student and daughter of a wealthy Buenos Aires family of European ancestry, falls in love with the almost adolescent maid, Ailín (or as called in the house: Guayi) (Mariela 'Emme' Vitale), a brunette descendant of the Guaraní who has escaped from a past of poverty, abuse and loneliness. Although their origins could not be more different, both women share the pain of coming from families destroyed by drugs or sexual perversion. The love between them is based on an exchange between two culturally distinct worlds: Lala understands neither Guaraní nor the brash behaviour of her friend on the dance floor; Guayi prefers to protect her friend from the real world and to tell her wonderful stories to hide her own unspeakable secrets.

Among the aspects of melodrama, thriller and road movie, the film tells a story of love and vengeance. The crime that Guayi had suffered as a child by being raped by her father will be revenged years later by Lala who, discovering that her own father is abusing Guayi as well, allows her father to unwittingly commit suicide with her own glass of poisoned milk. Meanwhile, Guayi also carries the burden of her own crime: the death of her son is so unbearable that she begins to invent fantastical stories full of magic in which she transforms her own dead infant into the Mítã'í Pira, a divinity of all drowned souls who protects children.

Along the roads heading from Asunción to Buenos Aires and back, the girls are looking for a habitable place far away from evil, where they can realize their love. In the terrestrial world, however, full of inequality, slander and exploitation, their love is an impossible one. It might, perhaps, become possible near the lagoon inhabited by Mítã'í Pira, where the villagers have long been leaving offerings at an old tree half submerged under water. Reminiscent of a Greek myth, in which the dog Cerberus guards the gates of the underworld, it is a dog here too, the aptly named Seraphim (a present given to Lala by Guayi), which guides the girls on their journey to the underwater realm beyond the real world. It is also a pack of hounds, trained by the character Vasco (Diego Velázquez), who will save Guayi from the world of forced prostitution, in an ending somewhat typical of an urban western.

The graphics in the title, cut in half simulating a water surface, indicates that the story takes place at the edge between two worlds:

Photo: Sebastián Puenzo

Lucía Puenzo: *El niño pez/The Fish Child*,
2009 © Sebastián Puenzo with friendly authorization.

reality and fiction. There are also two essential metaphors that structure the film in a double system and give both an atmosphere of lyricism and magic. One is water, present not only in the lagoon Ypoá but also in the numerous love scenes that take place in the bathroom. It is in the bathtub where Guayi gives birth to her child and it is when the two women are bathing in the tub that they imagine the house they will inhabit together one day.

Finally, discovering that Guayi has been imprisoned for her own crime, it is in the tub where Lala, in act of love towards her partner, will violently cut off her long, blonde hair – a symbol of the upper class in Argentina. As if it were the primordial liquid of all life, water is a metaphor for universal love and utopia. Another element contributing to the climate of surrealism of the film are the scenes of awakening. As hinges between wakefulness and sleep, they mark the passing of time within the film, which progresses in a broken narrative, slowly approaching death. In the first scene of the film we see Lala awakening after having killed her father with poisoned milk. In the same manner and just before discovering the story about pregnancy and abandonment of his daughter by Socrates Espina (Arnaldo André), Lala awakens with a figure of the fish child Mítã'í Pira in her hand. This gives her the idea that perhaps the underwater realm she has dreamt of really does exist. The real melts with the dream and the dream permits the characters to escape from the real.

But perhaps the most interesting aspect of the film by Lucía Puenzo, daughter of the famous Argentine film-maker Luis Puenzo, is not so much the Oedipal relationship of love, hate and crime among parents and children, but the sarcastic rewriting of a television genre which all girls of their generation grew up with: the soap opera. The film builds a narrative product that diverges from the classic archetypes of the genre, but keeps the multiplicity of interconnected storylines and the melodrama carried to the point of paroxysm. Instead of being the maid who falls for a handsome and wealthy young man, here it is the apparently good family teenager who falls in love with the maid. The instance of evil, often embodied in the television series by a wicked mother or a jealous rival woman, is here embodied by the male face of the law: Guayi's abusers and the triggers of the tragedy are Lala's father – a judge of the Republic (Pep Munné) – and the corrupt commissioner Pulido (Carlos Bardem). Finally, the fairy tale that often inspires the soap operas has nothing to do with the European *Cinderella* or *Snow White* here. *The Fish Child*, which incidentally could well be the title of a marvellous tale from Latin America, falls back on pre-Columbian myths and songs and legends of mermaids to rescue the lovers from the distorted real world. Together the women will head for the underwater place Guayi invented, where they hope to find a happy ending, 'swimming together to the bottom', even if that ending is very different from most fairy tales.

Karen Saban

Frida

Countries of Origin:

Canada
Mexico
United States

Studio/Distributor:

Miramax

Director:

Julie Taymor

Producers:

Jay Polstein
Lizz Speed
Nancy Hardin
Linday Flickinger
Roberto Sneider

Screenwriters:

Diane Lake
Gregory Nava
Ann Thomas

Cinematographer:

Rodrigo Prieto

Art Director:

Bernardo Trujillo

Synopsis

Based on the Kahlo biography by Hayden Herrera, *Frida* depicts the central highlights of the life and work of Frida Kahlo: it begins with Kahlo painting as a teenager, tied to a bed due to a bus accident. In search of an artistic mentor she meets the Mexican painter Diego Rivera whom she comes to know and love. During her subsequent marriage to Rivera, Kahlo, in light of her husband's open affairs, is initially jealous, but soon comes to terms with the situation and makes new acquaintances from the artistic milieu surrounding her husband. At the invitation of Nelson Rockefeller, she accompanies the now internationally prominent Rivera on a trip to the United States. Both artists become disillusioned with the political climate there and after the removal of Rivera's mural depicting Lenin from the Rockefeller Center, they return home. Back in Mexico, the marriage is shattered by Rivera's affair with Frida's sister Cristina. Frida turns her back on Rivera. A short time later, the couple receives the opportunity to provide Trotsky with shelter, resulting in an affair between Kahlo and Trotsky. At the invitation of Andre Breton, Kahlo travels to Paris, where the first exhibition of her work takes place. Kahlo's subsequent love affairs lead her to divorce her husband Rivera, then to the reconciliation and another wedding following soon after. The rapid decline in Kahlo's health is associated with an intense artistic creative phase, which lasts until her death.

Critique

Considered to be in the genre of biopics (biographical pictures), the movie is a Hollywood production that draws on Mexican cultural

Editor:

Françoise Bonnot

Composer:

Elliot Goldenthal

Duration:

124 minutes

Genres:

Biography
Drama
Romance

Cast:

Salma Hayek
Alfred Molina
Antonio Banderas
Valeria Golino
Ashley Judd
Mia Maestro
Edward Norton
Geoffrey Rush

Year:

2002

symbols, striving for creative, intense and self-sufficient imagery. So, we find in the dream sequences the use of 3D live painting animation technology that was still relatively new in 2002. Famous paintings and designs from Kahlo's work create very intensely coloured *tableaux vivants*. On the one hand there are those moving paintings of the film that refer to a surrealist aesthetic image, which was often attributed to Kahlo's work, although she herself rejected this. On the other hand, there is the reliance on symbols of Mexican culture, such as the Mexican *Día de los muertos* (Day of the Dead), from which she borrowed the skeletal animation characters, in order to create an atmospheric authenticity and eye-popping originality. This is closely based, at least formally, on Kahlo's image motifs.

Nevertheless, the film is historically rooted in Hollywood's film industry with its reproduction of current stereotypes about Mexico and Latin America. A key element of these stereotypes is a colourful exoticism that draws on popular notions of gender with the opulently dressed, singing and dancing Latina of Hollywood cinema in the 1930s and 1940s. (That cliché was portrayed, for example, by the Mexican actress Lupe Vélez.) Such exoticism projected on Kahlo is combined with the picture formed by Herrera's artist biography of a Kahlo excessively influenced by intense physical pain and sensual passion. Its cultural *otherness* in the form of an artistically, fashionably, physically and sexually exceptional personality is repeatedly enhanced by the cinematic imagery. Accordingly, Kahlo's homoerotic liaisons or her critical attitude towards capitalism are in no way excluded in the film. Rather, they serve to emphasize Kahlo's unconventionality and her difference, and thus again her personal and artistic exoticism. This happens for example when Kahlo, after she kisses the Italian photographer Tina Modotti, supposedly takes a strong swig from a bottle of Tequila. Or when the painting *Alla cuelga mi vestido/My dress hangs there* (1933), in which Kahlo's colourful and folkloric Tehuana dress is seen, stands out vibrantly against the bleak urban winter landscape of New York. This film also suggests an – albeit fictional – historicization of the origins of individual paintings. This leads to the same claims of historical authenticity, which Herrera's biography of Kahlo also claims for itself. It should not however, prevent us from seeing that Herrera's biography also contributed to form the dominant picture on which the phenomenon of Kahlo as an icon (of fashion, feminism) is substantially based. The film reinforces Kahlo's iconic character for its part, but attempts to lighten its narrative gravity with humour and entertainment value. For example, this happens in Kahlo's mind when she envisions Diego Rivera terrorizing New York as King Kong. In addition, the aesthetics of the film based on the innovative technical processes are also the basis of the public appeal of the film in the United States and Europe, whilst in Latin America – albeit being a US-American/Mexican co-production – it was critically received.

Beatrice Schuchardt

The Headless Woman

La mujer sin cabeza

Country of Origin:

Argentina

Language:

Spanish

Studios/Distributors:

El Deseo
D.A.S.L.U.
Teodora Film

Director:

Lucrecia Martel

Producers:

Pedro Almodóvar
Agustín Almodóvar
Esther García
Verónica Cura
Enrique Piñeyro
Lucrecia Martel

Screenwriter:

Lucrecia Martel

Cinematographer:

Bárbara Álvarez

Art Director:

María Eugenia Sueiro

Editor:

Miguel Schverdfinger

Composer/Sound Recordist:

Guido Berenblum

Duration:

87 minutes

Genres:

Drama
Mystery
Thriller

Cast:

María Onetto
Claudia Cantero
Inés Efrón
Daniel Genoud
César Bordon

Synopsis

Accident, hit-and-run, crime and effacement of the crime construct the filmic matrix of the movie, which tells the story of a neurotic female protagonist of the Argentine middle class who runs over a living being at the very beginning of the movie. Using the patterns of the classic thriller, the film unfolds revealing that the victim was an indigenous boy. While the female protagonist falls into a state of torpor, the male members of the family begin to efface the criminal act so efficiently that in the end she seems to acquire a new identity.

Critique

The Argentine film-maker Lucrecia Martel, who has become an internationally renowned film director of the Nuevo Cine Argentino with already two films *La ciénaga/The Swamp* (2001) and *La niña santa/The Holy Girl* (2004), screens with *The Headless Woman* once more the perspective of a female protagonist of the Argentine middle-class.

The movie shows numerous analogies to Martel's previous works. In the centre of the filmic attention is, as in the two previous movies of the so-called Salta-trilogy, the Argentine province La Salta, inhabited by a corrupt middle class and an indigenous population subservient and deprived of any rights.

Quoting filmic references from Alfred Hitchcock, Michelangelo Antonioni and David Lynch, the nervous breakdown of the protagonist is skillfully constructed. Close-ups reflecting the subjective perspective, the chromatic composition of the costumes, and the focus on the emotional vacuum of the protagonist constitute the main features of the filmic construction. In *The Headless Woman*, the film-maker succeeds again in rendering visible the political subtext in the aesthetics of the film as well as in drawing a critical portrayal of the corruption of the Argentine middle class.

International critics have acknowledged the latent nuance of the film and have interpreted it as a subtle cinema that commemorates the *desaparecidos* during the Argentine dictatorship of the 1970s. In this sense, the use of the song from the 1970s titled 'Mamy Blues' to which the female protagonist listens during a car accident, is not fortuitous. With this acoustic coding of the accident, the hit-and-run, the murder cover-up of the indigenous young boy Aldo, and the disappearance of his dead body implicitly refers to the atrocities committed by the Argentine military dictatorship during the 1970s and to the numerous disappeared victims, whose destiny is unknown even today. Lucretia Martel has underlined the political subtext of the film in numerous personal commentaries. The concealed crime, the guilt of murdering an innocent person carried by the female protagonist, is comparable to the guilt of numerous people during the Argentine dictatorship of the 1970s, as the defenselessness of the victims is equally comparable to the defenselessness of the poor and socially deprived of the contemporary era:

Lucrecia Martel: *La mujer sin cabeza/The Headless Woman*, 2008 © EL DESEO, D.A., S.L.U./María Gowland, Silvia Jänkel.

Guillermo Arengo
María Vaner

Year:

2008

The woman is going to carry this on her back of bones forever. In Argentina, I see people who still carry the weight of the really bad stuff that they did not denounce back when it happened under the dictatorship. [...] The same mechanism that we used in the past to ignore the suffering of others is still present today. (Lucrecia Martel, cited in Jubis 2010: 95)

Jubis identifies *The Headless Woman* as a 'political move', as a political turning point in Lucretia Martel's film career and underlines the socially critical tone of the film: 'I called it Martel's political move. Indeed, the film bracingly lays bare the mechanism by which the rich exercise their political power' (Jubis 2010: 96). One of the most interesting innovations of the film is its uncommon point of view, the perspective of the perpetrator. The spectator would want to distance himself or herself from the female protagonist and to prevent the identification with the villain's viewpoint. At the same time, the camera forces the spectator to identify with the perpetrator's perspective. Through this technique, the spectator becomes 'mujer sin cabeza', the 'headless woman' who ignores the pain of others and who covers up the committed crime. Amy Taubin underlines Martel's inconvenient invitation, which forces the spectator to identify with the perpetrator's perspective. This invitation cannot be easily avoided and thus summons the viewer not to look the other way:

> If, however, we resist Martel's invitation to identify, it is not simply because Vero is an unlikeable character or that we are ignorant of Argentine society. Rather, it is that we are all, to one degree or another, headless woman. I would not leave a dog or a child to die alone in the road, but the suffering I turn my back on every day is beyond measure. (Taubin 2009: 21–22)

Uta Felten

The Holy Girl

La niña santa

Countries of Origin:

Argentina
Spain
Italy

Language:

Spanish

Studios/Distributors:

Lita Stantic Producciones S.A.
El deseo D. A. y S. L. U.
Sanso

Director:

Lucrecia Martel

Producer:

Matías Mosteirín

Screenwriter:

Lucrecia Martel

Cinematographer:

Félix Monti

Art Director:

Graciela Oderigo

Editor:

Santiago Ricci

Composer:

Andrés Gerszenzon

Duration:

106 minutes

Synopsis

The erotic and spiritual desires of the teenager Amalia constitute the centre of the film's plot. In a mystical transfiguration, they are directed sometimes towards the divine bridegroom, sometimes towards the best girlfriend, and lastly towards an uptight doctor and patriarch who acts out his secret desires in the anonymous crowd, wants to use Amalia as an anonymous object of his sexual arousal, and becomes increasingly, against his will, the target of her freshly awakened erotic feelings.

The conflicts deliberately staged in the film grow to be more visible when the doctor, a guest in the hotel run by Amalia's family, becomes increasingly the pivotal point of Amalia's mother and Amalia's own erotic desire, while her best friend threatens to disclose the sexual secret of the stranger.

Critique

With her second feature film, the Argentine film-maker has produced another masterwork complementing her resounding success with *La ciénaga/The Swamp* (2001), which received an award, presented in competition at the 'Berlinale 2001'. The title of the movie can be read as an ironic play on words. The movie screens more the erotic desires of the youngest daughter than her mystical aspirations, even though the beginning of the film frames the latter in a virtuosic manner. The opening sequence shows a group of teenagers during a religious education class while they recite the mystical poetry of Saint Teresa of Avila and during the confession of religious experiences. Therefore, as in *The Swamp*, a post-Catholic, deconstructivist gesture dominates the narrative. After the realization of the two adolescent girls that every form of religious and mystical experience is impossible, they focus on their own and mutual erotic desires. As previously seen in *The Swamp*, Martel uses an aesthetic practice of modern cinema, as conceptualized by French philosopher Gilles Deleuze, which focuses not on action but on the sensual experience of the protagonist. The primacy of the haptic sense can be understood as a decoding of the

Lucrecia Martel: *La Niña santa/The Holy Girl*, 2004 © EL DESEO, D.A., S.L.U./Ivana Salfity.

Genre:

Drama

Cast:

Mercedes Morán
Carlos Belloso
Alejandro Urdapilleta
María Alché
Julieta Zylberberg

Year:

2004

classical hierarchy of senses. Sensual bodies in water, extensive hair combing, the tender contacts between the two friends, as well as the perverse touch of a hotel guest who reveals himself to be a hypocrite patriarch, are highlights of haptic experiences, which also actively involve the spectator. Martel uses here a refined *mise en abyme* of the voyeur situation, through which she places the spectator as the voyeur of the voyeur and confronts the spectator to the perpetuator's perspective.

As in *The Swamp*, the protagonists are not primarily agents, but visual and haptic filters, seeing and feeling agents who are exposed to optical and erotic temptation. The aesthetic of modern cinema, which Martel deliberately promotes, also suggests the abandonment of a filmic resolution in a closed form. Therefore, the end of the movie remains open. The question whether Amalia will start a scandal and reveal the unauthorized touch of the hotel guest, who at the same time is a hypocrite patriarch, or if she will shelter the secret of his perverse desire remains unanswered. Thus, the film also invites a sociological-political reading that exposes the hypocrisy of the Catholic nuclear family, which experiences its lust only in secret and whose survival is based on the silence of the victim. The critics, such as Eva-Lynn Jagoe and John Cant, have labelled Martel's film *The Holy Girl*, as an example of a post-Catholic cinema, inaugurating a screening of the corporeal beyond the established Catholic norms. They underline in *El cine argentino de hoy: entre el arte y la política* (2007) that Martel herself proposes that a post-Catholic culture of the body is possible. Amalia is the character who embodies this concept of a liberated culture of desire, while her mother and the uptight hotel guest, the patriarch Jano, further persist in the structures of a repressive, Catholic-based culture of repression. Jagoe and Cant continue, maintaining that 'the girl's progress towards a more human culture contrasts with the confusions and sufferings of her parents' generation, who struggle with the contradictions inherent to their traditional culture and their authoritarian, irrational, and guilt-ridden visions of love' (Jagoe and Cant 2007: 170).

The experience of a post-Catholic corporeal culture is revealed to the spectator through Martel's strategies of a cinema of the senses, a cinema that foregrounds the sensual perception of the body and haptic elements. Consequently, the film ends on this note with the sensual-erotic scene of the swimming pool, in which the two friends Josefina and Amalia are shown in a moment of joyful and liberated eroticism. Oscar Jubis detects that 'Amalia smiles broadly, thrilled to see her friend. Her face has never registered such joy and warmth before' and that 'the girls float on their backs, swimming slowly, enjoying each other's company, and the smell of orange blossoms' (Jubis 2010: 73).

Uta Felten

Madeinusa

Countries of Origin:

Peru
Spain

Languages:

Spanish
Quechua

Studios/Distributors:

Oberón Cinematográfica
Vela Producciones
Wanda Visión

Director:

Claudia Llosa

Producers:

Antonio Chavarrías
Claudia Llosa
José María Morales

Synopsis

The inhabitants of the small village of Manayaycuna in the Peruvian Andes are convinced that God is dead and everything is allowed between Good Friday and Easter Sunday. Their Easter festival therefore always turns into an orgy, during which a number of sins are committed. Fourteen-year-old Madeinusa is elected Immaculate Virgin for this year's festival, which is a great honour, but she also knows that her father, mayor of the little village, wants to deflower her during the festival as he did with her older sister Chale.

The arrival of a stranger – a rare event in this secluded village – changes the usual events. Salvador, a young man from Lima, is forced to spend the weekend in Manayaycuna due to road problems. The mayor wants to lock him up during Holy Time, but Salvador can escape and gets to know Madeinusa. The two young people fancy each other immediately and Madeinusa recognizes that Salvador is her chance to get away from the oppressive atmosphere of Manayaycuna and go to Lima, to which her beloved mother fled years before. When her choleric father realizes that Madeinusa has had sex with Salvador, he destroys the last keepsake Madeinusa possesses of her mother, a pair of earrings. Completely upset, Madeinusa kills her

Screenwriter:

Claudia Llosa

Cinematographer:

Raúl Pérez Ureta

Art Director:

Eduardo Camino Solís

Editor:

Ernest Blasi

Composer:

Selma Mutal

Duration:

100 minutes

Genre:

Drama

Cast:

Magaly Solier
Carlos Juan de la Torre
Juan Ubaldo Huamán
Yiliana Chong

Year:

2006

father by poisoning his soup. Salvador is horrified and wants to leave, but Madeinusa does not let the opportunity to get to the coast pass: together with her sister, she incriminates Salvador in the murder of her father and he is presumably lynched by the Andean community, while in the film's final scene, Madeinusa is on her way to Lima.

Critique

In this, her first movie, Claudia Llosa describes the social reality of the Peruvian Andes, focusing particularly on the role of women. She portrays this region, which could still be categorized as underdeveloped, and deliberately exaggerates certain aspects. The symbol for this region is the fictitious village Manayaycuna, in which the story is set. Llosa centres her movie on the three days of Easter, during which the inhabitants' strong religious feelings, formed by an odd syncretistic mixture of Christian and pre-Columbian features, are revealed. The residents of Manyaycuna believe that God is dead from Good Friday to Easter Sunday and cannot see what humans do. Everything, therefore, is permitted. The mayor of the village plans to use the Holy Time to deflower his daughter Madeinusa. This intended incest and all the committed misdeeds are used to show the backwardness of this Andean village with its superstitious beliefs that are mere excuses for the mentionned impious lifestyle.

This lifestyle can persist only because strangers hardly ever come to this village, as its name indicates: 'Manayaycuna' in Quechua means 'a village no one can enter' and is one of many highly symbolic names in the movie. This name, the village's secluded location and the archaic customs reveal the community as a dystopia, which is confirmed by Salvador's arrival and subsequent violent events.

Salvador comes from Lima, the Peruvian capital that symbolizes the remote village's counterpart. The movie thus also can be seen as a variant on a classic Latin American theme: the conflict between 'civilization' and 'barbarism'. Salvador brings modern technology to the underdeveloped village, symbolized by the camera with which he documents the local customs. These are completely new for him even though he lives in the same country. Madeinusa realizes that Salvador's arrival gives her the chance to get out of her oppressed life in the remote village and to live her lifelong dream of going to Lima. In order to seize this opportunity she does not hesitate to cause two deaths: she kills the two men that symbolize the two sides of 'civilization' and 'barbarism' in the movie. Madeinusa poisons her father, who represents the backward cult of the Andes, and incriminates Salvador, the representative of modern civilization. The fact that Madeinusa causes the death of Salvador is highly significant: the symbolic union between the man from the coast and the girl from the mountains, between the archaic and the modern civilization, does not occur. This is the surprise in a movie that for a long time seems to prepare for just that union. Additionally, this underscores that Llosa wants to show that an easy conciliation between the different parts of her native country is impossible.

Various parallels can be found between *Madeinusa* and Llosa's second movie, *La teta asustada/The Milk of Sorrow* (2009). Also noteworthy is the fact that the movie has certain parallels to the novel

Claudia Llosa: *Madeinusa*, 2006 © with kind permission of oberoncinematografica.

Lituma en los Andes/Death in the Andes (1993) by her uncle, Mario Vargas Llosa, which also concentrates on the backwardness and superstiousness of the Peruvian Andes. As was her uncle for his novel, Claudia Llosa has been criticized in her native country for her negative portrayal of the Andean region, and her movie, while praised by international critics, is controversial within Peru itself.

Matthias Hausmann

Man of Two Havanas

El hombre de las dos Habanas

Country of Origin:

United States

Languages:

English

Spanish

Studio/Distributor:

LatinoVision, LLC

Director:

Vivien Lesnik Weisman

Producer:

LatinoVision

Screenwriters:

Vivien Lesnik Weisman

Tirsa Hackshaw

Sarah Monso

Cinematographer:

Paul Maschall

Art Director:

Vivien Lesnik Weisman

Editor:

Tirsa Hackshaw

Composer:

Michael Wandmacher

Duration:

99 minutes

Genre:

Documentary

Cast:

Max Lesnik

Fidel Castro

Year:

2007

Synopsis

Man of Two Havanas is a feature-length documentary by Vivien Lesnik Weisman that examines the story of Weisman's father, Max Lesnik, widely considered to be the most controversial figure in the Cuban exile community. Max Lesnik is a complex figure: he was an early friend of Fidel Castro, an active Cuban migrant who established the magazine *Replica* (the biggest Spanish-language magazine of his time in the United States), and the director of Radio Miami. The documentary demonstrates the political difficulties and the inner disunity of a man who loved his home more than anything else. Although he was never an anti-Castroist, he was also against negotiations with the Soviet Union. He was not sympathizing with the communism but an animosity of short duration towards Castro was the main reason why he became the target for the American anti-communists. The documentary offers an intimate insight into his life through the eyes of his daughter.

Critique

Vivien Lesnik Weisman was born in Havana, Cuba. She graduated from Barnard College with a BA in Art History and from New York Law School with a Doctorate in Jurisprudence.

Her first documentary *Man of Two Havanas* arose because of a very personal sentiment. Her childhood was filled with assassination attempts on her father's life, and she wanted to know why her father had to make so many sacrifices. Weisman underlined that her dad cared a great deal. When he was back in Havana he was a revolutionary and fought alongside Castro for the freedom of the Cuban people. Then he had a falling out with his old friend and it was Miami where they went. Bombings, death threats and drive-by shootings were a daily occurrence in their home. And Weisman asked herself who would have done that to them because they were Americans. Consequently, for Weisman that must have been the communists but, by contrast, her father became the focal point of the anti-Castro terrorists. The documentary shows us that Max Lesnik always wanted Cuba to be free. By discovering his homeland as a child, Max began to understand that there was great misery among the Cuban people: he saw kids with big bellies and he started to realize that his Cuba was poor. His mother said that this was the 'key moment' for his further revolutionary career, the moment in which his love for Cuba was born. 'En los barrios mas pobres'– 'in the poorest districts' Max found his greatest friends. As a student he was a member of the orthodox party, as was the Cuban leader Fidel Castro, which is how they met each other.

The turning point of the documentary takes place when Max talks about the first year of Castro's revolution. He felt that freedom was in danger, because Castro had started to deal with the USSR. Max wanted sovereignty, liberty and independence, and he told Castro that he was neither a communist nor an anti-imperialist. This difference in ideology between Max Lesnik and Castro is the reason why the former left Cuba in January 1961. Of course it was not only

Max who had to leave Cuba; many families had to leave during the 1960s. What is left is a sense of incompleteness. When Max reconnected with Fidel after a long time, they had an open, positive conversation. Castro's first question was why Max had left Cuba. Max replied that he had not agreed with Castro's opinion on what Cuba's relationship with the Soviet Union should be and Castro answered him that if he had been in his place he would have done the same to save the revolution.

The documentary consists of a diversity of archival pictures, old photographs and interviews. It also contains highly controversial, top-secret audiotapes of a CIA-trained, Cuban terrorist living in exile. The audiotape excerpts are from a *New York Times* reporter who refuses to turn over the tapes. The never-before-heard audiotapes were hotly debated in the media.

The documentary and the narrative form chosen by Vivien Lesnik Weisman turned out very well, because the story of her family is highly interesting and shows how important it is to find an identity. Vivien found her father's identity through the lens of the camera, making it possible for others to empathize with her father, a person with a great competitive spirit.

Silke Paulitsch

The Milk of Sorrow

La teta asustada

Countries of Origin:

Peru
Spain

Languages:

Spanish
Quechua

Studios/Distributors:

Oberón Cinematográfica
Vela Producciones
Wanda Visión

Director:

Claudia Llosa

Producers:

Antonio Chavarrías
José María Morales
Claudia Llosa

Screenwriter:

Claudia Llosa

Synopsis

Young Fausta and her mother have come from a small village in the Andes to Lima, where they live in the poor suburbs with other families that have moved to Lima in search of a better life. The mother suffered badly in the Peruvian Civil War, during which she was raped. She passed her trauma to Fausta by the 'milk of sorrow', a Peruvian myth which says that mothers that have been raped transfer the sickness of fright to their daughters through their breast milk. Suffering this mythological disease, Fausta's life is filled with fear, especially of men, which is so great that she has inserted a potato into her vagina in order to bar intruders from entering her body.

When her mother dies, Fausta, who had lived in her own world to that point, is forced to face her fears, because she wants to bury her mother in her mother's native village. Since she does not have enough money, she overcomes her fear of strangers and starts to work as a maid for a well-known pianist. Ms Aida, who is suffering from a creative crisis, is impressed by the songs Fausta sings during work and strikes a bargain with her: for every song that Fausta performs she will give her a pearl, thus giving her the possibility of paying for the trip and Fausta's mother's funeral. Ms Aida has great success using Fausta's songs but refuses to give the maid the promised pearls. Upset by this deceit, Fausta acts deliberately on her own for the first time in her life: she breaks into the pianist's house, steals the pearls and, with the help of Noé, the gardener she had befriended, finally goes to hospital to have a doctor remove the potato from her vagina. The end of the movie shows Fausta on the way to bury her mother; it is obvious that she has turned into a self-confident woman.

Cinematographer:

Natasha Brier

Art Director:

Patricia Bueno

Editor:

Frank Gutierrez

Composers:

Selma Mutal
Susana Torres

Duration:

94 minutes

Genres:

Drama
Music

Cast:

Magaly Solier
Susi Sánchez
Efraín Solís
Marino Ballón
Delci Heredia
María del Pilar Guerrero

Year:

2009

Critique

Claudia Llosa's second movie won high international praise, winning the 'Berlin International Film Festival''s Golden Bear and garnering Academy Award nominations. This recognition made her one of the most important and best-known female film-makers in Latin America.

Many aspects in *The Milk of Sorrow* can be seen as a continuation of Llosa's first movie, *Madeinusa*. The same actress, Magaly Solier, plays a protagonist who once again has come from a small village in the Andes to Lima. She thus can be regarded as a woman in a situation similar to that Madeinusa will have to face following the latter's escape from her native village. Although *The Milk of Sorrow* shows how difficult life in Lima can be for people from the Andes, it ends on a more optimistic note than its precursor, as Fausta gains her independence without violence. Both movies can be regarded as emancipation films. This is especially clear in *The Milk of Sorrow*, where Fausta undergoes a profound change that leads her from fear to personal freedom.

At the beginning, Fausta is terrified of everything around her. Llosa shows this anxiety by breaking the mostly static visual approach of the movie with a few subjective sequences that follow the visibly nervous Fausta in tracking shots. At the end of one of these sequences Fausta reaches Ms Aida's house, the second setting of the film besides the poor barrio on the outskirts of Lima. This setup allows Llosa to show the different worlds of Lima: the wealth of the pianist's mansion, an oasis of tranquillity and nature, contrasts sharply with the hectic and

laudia Llosa: *La teta asustada/The Milk of Sorrow*, 2009 © with kind permission of
beroncinematografica.

loud barrio where Fausta lives. Ms Aida's house is fenced in. The gate is an important element for the film's action and a visible symbol for the separation of the Peruvian population and its social inequalities that Llosa criticizes sharply with her film.

It is important to note that the movie takes up a dark era of Peru's history by the use of the theme of the 'milk of sorrow': it refers to the battles between the Maoist Sendero Luminoso guerrillas and the government forces between 1980 and 2000, during which many women were raped, especially in the Andes. A 'Commission for Truth and Reconciliation', which had been set up to investigate these crimes, registered countless rapes alongside nearly 70,000 murders. One result of the violence against women has been the so-called 'milk of sorrow', a myth studied and named by anthropologist Kimberley Theidon in her book *Entre Prójimos* (2004). Theidon shows that the phenomenon was omnipresent during the period of the internal war. Claudia Llosa, who was impressed by Theidon's thesis, deals with this part of her country's history in her film. The movie opens with a song of Fausta's mother recounting the brutal events that led to the 'milk of sorrow'. For most of the song, the screen remains black. By keeping the outrages in this opening scene off-screen, Llosa underlines the fact that they are unspeakable crimes, not even talked about today. She follows this line, as the film never shows the crimes committed during the internal war. Nevertheless, the experiences of violence and rape are alive in every scene as Fausta, with her trauma, is a living reminder of these crimes.

Matthias Hausmann

The Swamp

La ciénaga

Country of Origin:

Argentina

Language:

Spanish

Studios/Distributors:

Lita Stantic Producciones
Cuatro Cabezas

Director:

Lucrecia Martel

Producers:

Lita Stantic
Diego Guebel
Ana Aizenberg
Mario Pergolini
José M. Morales

Synopsis

The central interest of the film, which can be summarized in a few sentences, lies not in the narrative but is directed essentially towards the intensive focus on sensorial perception (sight, touch, taste, smell and hearing).

The depression-prone Mecha, a 50-year-old representative of the Argentine middle class hit by economic decline, lives with her husband Gregorio and her four children in a hopeless existence divided between alcohol excesses and exhaustion states. On her estate 'La Mandragora' in the province La Salta, she resides in a derelict holiday home with a contaminated swimming pool. Her existence is occasionally interrupted by television broadcasts reporting spectacular apparitions of the Virgin Mary. The beginning and the end of the film are marked by two accidents: at the beginning Mecha, drunk, falls into the recently collected wine glasses, leaving her body covered with cuts. At the end of the film, the son of a befriended family (Luciano) falls off a ladder. The apparition of the Virgin Mary, desired by all the family members, fails to happen. Therefore, 'I did not see anything' is the last sentence that Momi, Mecha's daughter, pronounces, and through which she destroys every hope for redemption.

Screenwriter:

Lucrecia Martel

Cinematographer:

Hugo Colace

Art Director:

Graciela Oderigo

Editor:

Santiago Ricci

Composer/Sound Recordist:

Guido Beremblum

Duration:

102 minutes

Genres:

Comedy
Drama

Cast:

Graciela Borges
Mercedes Morán
Martín Adjemián
Diego Baenas
Leonora Balcarce
Juan Cruz Bordeu

Year:

2000

Critique

The highly codified film invites to multiple lectures and interpretations: a socio-political, perceptual-aesthetic and an epistemological reading. One of the best known readings of the film emphasizes the political aspect and is highly relevant, in particular for contemporary spectators. Even though the film contains no direct references to the corruption of the political class during the Menem era, the title of the movie, *The Swamp*, with its semantic connotations of mud, swamp and decay still suggests the degeneration and corruption of the Argentine political system. Protagonists' remarks such as 'here everything decomposes and rots' serve the same purpose as implicit references to the economic decline of the Argentine middle class. The subtlety of the film lies in the close linking of implicit political codes to the perceptual-aesthetical, epistemological and anthropological signs of the movie, so that an aesthetics of politics, in French philosopher Jacques Rancière's terms, is visible.

    Though, in French philosopher Gilles Deleuze's terms, *The Swamp* belongs to the modern tradition of European cinema, being defined as a 'cinema of seeing'. In this framework, optical situations proliferate and protagonists become seeing filters while their capacity of agency is undermined. At the same time, the film exceeds the historical limitations of the modern cinema of the 1960s through the stylization of its protagonists as perceptual bodies, which do not do anything else than receive and await visual, acoustic, haptic, olfactory and gustatory impulses. Their reactions to all these perceptual impulses are only numbness and exhaustion. A diversification of the various senses and an analysis of the diverse effects on the cinematic body show a break with the classical hierarchy of the senses. In fact, even the name of the La Mandrágora is an easy symbol for the protagonists' state of numbness. The family members' inert bodies numbed by sun, alcohol and sultry heat find themselves in a perpetual state of expectation, waiting for a spectacular visual impulse that is repeatedly announced by the television broadcast reporting the apparitions of the Virgin Mary in the province Salta. The end of the movie makes the same point through visual curiosity and the desired epiphany of the monstrosity, which pushes the youngest son to climb up a ladder to see a hideous African rat. The overlapping sexual and mystical codes become evident in the figure of the ladder, which serves as a symbol of the soul's ascent to God in the mystic tradition. However, the semantic connotations linked to this figure are not redeeming at all as the family members are denied not only the sight of the monstrous but also the visual drama of the apparition of the Virgin Mary. In this sense, the movie can be read as a post-Catholic, anti-redemption cinema. This meaning is revealed through the last sentence of the youngest daughter in the family: 'I have gone where the vision of Maria should be. I did not see anything.'

Uta Felten

Under the Same Moon

La misma luna

Countries of Origin:

Mexico
United States

Languages:

Spanish
English

Studios/Distributors:

Creando Films
Fidecine
Potomac Pictures

Director:

Patricia Riggen

Producers:

Patricia Riggen
Gerardo Barrera
Ligiah Villalobos

Screenwriter:

Ligiah Villalobos

Cinematographer:

Checco Varese

Art Directors:

Adriána Navarrete
Ángeles Moreno

Editor:

Aleshka Ferrero

Composer:

Carlo Siliotto

Duration:

106 minutes

Genre:

Drama

Cast:

Adrian Alonso
Kate del Castello
Eugenio Derbez
America Ferrera
Jesse Garcia

Year:

2007

Synopsis

When his grandmother dies, 9-year-old Carlitos decides to leave Mexico in order to reunite with his mother Rosario who has been working illegally in Los Angeles for the last four years. Weaving the parallel stories of Carlitos' perilous and adventurous quest for his mother and her weary and hard-working life as an illegal immigrant, this melodramatic road movie portrays the constant fear of discovery by the 'Migra' (a slang term for US Immigration and Customs Enforcement or other immigration law enforcement agencies) and the hope of a better life for mother and son.

Critique

In *Under the Same Moon*, although Carlitos (Adrian Alonso) and Rosario (Kate del Castillo) live far away from each other in different countries, they dream of being together 'under the same moon'. Every Sunday, Rosario calls her son from the same pay phone and describes to her son what she sees, and Carlos imagines himself being there. When they go to bed they picture themselves sleeping next to each other. The camera and editing techniques of split screens and harmonious shots and counter shots give us the illusion of closeness and proximity. However, the harmony is shattered by the sudden death of Carlitos' grandmother and his decision to cross the border in order to look for his mother.

The two different worlds and circumstances are visually underscored by contrasting approaches to movement, colour and light: whereas Rosario's urban and anonymous environment is filmed with little colour and very little camera movement, Carlitos' journey is more like modern-day road movies with expansive scenery, rich contrast, and bright and saturated colours. Handheld cameras, improvised movements, and wider lenses accentuate Carlitos' unpredictable quest for his mother. With the help of lower camera angles we see the world through the eyes of a child. At tense and dangerous moments like in the scene in which Carlitos is trying to cross the border – hidden under the floorboards of a minivan driven by two American students – the camera looks down on him and emphasizes his fragility and vulnerability. Due to some unfortunate events, Carlitos loses all his money, is nearly sold to a mean-looking man, but is helped by Reyna (María Rojo) who provides a hideout for illegal workers. Nearly caught by US Citizenship and Immigration Services agents, Carlitos stubbornly follows the illegal worker Enrique (Eugenio Derbez), who is more than reluctant to team up with him at first. Both sing along to the popular song 'La Abusadora' that is an homage to a similar scene in Mexico's first film with sound, *Alla en el Rancho Grande/Out on the Big Ranch* (Fernando de Fuentes, 1936).

Finally sympathizing with Carlitos, Enrique helps him to find his way to Los Angeles and even lets himself be caught by the Migra in order to distract the police from Carlitos. Miraculously, Carlos manages to get to the telephone booth from which his mother always calls him, and the two finally reunite. Although more a simplistic, far-fetched, heart-warming story than a political realistic drama, the film succeeds in raising empathy for illegal immigrants. It is entertaining not only because of its cast of famous Mexican actors but also because of its blend of popular Mexican music, ranging from ranchera, mariachi, trío, norteño and reggaeton. The well-known Mexican band Los Tigres del Norte not only composed a song for *Under the Same Moon*, they also appear in the film, giving Carlitos and Enrique a ride in their van and singing for them.

Heidi Denzel de Tirado

RECOMME
READING

Agramonte, Arturo and Castillo, Luciano (2008) *Entre el vivir y el soñar: Pioneros del cine cubano*, Camagüey: Ácana.

Agrasanchez, Rogelio (2001) *Cine Mexicano: Posters from the Golden Age 1936–1956*, San Francisco: Chronicle Books.

Aguilar, Gonzalo (2008) *Estudio crítico sobre El bonaerense: Entrevista a Pablo Trapero*, Buenos Aires: Picnic.

Alsina Thevenet, Homero (2006) *Más notas de cine*, Montevideo: Ediciones la Plaza.

Amado, Ana (2009) *La imagen justa: Cine argentino y política (1980–2007)*, Buenos Aires: Colihue.

Amador, María Luisa and Ayala Blanco, Jorge (2006) *Cartelera cinematográfica, 1980–1989*, México, DF: Universidad Nacional Autónoma de México.

Aprea, Gustavo (2008) *Cine y políticas en Argentina: Continuidades y discontinuidades en 25 años de democracia*, Los Polvorines/Buenos Aires: Universidad Nacional de General Sarmiento/Biblioteca Nacional.

Báez, Etzel (2007) *Cortometraje: Notas sobre el arte de hacer cine*, Santo Domingo: Universidad Autónoma de Santo Domingo.

Batlle, Diego, et al. (2008) *50 cineastas de Iberoamérica. Generaciones en tránsito, 1980–2008*, México, DF: Cineteca Nacional/Instituto Mexicano de Cinematografía.

Bedoya, Ricardo (2009) *El cine silente en el Perú*, Lima: Universidad de Lima.

Berg, Charles Ramirez (2002) *Latino Images in Film: Stereotypes, Subversion, and Resistance*, Austin, TX: University of Texas Press.

Berthier, Nancy (ed.) (2007) *Le cinéma d'Alejandro Amenábar*, Toulouse: PUM.

Biondi, Hugo (2007) *Sin renunciamientos: El cine según Leonardo Favio*, Buenos Aires: Corregidor.

Borrás, Eduardo (2006) *Las aguas bajan turbias*, Buenos Aires: Biblos/Argentores.

Branston, Gill in: Roberta Pearson and Ric Allsopp (eds) (2000) *Critical Dictionary of Film and Television Theory*, London: Routledge.

Bremme, Bettina (2000) *MOVIE-mientos: Der lateinamerikanische Film: Streiflichter von unterwegs*, Stuttgart: Schmetterling Verlag Gmbh.

Bremme, Bettina (2008) *Movie-mientos II: Der lateinamerikanische Film in Zeiten globaler Umbrüche*, Stuttgart: Schmetterling Verlag Gmbh.

Caballero, Rufo (2008) *Lágrimas en la lluvia: Crítica de cine, 1987–2007*, La Habana: ICAIC/Letras Cubanas.

Caballero, Rufo (2000) *Rumores del cómplice: Cinco maneras de ser crítico de cine*, La Habana: Letras Cubanas.

Caballero, Rufo//Pastrana, Mayra (1999) *A solas con Solás*, La Habana: Letras Cubanas.

Cabrera, Gustavo (2006) *Tita Merello (1904–2002): El mito, la mujer y el cine*, Buenos Aires: Marcelo Héctor Oliveri.

Caicedo, Andrés (2009) *Ojo al cine*, Bogotá: Norma.

Cangi, Adrián (ed.) (2007) *Favio: Sinfonía de un sentimiento*, Buenos Aires: Fundación Eduardo Constantini/Malba.

Carbone, Giancarlo (2007) *El cine en el Perú. El cortometraje: 1972–1992*, Lima: Universidad de Lima.

Castillo, Luciano (2007) *El cine cubano a contraluz*, Santiago de Cuba: Oriente.

Cavallo, Ascanio and Díaz, Carolina (2007) *Explotados y benditos: Mito y desmitificación del cine chileno de los 60*, Santiago de Chile: Uqbar.

Cavallo, Ascanio, Douzet, Pablo, and Rodríguez, Cecilia (2007) *Huérfanos y perdidos. Relectura del cine chileno de la transición 1990–1999*, rev. edn, Santiago de Chile: Uqbar.

Chanan, Michael (ed.) (1995) *Memories of Underdevelopment and Inconsolable Memories*, Piscataway Township, NJ: Rutgers University Press.

Chanan, Michael (2007) *The Politics of Documentary*, London: British Film Institute.

Cortés, María Lourdes (2007) *La pantalla rota: Cien años de cine en Centroamérica*, La Habana: Casa de las Américas.

Costa, Jaime Enrique (2008) *El cine tal cual era: Recuerdos desde la butaca*, Montevideo: Fin de Siglo.

Deborah, Jermyn in: Roberta Pearson and Ric Allsopp (eds) (2000) *Critical Dictionary of Film and Television Theory*, London: Routledge.

Donoso Pinto, Catalina (2007) *Películas que escuchan: Reconstrucción de la identidad en once filmes chilenos y argentinos*, Buenos Aires: Corregidor.

Douglas, María Eulalia (2008) *Catálogo del cine cubano 1897–1960*, La Habana: ICAIC.

Duno-Gottberg, Luis (ed.) (2008) *Miradas al margen: Cine y subalternidad en América Latina y el Caribe*, Caracas: Fundación Cinemateca Nacional.

España, Claudio/Fabbro, Gabriela (1994) *Cine argentino en democracia, 1983–1993*, Buenos Aires: Fondo Nacional de las Artes.

España, Claudio (ed.) (2005) *Cine argentino: Modernidad y vanguardias, 1957–1983*, vol. 2, Buenos Aires: Fondo Nacional de las Artes.

Eva-Lynn, Jagoe and Cant, John (2007) 'Vibraciones encarnadas en La niña santa de Lucrecia Martel', in: Viviana Rangil (ed.) *El cine argentino de hoy: entre el arte y la política*, Buenos Aires: Editorial Biblos, pp. 170–82.

Filippelli, Rafael (2008) *El plano justo. Cine moderno: de Ozu a Godard*, Buenos Aires: Santiago Arcos.

Fornet, Ambrosio (2007) *Las trampas del oficio: Apuntes sobre cine y sociedad*, La Habana: José Martí/ICAIC.

Foster, David William (1992) *Contemporary Argentine Cinema*, Columbia, MO: University of Missouri Press.

Foster, David William (2000) *Gender and Society in Contemporary Brazilian Cinema*, Austin, TX: University of Texas Press.

Foster, David William (2002) *Mexico City in Contemporary Mexican Cinema*, Austin, TX: University of Texas Press.

García Canalini, Nestor (2004): *Diferentes, desiguales y desconectados. Mapas de la interculturalidad*. Barcelona: Editorial Gedisa.

Geraghty, Christine (2000) 'Re-examining stardom: questions of texts, bodies and performance' in: Christine Gledhill and Linda Williams (eds): *Reinventing Film Studies*. London: Arnold, pp.183–201.

Gwenllian Jones, Sara in: Roberta Pearson/Ric Allsopp (2000) *Critical Dictionary of Film and Television Theory*, London: Routledge.

Herrera, Hayden (2002): *Frida: A Biography of Frida Kahlo*. New York: Harper Perennial.

Hershfield, Joanne and Maciel, David R (eds) (1999) *Mexico's Cinema: A Century of Film and Filmmakers*, Wilmington, DE: Scholarly Resources.

Huayhuaca, José Carlos (2006) *Cine escrito: Guiones para filmar*, Lima: Universidad de Lima.

Ibarra, Jesús (2006) *Los Bracho. Tres generaciones de cine mexicano*, México, DF: Universidad Nacional Autónoma de México.

Ibarra, Mirtha (2008) *Tomás Gutiérrez-Alea: Volver sobre mis pasos*, La Habana: Unión.

Johnson, Randal and Stam, Robert (1995) *Brazilian Cinema*, New York: Columbia University Press.

Jossner, Ulrich (2003), 'Mit der Idee im Kopf und der Kamera in der Hand', *Culturebase*, www.culturebase.net/artist.php?657. Accessed 23.02.1012.

Jubis, Oscar (2010) *The films of Lucrecia Martel: The Salta Trilogy*, Saarbrücken: VDM Verlag Dr. Müller.

Junge, Christian (2009) *Hollywood in Cannes: Die Geschichte einer Hassliebe 1939–2008*, Marburg: Schüren Verlag.

King, John (2000) *Magical Reels: A History of Cinema in Latin America*, London/New York: Verso Books.

Kriger, Clara (2009) *Cine y peronismo: El Estado en escena*, Buenos Aires: Siglo XXI.

Lizarazo Arias, Diego (2004) *La fruición fílmica: Estética y semiótica de la interpretación cinematográfica*, México, DF: Universidad Autónoma de México-Xochimilco.

Maldonado, Sonia (ed.) (2007) *Titón, más allá del cine: Exposición homenaje a Tomás Gutiérrez-Alea*, La Habana: ICAIC/Museo Nacional de Bellas Artes/Fundación Ludwig de Cuba.

Martin, Michael (ed.) (1997) *New Latin American Cinema: Volume 1. Theory, Practices and Transcontinenal Articulations*, Detroit: Wayne State University Press.

Martin, Michael (ed.) (1997) *New Latin American Cinema: Volume 2. Studies of National Cinemas*, Detroit: Wayne State University Press.

Martínez Molina, Julio (2008) *Haikus de mi emoción fílmica*, Cienfuegos: Mecenas.

Melo, Adrián (2008) *Otras historias de amor: Gays, lesbianas y travestis en el cine argentino*, Buenos Aires: Ediciones Lea.

Mignogna, Eduardo and Oves, Santiago Carlos (2007) *Sol de otoño*, Buenos Aires: Biblos.

Millán, Margara (1999) *Derivas de un cine en femenino*, México, DF: Miguel Ángel Porrúa.

Miquel, Ángel (2000) *Mimí Derba*, Texas/México, DF: Archivo Fílmico Agrasánchez/Filmoteca de la UNAM.

Miquel, Ángel (2009) *Placeres en imagen: Fotografía y cine eróticos, 1900–1960*, Morelos: Sin Nombre/Universidad Autónoma del Estado de Morelos.

Monaco, James (1991) *Film verstehen*, Reinbek bei Hamburg: Rowohlt Taschenbuch Verlag.

Mora, Carl J (2005) *Mexican Cinema: Reflections on Society, 1896–2004*, 3rd edn, Jefferson, NC: McFarland & Co.

Mora, Carl J (1990) *Mexican Cinema: Reflections of a Society, 1896–1988*, Berkeley: University of California Press.

Mora Lomelí, Raúl H (2005) *Dios en el cine*, Tlaquepaque, Jalisco: ITESO/Universidad Iberoamericana-León.

Nagib, Lucia (2003) *The New Brazilian Cinema*, London: I.B. Tauris.

Naudeau, Javier (2006) *Un film de entrevista: Conversaciones con David José Kohon*, Buenos Aires: Fondo Nacional de las Artes.

Neil, Claudia, et al. (2007) *Fotogramas Santafesinos*, Instituto de Cinematografía de la UNL, 1956–1976, Santa Fe: Universidad Nacional del Litoral.

Noriega, Chon A. (ed.) (2000) *Visible Nations: Latin American Cinema and Video*, Minneapolis: University of Minnesota Press.

Olson, Scott Robert (1999) *Hollywood Planet: Global Media and the Competitive Advantage of Narrative Transparency*, London: Routledge.

Ospina, Luis (2007) *Palabras al viento: Mis sobras completas*, Bogotá: Aguilar.

Oubiña, David (2004) 'Between Breakup and Tradition: Recent Argentinean Cinema', *Senses of Cinema*, 31, April/June, pp. 17–31.

Paranaguá, Paulo Antonio (ed.) (2003) *Cine documental en América Latina*, Madrid: Ediciones Cátedra.

Paranagua Paulo Antonio (ed.) (1996) *Mexican Cinema*, London: British Film Institute.

Padrón, Frank (2008) *Sinfonía inconclusa para cine cubano*, Santiago de Cuba: Oriente.

Pérez Turrent, Tomás, *Felipe Cazals* (2007) *Canoa*, México, DF: Universidad Autónoma Metropolitana/Casa Juan Pablos.

Pick, Zuzanna and Schatz, Thomas (1993) *The New Latin American Cinema: A Continental Project*, Austin, TX: University of Texas Press.

Pilcher, Jeffrey M (2001) *Cantinflas and the Chaos of Mexican Modernity*, Wilmington, DE: Scholarly Resources Inc.

Protzel, Javier (2009) *Imaginarios sociales e imaginarios cinematográficos*, Lima: Universidad de Lima.

Ramos, Alberto and Reloba, Xenia (eds.) (2006) *28 Festival Internacional del Nuevo Cine Latinoamericano*, 5–15 December, La Habana: Oficina del Festival Internacional del Nuevo Cine Latinoamericano.

Ramos, Alberto and Reloba, Xenia (eds.) (2007) *29 Festival Internacional del Nuevo Cine Latinoamericano*, 4–14 December, La Habana: Oficina del Festival Internacional del Nuevo Cine Latinoamericano.

Ramos, Alberto and Reloba, Xenia (eds.) (2008) *30 Festival Internacional del Nuevo Cine Latinoamericano*, 2–12 December, La Habana: Oficina del Festival Internacional del Nuevo Cine Latinoamericano.

Ramos, Alberto (ed.) (2005) *27 Festival Internacional del Nuevo Cine Latinoamericano*, La Habana: Oficina del Festival Internacional del Nuevo Cine Latinoamericano.

Ramírez Martínez, Juan (2008) *Luces y sombras*, Granma: Bayamo.

Rangil, Viviana (ed.) (2007) *El cine argentino de hoy: entre el arte y la política*, Buenos Aires: Biblos.

Rangil, Viviana (2005) *Otro punto de vista: mujer y cine en la Argentina*, Rosario: Beatriz Viterbo.

Rashkin, Elissa (ed.) (2001) *Women Filmmakers in Mexico: The Country of Which We Dream*, Austin, TX: University of Texas Press.

Reader, Keith (1999) "Review of Time Regained" in: *Sight and Sound*, 61.

Rodriguez, Clara E (2004) *Heroes, Lovers, and Others: The Story of Latinos in Hollywood*. Washington, DC: Smithsonian Books.

Rodríguez Triana, Mariví (2007) *Catálogo de la producción fílmica de la Escuela Internacional de Cine y Televisión, 1987–2002*, Córdoba/La Habana: Diputación de Córdoba/Fundación del Nuevo Cine Latinoamericano.

Rodríguez, Alejandra and López, Marcela (2009) *Un país de película: La historia argentina que el cine nos contó*, Buenos Aires: Del Nuevo Extremo.

Román Pérez, Ernesto (2006) *El cine pornográfico mexicano de los '90*, México, DF: Cineteca Nacional.

Ruffinelli, Jorge (2008) *El cine de Patricio Guzmán: En busca de las imágenes verdaderas*, Santiago de Chile: Uqbar.

Rulfo, Juan (1980) *El gallo de oro y otros textos para cine*, México, DF: Era.

Río, Joel del/Cumaná, María Caridad (2008) *Latitudes del margen. El cine latinoamericano ante el tercer milenio*, La Habana: ICAIC.

Santovenia, Rodolfo (2006) *Diccionario de cine: Términos artísticos y técnicos*, La Habana: Arte y Literatura.

Sartora, Josefina and Rival, Silvina (eds) (2007) *Imágenes de lo real: La representación de lo político en el documental argentino*, Buenos Aires: Libraria.

Schenk, Irmbert, Tröhler, Margit, and Zimmermann, Yvonne (2010), *Film – Kino – Zuschauer: Filmrezeption. Zürcher Filmstudien Nr 24*, Marburg: Schüren Verlag.

Anon. (et.alt) (2009) *Cinémas du réel en Amérique latine* (XXIe siècle), Toulouse: Presses Universitaires du Mirail.

Schulze, Peter W (2005) *Transformation und Trance: Die Filme des Glauber Rocha als Arbeit am postkolonialen Gedächtnis*, Remscheid: Gardez!

Schulze, Peter W and Schumann, Peter B (2011) *Glauber Rocha e as culturas na América Latina*, Frankfurt: TFM.

Sidorkovs, Nicolás (1994) *Los cines de Caracas en el tiempo de los cines*, Caracas: Armitano.

Solórzano, Enrique (2007) *Entre la luz y el silencio: Lupe Vélez y su tiempo*, México, DF: Cabos Sueltos.

Soutar, Jethro (2008) *Gael García Bernal and The Latin American New Wave*. New York: Portico.

Stam, Robert (1997) *Tropical Multiculturalism: A Comparative History of Race in Brazilian Cinema and Culture*, Durham, NC: Duke University Press.

Stevens, Donald F. (ed.) (1998) *Based on a True Story: Latin American History at the Movies*, Wilmington, DE: Scholarly Resources.

Stock, Anne Marie and Fornet, Ambrosio (ed.) (1997) *Framing Latin American Cinema: Contemporary Critical Perspectives*, Minneapolis: University of Minnesota Press.

Tal, Tzvi (2005) *Pantallas y revolución: Una visión comparativa del cine de liberación y el cinema novo*, Buenos Aires/Tel Aviv: Lumiere/ Universidad de Tel Aviv.

Taubin, Amy (2009) 'Identification of a woman', *Film Comment*, July/ August, pp. 21–22.

Teissl, Verena (2007) *Filmland Argentinien – Gegen die Gewohnheit*, in: *ray Filmmagazin*, September.

Teissl, Verena (2008) 'La conquista del espacio urbano, último tabú del cine mexicano: las identidades cinematográficas de la Ciudad de México', in: Susanne Igler and Thomas Stauder (eds) *Negociando identidades, traspasando fronteras*, Madrid/ Frankfurt: Iberoamericana/Vervuert, pp. 229–245.

Teissl, Verena (2010) 'Filmbetrieb und Interkulturalität: Betrachtungen eines Verhältnisses', in: Theo Hugh and Andreas Kriwak (eds) *Visuelle Kompetenz*, Innsbruck: University Press.

Torre, Gerardo de la (2007) *Vicente Leñero: vivir del cine*, Guadalajara: Universidad de Guadalajara.

Toscan du Plantier, Daniel (1996) *La emoción cultural*, México, DF: CONACULTA.

Trelles Plazaola, Luis (1975) *El cine visto en Puerto Rico (1962–1973)*, San Juan: Universidad de Puerto Rico.

Turan, Kenneth (2003) *Sundance to Sarajevo: Film Festivals and the World they Made*, Berkeley, CA: University of California Press.

Ulive, Ugo (2007) *Memorias de teatro y cine*, Montevideo: Trilce.

Valck, Marijke de (2007) *Filmfestivals: From European Geopolitics to Global Cinephilia*, Amsterdam: Amsterdam University Press.

Vega Alfaro, Eduardo de la (2001) *Microhistorias del cine en México*, Guadalajara/México, DF: Universidad de Guadalajara/UNAM/ Cineteca Nacional.

Vite, Omar (2007) *La gran sangre: Confidencial*, Lima: Norma.

Winter, Rainer and Nestler, Sebastian (2010) '"Doing cinema": Filmanalyse als Kulturanalyse in der Tradition der Cultural Studies', in: Irmbert Schenk, Margit Tröhler and Yvonne Zimmermann (eds) *Film – Kino – Zuschauer: Filmrezeption. Zürcher Filmstudien Nr 24*, Marburg: Schüren Verlag, pp. 99–116.

Wood, Jason (2006) *The Faber Book of Mexican Cinema*, London: Faber and Faber.

Xavier, Ismail (1997) *Allegories of Underdevelopment: Aesthetics and Politics in Modern Brazilian Cinema*, Minneapolis: University of Minnesota Press.

Newspaper and Online Articles (listed chronologically)

'Priest scandal picture shatters Mexican box office records', in: *Screen International*, 19th August 2002.

Geoff Andrew and Walter Salles (Guardian interviews at the BFI, 2004), http://www.guardian.co.uk/film/2004/aug/26/features. Accessed 26.2.2012.

Reicher, Isabella (2004): „Reisen-in-der-Luftblase"/"To travel in a bubble", http://derstandard.at/1146147/Reisen-in-der-Luftblase. Accessed 26.2.2012.

'The New York Daily News as referenced in 'The Motorcycle Diaries: What to say about ...', in: *The Guardian*, 24th August 2004, p.16.

'Guardian NFT Interview: Gael Garcia Bernal', 16th October 2006. Accessed online at http://www.guardian.co.uk/film/2006/oct/16/ guardianinterviewsatbfisouthbank. Accessed at 26.2.2012.

'Bernal has the magic movie touch Mexican star keeps picking cult classic winners', in: *Evening News*, 19th January 2007, p.12.

'The political pin-up: Gael Garcia Bernal has no interest in becoming a Hollywood star – he's on a mission to put Mexican cinema on the map, finds Charlotte Higgins', in: *The Guardian*, 22nd May 2007, p. 23.

"SWINE FLU?; IT WAS GOOD FOR MEXICO: He's clever, good-looking and, as he showed in 'Amores Perros', ridiculously talented. But instead of carving out a career as the new Tom Cruise the Mexican actor Gael Garcia Bernal is busy avoiding Hollywood pay cheques and saving his homeland from the 'poison' of celebrity", in: *The Sunday Telegraph*, 5th July 2009, p. 10.

"Spurning Hollywood's advances; 'My love is for acting, not money', says Mexican star Gael Garcia Bernal". In: *Edmonton Journal*, 9th July 2009, Arts and Entertainment, p. 4.

"'It's a big road. And who knows where it will take me?'; He's handsome, he's talented and he sees politics in everything - even football. The Mexican actor Gael García Bernal speaks to Kevin Maher", in: *The Times*, 25th June, 2009, T2, features p.1.

LATIN AMERICAN CINEMA RESOURCE ONLINE

Fantastic source of the following sites: http://www.cinelatinoamericano.org/

Digital magazines

Contrapicado.net
Revista Sunrise
Cineismo, Argentina
Espacio Cine Independiente, Argentina
El Amante, Argentina, Buenos Aires
Cinestesia, Brasil
Enrodaje, Colombia
Número, Bogotá, Colombia
Miradas, Cuba, San Antonio de los Baños
La fuga, Chile
Mabuse, Chile
Telón, Chile
Voraz, Chile
Cinegrama, Chile, Santiago de Chile
OnOff, Chile, Santiago de Chile
Racontto, Chile, Valparaíso
Área Visual, España
Aurora Bitzine, España
Fotogramas, España
Miradas de cine, España
Revista Cine Iberoamericano, España
Video Popular, España
Cine por la Red, España, Madrid

Cine y Tele, España, Madrid
Cinevideo 20, España, Madrid
Revista Acción Cine-Video, España, Madrid
Anika Cine Magazine, España, Valencia
La Butaca, España, Valencia
American Cinematographer, Estados Unidos de América, California
8 y Medio. Revista electrónica de cine, México
El ojo que piensa. Revista virtual de cine iberoamericano, México, Guadalajara
Cinemanía, México, DF

Filmsites
Babadú
CanalDocumental
LatAm cinema
Cine Nacional, Argentina
Adorocinemabrasileiro, Brasil
Cinema Net, Brasil
Cinemaemcena, Brasil
Cineweb, Brasil
Mnemocine, Brasil
Movie Review Querie Engine, Canadá
Proimagenes Colombia, Colombia, Bogotá
Portal Centro-americano de cine, video y animación, Costa Rica, San José
CUBACINE, Cuba, Ciudad de La Habana
Ser Indígena – Portal de las Culturas Originarias de Chile, Chile
Todo un cine, Chile
Chileaudiovisual, Chile, Santiago de Chile
Cinestel, España
Cineuropa, España
El Multicine, España
Filmin, España
Nuestro Cine, España
Tercer-ojo, España
TodoCine, España
Festivales.com, España, Barcelona
La Higuera, España, León
ABCguionistas, España, Madrid
Noticine, España, Madrid
Ahora Cine, España, Navarra
Film Quarterly, Estados Unidos de América
Internet Movie Data Base (IMDB), Estados Unidos de América
Casa Comal Arte y Cultura, Guatemala, Guatemala
DeCine, México
Cine Butaca, México, DF, México
Cinencuentro, Perú
UK Film Council, Reino Unido, Londres
WebCinema, República Checa
Arte 7, Uruguay
Fundavisual Latina, Venezuela, Caracas

Bulletins

Estrellas en la noche
La Gaceta del Cine
Página/12, Argentina, Buenos Aires
Gacemail, Argentina, Buenos Aires, CF
Boletín Filme B, Brasil, Rio de Janeiro
Bogocine, Colombia, Bogotá

Cine blogs

Blog de cine latinoamericano
Cine Indígena
Filmoscopio
OtrosCines
Ardito Documental, Argentina
Celuloide, Argentina
Nistagmus, Argentina
Cine Argentino, Argentina, Buenos Aires
La Latina, Brasil
Cinéfagos.net, Colombia
Film Nacional, Chile
La bitácora de la Escuela de Cine, Chile
Cinerama, Ecuador
Cine Latino, España
La ventana indiscreta, España
Tu Blog de Cine, España
Moloch Tropical, Haití
Cinebits, México
Rodandocine, México
Cinencuentro, Perú
La Cinefilia no es Patriota, Perú
La Trinchera del Cine, Perú
Blogacine, Venezuela

Institutions

Ar Detroy, Argentina
ARTEUNA. Sitio de arte en la web, Argentina
ßeta_test, Argentina
Centro Cultural General San Martín, Argentina, Buenos Aires
Centro Cultural Ricardo Rojas de la Universidad de Buenos Aires, Argentina, Buenos
    Aires
FIAPF – International Federation of Film Producers Associations
Fundación para un Nuevo Periodismo Iberoamericano – FNPI, Colombia, Cartagena de
    Indias
Escuela de Cine y Vídeo de Andoain, España, Gipúzkoa
Ars Animación, España, Madrid
Arte 4 Estudio de Actores, España, Madrid
Escuela de Imagen y Sonido de Vigo, España, Vigo
American Film Institute, Estados Unidos de América, Los Angeles
Asociación de Productores de Puerto Rico, Puerto Rico
Archivo Nacional de la Imagen-Sodre, Uruguay, Montevideo

Regional bodies

Conferencia de Autoridades Audiovisuales y Cinematográficas de Iberoamerica (CAACI)
Secretaría Ejecutiva de la Cinematografía Iberoamericana (SECI)
TAL – Televisión América Latina
Unión Latina de Economía Política de la Información, la Comunicación y la Cultura (ULEPICC)
Federación Internacional de Archivos Fílmicos (FIAF), Bélgica, Bruselas
Coordinadora Latinoamericana de Cine y Comunicación de los Pueblos Indígenas
     (CLACPI), Bolivia
Convenio Andrés Bello, Colombia, Bogotá
Fondo de Fomento al Audiovisual de Centroamérica y Cuba (CINERGIA), Costa Rica,
     San José
Oficina Regional de Cultura para América Latina y el Caribe de la UNESCO, Cuba,
     Ciudad de la Habana
Federación de las Escuelas de la Imagen y el Sonido de Latinoamérica (FEISAL), Chile,
     Santiago de Chile
Federación Iberoamericana de Productores de Cine y Audiovisuales (FIPCA), México
Fondo de desarrollo de las Naciones Unidas para la Mujer (UNIFEM), México
Comunidad Andina, Perú, Lima

Governing bodies

Instituto Nacional de Cine y Artes Audiovisuales (INCAA), Argentina, Buenos Aires
Australian Films Institute, Australia, Melbourne
Consejo Nacional de Cine (CONACINE), Bolivia, La Paz
Secretaria do Audiovisual. Ministério da Cultura, Brasil, Brasilia
Agência Nacional do Cinema (ANCINE), Brasil, Río de Janeiro
National Film Board of Canada, Canadá, Montreal
Consejo Nacional de las Artes y la Cultura en Cinematografía (CNACC). Ministerio de
     Cultura de Colombia, Colombia, Bogotá
Korean Film Council, Corea del Sur, Corea del Sur
Centro Costarricense de Producción Cinematográfica (CCPC), Costa Rica, San José
Instituto Cubano del Arte e Industria Cinematográficos (ICAIC), Cuba, La Habana
Consejo del Arte y la Industria Audiovisual – Consejo Nacional de Cultura y Artes
     (CNCA), Chile, Santiago de Chile
Consejo Nacional de Cinematografía del Ecuador (CNCINE), Ecuador, Quito
Instituto de Cinematografía y de las Artes Audiovisuales, A.C. (ICAA). Ministerio de
     Cultura de España, España, Madrid
Centro Nacional de Cinematografía (Francia), Francia, París
Dirección de Cine y Audiovisual. Secretaría de Cultura, Artes y Deportes, Honduras
National Film Development Corporation (India), India
UniJapan Film, Japón, Tokyo
Instituto Mexicano de Cinematografía (IMCINE), México, México, DF
Asociación Nicaragüense de Cinematografía (ANCI), Nicaragua, Managua
Viceministerio de Cultura, Paraguay, Asunción
Consejo Nacional de Cinematografía (CONACINE), Perú, Lima
Instituto do Cinema e do Audiovisual (ICA), Portugal, Lisboa
Corporación para el Desarrollo del Cine en Puerto Rico (Puerto Rico Film Commission),
     Puerto Rico, San Juan
Dirección Nacional de Cine (DINAC), República Dominicana, Santo Domingo
National Film and Video Foundation (Sudáfrica), Sudafricana, República, Johannesburg
Instituto Nacional del Audiovisual de Uruguay (INA), Uruguay, Montevideo
Centro Nacional Autónomo de Cinematografía (CNAC), Venezuela, Caracas

Film archives

Fundación Cinemateca Argentina, Argentina, Buenos Aires
Museo del Cine Argentino, Argentina, Buenos Aires
Cinemateca Boliviana, Bolivia, La Paz
Cinemateca del Museo de Arte Moderno de Río de Janeiro, Brasil, Río de Janeiro
Cinemateca Brasileña de São Paulo, Brasil, São Paulo
Cinemateca Distrital de Bogotá, Colombia, Bogotá
Fundación de Patrimonio Fílmico Colombiano, Colombia, Bogotá
Cinemateca de Cuba, Cuba, La Habana
Cinemateca Virtual de Chile, Chile
Cinemateca Santiago de Chile, Chile, Santiago de Chile
Fundación Chilena de las Imágenes en Movimiento, Chile, Santiago de Chile
Cinemateca Nacional del Ecuador, Ecuador, Quito
Filmoteca de Asturias, España, Asturias
Filmoteca de la Generalitat de Catalunya, España, Barcelona
Filmoteca de Andalucía, España, Córdoba
Filmoteca Canaria, España, Las Palmas
Filmoteca Española, España, Madrid
Filmoteca Regional Francisco Rabal, España, Murcia
Filmoteca Balear, España, Palma de Mallorca
Filmoteca Regional de Castilla y León, España, Salamaca
Filmoteca Vasca Euskadiko Filmategia, España, San Sebastián
Filmoteca de la Generalitat Valenciana, España, Valencia
Filmoteca de Zaragoza, España, Zaragoza
Latin American Film and Video Archives, Estados Unidos de América
Cinemateca Universitaria Enrique Torres. Universidad de San Carlos. Guatemala,
     Guatemala, Ciudad de Guatemala
Filmoteca de la UNAM, México, México, DF
Fundación Carmen Toscano I.A.P. Archivo Histórico Cinematográfico, México, México, DF
Cineteca Nacional, México, México, DF.
Cinemateca Nacional de Nicaragua, Nicaragua, Managua
Filmoteca de la Pontificia Universidad Católica del Perú, Perú, Lima
Filmoteca de Lima/Museo de Arte, Perú, Lima 1
Cinemateca Nacional. República Dominicana, República Dominicana, Santo Domingo
Cinemateca Uruguaya, Uruguay, Montevideo
Fundación Cinemateca Nacional, Venezuela
Biblioteca Nacional de Venezuela, Venezuela, Caracas

Schools

German Federal Film Board, Alemania, Berlín
Buenos Aires Comunicación. Escuela de Cine, Televisión y Video, Argentina, Buenos Aires
Centro de Investigación y Experimentación en Video y Cine (Cievyc), Argentina, Buenos
     Aires
Escuela Nacional de Experimentación y Realización Cinematográfica (ENERC),
     Argentina, Buenos Aires
Escuela Profesional de Cine, Argentina, Buenos Aires
Escuela Superior de Cinematografía, Argentina, Buenos Aires
Fundación Taller Escuela de Buenos Aires (TEBA), Argentina, Buenos Aires
Taller de Cineme Contporáneo, Argentina, Buenos Aires
Universidad del Cine, Argentina, Buenos Aires
Centro de Estudios de Imagen y Sonido (CEIS), Argentina, Córdoba

Departamento de Cine y TV – Universidad Nacional de Córdoba, Argentina, Córdoba
La Metro. Escuela de Comunicación Audiovisual, Argentina, Córdova
Taller de Cine 'El Mate', Argentina, Provincia de Buenos Aires
Escuela Provincial de Cine y Televisión, Argentina, Rosario
Instituto Superior de Cine y Artes Audiovisuales de Santa Fe (ISCAA), Argentina, Santa Fe
Escola de Comunicaçoes e Artes da Universidade de São Paulo, Brasil, São Paulo
Universidade Metodista de São Paulo (UMESP), Brasil, São Paulo
Corporación Universitaria Nueva Colombia, Colombia
Universidad Autónoma del Caribe. Dirección y Producción de Radio y Televisión,
        Colombia, Barranquilla
Corporación Unificada Nacional de Educación Superior (CUN) Cine, Televisión y Video,
        Colombia, Bogotá
Corporación Universitaria Unitec, Cine y Televisión, Colombia, Bogotá
Escuela de Cine Black María, Colombia, Bogotá
Escuela de Cine y Televisión de la Universidad Nacional, Colombia, Bogotá
Corporación Universitaria Autónoma de Occidente, Colombia, Cali
Universidad de Caldas. Taller de Radio y Televisión, Colombia, Manizales
Universidad de Manizales. Comunicación Social y Periodismo, Colombia, Manizales
Corporación Academia Tecnológica de Colombia Comunicación Social, Colombia,
        Medellín
Politécnico Jaime Isaza Cadavid. Escuela de Comunicación Audiovisual, Colombia,
        Medellín
Escuela Internacional de Cine y Televisión San Antonio de los Baños (EICTV), Cuba, La
        Habana
Instituto Superior de Arte (ISA), Cuba, La Habana
Comunicación Audiovisual (UNIACC), Chile, Santiago de Chile
Escuela de Cine de Chile, Chile, Santiago de Chile
Escuela de Cine y Televisión. Universidad ARCIS, Chile, Santiago de Chile
Facultad de Comunicación. Pontificia Universidad Católica de Chile, Chile, Santiago de
        Chile
Instituto de la Comunicación e Imagen. Universidad de Chile, Chile, Santiago de Chile
Mediart Institute, España
Centro de Imagen y Nuevas Tecnologías (CINT). Ayuntamiento de Vitoria, España, Álava
Universidad de Alicante (Taller de la Imagen), España, Alicante
Centro de Estudios Cinematográficos de Catalunya (CECC), España, Barcelona
Escola Municipal d'Ensenyement Secundari Mitjans Audiovisuals (EMAV), España,
        Barcelona
Escuela de Altos Estudios de la Imagen y el Diseño (IDEP), España, Barcelona
Escuela Lagares, España, Barcelona
Escuela Superior de Cine y Audiovisuales de la Universidad de Catalunya (ESCAC),
        España, Barcelona
Instituto de Ciencias de la Educación. Universidad Politécnica de Catalunya, España,
        Barcelona
Microfusa. La Escuela de Sonido, España, Barcelona
Quince de Octubre – Academia de Cine, España, Barcelona
Universidad Autónoma de Barcelona Facultad de CC de la Información, España,
        Barcelona
Universitat Pompeu Fabra Institut Universitari Audiovisual, España, Barcelona
Universitat Ramon Llul – Facultad de Ciencies de la Comunicaciò, España, Barcelona
Centros de Estudios Audiovisuales (IMVAL), España, Bilbao
Kinema. Escuela de Cine de Bilbao, España, Bilbao
Centro Gallego de las Artes de la Imagen, España, Galicia

Aula de Cine de la Universidad de Granada, España, Granada
Escola de Imaxe e Sonido, España, La Coruña
Escuela de Cinematografía y Artes Visuales. Universidad de León, España, León
Centro de Estudio del Video y de la Imagen (CEV), España, Madrid
Centro Municipal de Tecnologías Audiovisuales (CEMTAV), España, Madrid
Escuela de Artes Visuales (EAV), España, Madrid
Escuela de Cinematografía y del Audiovisual de la Comunidad de Madrid (ECAM),
    España, Madrid
Escuela de Imagen y Sonido (CES), España, Madrid
Escuela Internacional de Medios Audiovisuales, España, Madrid
Escuela Superior de Artes y Espectáculos, España, Madrid
Escuela Superior de Dibujo Profesional Comunicación e Imagen (ESDIP), España, Madrid
Escuela Trazos, España, Madrid
Instituto del Cine de Madrid, España, Madrid
Instituto Oficial de Radio y Televisión (IORTV), España, Madrid
La Escuela de Radio y Televisión, España, Madrid
Metropolis. Escuela de Artes Audiovisuales de Madrid, España, Madrid
Ondas Escolares y Universitarias, España, Madrid
Septima Ars. Escuela de Cinematografía y Audiovisuales, España, Madrid
Universidad Complutense de Madrid. Facultad de Ciencias de la Información, España,
    Madrid
Universidad Europea de Madrid (UEM), España, Madrid
Universidad de Málaga. Facultad de Ciencias de la Información, España, Málaga
Universidad de Navarra. Facultad de Ciencias de la Información, España, Pamplona
Escuela Superior de Artes Cinematográficos de Galicia, España, Pontevedra
Universidad de Sevilla. Facultad de Ciencias de la Información, España, Sevilla
Fundación para la Investigación del Audiovisual (FIA), España, Valencia
Toon Factory – Centro de Formación de Dibujos Animados y Nuevas Tecnologías,
    España, Valencia
Universidad de Valladolid. Cátedra de Historia y Estética de la Cinematografía, España,
    Valladolid
Escuela de Cine de Aragón, España, Zaragoza
Instituto Cinematográfico Lumiere, México, México, DF
Instituto Ruso Mexicano de Arte, Cine y Teatro Sergei Einsestein, A.C., México, México, DF
Centro de Capacitación Cinematográfica (CCC). Centro Nacional de las Artes, México,
    México, DF
Centro Internacional de Guionismo de Cine (Cigcite), México, México, DF
Academia Mexicana de Ciencias y Artes Cinematográficas, México, México, DF
Universidad del Cine (AMCI), México, México, DF
Grupo Experimental de Cine Universitario. Universidad de Panamá, Panamá, Ciudad
    Panamá
Universidad de Lima. Facultad de Comunicación, Perú, Lima
Universidad de Aveiro. Departamento de Comunicación y Artes, Portugal, Aveiro
Facultad de Letras de la Universidad de Coimbra. Estudios Artísticos, Portugal, Coimbra
Escola Superior de Teatro e Cinema, Portugal, Lisboa
Escuela de las Artes. Sonido e Imagen. Universidad Católica de Portugal, Portugal, Porto
Centro de Estudios en Comunicación Audiovisual (CENECA), República Dominicana,
    Santo Domingo
Escuela de Cine, TV y Fotografía. Universidad Autónoma de Santo Domingo, República
    Dominicana, Santo Domingo
Escuela de Cine del Uruguay, Uruguay, Montevideo.
Escuela de Cine y Televisión en Venezuela, Venezuela, Caracas

Other institutions

Yoochel Kaaj

Asociación Argentina de Productores de Cine y Medios Audiovisuales, Argentina,
    Buenos Aires

Directores Argentinos Cinematográficos (DAC), Argentina, Buenos Aires

Centro de Formación y Realización Cinematográfica, Bolivia

Coordinadora Audiovisual Indígena-Originaria de Bolivia, Bolivia

PRAIA, Bolivia

Video nas Aldeias/Video en las Aldeas, Brasil

Asociación Brasileña de Cinematografía, Brasil, São Paulo

Fundación Teoría y Práctica de las Artes, TYPA, Colombia, Bogotá

Centro Cultural 'Pablo de la Torriente Brau', Cuba, Ciudad de La Habana

Fundación del Nuevo Cine Latinoamericano (FNCL), Cuba, La Habana

Museo Chileno de Arte Precolombino, Chile

Confederación de Nacionalidades Indígenas del Ecuador (CONAIE), Ecuador

Academia de las Artes y las Ciencias Cinematográficas de España, España

Asociación ProDocumetales Cine y TV, España, Albacete

Fundación Ciencias de la Documentación, España, Cáceres

Asociación de Televisión Educativa y Cultural Iberoamericana ATEI-TEIb, España, Madrid

Casa de América, España, Madrid

Egeda, España, Madrid

Programa Ibermedia, España, Madrid

Fundación Audiovisual de Andalucía, España, Sevilla

All Roads Film Project (National Geographic), Estados Unidos de América

Sundance Institute Native American Program, Estados Unidos de América, Beverly Hills, CA

National Museum of the American Indian Film and Video Center, Estados Unidos de
    América, New York, NY

American Indian Film Institute (AIFI), Estados Unidos de América, San Francisco

Unión Latina, Francia, Paris

Cinecittá, Italia, Roma

Comisión Nacional para el Desarrollo de los Pueblos Indígenas de México
    Departamento de Cine y Video, México

Ojo de Agua Comunicación, México

Yoochel Kaaj: Cine Video Cultura, A.C., México

Asociación NOMADAS – cine itinerante en Latinoamérica, Perú, Lima

Asociación de Productores de Uruguay (ASOPROD), Uruguay, Montevideo

MERCOSUR, Uruguay, Montevideo

Reunión Especializada de Autoridades Cinematográficas y del Audiovisual del
    MERCOSUR (RECAM), Uruguay, Montevideo

Fundación Villa del Cine, Venezuela

Fundavisual Latina, Venezuela, Caracas

FUNDEARC – Fundación para el Desarrollo de las Artes y la Cultura, Venezuela, Mérida

Associations of audiovisual investigation

Sociedad Argentina de Información, Argentina

Consejo Latinoamericano de Ciencias Sociales (CLACSO), De carácter Internacional

Asociación Latinoamericana de Investigadores de la Comunicación (ALAIC), De carácter
    Regional

Diálogo Regional sobre la Sociedad de la Información (DIRSI), De carácter Regional

Federación Latinoamericana de Facultades de Comunicación Social (FELAFACS), De
    carácter Regional

Federación Latinoamericana de Semiótica (FELS), De carácter Regional
Instituto Latinoamericano de la Comunicación Educativa (ILCE), De carácter Regional
Red de Investigación y Comunicación Compleja (RICC), De carácter Regional

Organizations of investigation

Centro de Investigaciones en Estudios Culturales, Educativos y Comunicacionales (CIECEC), Argentina
Instituto de Investigaciones Gino Germani, Argentina
Centro de Investigación Cinematográfica (CIC), Argentina, Buenos Aires
Universidad de los Andes. Facultad de Humanidades y Educación, Bolivia, Mérida
Facultad de Biblioteconomía e Comunicação. Universidade Federal do Rio Grande, Brasil
Laboratório de Estudos Avançados em Jornalismo (Labjor). Universidade Estadual de Campina, Brasil
Núcleos de Estudos e Projetos em Comunicação (NEPC), Brasil
Centro de Investigaciones de la Universidad de Manizales, Colombia
Centro de Investigaciones en Periodismo y Publicidad (CIPP), Chile
Instituto de Estudios Mediales, Chile
Centro Internacional de Estudios Superiores de Comunicación (CIESPAL), Ecuador
Instituto Superior de Investigación de la Facultad de Comunicación Social (ISICS) de FACSO, Ecuador
Universidad Internacional SEK. Facultad de Ciencias de la Información, Ecuador, Quito
Asociación Mexicana de Investigadores de la Comunicación (AMIC), México
Cátedra de Investigación en Medios Audiovisuales y Globalización en América del Norte (CIMAGEN), México
Centro Avanzado de Comunicación (CADEC), México
Centro de Investigación y Estudios Cinematográficos (CIEC), México
Consejo Nacional para la Enseñanza y la Investigación de las Ciencias de la Comunicación (CONEICC), México
Estudios Cine Mexicano, México, Cuernavaca
Centro de Estudios Cinematograficos INDIe, México, México DF.
Centro Universitario de Estudios Cinematográficos (CUEC), México, México DF.
Centro de Documentación (CEDOC), Perú
Centro de Investigación de la Comunicación. Universidad Católica Andrés Bello (CIC-UCAB), Venezuela
Instituto de Investigaciones de la Comunicación (ININCO), Venezuela

Audiovisual observatories

Observatorio Cultural de la Universidad de Buenos Aires, Argentina, Buenos Aires
Observatorio de Industrias Culturales (Argentina), Argentina, Buenos Aires
Observatorio del Mercosur Audiovisual (OMA), Argentina, Buenos Aires
O.C.A. Observatório brasileiro do cinema e do audiovisual, Brasil
Canadian Cultural Observatory, Canadá
L'Observatoire de la Culture et des Communications du Québec, Canadá, Québec
L'Observatoire du Quebec, Canadá, Quebec
Observatorio de Cultura Urbana de Bogotá, Colombia
Observatorio del Caribe colombiano, Colombia
Sistema Nacional de Información Cultural de Colombia (SINIC), Colombia
Observatorio Europeo de la Televisión Infantil (OETI), España
Observatorio de Cine, España, Barcelona
Observatorio del Audiovisual Gallego, España, La Coruña
Observatorio Europeo del Audiovisual, Francia

Observatorio de Políticas Culturales (L'Observatoire del Politiques Culturelles), Francia,
    Grenoble
Regional Observatory of Financing Culture in East-Central Europe. The Budapest
    Observatory, Hungría
Osservatorio Culturale del Piemonte, Italia
Osservatorio Culturale e Reti Infornmative. Direzione Generale Culture, Identitiá e
    Autonomie Regione Lombardia, Italia
Sistema de Información Cultural de México (SIC), México
Observatório das Actividades Culturais da Universidade Lisboa, Portugal
Iniciativa Latinoamericana, Uruguay
Innovarium – Observatorio de Políticas Culturales, Viet Nam

Festivals

'¡Viva! Spanish & Latin American Film Festival', Reino Unido, Manchester
'ABFF – American Black Film Festival', Estados Unidos de América, New York
'ACE – Asociación de Cronistas de Espectáculos de Nueva York', Estados Unidos de
    América, New York
'ADocS – Muestra Documentales y Fotografías de América Latina', España, Albacete
'AFI Fest Estados Unidos de América', Los Angeles, California
'African American Women in Cinema', Estados Unidos de América, New York
'Alcine – Festival de Cine de Alcalá de Henares', España, Madrid
'ALMA Awards – American Latino Media Arts Awards', Estados Unidos de América, California
'Ambulante Gira de Documentales', México
'Anima – Festival Internacional de Animación de Córdoba', Argentina, Córdoba
'Anima Basauri – Festival Internacional de Cine de Animación de Basauri – Bizkaia',
    España, Bilbao
'Anima Mundi – Festival Internacional de Animaçao do Brasil', Brasil, Río de Janeiro
'Animagyc – Festival Internacional de Animación', Perú, Lima
'ANIMEC – Festival Internacional de Animación en Ecuador', Ecuador, Quito
'APCA – Associçao Paulista de Críticos de Artes', Brasil, São Paulo
'AsoloCartoonFestival – Concorso Internazionale del Cortometraggio', Italia, Asolo
'AXN Film Festival', Venezuela, Caracas
'BAFICI – Buenos Aires Festival Internacional de Cine Independiente', Argentina,
    Buenos Aires
'BAFTA Awards. Orange British Academy Film Awards', Reino Unido, Londres
'Bangkok International Film Festival', Tailandia, Bangkok
'Belize Internacional Film Festival', Belice, Belice
'Berlinale – Internationale Filmfestspiele Berlin', Alemania, Berlín
'Bermuda International Film Festival Bermudas', Islas, Bermudas
'BIFA – British Independent Film Awards', Reino Unido, London
'Birds Eye View Film Festival – Emerging Women Filmmakers', Reino Unido, London
'Bodilprisen (Premios Bodil)', Dinamarca, Copenhagen
'Boston Latino International Film Festival', Estados Unidos de América, Boston
'Brazilian Film Festival of Miami Estados', Unidos de América, Miami, Florida
'Brussels International Film Festival of Fantastic Film', Bélgica, Bruselas
Cannes International Film Festival, Cannes, France
'Cairo International Film Festival', Egipto, El Cairo
'Camerimage – International Film Festival of the Art of Cinematography,' Polonia, Lódz
'Cero Latitud – Festival de Cine de Quito', Ecuador, Quito
'Ciclo de Cine Centroaméricano de Viena', Austria, Viena
'Cine Ceará. Festival Ibero-Americano de Cinema e Vídeo Brasil Fortaleza', Brasil, Ceará
'Cine Fest Brasil – Madrid', España, Madrid

'Cine Las Americas International Film Festival', Estados Unidos de América, Texas
'CineEnCorto – Festival Internacional de Cortometrajes', México, Tamaulipas
'CineLatino', Alemania, Tüebingen
'Cinema Caraïbe – St Barth Film Festival', St. Barthelemy
'Cinéma du Réel international documentary film festival', Francia, Paris
'Cinema Jove – Festival Internacional de Cine de Valencia', España, Valencia
'Cinema Novo Festival', Bélgica
'Cinemafest Puerto Rico', Puerto Rico, San Juan
'Cinemaissí – Festival de Cine Latinoamericano y Caribeño de Finlandia', Finlandia, Helsinki
'CinemaLatino – Muestra Latinoamericana de Cine de Guayaquil', Ecuador, Guayaquil
'Cinequest San Jose Film Festival Estados', Unidos de América San Jose, California
'CINESUL – Festival Iberoamericano de Cinema e Video', Brasil, Río de Janeiro y São Paulo
'Concurso de Cortometrajes on-line Nontzefilm', España, Bilbao
'Cortópolis – Festival Nacional de Cortometrajes', Argentina, Córdoba
'Critics' Choice Movie Awards', Estados Unidos de América, Santa Monica
'Cubanima – Festival Internacional del Audiovisual para la Niñez y la Adolescencia', Cuba, Ciudad de La Habana
'Chicago International Film Festival Estados', Unidos de América, Chicago
'Chicago Latino Film Festival Estados', Unidos de América, Chicago
'Chilereality – Festival de Cine Documental de Chillán', Chile, Chillán
'Davis Feminist Film Festival Estados', Unidos de América, California
DerHumALC – Festival Internacional de Cine de Derechos Humanos', Argentina, Buenos Aires
'Diosa de Plata – Periodistas Cinematográficos de México', México, México, DF
'Discover Screenwriting Award', Estados Unidos de América
'Divercine – Festival Internacional de Cine para Niños y Jóvenes', Uruguay, Montevideo
'DOC.BOL – Muestra Internacional de Cine y Video Documental', Bolivia, La Paz
'DocBsAS – Muestra Documental Buenos Aires', Argentina, Buenos Aires
'DOCLATXXI – Encuentro de Documentalistas Latinoamericanos del Siglo XXI', Ecuador, Quito
'DocsDF – Festival Internacional de Cine Documental de la Ciudad de México', México, México DF
'DOCUMENTA – Muestra de Cine documental', Ecuador, Quito
'Documenta Madrid – Festival Internacional de Documentales de Madrid', España, Madrid
'DOK Leipzig – International Leipzig Festival for Documentary & Animated Film', Alemania, Leipzig
'DOK.FEST – Internationales Dokumentar Film Festival München', Alemania, Munich
'É Tudo Verdade – Festival Internacional de Documéntarios', Brasil, São Paulo
'EcoBahia – Festival Internacional de Audiovisual Ambiental', Brasil, Río de Janeiro
'ECU – The European Independent Film Festival', Francia, Venue
'Edinburgh International Film Festival', Reino Unido, Scotland
'EDOC – Encuentros del Otro Cine. Festival Internacional de Cine Documental', Ecuador, Quito
'EFA – European Film Awards', Alemania, Berlin
'Encuentro Hispanoamericano de Cine y Video Documental Independiente', México, Ciudad de México
'ExpoToons Festival Internacional de Animación', Argentina, Buenos Aires
'Expresión en Corto – Festival Internacional de Cortometraje', México, Guanajuato
'FAM – Florianópolis Audiovisual Mercosul', Brasil, Florianópolis
'Famafest – Festival Internacional de Cinema e Vídeo de Famalicão', Portugal, Famalicão

'FANTASPORTO – Festival Internacional de Cinema do Porto', Portugal, Porto
'FECOVEN – Festival de Cortometrajes Venezuela', Venezuela
Viennale, Vienna, Austria

Other sites:

General
Latin American Video Archives:
http://www.lavavideo.org/
> The place to locate and purchase Latin American- and US Latino-made film and
> video. The *Latin American Video Archives* has been created with support from the
> John D. and Catherine T. MacArthur Foundation, The Rockefeller Foundation, the
> New York State Council on the Arts, and the National Video Resources to facilitate
> the distribution of Latin American and US-Latino films and videos in the United States.

Hollywood Inc, Latin America
http://www.zonalatina.com/Zldata155.htm
> Site by Zona Latina on the popularity of Hollywood films in Latin America,
> and in addition a large variety of Latin American cinema links. 'Looking at the
> WorldwideBoxOffice.com ranking of all-time movie box office receipts, it is clear that
> the global film market is dominated by products made in Hollywood, USA. Why are
> Hollywood products so popular? In his book, Scott Robert Olson proposes the United
> States' competitive advantage in the creation and global distribution of popular
> taste is due to a unique mix of cultural conditions that are conducive to the creation
> of 'transparent' texts – narratives whose inherent polysemy encourage diverse
> populations to read them as though they are indigenous […] these narratives have
> meaning to so many different cultures because they allow viewers in those cultures to
> project their own values, archetypes, and tropes into the movie or television program,
> thus enabling the import to function as though it were an indigenous product.'

Latin American Cinema in the 90th by Michael Chanan
http://www.tau.ac.il/eial/IX_1/chanan.html

Latin-America Cinemateca of Los Angeles – LACLA Ressources
http://www.lacla.org/resources.html

Recent Colombian Cinema comes to Boston, MFA
http://www-tech.mit.edu/V110/N29/mfa.29a.html

Cinema in Latin America (University of Texas Latin American Network Information Center)
http://lanic.utexas.edu/la/region/cinema/
> Film-related country resources, grouped by country in alphabetical order. Also:
> listings of educational and distribution resources, film festivals, international and
> regional resources. Also accessible in Spanish and Portuguese. Well worth a visit.

LatinoLA
http://www.latinola.com/
> "Latino voices, lives and souls"

Southern California's Latino Arts portal.
http://www.latinheat.com/

Latino Review
http://www.latinoreview.com/
>Los Angeles and New York-based web site featuring reviews of the latest American movies to the English speaking Latin-American audience. Reviewers are young Latinos (Puerto Rico, Mexico, Colombia) based in Los Angeles and New York, offering a fresh perspective on movies from the nation's fastest growing markets.

NALIP (National Association of Latino Independent Producers)
http://www.nalip.org/
>Membership organization dedicated to the advancement, development, and funding of Latino and Latina film and media arts in all genres.

NHMC (National Hispanic Media Coalition)
http://www.nhmc.org/
>Dedicated to improving the image of Hispanic-Americans as portrayed by the media and increasing the number of Hispanic-Americans employed in all facets of the media industry. A great example of nationwide media policy activism.

ALMA Awards
http://www.almaawards.com/
>American Latino Media Awards for positive portrayals of Latino people and culture.

El Amante
http://www.elamante.com/
>Argentinean online journal (in Spanish).

Miradas
http://www.eictv.co.cu/miradas/
>Quarterly digital magazine from the prestigious International School of Film & Television San Antonio de los Baños, Cuba. Offers a wide range of rare interviews with Latin American film-makers, essays by well-known international film theorists, and dossiers on specific subjects such as experimental cinema, new Latin American cinema, underground Cuban cinema, etc. (in Spanish).

Specific countries

Argentine Cinema History
http://www.surdelsur.com/cine/cinein/indexingles.html
>Gives an overview of the history of Argentine cinema, from 1896 to the present day.

Historia y critica del cine espanol
http://www.cervantesvirtual.com/portal/LGB/enlaces_art.shtml
>Contains some articles also on Latin American cinema.

Cine Brazil Movie Database
http://cinemabrasil.org.br/indexen.html
>Database containing over 500 Brazilian feature films. Site of the Brazilian Ministry of Culture that gives information on contemporary Brazilian films, covering both the art and business of film-making, with a few side steps into history. Available in English, French or Portuguese.

Buscacine.com

http://www.buscacine.com/

Cine Chileno
http://cinenacional.blogspot.com/
    The history of Chilean Cinema.

Cine Argentino
http://www.surdelsur.com/cine/cinein/
    The history of Argentinean Cinema.

Women Cinema
Fantastic source of the following sites: http://www.cinelatinoamericano.org/

Films related to women
Curt nimuendaju e icatu, puestos indígenas (Nilo de Oliveira Vellozo and Harald Schultz,
    1942)
Los chipayas: vuelve Sebastiana (Jorge Ruiz and Augusto Roca, 1954)
Manuela (Humberto Solás, 1966)
Lucía (I – III) (Humberto Solás, 1968)
Andean women/Mujer andina (Hubert Smith, 1974)
Dionisia potiere otomi (Claude Stresser Pean and Lagarde V, 1974)
Los kuna (Robert Huber and Marianne Huber, 1975)
Sabina Sánchez and the art of embroidery/Sabina Sánchez y el arte de bordar (Judith
    Bronowski and Robert Grant, 1976)
Dança das mulheres (Grzegorz Denys, 1977)
Huancayo (Paul Saltzman and Deepa Saltzman, 1978)
Aquella larga noche (Enrique Pineda Barnet, 1979)
Dominga (Guy L. Cote, 1979)
María Sabina, mujer espíritu (Nicolás Echevarría, 1979)
Mineurs et indiens (Alain Labrousse, 1979)
Retrato de Teresa (Pastor Vega, 1979)
Peruvian Weaning/Textiles peruanos (John Cohen, 1980)
Soutaji Wayuu (Gerson Bermúdez, 1980)
Tiempo de mujeres (Mónica Vásquez, 1980)
Working women: pottery making in Amatenango del valle/Mujeres alfareras en Amatenango
    (David Pentecost, Lyn Tiefenbacher, Denice Dilanni and Mike Bruno, 1980)
A india vestida (Berta Ribeiro and Federico F. Ribeiro, 1981)
Le derniere rire (Marie-Claire Deffarge and Gordian Troeller, 1981)
Uso e fio (Berta Ribeiro and Federico F. Ribeiro, 1981)
Xingú terra (Maureen Bisilliat, 1981)
Doña Helena Palliri (César Alarcón, 1983)
Frida/Frida, naturaleza viva (Paul Leduc, 1983)
Hasta cierto punto (Tomás Gutiérrez Alea [Titón], 1983)
India, a Filha do Sol (Fabio Barreto, 1983)
Camila (María Luisa Bemberg, 1984)
Intima raíz (Patricia Howell Aguilar, 1984)
A hora da estrela (Suzana Amaral, 1985)
Mulher india (Eliane Bandeira, 1985)
Oriana (Fina Torres, 1985)
Rigoberta (Rebeca Chávez, 1985)

When the mountains tremble/Cuando tiemblan las montañas (Tom Sigel and Pamela
    Yates, 1985)
Eu sei que vou te amar (Arnaldo Jabor, 1986)
Gerónima (Raúl Tosso, 1986)
A festa da moça (Vincent Carelli, 1987)
La vida de una familia Ikoods (Teófila Palafox, 1987)
Luisa Gerónima (Adauto dos Santos and Vik dos Santos, 1987)
Tejedoras de Ñanduti (Ana Montes de González, 1987)
Tejiendo mar y viento (Luis Lupone, 1987)
El verano de la señora Forbes (Jaime Humberto Hermosillo, 1988)
Mujer aymara en Perú (Bianca Casagrande, 1988)
La bella del Alhambra (Enrique Pineda Barnet, 1989)
Zulay frente al siglo XXI (Jorge Prelorán, Mabel Prelorán and Zulay Saravino, 1989)
Domitila y la mina (Carmen Sarmiento García, 1990)
Doña Odilia y sus compas (Roberto Triana, 1990)
En el volcán (Carmen Sarmiento García, 1990)
Funeral mentuktire: nascimento kamaiura/Funeral mentuktíre: nascimiento kamaiurá
    (Yoshikuní Takahashi, 1990)
La mujer indígena (Carmen Sarmiento García, 1990)
La tarea (Jaime Humberto Hermosillo, 1990)
María Antonia (Sergio Giral, 1990)
Muyushina (María Augusta Calle, 1990)
Wayúu: por el camino de los sueños (Eduardo Martínez, 1990)
Weavers in Ahuiran/Tejedoras en Anuiran (Beate Engelbrecht and Ulrike Keyser, 1990)
El embarazo (Ivonne Muñoz Cañedo, 1991)
El hablar de las mujeres (José Antonio Portugal, 1991)
Lady Marshall (Martha Clarissa Hernández, 1991)
Manteniendo el fuego vivo (José Armijo, 1991)
Mujeres artesanas de si mismas (Julio Barco, 1991)
Nube de lluvia (Patricia Mora, 1991)
Sueños de cultrun (Pablo Rosenblatt, 1991)
Warmin arupa: palabra de mujer (serie I) (Iván Sanjinés and Cecilia Quiroga, 1991)
Warmin arupa: palabra de mujer (serie II) (Iván Sanjinés and Cecilia Quiroga, 1991)
El trabajo silencioso de la mujer añú (Reina Taylhardat, 1992)
Grandmother told me/Abuela háblame (Jon Sletbak, 1992)
La deesse lune (Francois Robert Zacot, 1992)
Mujeres del Valle del Mezquital (Salvador Morelos Ochoa, 1992)
Kaxinawa the real people (Siã Runikuí, 1993)
Sobada and manteada/Parteras mexicanas (Laura Cao Romero, 1993)
Carmen Miranda: Bananas Is My business (Helena Solberg-Ladd, 1994)
Carlota Joaquina, Princesa do Brasil/Carlota Joaquina, princesa de Brasil (Carla de
    Andrade Camurati, 1995)
Tieta do Agreste (Carlos Diegues, 1996)
Central Do Brasil (Walter Salles, 1998)
Eu, tu, Eles (Andrucha Waddington, 2000)
Tan de repente (Diego Lerman, 2002)
Las mantenidas sin sueño (Vera Fogvill, 2005)
Maria Bethânia: música é perfume/Maria Bethânia: música y perfume (Georges Gachot, 2005)
Maroa (Solveig Hoogesteijn, 2005)
Bajo Juárez, la ciudad devorando a sus hijas (José Antonio Cordero and Alejandra
    Sánchez, 2006)
Pan's Labyrinth/El laberinto del fauno (Guillermo del Toro, 2006)
Antiguos sueños de mujeres Kichwas (Santiago Carcelén Cornejo, 2007)

Jogo de cena (Eduardo Coutinho, 2007)
Una novia errante (Ana Katz, 2007)
XXY (Lucía Puenzo, 2007)
1, 2 y 3 mujeres (Andrea Herrera, Anabel Rodríguez and Andrea Ríos, 2008)
Backyard/El traspatio (Carlos Carrera, 2008)
En defensa propia (Claudia Barril, 2008)
Hace mucho tiempo que te quiero (Philippe Toledano, 2008)
Linha de Passe (Walter Salles and Daniela Thomas, 2008)
Lluvia (Paula Hernández, 2008)
Precious: Based on the novel Push *by Sapphire* (Lee Daniels, 2008)

Festivals and events dedicated to female directors

'FICCI – Festival Internacional de Cine de Cartagena de Indias', Colombia, Cartagena de Indias
'Festival International de Films de Femmes', Francia, Créteil
'Birds Eye View Film Festival – Emerging Women Filmmakers, Reino Unido, London
'Tricky Women International Animation Festival, Austria, Vienna
'The Female Eye Film Festival, Canadá, Toronto
'Davis Feminist Film Festival, Estados Unidos de América, California
'Internationales Frauen Film Festival Dortmund | Köln, Alemania, Dortmund | Cologne
'O Femina – Festival Internacional de Cinema Feminino, Brasil, Río de Janeiro
'Miradas Madrid Festival International de Cine y Mujeres, España, Madrid
'St Johns´s International Women Festival, Canadá, St. John
'WOW Film Festival, Australia
'Mujeres en Dirección. Semana Internacional de Cine Ciudad de Cuenca', España, Cuenca
'Muestra Internacional de Mujeres en el Cine y la Televisión México', México, México DF
'International Women's Film Festival "KIN"', Armenia, Yerevan
'African American Women in Cinema', Estados Unidos de América, New York
'Certamen de Artes Plásticas y Visuales Mujeres y Arte, España, Madrid

Publications dedicated to female directors

Ciuk, Perla, Diccionario de Directores del Cine Mexicano (Mexico City: Consejo Nacional para la Cultura y las Artes (CONACULTA)/Cineteca Nacional, 2009)
D'Atri, Andrea/ Funes, Bárbara, *Luchadoras. Historias de mujeres que hicieron historia* (Buenos Aires: Ediciones del IPS, 2006)
Ravelo, Aloyma, *40 preguntas sobre sexo* (La Habana: Editorial de la Mujer 2009)
Ravelo, Aloyma, *Enigmas de la Sexualidad Femenina* (La Habana: Editorial de la Mujer 2006)
Richard, Nelly, *Campos cruzados. Crítica cultural, latinoamericanismo y saberes al borde* (La Habana: Fondo Editorial Casa de la Américas, 2009)
Stock, Ann Marie, *On Location in Cuba: Street Filmmaking during Times of Transition* (Chapel Hill: The University of North Carolina Press, 2009)
Torres Falcón, *Marta: La violencia en casa* (Barcelona: Paidós, 2002)
Torres, San Martín Patricia (ed.), *Mujeres y Cine en América Latina* (Guadalajara: Universidad de Guadalajara, 2004)
Vasallo, Norma, *Mirar de otra manera* (La Habana: Editorial de la Mujer, 2008)
Velázquez, Susana, *Violencias cotidinas, violencias de género* (Barcelona: Paidós, 2003)

TEST YOUR KNOWLED

Questions

1. Which photo travelled around the world?
2. Who won an Oscar for his supporting role in *Biutiful*?
3. Who/what is called a chocolate in Carlos Soríns movie *Bombón*?
4. In which movies can we see Magaly Solier?
5. Who directed *Babel*?
6. What does the word 'boludos' mean in *Chinese Take-Away*?
7. What falls from the sky in *Chinese Take-Away*?
8. *Mami te amo* was the first feature film of which film-maker?
9. Who filmed 'football histories'?
10. What did Raúl Fornet-Bétancourt investigate?
11. Where is the secret in Juan José Campanella's Oscar-awarded film?
12. Who is 'Frida' in July Taymor's film?
13. Who is her husband?
14. Which documentary is about the Uruguayan doctor and scientist Henry Engler?
15. Where was Alejandro Alonso born?
16. Who said 'May you never get used to the absurd'?
17. In which film does Alberto González enter the lives of five teenagers in a musical band?
18. Who filmed *The Swamp*?
19. When was Cuban comedy *Alice in Wondertown* screened at the 'Berlin International Film Festival'?
20. Paula Markovitch was the screenwriter for which film?
21. Which genre deals with the absurd elements of life?
22. What is the animal of the 'Berlinale' festival?
23. Who talked about 'symbolic capital'?
24. In which film do Lala and Guayi love each other?
25. To what genre do *The Class* by Laurent Cantet and *Gomorra* by Matteo Garrone belong?
26. What is Guillermo del Toro's predilection for?
27. In which film does a deadly and highly contagious virus spreads across the world?
28. What was Solveig Hoogesteijn's film-making debut?
29. Which are the three best known films by Lucretia Martel?

30. Who made *I, the Worst of All*?
31. Which actor is a 'serious actor and political pin-up'?
32. When was the premiere of Sandra Wernecks *Pequeno Dicionário Amoroso/Little Book of Love*?
33. What was the first feature film in Venezuelan film history?
34. Who created *Cuando besa mi marido* (1950)?
35. The plot of which film pretends to document the power of pornography?
36. The three people in *Intimate Stories* journey 200 miles from the small town of Fitz Roy in Argentina's southern region of Patagonia to which city?
37. Who is an overweight high school student and a prototypical freak/geek, avid reader, collector and fan of comic-book series and films like *Star Wars*?
38. With what event ended the time of ideological agitation films that dominated Latin American Cinema in the 1960s and 1970s?
39. When did the fascination for war and struggle start for Che Guevara?
40. What is the classical drama based on?
41. Who is the usual screenwriter of Alejandro González Iñárritu films?
42. What would René Descartes say if he were alive today?
43. Where does Pedro Machuca live?
44. Who made *Possible Lives*?
45. Who wrote the novel that *The Secret in Their Eyes* is based on?
46. By what kind of stories are Colombian thrillers frequently dominated?
47. What do Aurora (Tamara Shanath) and her lovable grandfather Jesús Gris (Federico Luppi) find in an old statue of an archangel?
48. Who is an overweight nurse who takes care of terminally ill old patients and struggles to earn a living for herself and her two children?
49. What is the first feminist film group in Venezuela called?
50. Where can you find one of the most important online forums for Latin American Cinema?

Answers

1. 'Che Guevara' by Alberto Korda
2. Javier Bardem
3. A dog
4. *The Milk of Sorrow*
5. Alejandro González Iñárritu
6. 'Jerk'
7. A cow
8. Elisa Eliash
9. Andrés Wood
10. Interculturality
11. In the eyes
12. Frida Kahlo
13. Diego Rivera
14. *El círculo*
15. Argentina
16. Daniel Díaz Torres
17. *Havana Kidz II*
18. Lucrecia Martel
19. 1991
20. *Duck Season*
21. Comedy
22. A bear
23. Pierre Boudieu
24. *The Fish Child*
25. Docufiction
26. Fantasy and horror
27. *Phase 7*
28. The documentary *Vasilis* (1970)
29. *The Swamp, The Holy Girl, The Headless Woman*
30. María Luisa Bemberg
31. Gael García Bernal
32. 1996
33. Antonio Delgado Gómez's *El rompimiento* (1939)
34. Carlos Schliepper
35. Jaime Humberto Hermosillo's *La tarea* (1990)
36. The district capital of San Julián
37. Roberto Rodríguez in *Promedio Rojo* (2004)
38. With the collapse of the Soviet Union
39. At the age of 10 when he heard from his father about the Spanish Civil War
40. The Greek theatre
41. Guillermo Arriaga
42. 'I am on TV, therefore I exist.'
43. Santiago de Chile
44. Sandra Gugliotta
45. Eduardo Sacheri
46. By gritty urban stories about drug and gang violence
47. A golden mechanical device
48. Coral Fabré
49. The Grupo Feminista Miércoles (Feminist Group Wednesday)
50. http://www.cinelatinoamericano.org/index.aspx

NOTES ON CONTRIBUTORS

The Editor

Isabel Maurer Queipo is Assistant Professor of French, Spanish and Latin American Literature, Culture and Media Studies at the University in Siegen (Germany). After her doctoral thesis about Pedro Almodóvar she worked on surrealism and intermediality in Europe and Latin America. Currently she is preparing a postdoctoral lecture qualification about the influence of dreams and nightmares on the different arts.

Contributors

Paul Becker studied English and Philosophy at the University of York (United Kingdom) and translation at the the Heinrich-Heine-University of Düsseldorf (Germany). He works as a freelance translator of English and German.

Verena Berger teaches Spanish and Latin American Studies at the University of Vienna/ Austria, with a focus on theatre and film. She is the co-editor of *Montréal-Toronto: Stadtkultur und Migration in Literatur, Film und Musik* (Berlin: Weidler Buchverlag, 2007), *Escenarios compartidos: Cine y teatro en España en el umbral del siglo XXI* (Münster/ Berlin/Wien/Zürich/London: Lit Verlag, 2009) and *Polyglot Cinema: Migration and Transcultural Narration in France, Italy, Portugal and Spain* (Münster/Berlin/Wien/Zürich/ London: Lit Verlag, 2010). Her current research includes a publication on Latin American Cinema.

Wolfgang Bongers is Associate Professor of Literature and Film Studies at Catholic University of Chile. He specializes in intermedial configurations and has published books and articles on European and Latin American Literature and Film.

Claudia Cabezón Doty is a lecturer in Latin American and Translation Studies at the Institute for Translation and Interpreting of Heidelberg University. Her main area of expertise is Latin American Literature and Cinema, with a focus on Comparative Literature and Adaptation's History and Theory. She is the author of *Literatur und Film Lateinamerikas im intermedialen Dialog* (Frankfurt am Main: Peter Lang Verlag, 2000) and many articles about the relationship between Latin American literature, film and television. She is currently working on a book about the History of Literary Adaptation.

Maribel Cedeño Rojas holds a PhD in Audiovisual Translation and Hispanic Studies from the Ruprecht-Karls-Universität Heidelberg (Germany). Her research and teaching activities focus on Literature and Audiovisual Translation, Spanish language and Cinema in Latin America.

Justyna Cempel is a lecturer and freelance writer with a degree in French/English linguistics and literature from the University of Siegen (Germany). Her areas of research are surrealisms, representation of violence and sexuality on screen, cinema brut, the French cinema of transgression/new extremism and media aesthetics. She is currently working on her doctoral thesis about Catherine Breillat.

Claudio Cifuentes-Aldunate is Associate Professor at the Institut for Literature, Culture and Media at the University of Southern Denmark. He has a PhD in Latin American Literature of Université de Fribourg, Switzerland. His research areas are Spanish and Latin American culture, literature and film.

Heidi Denzel de Tirado is Assistant Professor at Georgia State University (United States). She has published several articles on Spanish and French film and is currently working on a book about the depiction of Latino immigrants in film and TV.

Marijana Erstic is a research associate at the University of Siegen (Germany). She has a PhD in Film Studies (cinematic work of Luchino Visconti), and various publications about futurist, Italian, German, French and Hollywood cinema.

Tom Fallows is a writer and infrequent film-maker based in Stoke-on-Trent. After studying Film Journalism with the BFI in London, he went on to co-author a biography on zombie king George A. Romero for Pocket Essentials and continues to contribute to numerous film blogs around the globe, including the Rondo-nominated Classic-Horror. He is currently working on the short film *Charlie on the Streets*.

Uta Felten is Professor for Romance Literature, Culture and Medias at the University of Leipzig (Germany). Her research areas are, among others, the modern cinema in France and Italy, Gender, and Latin American Studies.

Anna Paula Foltanska is a degree student of Hispanic Literature, Culture and Media, at the University of Siegen (Germany). She lived in Mexico and in Cuba, where she also made a certification on scriptwriting, video production and cinema history. Among her areas are Latin American Culture and Arts.

Dietmar Frenz is Lecturer in Romance Studies at the University Frankfurt am Main (Germany) with a focus on animation and comics.

Javier Gutiérrez-Rexach is Professor of Spanish and Linguistics at the Department of Spanish and the Center for Latin American Studies at Ohio State University (United States). He was co-founder, member of the editorial board, and coordinating editor of the journal *Música de Cine*, from 1990 to 1997. He has served in the selection committee for the 'Valencia Film Festival', and has written film reviews for several outlets. His research interests are in the cognitive sciences and the analysis of audiovisual cultures.

Jenny Haase teaches Spanish and Latin American Literature at the Humboldt University of Berlin. She spent research periods in Santiago de Chile and Buenos Aires, wrote her doctoral thesis about representations of Patagonia in travel literature and historic novels of the late twentieth century, and has published articles on Patagonia in Argentinean and Chilean cinema. Other research interests post-colonial theory and postmodern theory, gender studies, and intermediality.

Matthias Hausmann is Assistant Professor of French and Spanish Literature at the University of Vienna (Austria). After his doctoral thesis about nineteenth century French utopian literature he has centred his interests on contemporary Latin American literature and particularly in Latin American film. Currently he is preparing a postdoctoral lecture qualification about the influences of movies on the literature of Argentine author Adolfo Bioy Casares.

Roberto Herrera graduated as Director of Photography at the Cinema School in Barcelona (Spain) (CECC-Centro de Estudios Cinematográficos de Catalunia). His experience as film critic started in a magazine in Barcelona. After he finished his studies he worked as film consultant for a Brazilian distributor through the 'Venice', 'San Sebastian' and 'Rotterdam' film festivals. Currently he is working as a freelance in video productions and is shooting his short film 'Gitanic'.

Kerstin Hörmann studies translation at Heinrich-Heine-University in Düsseldorf (Germany). She spent a semester at a private university in Montevideo (Uruguay) and worked on Uruguayan films.

Joanna Jaritz is graduated from the University of Heidelberg (Germany) in French and Spanish Literature. She has worked for the German radio and television channel SWR and is currently completing a doctorate on an intermedial approach to Marcel Proust's *Time Regained*.

Victoria Kearley has been studying for a PhD in Film, part-time at the University of Southampton since October 2008. The representation of Hispanic masculinity in contemporary Hollywood cinema is the subject of her doctoral thesis. She has worked as a part-time lecturer at the University of Portsmouth and the University of Southampton and has served as a postgraduate representative for the Society of Cinema and Media Studies' Latino/a Caucus.

Nicole Kretschmer studies at the Romance Department of the Universities of Aachen and Siegen (Germany), and worked on Latin American Cinema, especially Peruvian cinema.

Kerstin Küchler is a research assistant and PhD student at the Institute of Romance Studies at the University of Leipzig (Germany). Her main area of research is currently French Cinema. She intends to pursue a postdoctoral project in Spanish and Latin American Studies.

Silke Paulitsch is writing her doctorate at the University of Vienna (Austria), Department of Communication Science. Her field of research is the Caribbean Documentaries, specifically the documentaries of Cuba and Jamaica. She spent a long time in the Caribbean and worked together with the Caribbean Institute of Media and Communication in Kingston, Jamaica, and the Instituto Superior de Arte in Havana, Cuba.

Iván Pinto Veas is Professor of Theory and History of (Documetal) Cinema at Cinema School, University of Chile and Catholic University of Chile. He is a critic of cinema and editor of the website *laFuga* (http://lafuga.cl) specializing in contemporary cinema. He co-edited an anthology about the work of Raúl Ruiz and collaborates at different international forums. Currently he is investigating Chilean documental cinema and completing a work about Rock 'n' Roll in Cinema.

Sven Pötting studies at the Department of Theatre, Cinema and Television and is Assistant Teacher at the University of Cologne (Germany). He is completing his doctoral thesis on movies about the Falkland War. He works on cinema and leads an internet portal about Latin American Cinema (www.kinolatino.de).

Laia Quílez Esteve has an MA in Media Studies from the Universitat Autònoma de Barcelona (Spain) and in Comparative Literature & Literary Theory from the Universitat de Barcelona (Spain). She has a PhD in Communication Sciences by the Universitat Rovira i Virgili where currently she is a lecturer.

Ivo Ritzer is a lecturer in Media and Film Studies. His main research interests are popular genres in Hollywood, East Asian and European Cinema. He focuses on textual analysis as well as cultural theory and has published extensively on narrative film, questions of cultural globalization, and TV aesthetics.

Zachariah Rush is a prize-winning poet, essayist, film-maker and freelance film critic having regularly contributed to *Film International* and several volumes of the *Directory of World Cinema* including: *Japan Vol. 2*, *East Europe*, *Sweden*, *Belgium*, *France*, *India* as well as the *Paris* and *Las Vegas* volumes of Intellect's *World Film Locations* series. He is completing a book on dialectical dramaturgy to be published by McFarland and is currently adapting Albert Camus' novel *L'étranger* into a libretto for Gallimard, Paris.

Karen Saban graduated from the National University of Buenos Aires and finished a PhD in Romance Literature at the University of Heidelberg. She works as a lecturer in Spanish and translator. Her main area of expertise is memory and representation in Argentinean Literature which she is currently extending into Cinema. She is also editor of *HeLix*, a German electronic journal for Romance Literature and Cultural Studies.

Verena Schmöller is an assistant professor in the Roman Literatures and Cultures Department at Passau University, where she teaches literature, cultural and film studies, and works on her doctorate about narrative structures in contemporary film. She is on the board of cineforum e.V. (an association that promotes Iberoamerican cinema in Germany) and founder of the 'muestra! Iberoamerikanisches Filmfest Passau' (film festival presenting Iberian and Latin American Cinemas). In addition to various articles on film and culture focusing on Latin America, she wrote a book about Chilean Cinema.

Beatrice Schuchardt is Lecturer at Siegen University (Germany) where she teaches Latin American, Spanish, and French Literature, Cultural, and Media Studies. One of her main fields of research is Intercultural Border Crossing in Literature and the Movies, mainly focusing on adaptations of the life and work of Frida Kahlo. She has published various articles in this field. In cooperation with the Universities of Leipzig and Jerusalem, she is currently working on the international research project 'New Diasporas', focusing on global diasporas in the work of Chilean author Roberto Ampuero.

Peter W. Schulze teaches Film at the Gutenberg-Universität Mainz (Germany). His doctorate deals with the connection between Brazilian Modernism and Cinema Novo. His publications focus on the oeuvre of Glauber Rocha and his impact on Latin American, and contemporary Latin American Cinema.

Daniel A. Verdú Schumann is a lecturer in Film History. His main research field is Postmodern Cinema and particularly the construction of History in contemporary film, a topic on which he has published several papers. He holds an MA in Latin American Literature and Culture from the University of London, and has also worked on identity issues in Latin American art.

Lorenzo Javier Torres Hortelano is Associate Professor (tenure) at Universidad Rey Juan Carlos (Spain). He teaches Audiovisual Language and Analysis and Film Theories. Books: *Directory of World Cinema: Spain* (ed.) (Bristol: Intellect, 2011), *World Film Locations: Madrid* (Bristol: Intellect, 2011) and *'Primavera tardía' de Yasujiro Ozu: cine clásico y poética Zen* (Valladolid, Caja España, 2006). Research: textual analysis of all kinds of world cultural tests. He is a regular contributor to the journal *Trama & Fondo* (www.tramayfondo.com).

Christian von Tschilschke is Chair of Romance Literature at the University of Siegen (Germany). His primary research interests include the relationship between literature and media (film/television), theory and practices of intermediality, documentarism and docufiction. He has published numerous articles on French, Spanish and Latin American Cinema.

Marlene Christine Sommer is a student of Spanish and English Language and Literature at the University of Siegen (Germany). She has lived and studied in the United States and Latin America for several months and worked on Latin American Cinema.

Marcus Stiglegger teaches Film Studies at the University of Siegen, Germany. His writings include books and articles on film aesthetics, history and theory. His doctorate 'Sadiconazista' (1999) will be published in English in Spring 2012 ('"Nazi Camp": Fascist Aesthetics in Cinema & Popular Culture'). His further publications deal among others with the seduction theory of film. He is editor of the cultural magazine : *Ikonen* : (www.ikonenmagazin.de) and contributor of international magazines.

Esther Marie Stienen is a student of Spanish Language and Literature and Social Science at the University of Siegen (Germany). She lived and worked in El Salvador and worked on Latin American Cinema.

Verena Teissl is Professor of Science and Management of Culture at the University of Applied Science and Arts in Kufstein (Austria). She founded the 'International Film Festival Innsbruck' and worked for the 'Viennale' – the international film festival in Vienna (Austria). She has published and edited various works on Cinema.

Valentina Vazzano is a student of English and Spanish at the University of Siegen (Germany) with a focus on Latin American Cinema.

Regine Wenzel is a journalist on the staff of a regional German newspaper. She studied German, English and Psychology at the Universities of Kassel (Germany) and Manchester (United Kingdom). Her areas of work are arts, cinema and culture.

Gerhard Wild is Professor of Ibero-Romance Studies at Goethe University Frankfurt, co-editor of the German *Catalan Review* and of a world literature dictionary (*Kindlers Literaturlexikon*). He is the author of a book about the intercultural aesthetics in Alejo Carpentier works. Among his articles are texts on photography, on French, Portuguese, Spanish and Latin-American Cinema, and on the relationship of poetry and painting. His chosen research field is the literary production of vanguard painters.

Acta general de Chile (Miguel Littín, 1986)

Alice in Wondertown/Alicia en el pueblo de maravillas (Daniel Díaz Torres, 1991)

The Aura/El aura (Fabián Bielinsky, 2005)

Babel (Alejandro González Iñárritu, 2006)

Battle in Heaven/Batalla en el cielo (Carlos Reygadas, 2005)

My best enemy/Mi mejor enemigo (Alex Bowen, 2005)

Biutiful (Alejandro González Iñárritu, 2011)

The Blonds/Los rubios (Albertina Carri, 2003)

Bombón: El Perro (Carlos Sorín, 2004)

Carancho (Pablo Trapero, 2010)

Che Guevara Where You'd Never Imagine Him/Che Guevara, donde nunca jamás se lo imaginen (Manuel Pérez, 2004)

Chinese Take-Away/Un Cuento chino (Sebastián Borensztein, 2011)

Chronicles/Crónicas (Sebastián Cordero, 2004)

The Circle/El círculo (José Pedro Charlo, 2008)

Clouds/La nube (Fernando Solanas, 1998)

Cronos (Guillermo del Toro, 1993)

Danzón (Maria Novaro, 1991)

Deep Crimson/Profundo carmesí (Arturo Ripstein, 1986)

The Devil's Backbone/El espinazo del diablo (Guillermo del Toro, 2001)

Duck Season/La temporada de patos (Fernando Eimbcke, 2004)

Embodiment of Evil/Encarnação do Demônio (José Mojica Marins, 2008)

Empty nest/El nido vacío (Daniel Burman, 2008)

Extraordinary Stories/Historias extraordinarias (Mariano Llinás, 2008)

Frida (Julie Taymor, 2002)

Frida/Frida, naturaleza viva (Paul Leduc, 1986)

The Fish Child/El niño pez (Lucía Puenzo, 2009)

La gata borracha (Román Chalbaud, 1983)

Giant/Gigante (Adrián Biniez, 2009)

Gringuito (Sergio Castilla, 1998)

Havana Kidz 2 (Alberto Gonzales, 2008)

The Headless Woman/La mujer sin cabeza (Lucrecia Martel, 2008)

Hell' Highway: KM31/Km 31: Kilómetro 31 (Rigoberto Castañeda, 2006)

Highway Patrolman/El patrullero (Alex Cox, 1991)

Hitting Bottom/En la puta calle (Enrique Gabriel, 1997)

The Holy Girl/La niña santa (Lucrecia Martel, 2004)

The Journey/El viaje (Fernando E. Solanas, 1992)

Last Days of the Victim/Los últimos días de la víctima (Adolfo Aristaráin, 1982)

Like Water for Chocolate/Como agua para chocolate (Alfonso Arau, 1992)

Lost Embrace/El abrazo partido (Daniel Burman, 2004)

Love in the Time of Hysteria/Sólo con tu pareja (Alfonso Cuarón, 1991)

M (Nicolás Prividera, 2007)

Machuca (Andrés Wood, 2004)

Madeinusa (Claudia Llosa, 2006)

The Maid/La nana (Sebastián Silva, 2009)

Man Of Two Havanas/El hombre de las dos Habanas (Vivien Lesnik Weisman, 2007)
Y tu mamá también (Alfonso Cuarón, 2001)
Martin (Hache)/Martín (Hache) (Adolfo Aristaráin, 1997)
The Milk of Sorrow/La teta asustada (Claudia Llosa, 2009)
Intimate Stories/Historias mínimas (Carlos Sorin, 2001)
The Moon in the Mirror/La luna en el espejo (Silvio Caiozzi, 1990)
Avellaneda's Moon/Luna de Avellaneda (Juan José Campanella, 2004)
The Motorcycle Diaries/Diarios de motocicleta (Walter Salles, 2004)
Nine Queens/Nueve reinas (Fabián Bielinsky, 2000)
No return/Sin retorno (Miguel Cohan, 2010)
Pan's Labyrinth/El laberinto del fauno (Guillermo del Toro, 2006)
Phase 7/Fase 7 (Nicolás Goldbart, 2011)
A Photo That Travels Around the World/Una foto recorre el mundo (Pedro Chaskel, 1981)
A Place in the World/Un lugar en el mundo (Adolfo Aristaráin, 1992)
Promedio rojo (Nicolás López, 2004)
Red Bear/Un oso rojo (Adrián Caetano, 2002)
Same Love, Same Rain/El mismo amor, la misma lluvia (Juan José Campanella, 1999)
The Secret in Their Eyes/El secreto de sus ojos (Juan José Campanella, 2009)
The Signal/La señal (Ricardo Darín/Martín Hodara, 2007)
Son of the Bride/El hijo de la novia (Juan José Campanella, 2001)
Havana Suite/Suite Habana (Fernando Pérez, 2003)
The Swamp/La ciénaga (Lucrecia Martel, 2001)
Time for revenge/Tiempo de revancha (Adolfo Aristaráin, 1981)
Marcel Proust's Time Regained/Le temps retrouvé, d'après l'oeuvre de Marcel Proust (Raoul
     Ruiz, 1999)
Tony Manero (Pablo Larrain, 2008)
Under the Same Moon/La misma luna (Patricia Riggen, 2007)
La vida loca (Toño Chavez, 1999)
The Waiting List/Lista de espera (Juan Carlos Tabío, 2000)
The Wind Journeys/Los viajes del viento (Ciro Guerra, 2009)
Wind with the Gone/El viento se llevó lo que (Alejandro Agresti, 1998
The Window/La ventana (Carlos Sorin, 2008)
Without Name/Sin nombre (Cary Fukonaga, 2009)
The Zone/La zona (Rodrigo Plà, 2007)